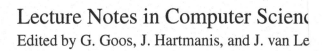

Lecture Notes in Computer Science

Edited by G. Goos, J. Hartmanis, and J. van Le

T0237818

Berlin
Heidelberg
New York
Barcelona
Hong Kong
London
Milan
Paris
Singapore
Tokyo

Jean-Jacques Quisquater
Bruce Schneier (Eds.)

Smart Card
Research and Applications

Third International Conference, CARDIS'98
Louvain-la-Neuve, Belgium, September 14-16, 1998
Proceedings

Series Editors

Gerhard Goos, Karlsruhe University, Germany
Juris Hartmanis, Cornell University, NY, USA
Jan van Leeuwen, Utrecht University, The Netherlands

Volume Editors

Jean-Jacques Quisquater
UCL, Microelectronic Laboratory
Place du Levant 3, 1348 Louvain-La-Neuve, Belgium
quisquater@dice.ucl.ac.be

Bruce Schneier
CTO and Founder, Counterpane Internet Security, Inc.
3031 Tisch Way, Suite 100 PE
San Jose, CA 95128, USA
E-mail: schneier@counterpane.com

Cataloging-in-Publication Data applied for

Die Deutsche Bibliothek - CIP-Einheitsaufnahme

Smart card research and applications : third international conference ;
proceedings / CARDIS'98, Louvain-la-Neuve, Belgium, September 14 -
16, 1998. Jean-Jacques Quisquater ; Bruce Schneier (ed.). - Berlin ;
Heidelberg ; New York ; Barcelona ; Hong Kong ; London ; Milan ; Paris ;
Singapore ; Tokyo : Springer, 2000
    (Lecture notes in computer science ; Vol. 1820)
    ISBN 3-540-67923-5

CR Subject Classification (1998): E.3, K.4.4, K.5, K.6.5, D.4.6, C.2

ISSN 0302-9743
ISBN 3-540-67923-5 Springer-Verlag Berlin Heidelberg New York

Springer-Verlag Berlin Heidelberg New York
a member of BertelsmannSpringer Science+Business Media GmbH
© Springer-Verlag Berlin Heidelberg 2000
Printed in Germany

Typesetting: Camera-ready by author, data conversion by PTP-Berlin, Stefan Sossna
Printed on acid-free paper   SPIN: 10721064   06/3142   5 4 3 2 1 0

Preface

Smart cards have been driven by the need for a secure, portable, computing platform. Hence it is no surprise that security considerations dominated their research. The CARDIS conferences were created to provide a forum for this research.

CARDIS 1998 is the third international conference on Smart Card Research and Advanced Applications, held in Louvain-la-Neuve, Belgium, 14-16 September 1998. The first CARDIS was held in Lille, France in November 1994, and the second was held in Amsterdam, The Netherlands in September 1996. The fourth CARDIS is scheduled to take place in Bristol, UK in September 2000 (http://www.cardis.org).

This volume contains the refereed papers presented at CARDIS 1998. These 35 papers were first published in a pre-proceedings and distributed to the attendees at the conference; they have subsequently been revised and updated for this volume.

The papers discuss all aspects of smart-card research: Java cards, electronic commerce applications, efficiency, security (including cryptographic algorithms, cryptographic protocols, and authentication), and architecture. Submissions from Europe, the U.S., Asia, and Australia show that this is indeed an international area of research, and one that is becoming more popular as practical demand for smart cards increase.

We wish to thank the Program Committee members who did an excellent job in reviewing papers and providing feedback to the authors.

All credit for the smooth editing submission process goes to Damien Giry, who handled all aspects and delivered a convenient directory full of submissions and editing postscript, PDF (and Troff !) submissions so that they would view and print acceptably; Catherine Rouyer, Patricia Focant and Catherine Konstantinidis for secretarial help, particulary in helping to organize the whole conference.

We also thank Professor Benoit Macq for the involving of his group during the conference.

Finally, we wish to thank all the authors who submitted papers, making this conference possible, and the authors of accepted papers for updating their papers with care and patience during the lengthy production of these proceedings.

June 2000

Jean-Jacques Quisquater
Bruce Schneier
Program Chairs
CARDIS '98

CARDIS '98

September 14 – 16, 1998, Louvain-la-Neuve, Belgium

Sponsored by
Belgacom
Europay International

Program Chairs

Jean-Jacques Quisquater, UCL, Belgium
Bruce Schneier, Counterpane, USA

Program Committee

William Caelli . . . . QUT Brisbane, Australia
Vincent Cordonnier . . . . R2DP Lille, France
David Chan . . . . HP Labs Bristol, UK
Jean-François Dhem . . . . Belgacom, Belgium
Jan Eloff . . . . RAU, South Africa
Marc Girault . . . . CNET, France
Louis Guillou . . . . CNET, France
Pieter Hartel . . . . Southampton, UK and Amsterdam, Netherlands
Peter Honeyman . . . . Michigan Univ, USA
Pierre Paradinas . . . . Gemplus, France
Sihan Qing . . . . Acad. Sciences Beijing, China
Michel Ugon . . . . Bull CP-8, France
Doug Tygar . . . . Carnegie-Mellon Univ., USA
Anthony Watson . . . . ECU Perth, Australia
Wijang Zhang . . . . Shangai, China

Steering Committee

Vincent Cordonnier, R2DP Lille, France

Local Organizing Committee

Catherine Rouyer, UCL, Belgium
Patricia Focant, UCL, Belgium
Catherine Konstantinidis, UCL, Belgium
Benoît Macq, UCL, Belgium
Damien Giry, UCL, Belgium (editing and printing)

Table of Contents

Session 5: Authentication

Session 6: Cryptography and Applications

Session 7: Advanced Encryption Standard

User-Defined Divisibility of Ecash and a Practical Implementation

Eli Biham and Amichai Shulman

Computer Science Department
Technion
Haifa 32000, Israel
biham@cs.technion.ac.il

Abstract. We propose a new electronic cash scheme with divisible coins which can be implemented on smartcards. In this scheme, the division of coins is not restricted to withdrawal-time choices, and can be done during off-line payments in any convenient way. It is the first divisible-coin scheme in which the amount of required storage is small (about 1000 bytes) regardless of the division of the coins.

1 Introduction

An electronic cash (ecash) system is a system in which digital information, manipulated by electronic devices (such as personal computers, cash registry and smartcards), is used to replace the everyday use of cash money. Behind any ecash system stands a set of data structures and algorithms that imitate the main protocols of withdrawal, payment and deposit. These protocols involve three parties: a consumer (user), a shop (payee) and the bank.

The first off-line ecash system relying on cryptographic tools (rather than tamper-proof devices) was introduced in [ChFN90]. The ecash systems introduced in the cryptographic literature (unlike systems used in commercial applications) since then [AmCr94, Bra94, EO94, Fer94, FrYu93, Ok95, OO89, Ya94] use the concept of "coins". Each coin is a piece of information, obtained by the user at the time of withdrawal, and represents a fixed amount of money. The coin is usually a combination of random elements chosen by the user and digital signatures of the bank. In a typical payment protocol, the user uses the signatures to convince the payee that the coin is authentic, and then signs a nonce (generated by the payee) with the random elements. During deposit the payee hands to the bank all the information obtained in the payment protocol. The bank verifies the authenticity of the coin and the signature generated by the user, and then credits the shop's account. The different ecash methods described in the cryptographic literature differ in the features they offer and the performance they deliver. Table 1 compares the main features and performance issues of some of the ecash systems, before going into a more detailed description of ecash systems that offer divisibility.

J.J. Quisquater and B. Schneier (Eds.): CARDIS 2000, LNCS 1820, pp. 1–18, 2000.

Table 1: Comparison of Ecash Methods

	Bra94	EO94	Fer94	OO89	Ok95	Ya94	Our System
Anonymity	+	+	+	+	+	+	+
Unlinkability	+	Partial	+	-	-	+	Partial
Divisibility	-	Partial	-	Partial	Partial	-	Full
Transferability	-	-	-	-	-	-	-
Computational Requirements	Low	High	Low	High	Med*	High	Med
Storage Requirements	High	High	High	High	Low	High	Low

* Improving the unlinkability in this system increases the computational requirements dramatically.

1.1 Ecash Systems That Support Divisibility

The system described in [EO94] offers divisibility via a binary division tree. In the first level, the original coin can be divided into two sub-coins, in the next level each sub-coin can be further spliced in two, and so on. The depth of the division tree is chosen during the withdrawal protocol together with the monetary value of the leaves (the value of a node is the sum of the values of its direct descendents). The system suggests a tradeoff between extensive computation (by the user) during the payment and non-feasible memory requirements. The computational requirements as well as the storage requirements are strongly related to the depth of the division tree. The withdrawal protocol for each coin requires a huge number of modular exponentiations. This number is exponential in the height of the division tree.

The system in [OO89] uses disposable zero-knowledge certificates to implement ecash. In this system the division is restricted to one level with all sub-coins having the same monetary value. The number of sub-coins is a system parameter. This system requires a huge amount of storage, both for a constant overhead and for each of the coins. The payment and withdrawal protocols require a large number of exponentiations. The system offers no unlinkability since all coins of one user can be related to each other.

The system in [Ok95] uses a binary tree approach to the division of coins. The withdrawal protocol in this system is very efficient assuming that a user has an approved electronic license. The payment protocol requires a small number of modular exponentiations (approximately 20 for a system that supports reasonable monetary resolution). The system offers no unlinkability because it depends on a computation extensive protocol for receiving the electronic license, and therefore the same license is used for all the coins used by a single user. The divisibility is limited as in all systems that use binary division trees. Recently this system was improved in [CFT98]. The improved version is considerably more efficient, but still cannot be applied in practice.

1.2 Our New Ecash System

Our new system offers a novel solution to the memory requirements and coin division. The system offers full anonymity and full divisibility. The withdrawn coin can be easily divided into any number of sub-coins with arbitrary values. The sub-coins can be divided further (with any arbitrary monetary division) during payments as many times as required. The unlinkability is partly compromised since all the payments made with the same coin could be related to each other. The system does not offer transferability.

In our system, at the time of withdrawal, the user *arbitrarily* decides how to divide the coin into sub-coins in the first level. The amount of memory required for storing the withdrawn coin is small, and can be compared to the amount of memory required for a single (undivisible) coin in [Bra94] and [Fer94]. A user can now use each of the sub-coins for payment. A user can even split an unused sub-coin into smaller arbitrary monetary values at *any time*. The spliced sub-coins can be divided further by the user, generating a division tree of an arbitrary depth. The additional storage required for splitting sub-coins is negligible. Moreover, unlike other systems, only a small part of the division tree should be kept in memory, since nodes cannot be kept before their generation, nor should be kept after their full payment.

Using this unique feature of our system a user decides on the division during payment. For example, assume that originally a $100 coin is divided into two $20 sub-coins, five $10 sub-coins, and two $5 sub-coins, and the amount to be paid is $17.53. The user can divide a $20 sub-coin into one $17.53 sub-coin to be paid, and several additional sub-coins with arbitrary values, whose total value is $2.47. Alternatively, the user can pay with sub-coins of $10 and $5, and divide another sub-coin to pay the remaining $2.53.

In some situations, "advance-division" techniques can be implemented. For example: users who regularly ride in a bus or use pay phones need to pay the same amount several times. In our system, when a sub-coin is divided in order to pay a bus ticket, it is possible to divide the rest of the original sub-coin into additional sub-coins of the same value which can later be used for the same purpose. This technique is expected to reduce the number of future division and the total number of spent coins, and thus increase the system's efficiency.

The required amount of computations in our system is smaller than that required for the systems described in Section 0. The amount of calculation required for withdrawal is constant and does not depend on the number of sub-coins. The amount of calculation required for a payment is independent of the number of sub-coins in each level of division, and is linear in the depth of the sub-coin in the division tree. The total amount of memory required by our system easily fits in today's smartcards. The main drawback in this system is slow smartcard performance. However, we believe that next-generation smartcard processors will be much faster, and thus enable the implementation of our system with reasonable speed.

In our system the user commits to a series of pseudo-random numbers during the withdrawal protocol, the knowledge of which can be easily proven by the user without the disclosure of the numbers themselves. This series is based on a random number generator and the knowledge of a discrete logarithm modulo a composite. The payments in our system are based on a variation of Schnorr's signature scheme ([Sch91]), which uses a composite modulus instead of a prime number. A description of this signature scheme is given in Section 0. Payments with each sub-coin are done using a unique random element, and thus double spending of a sub-coin can be identified, and reveal the secret key and the identity of the user.

2 Schnorr's Signature Scheme with an RSA Modulus

In [Sch91] Schnorr suggests an efficient signature scheme that uses a large prime modulus p and a prime divisor q of $p-1$. All the exponents in Schnorr's system are calculated modulo the factor q.

We describe a variant of Schnorr's signature scheme in which the modulus p is replaced with an RSA modulus n. The factor q should be replaced in our system with a term whose knowledge does not contribute to the factorization of n. We chose to replace the term q with another RSA modulus n_1.

2.1 Generation of Signature Keys

The signature scheme requires four large prime numbers p_1, q_1, p_2, q_2, such that $p = 2p_1p_2 + 1$ and $q = 2q_1q_2 + 1$ are also prime numbers. We then calculate the RSA moduli as $n = pq$ and $n_1 = p_1q_1$. The numbers p_1 and q_1 are chosen to have the same size, and the numbers p_2 and q_2 are chosen to have the same, much larger size. We suggest to chose the primes p_2, q_2 at least 100 bits longer than p_1, q_1. The primes p_1, q_1 should be sufficiently large to make the factorization of n_1 difficult.

To complete the system setup, we select a term g of order n_1 in Z_n^*. The terms g, n, n_1 are then published as system parameters.

A user who wants to sign messages selects a random number $s \in Z_{n_1}$ and calculates $h \equiv g^s \bmod n$. The term h constitutes the public key of the signer, and s is the signer's private key. Notice, that the signer does not need to know the factorization of neither n nor n_1.

2.2 Signing a Message

The signature protocol is the same as Schnorr's. Given a message m, the signer selects a random term $r \in Z_{n_1}$ and calculates $x \equiv g^r \bmod n$ and $y \equiv r + sf(x,m) \bmod n_1$, where f is a one way collision intractable hash function. The signature of the message is the tupple (x, y). The verification of the signature is done by checking whether the equation $g^y \equiv h^{f(x,m)} x \pmod{n}$ holds.

2.3 Security

The safety of Schnorr's original scheme is based on the difficulty of calculating DLOG modulo a prime number. Calculating DLOG modulo a composite number is not an easier problem, and therefore our variation of the signature scheme is at least as safe. Moreover, calculating DLOG modulo a prime number does not imply calculating DLOG modulo a composite number without knowing its prime factors.

Therefore, our scheme remains safe even if the DLOG problem is found to be easy. Note also that solving only the factorization problem does not help in attacking our signature scheme either.

A slight variant of this signature scheme in which the small modulus n_1 is removed, n is any RSA composite, and y is instead computed non-modularly (with large random r's) has the feature that finding the secret key s is as difficult as factorization: The attacker generates a signature key with some large secret key s of his choice, and signs as many messages as required for the attack. Then he applies the algorithm which recovers the secret key. Note that such an attack cannot distinguish between the chosen s and $s+i\ (n)$ for any integer i. Thus, the algorithm finds $s+i\ (n)$, and the attacker subtracts his chosen s and receives a multiple of (n), which suffices to factor n.

Note that a similar signature scheme with composite moduli was suggested by Girault [Gi90]. We discuss some properties of it in Section 0. This scheme could be used as an alternative to our scheme in the ecash system introduced in this paper.

3   The System

3.1   System Setup

The bank selects four prime numbers p_1, q_1, p_2, q_2 and constructs the terms n, n_1 and g as described in Section 0. We recommend using 384-bit p_1 and q_1, and 490-bit p_2 and q_2. The bank then picks a set of RSA signature keys, d_b and e_b, such that $d_b e_b\ \ 1(\mathrm{mod}\ (n))$. These keys are then used by the bank to sign the coins.

The bank publishes n, n_1, g and e_b. It also publishes two one-way collision-intractable hash function $f : \{0,1\}^* \quad Z_n^*$ and $f_1 : \{0,1\}^* \quad Z_{2^a}$, where a is a parameter of the system whose recommended value is 128. Finally, the bank publishes a hash function H that maps it's input into Z_{2^t}, where t is a security parameter of the system (setting t to be 48 seems enough for coins of up to \$100). The function H can be implemented using the function f, but for reasons of clarity we distinct the two functions in the following discussion.

The bank also sets another security parameter s whose recommended value is 80. This parameter affects the withdrawal protocol and contributes both to its safety and to the anonymity of the user.

3.2   Representation of a Coin

Each coin consists of four elements defined by two secret terms and five public terms. The first element is the user's signature keys. In our system the user's secret key is the term U, constructed as $I \| x$ where I is a unique identifier of the coin selected by the bank and x is a random number known only to the user. Using 64-bit identifiers suffice for any practical purposes. The user's public key is the term h_U, calculated from the secret key as $h_U \quad g^U \pmod{n}$.

The second element is a description of the coin's division into smaller coins (sub-coins). Such a description includes the number of sub-coins and the denomination of each sub-coin. This information is represented by the term D, called the *division string*. If a sub-coin j is divided into smaller sub-coins then another division string, D_j, describes this division. Further sub-divisions of the l'th sub-coin in D_j have their own division strings $D_{j,l}$, and so on. The division strings define a denomination w_j for each sub-coin j, a denomination $w_{j,l}$ for each smaller sub-coin l of a sub-coin j, and so on. The only limitation on division strings is that the total sum of the sub-coins equals the worth of the divided coin or sub-coin ($w = \quad w_j$).

$$j$$

The third element is a sequence of random numbers used for signing transactions. In the proposed system, the sequence is defined as $r_j \quad k^{H(c,D,j)} \bmod n_1$ for each sub-coin j where the public term c is a random seed selected by the user, D is the division string and the secret term k is an element of $Z_{n_1}^*$. The sequence is also used further to split sub-coins, where $r_{j,l} \quad k^{H(c,D,j,D_j,l)} \bmod n_1$ corresponds to the l'th sub-coin of the j'th sub-coin. The secret term k defines the public term $h_k \quad g^k \pmod{n}$.

The last element of the coin is the bank's signature. The bank signs the public terms c, D, h_U and h_k during the withdrawal protocol. The bank's signature S_c is an RSA signature constructed as $(S_c)^{e_b} \quad h_U f(c,D,h_U,h_k) \pmod{n}$. The public terms of the coin are transferred between parties during the different protocols. We denote this public information as $C = (c,D,h_U,h_k,S_c)$.

3.3 The Procedure Prove_DLOG

During the payment protocol the user proves to the verifier that the DLOG of a certain term is known to the user and is a power of a signed secret key. In order to do that, the payment protocol makes use of a special procedure we call Prove_DLOG(h_x,h_y,h_{xy}). The procedure is a protocol between a prover and a verifier. The inputs are $h_x \quad g^x \pmod{n}$, $h_y \quad g^y \pmod{n}$ and h_{xy}, where x and y are known only to the prover. The prover proves to the verifier that $h_{xy} \quad g^{xy} \pmod{n}$.

Given the inputs, the verifier selects two random blinding elements $\quad$, $Z_{n_1}^*$, calculates $u \quad g \ h_x \bmod n$, and sends u to the prover. The prover computes $v \quad u^y \bmod n$ and gives the answer to the verifier. The verifier is convinced that h_{xy} is correct if the equation $v \quad h_y h_{xy} \pmod{n}$ holds. The procedure Prove_DLOG is given in Fig. 1.

On input h_x $g^x \pmod{n}$, h_y $g^y \pmod{n}$ and h_{xy}

Prover | Verifier

$$Z_{n_1}^*$$

$$u \quad g\ h_x \bmod n$$

$$u$$

$$v \quad u^y \bmod n$$

$$v$$

$$v \overset{?}{=} h_y\, h_{xy} \pmod{n}$$

Fig. 1: Procedure Prove_DLOG

3.4 Basic Payment Protocol

The payment protocol is a variation of Schnorr's signature protocol. For each coin, the user's key and random element are fixed at the withdrawal time, and the message includes the data of the transaction (amount, participants' ids and a time stamp).

Given a payment of *amount* dollars, the user selects a coin C and a sub-coin j of C whose worth, w_j, is equal to the amount paid. The user sends to the payee the coin and the index j. The payee checks the bank's signature on the coin by verifying the equation $(S_c)^{e_b} \overset{?}{=} h_U\, f(c,D,h_U,h_k) \pmod{n}$. The payee also checks that the sub-coin j is of the correct amount to be paid ($w_j = amount$). The user and the payee can both calculate now $R \quad H(c,D,j)$, from which the user calculates the sequence element $r \quad k^R \bmod n_1$, and $b \quad g^r \bmod n$. Using the interactive procedure Prove_b(R,b,h_k), the user proves to the payee that $b \quad g^{(k^R)} \pmod{n}$ without revealing neither k nor r. The elements r and b are then used to sign the message $R\,|\,timestamp\,|\,shop$, using the procedure Schnorr_Sign$(R,b,R\,|\,timestamp\,|\,shop)$. If the signing procedure succeeds then the payment is accepted by the payee who keeps the description of the coin and the signature on the transaction. An overview of the payment protocol is given in Fig. 2.

The procedure Prove_b is the core of the payment protocol. Its inputs are an exponent R, an element $h_k \quad g^k \pmod{n}$ where k is known only to the prover and an element b. Prove_b's goal is to convince the payee that $b \quad g^{(k^R)} \pmod{n}$. The procedure includes a main loop that has one iteration for each bit of R, and a final step that proves all the 1 bits of R.

The equation $h_{i+1} \quad g^{e_{i+1}} \pmod{n}$ holds at the beginning of each iteration i, where e_{i+1} is known only to the prover. The prover then calculates $h_i \quad g^{e_{i+1}^2} \bmod n$ and

User | Payee

j s.t. $w_j = amount$

C, j

$(S_c)^{e_b} \overset{?}{\ } h_U f(c, h_U, h_k) \pmod{n}$

$w_j \overset{?}{=} amount$

$R \quad H(c, D, j)$

$r \quad k^R \bmod n_1$ $\qquad$ $R \quad H(c, D, j)$

$b \quad g^r \bmod n$

Prove_b(R, b, h_k) $\qquad$ Prove_b(R, b, h_k)

Schnorr_Sign$(R, b, R \mid timestamp \mid shop)$ $\qquad$ Schnorr_Sign$(R, b, R \mid timestamp \mid sho$

Fig. 2. Payment Protocol - Overview

uses the interactive procedure Prove_DLOG(h_{i+1}, h_{i+1}, h_i) to show that h_i is correct. If the i'th bit of R is 1 then the prover also calculates $h_i \quad g^{(ke_{i+1}^2)} \bmod n$ and sends it to the verifier without a proof. At the end of each iteration, the prover sets $e_i \quad \begin{matrix} e_{i+1}^2 \bmod n_1, & \text{if R}[i]=0; \\ ke_{i+1}^2 \bmod n_1, & \text{if R}[i]=1 \end{matrix}$ and the verifier sets $h_i \quad \begin{matrix} h_i, & \text{if R}[i]=0; \\ h_i, & \text{if R}[i]=1 \end{matrix}$.

After the last iteration of the loop, the prover uses a single execution of Prove_DLOG to prove all the elements h_i. To do that, the verifier selects a random element $\ _i \quad Z_{n_1}^*$ for each bit of R that is set to 1. The verifier sends the product $\underset{R[i]=1}{\ } h_i^{\ i} \bmod n$ to the prover. The prover calculates $\tilde{h} \quad \underset{R[i]=1}{\overset{k}{\ }} h_i^{\ i} \bmod n$, and they both execute Prove_DLOG($\underset{R[i]=1}{\ } h_i^{\ i}, h_k, \tilde{h})$. If the procedure succeeds, the verifier checks that the equation $\tilde{h} \quad \underset{R[i]=1}{\ } h_i^{\ i} \pmod{n}$ holds.

Prover	Verifier

$e_{t-1} \quad k$ $\qquad\qquad\qquad\qquad\qquad\qquad\qquad\qquad h_{t-1} \quad h_k$

For $i = (t-2)$ Down To 1 Do :

$\qquad h_i \quad g^{e_{i+1}^2} \bmod n$

$\qquad\qquad \text{Prove\_DLOG}(g^{e_{i+1}}, g^{e_{i+1}}, h_i) \quad \text{Prove\_DLOG}(h_{i+1}, h_{i+1}, h_i)$

$\qquad \text{If } R[i] = 1 \text{ then } h_i \quad (h_i)^k \bmod n$

$\qquad\qquad\qquad\qquad\qquad h_i$

$\qquad e_i \quad \begin{cases} e_{i+1}^2 \bmod n_1, & \text{if } R[i] = 0; \\ k e_{i+1}^2 \bmod n_1, & \text{if } R[i] = 1 \end{cases} \qquad h_i \quad \begin{cases} h_i, & \text{if } R[i] = 0; \\ h_i, & \text{if } R[i] = 1 \end{cases}$

$\qquad\qquad\qquad\qquad\qquad\qquad\qquad\qquad R[i] = 1 \qquad _i \quad Z_{n_1}^*$

$\qquad\qquad\qquad\qquad h_i \quad ^i$
$\qquad\qquad\qquad\qquad _{R[i]=1}$

$\qquad\qquad k$

$\tilde{h} \qquad h_i \quad ^i \quad \bmod n$
$_{R[i]=1}$

$\qquad\qquad \text{Prove\_DLOG}(\quad h_i \quad ^i, h_k, \tilde{h}) \quad \text{Prove\_DLOG}(\quad h_i \quad ^i, h_k, \tilde{h})$
$\qquad\qquad\qquad _{R[i]=1} \qquad\qquad\qquad\qquad\qquad _{R[i]=1}$

$\qquad\qquad\qquad\qquad\qquad\qquad\qquad\qquad \tilde{h} \overset{?}{\quad} h_i \quad ^i \pmod n$
$\qquad\qquad\qquad\qquad\qquad\qquad\qquad\qquad\quad _{R[i]=1}$

$\qquad\qquad\qquad\qquad\qquad\qquad\qquad\qquad h_1 \overset{?}{\quad} b \pmod n$

Fig. 3. Payment Protocol - Procedure Prove_b

At the end of Prove_b, the verifier knows that $h_1 \quad g^{(k^R)} \pmod n$ and checks that $b \quad h_1$ holds. The procedure Prove_b is given in Fig. 3.

The procedure Schnorr_Sign used at the last step of the payment protocol is an implementation of the Schnorr signature protocol using composite numbers, as described in section 0. Its inputs are R and b such that $b \quad g^{(k^R)} \pmod n$, and a string *message* to be signed. The signer uses $k^R \bmod n_1$ as the secret random element in the signature protocol. Procedure Schnorr_Sign is given in Fig. 4.

Signer	Verifier
$y \quad \left(k^R + Uf(b, message)\right) \bmod n_1$	
y	
	$g^y \overset{?}{=} bh_U^{f(b, message)} \pmod{n}$

Fig. 4. Payment Protocol - Procedure Schnorr_Sign

3.5 Splitting a Sub-Coin

In this system sub-coins can be divided into smaller sub-coins at any time. A sub-coin j of a coin C can be divided to any number of sub-coins with the same total value as the original sub-coin. However, we must ensure that a sub-coin can either be divided or be paid, but not both.

In order to split a sub-coin the user decides how to divide it (the number of smaller sub-coins and their values) and marks the sub-coin as split. When a sub-coin, l of a sub-coin j is used for payment, the user first proves the division of the sub-coin j to the payee and then pays its l'th sub-coin. The way a specific sub-coin is split, must be fixed by the user when the sub-coin is spliced for the first time.

The protocol for paying with a sub-coin of another sub-coin is a two stage protocol. Each of the stages is a slight variation of the original payment protocol. The first stage of the protocol proves the division of a sub-coin j of a coin C. This stage is very similar to paying with that sub-coin. The difference is that the user declares at the beginning that this is a split sub-coin, and the signature at the end of the protocol is constructed by: $y \quad k^R + Uf(b, R \mid D_j) \bmod n_1$, where D_j is a division string that describes how the sub-coin is spliced (this string has the same format as the division string D). The description string D_j is given to the payee at the beginning of the protocol. The payee can check the signature and that D_j describes a valid partition of the sub-coin (i.e., that the total value of the smaller sub-coins equals the value of the original sub-coin). The user must use the same string D_j each time the sub-coin j is being used, otherwise the identity of the user could be exposed in the same way as with double spending.

In the second stage of the splitting protocol, the user makes a payment, using a sub-coin l of the spliced sub-coin j. Again this protocol is very similar to the original payment protocol, with the only difference that the value R is calculated by $R \quad H(c, D, j, D_j, l)$. Fig. 5 describes a payment protocol using a sub-coin of another sub-coin.

A sub-coin of another sub-coin can be further subdivided in the same manner. For example, using the m'th sub-coin of the l'th sub-coin of a sub-coin j, requires proving the division of the sub-coin j using a division string D_j, proving the division of the sub-coin l using another division string $D_{j,l}$ and finally paying with it's m'th sub-coin, where the value R is calculated as $r \quad H(c, D, j, D_j, l, D_{j,l}, m)$. In the general

User	Payee
j, l s.t. $w_{j,l} = amount$	

C, j, l

$(S_c)^{e_b} \overset{?}{=} h_U \, f(c, h_U, h_k) \,(\bmod n)$

$w_{j,l} \overset{?}{=} amount$

User	Payee
$R_1 \quad H(c,D,j)$	
$r_1 \quad k^{R_1} \bmod n_1$	$R_1 \quad H(c,D,j)$
$b_1 \quad g^{r_1} \bmod n$	

$\text{Prove\_b}(R_1, b_1, h_k) \quad \text{Prove\_b}(R_1, b_1, h_k)$

$\text{Schnorr\_Sign}(R_1, b_1, R_1 \mid D_j) \quad \text{Schnorr\_Sign}(R_1, b_1, R_1 \mid D_j)$

User	Payee
$R_2 \quad H(c,D,j,D_j,l)$	
$r_2 \quad k^{R_2} \bmod n_1$	$R_2 \quad H(c,D,j,D_j,l)$
$b_2 \quad g^{r_2} \bmod n$	

$\text{Prove\_b}(R_2, b_2, h_k) \quad \text{Prove\_b}(R_2, b_2, h_k)$

$\text{Schnorr\_Sign}(R_2, b_2, R_2 \mid timestamp \mid shop) \quad \text{Schnorr\_Sign}(R_2, b_2, R_2 \mid timestamp \mid shop)$

Fig. 5. Payment Protocol - Using a Split Sub-Coin

case, the division path from the original coin down to the sub-coin being paid should be proven before paying the sub-coin itself. This feature maximizes the flexibility in spending the original coin.

3.6 Withdrawal Protocol

In the withdrawal protocol, the user gets a valid coin $C = (c, D, h_U, h_k, S_c)$. During the protocol a coin is constructed, including the signature, without disclosing the coin itself. We take advantage of the multiplicative property of the RSA signature to construct the bank's signature on h_U in a number of iterations. Then we add to it a signature on the hash value $f(c, D, h_U, h_k)$. Since the public key h_U appears in the signature outside a hash value, we must use the same modulo n in all the other calculations in the system, including the user's signature on transaction.

To begin the construction of the coin, the bank generates a unique coin identifier, id, and a random number $x \in Z_{2^a}$, and sends them to the user. Both the bank and the user compute the terms $x_1 \ldots x_{2s}$ as $x_i = f(x, id, time, i)$. The terms x_i are used to construct the terms $U_1 \ldots U_{2s}$, where $U_i = 0 \parallel id \parallel x_i$ (the length of the padding zeros string should be at least $\log_2 s$ to ensure that no overflow occurs when we add-up s

U_i's). The user selects a random string of bits, T, of length s, and calculates

$$h_U \prod_{i=1}^{s} g^{U_{2i} \, T[i]} \bmod n .$$ The user also picks a random number $c \quad Z_{2^t}$, an exponent

$k \quad Z_{n_1}^*$ and a blinding element $\quad Z_n^*$. In addition, the user chooses the way the coin is spliced into sub-coins, and constructs an appropriate division string D. The user calculates $h_k \quad g^k \bmod n$, and gives the bank the result of calculating $^{e_b} f(c, D, h_U, h_k) \bmod n$. Notice that there is no way for the bank to check the blinded hash value during the withdrawal protocol but the construction of the signature is such that supplying a false hash value results in an invalid coin that cannot be used for payment. This idea is very similar to that shown in Ferguson's randomized blind signature. The bank can neither check that D is a valid division string, but an invalid string would be rejected during payment.

For the second stage of the withdrawal protocol, the bank selects a set of random blinding elements $_1 \ldots {}_s \quad Z_n^*$, and calculates $\prod_{i=1}^{s} {}_i \bmod n$. This stage includes s iterations of an oblivious transfer protocol. In each iteration, i, the user receives from the bank a partial blinded signature denoted by S_{c_i}. The user can choose in each iteration one of two signatures. The choice is made according to the bits of the string T, as follows: $S_{c_i} \quad {}_i \, g^{U_{2i} \, T[i]}{}^{d_b} \bmod n$. In the last iteration, the bank incorporates the rest of the information in the signature. In this iteration, the information received by the user is the following: $S_{c_s} \quad {}_s \, g^{U_{2s} \, t[s]} \, {}^{e_b} f(c, D, h_U, h_k)^{d_b} \bmod n$.

After the last iteration, the bank deducts the value of the coin from the user's account, keeps the coin's identifier together with the identity of the user in a database, and sends to the user the product, , of the blinding elements. The user then calculates the signature for the coin as $S_c \quad \prod_{i=1}^{s} S_{c_i} {}^{1} \, {}^{1} \bmod n$, and checks it

using the equation $\left(S_c\right)^{e_b} \stackrel{?}{=} h_U f(c, D, h_U, h_k) \pmod n$. The withdrawal protocol is shown in Fig. 6.

User	Bank

Fig. 6. Withdrawal Protocol

<u>Payee</u>   <u>Bank</u>

$$C,$$
$$j,b,$$
$$shop, time,$$
$$y$$

$$(S_c)^{e_b} \stackrel{?}{=} h_U f(c, D, h_U, h_k) \pmod{n}$$
$$r = H(c, j)$$
$$g^y \stackrel{?}{=} bh_U^{f(r,b,shop,time)} \pmod{n}$$

Fig. 7. Deposit Protocol

3.7 Deposit Protocol

In the deposit protocol, the payee gives the coin C to the bank together with the information on the transaction (j, b, *shop*, *time*) and the signature y. The bank first checks the validity of the coin. Then the bank checks the signature by verifying the equation $g^y \stackrel{?}{=} bh_U^{f(r,b,shop,time)} \pmod{n}$. If both are successful, the bank credits the account of the payee, and stores the transaction in a database. The full description of the deposit protocol is given in Fig. 7. After the deposit, the bank checks that the transaction does not involve a sub-coin that was already used earlier. If so, the bank applies the algorithm for exposure of double spenders described in the next section.

In order to deposit a sub-coin of another sub-coin, the payee gives to the bank the information about splitting the sub-coin (j, b, D_j, y) and the information about paying with the smaller sub-coin (l, b', *shop*, *time*, y'), in addition to the coin C. In the more general case, the payee gives the bank all the information about the full path from the original coin to the deposited sub-coin.

3.8 Exposure of Double Spenders

For the exposure of the double spender we use the property of Schnorr's signature scheme, that signatures of two different messages with the same secret key and same random element expose the secret key. This is a property that exists in all the ElGamal type signature schemes ([El85]). The bank detects double-spending of a coin if the same sub-coin j of a coin C, appears in more than one payment transaction. The bank then selects two transactions involving the same sub-coin j. Given both transaction information, and given $m_i = f(r, b, shop_i, time_i)$ for $i \in \{1,2\}$, the bank computes the user's secret key by calculating $U = (y_1 - y_2)(m_1 - m_2)^{-1} \bmod n_1$. By construction of the withdrawal protocol, the upper bits of secret key U contain a coin identifier that can be matched by the bank with an identity of a user.

The same method is used to expose a user that exploited a sub-coin both for payment and for splitting, or spliced the same sub-coin in two different ways. In the first case, we have two messages $m_1 = f(r,b,shop,time)$ and $m_2 = f(r,b,D_j)$ with their respective signatures y_1, y_2. In the second case the different messages are $m_1 = f(r,b,D_j)$ and $e_2 = f(r,b,D_j)$.

4 Cryptographic Safety of the System

The system is based on two number theoretic problems: DLOG and factorization of large numbers. In [BrMc92], [Gi90] and [Sa90], identification schemes are described that combine the two problems. We combine the two problems in a different way.

4.1 Computing DLOG Modulo Composite Numbers

The problem of computing DLOG modulo a prime number is considered difficult. It is obvious that the problem of computing DLOG modulo a product of prime numbers is not weaker than the finding DLOG modulo each of these primes. It can be easily shown that computing DLOG modulo a composite number leads to factorization. In the procedure Prove_DLOG we rely on an extended Diffie-Hellman assumption modulo a composite number. A proof is given in [Sh85] for the fact that cracking the Diffie-Hellman system modulo an RSA number is at least as hard as factorization. We can also prove that given the series of numbers $g, g^k, g^{(k^2)}, g^{(k^3)} \ldots g^{(k^r)}$ modulo an RSA number n, finding the secret exponent k or any power of it leads to the factorization of that number. An even more general result can be found in [BBR97].

4.2 The Construction of the Composite Number

In our system we use stronger assumptions, and thus the above mentioned proofs are not valid any more: (1) The composite n is chosen in a specific way, thus it is unknown if it can be factored easily. However, p and q seem to be very strong primes and thus n seems difficult to factor. (2) We publish a factor n_1 of (n), which might help factorization, although it seems that it does not. In particular, factorization algorithms using (n) to factor n are not applicable when only divisors of (n) are known. (3) Our generator g is of order n_1, rather than (n). Therefore, the reductions from 0 would yield n_1 rather than (n), which gives nothing to the attacker.

In our system the composite n_1 is not a factor of either p 1 or q 1. If all prime numbers p_1, q_1, p_2, q_2 are of the same size then

$$\frac{n}{n_1} = \frac{(2p_1p_2+1)(2q_1q_2+1)}{p_1q_1} = 4p_2q_2 + \frac{p_2}{q_1} + \frac{q_2}{p_1} + \frac{1}{p_1q_1} = 4p_2q_2 + \quad \text{where} \quad \text{is a small}$$

integer. Thus, $p_2 q_2$ can be retrieved, as well as (n) and the factorization of n. Therefore it is required that p_2, q_2 are much larger than p_1, q_1. We recommend that they should be at least 100 bits longer. Unlike in [Gi90], bits of $p_2 + q_2$ are not revealed.

For the factorization of the smaller modulo, n_1, to be difficult, we have to choose it's prime factors, p_1 and q_1, to be at least 384 bits long. Following the reasoning of the previous paragraph, we recommend choosing the larger primes p_2 and q_2 to be 490 bits long. Given the sizes of the prime numbers we result with n_1 of size 768 bits, n of size 1750 bits and each of the prime factors of n of size 875 bits.

4.3 Safety of the Signatures

In [BrMc92] a proof is given that breaking the identification scheme leads to factorization. Such a proof is not given in the case of the signature scheme described in the same paper. The reason for that is evident when looking at the calculation of the signature: y $r + se$. In the identification scheme the term e is randomly selected by the verifier. In the case of the signature scheme, the term e is not chosen at random, but partly determined by the value of the term r.

The main attack on the system is by collecting a set of signatures from the same coin, and solving the equation set: y_l $k^\eta + Ue_l \pmod{n_1}$. Solving this set of equations is easy if the difference between two r values is either small or constant. Another attack on the system is by using the algorithm for finding messages in small-exponent RSA described in [CFPR96]. This algorithm can be used to attack the system given three equations. We first remove the terms Ue_l from the first two equations by subtracting multiples of the third equation. Then we view the resultant two equations as polynomials in k, whose (probably unique) common root is secret. By computing gcd of the two polynomials, the root can be computed.

To overcome the two types of attack we generate the r values using the hash function H. This way, the hamming distance between any two values is high and the difference between any two values seems random. We need the output of H to be long enough to achieve good distribution of the values for one coin. According to the estimations in [CFPR96], the attack is applicable to r's up to size of 32 bits. Taking into consideration that for a coin of value \$100, there is an upper bound of 10^4 2^{14} on the number of payments (the number of required r values), we recommend using of r's of size 48 bits (i.e., the value of the security parameter t is 48).

We can further enhance the safety of the system if we replace the term k^r with a more complex polynomial in k. This has no effect on the efficiency of the system if the additional terms are collected from the powers of k computed anyway during the payment protocol.

5 Summary

We described a very practical and flexible coin-based ecash protocol. It can be implemented on smartcards with the following computation times:

Modulo Construction Method	Withdrawal Protocol	Payment Protocol
Long Numbers	55	54
Short Numbers	18	18
Girault's Method	4.6	4.5

We anticipate that these times will be greatly reduced in the next generation of smartcards. In the full paper we will describe other security features of this protocol, and its immunity to various attacks.

References

AmCr94 S. D'Amiano, G. Di Crescenzo, "Methodology for Digital-Money Based on General Cryptographic Tools", Advances in Cryptology Proceeding of EUROCRYPT '94, Lecture Notes in Computer Science, pp. 156-170, Springer-Verlag, 1995.

BBR97   E. Biham, D. Boneh, O. Reingold, "Generalized Diffie-Hellman Modulo a Composite is not Weaker than Factoring", Electronic Colloquium on Computational Complexity, http://www.eccc.uni-trier.de/eccc ,TR97-061, 1997.

Bra94   S. Brands, "An Efficient Off-line Electronic Cash System Based on the Representation Problem in Groups of Prime Order", Advances in Cryptology, Proceedings of CRYPTO '93, Lecture Notes in Computer Science, pp. 302-318, Springer-Verlag, 1994.

BrMc92 E. F. Brikell and K. S. McCurley, "An Interactive identification scheme based on discrete logarithms and factoring", Journal of Cryptology, Vol 5, No. 1, pp. 29-40, 1992

ChFN90 D. Chaum, A. Fiat, M. Naor, "Untraceable Electronic Cash", Advances in Cryptology, Proceedings of CRYPTO '88, Lecture Notes in Computer Science, pp. 319-327, Springer-Verlag, 1990.

CFPR96 D. Coppersmith, M.K. Franklin, J. Patarin, M.K. Reiter, "Low-exponent RSA with related messages", Advances in Cryptology, Proceedings of EUROCRYPT '96, Lecture Notes in Computer Science, pp. 1-9, Springer-Verlag, 1997.

CFT98   A. Chan, Y. Frankel, Y. Tsiounis, "Easy Come - Easy Go Divisible Cash", Advances in Cryptology, Proceedings of EUROCRYPT '98, Lecture Notes in Computer Science, pp. 561-575, Springer-Verlag, 1998.

El85   T. ElGamal, "A public Key Cryptosystem and a Signature Scheme based on Discrete Logarithms, IEEE Trans. On Information Theory, Vol. IT-31 No. 4, pp. 469-472, July 1985.

EO94   T. Eng, T. Okamoto, "Single-Term Divisible Electronic Coins", Advances in Cryptology, EUROCRYPT '94, Lecture Notes in Computer Science, pp. 311-323, Springer-Verlag, 1995.

Fer94   N. Ferguson, "Single Term Off-line Coins", Advances in Cryptology, EUROCRYPT '93, Lecture Notes in Computer Science, pp. 318-328, Springer-Verlag, 1994.

FrYu93   M. Frankling, M. Yung, "Secure and Efficient Off-Line Digital Money", Proceedings of ICALP '93, Lecture Note is Computer Science, pp. 265-276, Springer-Verlag, 1993.

Gi90   M. Girault, "An Identity-based Identification Scheme based on Discrete Logarithms Modulo a Composite Number", Advances in Cryptology, EUROCRYPT '90, Lecture Notes in Computer Science, pp. 481-486, Springer-Verlag, 1991.

Ok95   T. Okamoto, "An Efficient Divisible Electronic Cash Scheme", Advances in Cryptology, CRYPTO '95, Lecture Notes in Computer Science, pp. 438-451, Springer-Verlag, 1996.

OO89   T. Okamoto, K. Ohta, "Disposable Zero-Knowledge Authentication and Their Application to Untraceable Electronic Cash", Advances in Cryptology, Proceedings of CRYPTO '89, Lecture Notes in Computer Science, pp. 481-495, Springer-Verlag, 1990.

Sa90   Saryazdi, "An Extension to ElGamal Public Key Cryptosystem with a New Signature Scheme", Communication, Control, and Signal processing, Elsevier, pp. 195-198, 1990.

Sch91   C.P. Schnorr, "Efficient Signature Generation by Smart Cards", Journal of Cryptology, Vol. 4, No. 3, pp. 161-174, 1991.

Sh85   Zehava Shmuely, "Composite Diffie-Hellman Public-Key Generating Systems are Hard to Break", Technical Report #356, Computer Science Detp., Technion - Israel Institute of Technology, February 1985.

Sha79   A. Shamir, "How to Share a Secret", Communications of the ACM, Vol. 22, No. 11, pp. 612-613, 1979.

Ya94   Y. Yacobi, "Efficient Electronic Money", Advances in Cryptology, ASIACRYPT '94, Lecture Notes in Computer Science, pp. 131-139, Springer-Verlag, 1995.

Graz98   Graz University of Technology, "Scaleable Cryptography for Smartcards", http://www.iaik.tu-graz.ac.at/RESEARCH/CRISP, 1998.

An Operational Model of QuickPay

Extended Abstract

Pieter H. Hartel[1], Jake Hill[2], and Matt Sims[2]

[1] Dept. of Electronics and Computer Science, Univ. of Southampton, UK,
phh@ecs.soton.ac.uk
[2] BT Laboratories, Martlesham Heath, Ipswich, UK,
{Jake.Hill, Matt.Sims}@bt-sys.bt.co.uk

Abstract. QuickPay is a system for micro payments aiming to avoid the cost of cryptographic operations during payments. An operational model of the system has been built to assist in the search for weaknesses in the protocols. As a result of this model building activity, one minor weakness has been found. Another more serious weakness has been re-discovered and a number of solutions are proposed.

The full paper gives the details of the model.

1 Introduction

QuickPay is a micro payment scheme with pre-payment [1,6]. The customer must register with the broker to obtain an electronic *carnet* with *value* tokens before a sale may take place. It is possible to acquire additional value tokens, or to refresh the value tokens at any time. A merchant must also register with the broker to obtain an electronic *till* with *authentication* tokens. This will enable the merchant to validate the tokens presented by the customer. Once customer and merchant are registered, a sale may proceed as follows. First the customer presents one or more value tokens to the merchant. The merchant then authenticates himself [1] with the broker and presents the customers value tokens to the broker for validation. The broker decides whether the customers tokens are valid. If the merchant is satisfied that the tokens are valid, goods/services may be delivered. The customer takes delivery but does not receive a receipt.

The QuickPay philosophy is to make transactions cheap in two ways. Firstly, offline payments are allowed although they are less secure than online payments. Secondly, payment does not require cryptographic computations. This is achieved by using real (as opposed to pseudo) random numbers as tokens. A sequence of random numbers is generated, encrypted and transferred when the customer or the merchant register with the broker. Creating the random numbers is efficient, as a hardware device (a noisy diode) is used rather than an computationally intensive algorithm. Encrypting and transmitting a sequence

---

[1] We refer to a customer using the words 'her' or 'she' and we refer to a merchant using the words 'his' or 'he'.

J.-J. Quisquater and B. Schneier (Eds.): CARDIS 2000, LNCS 1820, pp. 19–28, 2000.

of random numbers can be relatively inefficient. However, this is only done during registration; during payment transactions only a single random number is transferred in clear. Systems that use cryptographic computations during every transaction, such as Millicent [2] and Mini-Pay [5], are inherently less efficient than QuickPay but possibly more secure.

Micro payment systems raise a number of interesting questions because they differ from normal payment systems. The present paper makes the following contributions to the understanding of micro payment systems in general, and to that of QuickPay in particular:

– to introduce an operational model for the QuickPay protocols, which allows real life scenarios to be studied at an appropriate level of abstraction.
– to investigate an essential optimisation to the basic protocol, which allows multiple token payments to be replaced by a single token payment.

The operational model of QuickPay is written with the aid of the latos [3] tool, which provides type checking and animation of specifications. The type checking facility of the tool has been used to avoid inconsistencies in the model, and the animation facilities have been used to explore various transaction sequences.

The next section briefly presents the prototype implementation of QuickPay. Section 3 sketches the model of QuickPay; the complete specification is given in the full paper [4]. Section 4 presents a sample scenario, showing how QuickPay transactions can be studied using the model and the latos tool. Further scenarios are explored in full paper. Two problems and a number of solutions to one of the problems are briefly sketched in Section 5; the full paper giving the details and the proof. The last section presents conclusions and discusses further work.

2   Prototype

The QuickPay prototype has been tested on making payments over the internet. The prototype works as follows. The customer first starts her carnet application, which puts up a window to inform the customer about her balance as shown below.

The customer also starts up an unrelated application that might require payment, such as an intelligent agent that is going to make some purchases on

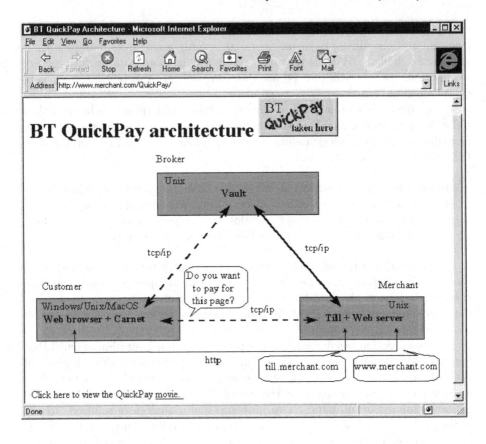

Fig. 1. The architecture of the QuickPay prototype showing how a customer might be asked to pay for access to a web server operated by a merchant.

her behalf. For the purpose of this example we will use a web browser, which is being used to select a page of information from a web server, for example http://www.merchant.com. Figure 1 shows the information provided by the server, as it appears on the customers work station. The Web page she is looking at is actually a schematic diagram of the QuickPay prototype. The diagram shows the three main parties and the (TCP/IP) connections between them.

If a page contains links that require payment, the web browser sends an http request to http://till.merchant.com/. The merchants till application opens a TCP/IP connection to the carnet at the customer site (identified by her IP address) and the carnet puts up a window asking the customer to confirm the sale. When the customer agrees, the merchant receives the tokens over the TCP/IP connection and clears them with the vault application at the brokers site. The carnet can be customised to designate merchants as permanently trusted, or trusted for the current session. Such merchants can help themselves to tokens without confirmation from the customer.

If the turn over of the merchant is high, a permanent TCP/IP connection (solid arrows) is used, otherwise a transient connection would be better. When the merchant is satisfied that the tokens have cleared, the till sends the page to the customer as a reply to the original http request.

The model to be described in the next section takes into account the core aspects of the implementation, but abstracts away from as much detail as possible. This strategy makes it possible to concentrate on the essentials, keeping the model simple and elegant. Once finished, it would be possible to refine the model so as to take on board more detail. Ultimately this process of refinement would lead to a finely detailed model that is able to describe every aspect of the implementation. The present work is the starting point for the refinement process.

The model takes into account the transactions that rely on the TCP/IP connections, but abstracts away from the actual protocol implementation. The model also takes into account the three parties but it is not concerned with the Web browser/server. These components can be replaced by other client/server applications and are therefore not relevant to the model. The model abstracts away from the internal representations of data and messages in the carnet, till and vault applications.

3   Model

The model represents the QuickPay book keeping by a state, and the messages exchanged by the QuickPay protocols are represented by a list of transactions. Each transaction causes a transformation to be applied to the state, modelling the change in the book keeping as a result of a message exchange in the real system.

The state of the model is described by a number of data type definitions. The transactions that can take place are described by a set of logical inference rules operating on that data. Transactions and state are bound together in a configuration, which records the present state of the system as well as the sequence of transactions that have yet to take place. The collection of inference rules defines a relation over configurations. The model is animated by computing the transitive closure of the relation.

In subsequent sections we introduce the state (s), the transactions (tr), the relation ($\overset{qp}{\Rightarrow}$) and its closure ($\overset{qp}{\Rightarrow}*$).

3.1   State

The state s of the model is represented by a 3-tuple consisting of the book keeping of the customers (cs), brokers (bs), and merchants (ms).

$$s \equiv (cs, bs, ms);$$

This rather innocent looking tuple represents the major abstraction of the model with respect to the prototype. The latter distributes the information with the protocol taking care that appropriate information is exchanged between the parties, but no more. The model in principles allows unlimited access to information. However, the model has been designed in such a way that it is easy to see (and prove) where and when information is accessed.

The full paper gives the details of the mappings cs (from customer ids id_c to customer records), bs (from broker ids id_b to broker records), and ms (from merchant ids id_m to merchant records).

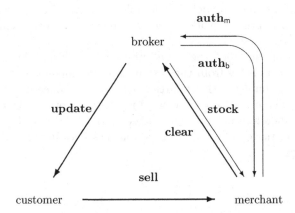

Fig. 2. The QuickPay parties and transactions. Thick arrows represent value token transfer and thin arrows represent authentication token transfer.

3.2   Transactions

The model represents transactions as separate actions and reactions. This permits actions be modelled whilst the reaction is not forthcoming. Each transaction is labelled and carries a number of parameters to identify the parties involved. Some transactions require further information, such as a token count n. The definitions below represent 'control' information of the messages transmitted in the actual prototype; we abstract away from actual 'payload' of the real messages (i.e., the lists of tokens).

$$tr \equiv \mathbf{update}(id_c,\ id_b,\ n)\ |\ \mathbf{sell}(id_m,\ id_c,\ n)\ |$$
$$\mathbf{clear}(id_b,\ id_m,\ id_c)\ |\ \mathbf{stock}(id_m,\ id_b,\ n)\ |$$
$$\mathbf{auth}_m(id_m,\ id_b)\ |\ \mathbf{auth}_b(id_b,\ id_m);$$

Figure 2 illustrates which parties are involved in each of the transactions. Value tokens (indicated by thick arrows) flow from the broker to the customer (**update**) and then via the merchant (**sell**) back to the broker (**clear**). The authentication tokens (thin arrows) flow from the broker to the merchant (**stock** and **auth$_b$**) and from the merchant to the broker (**auth$_m$**).

The notion of a configuration augments the (static) state s with a (dynamic) list of transactions [tr]. A configuration is represented as a tuple of the form $\langle[\text{tr}], \text{s}\rangle$. We can now formulate the model of QuickPay as a relation $\overset{qp}{\Rightarrow}$ over configurations. The type of the relation is:

$$\overset{qp}{\Rightarrow} :: \langle[\text{tr}], \text{s}\rangle \leftrightarrow \langle[\text{tr}], \text{s}\rangle;$$

The full paper gives the complete set of rules defining the relation $\overset{qp}{\Rightarrow}$.

3.3   Closure

The model is animated by computing the transitive closure $\overset{qp}{\Rightarrow}*$ of the relation as shown by the function animate below. This function takes an initial configuration and delivers a list of configurations showing the remaining transactions and the state of the system after each transaction. The initial configuration is prepended to the result to show the starting point of the animation.

$$\text{animate} \qquad :: \langle[\text{tr}], \text{s}\rangle \rightarrow [\langle[\text{tr}], \text{s}\rangle];$$
$$\text{animate}\langle\text{trs}, \text{s}\rangle = \langle\text{trs}, \text{s}\rangle : \langle\text{trs}, \text{s}\rangle \overset{qp}{\Rightarrow} *;$$

A complete model of QuickPay has now been sketched. The next section presents an example of use.

4   A Scenario: Double Spending

QuickPay has been designed to be customer friendly. She can refresh her carnet at any time, and even if she looses the carnet, she promptly receives fresh tokens. We will now use the model to study a scenario which mis-uses this facility. Suppose that a customer makes a purchase, and then immediately refreshes her carnet. Refreshing the carnet will invalidate the tokens just offered to the merchant, so that the latter is unable to clear the tokens. The customer will only benefit from her bad behaviour if the merchant delivers the goods/services before clearing the tokens. The merchant may wish to do so in order to clear tokens in batch, and thus to amortise the cost of a clear transaction over a larger number of tokens.

An animation as computed by the animate function from Section 3.3 consists of a series of snapshots, which show in detail how each transaction alters the state of the system. To save space customers or merchants with empty token lists are suppressed. Similarly, if the book keeping of any customer, broker or merchant is unaffected by a transaction then that information is suppressed.

In the animations of the model we have used subsequences of the natural numbers by way of random sequence.

The first step initialises the list of random numbers for the broker (called bank1), as shown below:

bank1   [10 11 12 13 14 15 16 17 18 19]

→ update(alice, bank1, 2) →
After the update transaction, the carnet of customer alice contains two value
tokens, [10, 11] (first line below). The brokers vault contains the duplicates and
shows that the customers budget is now 98 (shown indented on the third line
below):

alice   [10 11]
bank1   [12 13 14 15 16 17 18 19]
          alice   ([10 11],98)

→ stock(shopx, bank1, 4) →
After the stock transaction, the till of the merchant shopx contains four authentication tokens, [12, 13, 14, 15] (last line below). The brokers vault contains the
duplicates and shows that the merchants account is 0 (shown indented on the
third line below):

bank1   [16 17 18 19]
          alice   ([10 11],98)
          shopx   ([12 13 14 15],0)
shopx   [12 13 14 15]

→ sell(shopx, alice, 1) →
The merchant has received the token 10 as payment from the customer. There
is only one token (11) left in her carnet.

alice   [11]
shopx   [12 13 14 15]
          alice   [10]

→ update(alice, bank1, 0) →
The customer updates her carnet, receiving two fresh tokens [16, 17]. The customer's budget is still 98. The broker's record also shows the new state of the
carnet.

alice   [16 17]
bank1   [18 19]
          alice   ([16 17],98)
          shopx   ([12 13 14 15],0)

→ sell(shopx, alice, 1) →
The customer makes another purchase, this time spending token 16. The merchant holds the old, invalid token 10 as well as a new, valid token 16:

alice   [17]
shopx   [12 13 14 15]
          alice   [16 10]

$\rightarrow$ auth$_m$(shopx, bank1) $\rightarrow$

The broker accepts that the merchant is authentic by agreeing that 12 is the first authentication token:

```
bank1    [18 19]
         alice      ([16 17],98)
         shopx      ([13 14 15],0)
shopx    [13 14 15]
         alice      [16 10]
```

$\rightarrow$ auth$_b$(bank1, shopx) $\rightarrow$

The merchant also accepts that the broker is authentic, using token 13:

```
bank1    [18 19]
         alice      ([16 17],98)
         shopx      ([14 15],0)
shopx    [14 15]
         alice      [16 10]
```

$\rightarrow$ clear(bank1, shopx, alice) $\rightarrow$

At this stage the clearing fails because [16, 10] does not match [16, 17]. The merchant account is not credited. The ability to generate sample scenarios helps to study the protocol, to discover problems and to experiment with possible solutions.

5   Problems and Solutions

One of the main concerns in the design of QuickPay has been to make the protocols as efficient as possible. This has resulted in a design that uses random numbers instead of compute intensive cryptography and small messages instead of large ones. The strive for efficiency has brought with it some (potential) problems that we should like to address in this section.

5.1   Asymmetric Authentication

We discovered a hitherto unknown problem whilst building the model of Quick-Pay. The **stock** transaction serves to provide the merchant with authentication tokens. These tokens are used both to authenticate the broker with the merchant and vice versa. It is conceivable that a broker may take advantage of the knowledge how these tokens are computed to trick the merchant. This danger would not arise if both the broker and the merchant would create their own list of tokens, which they would then use to authenticate the other party. We have not found a practical example that exploits this weakness.

5.2   Selecting Lossy Compression

To reduce the amount of data transmitted during a multiple token transfer, the prototype implementation of QuickPay optimises payments of $n > 1$ value tokens in the following way. Instead of transferring a list of tokens $[v_1, \ldots v_n]$ the implementation transfers just the last one, v_n. We have termed this the *selecting lossy compression*, because the optimisation compresses by selecting a token.

When clearing, the broker has a duplicate of the customers carnet. The broker is thus able to look the token v_n up in the duplicate. Normally, the token will be found at the n-th place, thus confirming both that the token is valid, and that it represents n tokens.

In the full paper, we give a scenario that shows why the optimisation is not correct.

Whilst building the QuickPay model we (re) discovered that the selecting lossy compression optimisation was incorrect. We also found a different optimisation (*adding lossy compression*) which causes the scenario above to behave correctly. To study this new optimisation we applied it to the model, uncovering another problem. This lead us to a generalisation of compressing tokens, as well as a range of optimisations.

The full paper explores these issues in detail, giving necessary conditions on the compression function so that the optimised protocol can be proved correct with respect to the unoptiomes protocol.

6   Conclusions and Future Work

A formal model of the QuickPay micro payment system has been built that makes it possible:

- to describe clearly and concisely the transactions of the system.
- to animate sample transaction sequences so as to illustrate the concepts and to explore scenarios of incorrect uses of the system.
- to identify potential problems and to study possible solutions to these problems. A new problem has been identified and an old problem (selecting lossy compression) has been re-discovered. Various solutions to the old problem are given, ranging from a provably correct solution (lossless compression) to an efficient, but not formally correct solution (adding lossy compression).

The model has helped us to analyse the behaviour of the protocols, leading to the conclusion that QuickPay is:

- attractive for the customer. Even if she looses her tokens, they will be promptly replaced.
- attractive for the broker. Like all pre-paid schemes, the broker is able to dispose of the (real) money of the customer for a certain period of time.
- less attractive for the merchant. All problems that we have studied are to the disadvantage of the merchant. However, presently a merchant providing electronic services receives voluntary contributions at best. With QuickPay the merchant might expect an increase in revenue.

The model has been formulated rather abstractly, so that in the prototype implementation there may well be problems that are not captured by the model. The model could be extended to cover more detail.

The model could also be extended to study the costs of the transactions and to compare these costs to that of the tokens being processed.

The model could be extended to capture histories of customer and merchant behaviour. Such histories could be used to decide if and when clearing of tokens is needed, as well as other possible optimisations to the protocol. The histories could also be used to assess to what extent the merchant may take advantage of the knowledge of customer behaviour.

Finally, the model could be generalised to capture other micro payment systems, such as Mini-Pay, Millicent and Payword/Micromint. Such a general model would enable different micro payment systems to be compared on the same formal footing.

Acknowledgements. This work was supported by a short-term research fellowship from BT laboratories, Martlesham Heath, UK, contract number STRF97/33. The help and support of Michael Butler, John Regnault and Tim Hart is gratefully acknowledged.

References

1. UK BT Research laboratories, Martlesham Heath. Transaction system. In *GB Patent application no. 9624127.8*. 1996.
2. S. Glassman, M. Manasse, M. Abadi, P. Gauthier, and P. G. Sobalvarro. The millicent protocol for inexpensive electronic commerce. In *4th Int. World Wide Web Conf.*, pages 603–618, Boston, Massachusetts, Dec 1995. World Wide Web J. www.research.digital.com/ SRC/ staff/ msm/ bio.html.
3. P. H. Hartel. LATOS – a lightweight animation tool for operational semantics. Technical report DSSE-TR-97-1, Dept. of Electr. and Comp. Sci, Univ. of Southampton, England, Oct 1997. www.ecs.soton.ac.uk/ ~phh/ latos.html.
4. P. H. Hartel, J. Hill, and M. Sims. An operational model of QuickPay. Declarative Systems & Software Engineering Technical Reports DSSE-TR-98-4, Univ. of Southampton, Sep 1998. www.dsse.ecs.soton.ac.uk/ techreports/ 98-4.html.
5. A. Herzberg and H. Yochai. Mini-Pay : Charging per click on the web. *Computer networks and ISDN systems (Proc. 6th Int. WWW Conf.)*, 29(8-13):939–951, Apr 1997.
6. J. Hill and M. Sims. QuickPay: Prepaid micropayments. Technical report in preparation, BT Research laboratories, Martlesham Heath, UK, 1998.

Interoperable and Untraceable Debit-Tokens for Electronic Fee Collection

Cristian Radu*, Frederic Klopfert, and Jan De Meester

Integri N.V.
Leuvensesteenweg 325, B-1932 Zaventem, Belgium
`cradu@integri.be`

Abstract. In this paper we propose a pre-paid payment scheme suitable for Electronic Fee Collection in road pricing applications. The payment instrument used is implemented as a pair secret key/public key of an identity-based version of the Guillou-Quisquater identification/signature scheme. This design choice allows for interoperability among issuers of payment instruments and road services providers in the system, while the payment transaction can be carried out in a short time. This is the main contribution of our paper. A payment instrument is untraceable in the sense that it cannot be linked to a user. The untraceability feature can be revoked under the decision of a court. The privacy mechanism is based on the concept of revocable pseudonyms, the withdrawal stage of which is realized with an original protocol.

1 Introduction

In an Electronic Fee Collection (EFC) system for road pricing, the user and the road services provider (SP) – playing the role of the payer and payee – carry out the payment transaction by *remote interaction*. At the physical level, the service provider is represented by a Road Side Equipment (RSE) and the user is represented by a combination of two devices: an *On-Board Unit* (OBU) and a *smart card* (SC). The OBU is designed in such a way that: it ensures transmission and reception of data going to, and coming from, the Road Side Equipment within the Dedicated Short Range Communication ($DSRC$) standard [4]; it stores the public representation of the payment instrument; and it manages the man-machine interface with the user. When a pre-payment mode with local account is adopted, the SC of the user stores the balance of the local account and the secret information related to the electronic payment instrument. The Road Side Equipments are connected in a network; their subsystem named the *Operating Network Device* is responsible for establishing the network communication between the service provider and its acquiring bank during the deposit transaction of the payment transcripts and during the updating of the parameters belonging to the issuers subscribing in the EFC system.

---

* Part of this research was supported from the doctoral scholarship granted by the Katholieke Universiteit Leuven.

J.-J. Quisquater and B. Schneier (Eds.): CARDIS 2000, LNCS 1820, pp. 29–42, 2000.

The equipment of the user and of the service provider, and their communication, is shown in Figure 1.

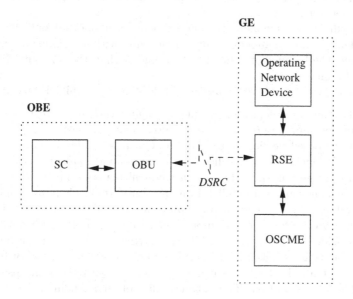

Fig. 1. Equipment used for the EFC system.

The payment scheme presented in this paper aims to answer the requirement of interoperability among service providers, issuers, and acquirers participating in the EFC system. It is suitable, for example, to answer the requirements of an European traveler that has obtained payment instruments validated by an issuing bank in Belgium and wants to spend them for road services during a trip to the south of Italy. If the instruments are validated correctly by an issuing bank subscribing to the EFC system, then they should be accepted by road services providers from Germany, Austria, and Italy, which are clients of acquiring banks other than the issuing bank. This should happen without the need of establishing bilateral business agreements among issuers, acquirers, and service providers, which would involve important management costs. However, banks (issuers/acquirers) and service providers should have signed before a Memorandum of Understanding (MoU), stating the acceptability of the same payment method: payment mode and payment instrument. A specialized association of road services providers, like the European Association of the Motorway Operators (ASECAP), can play the role of a Trusted Third Party (TTP)in the EFC system. Among its functions one can enumerate the management of the MoU and running of a Certification Authority (CA) server.

The payment mode of the proposed scheme can be characterized as:

- off-line – there is no interaction between the SP and the issuer of the payment instrument during the payment transaction;
- local account – the user has a tamper-resistant SC that keeps the balance of her local account;
- pre-payment – a payment transaction can be supported only if the user transferred enough money from her account with the issuer in the local account, the balance of which must be higher than the amount claimed by the SP; and
- payment per event – every passing of a tolling gate is billed separately.

The electronic payment instruments are *signature-based debit-tokens* [11]. A debit-token, or simply a *token*, is represented as a pair secret key/ public key of an identity-based version of the Guillou-Quisquater identification/signature scheme [7]. When a token is validated by the issuing bank it can be used to produce a signature as an evidence in a payment transaction. It can be seen as a reusable cheque that can be filled in many times. Its use is limited only by an imposed value threshold and by an expiration date. We show that this design choice allows for interoperability among issuers of payment instruments and road services providers in the system, while the payment transaction can be carried out in a short time. A token is untraceable, in the sense that it cannot be linked to a user, but all the tokens issued in connection with the same pseudonym are linkable to one another. The untraceability of payment instruments can be revoked under the decision of a court. The privacy mechanism is based on the concept of revocable pseudonyms, the withdrawal stage of which is realized with an original "cut-and-choose" protocol involving tamper-resistance devices. The user can obtain both a revocable pseudonym and untraceable tokens linked to this pseudonym running a client on her work station equipped with a smart card reader. The issuer runs a server on its host mainframe equipped with a Secure Application Module (SAM). The client-server communication can be realized over the Internet. The road services provider has no need of tamper-resistant devices in the Road Side Equipment.

The remainder of the paper is organized as follows. Section 2 introduces the main idea behind the design of the proposed EFC payment scheme. This idea consists of the use of implicitly certified public keys in order to reduce both the communication and computational effort during the payment transaction. Section 3 presents the form of the implicitly certified debit-tokens in the framework of the Guillou-Quisquater identification/signature scheme, and the protocol to issue them. The same section outlines the protocol of the payment transaction in the EFC system. Section 4 gives a detailed description of the protocol for obtaining a revocable pseudonym. Finally, our conclusion is derived.

2   Implicitly Certified Public Keys

The two major functional requirements of the user in the EFC system are that the duration of the payment transaction must be very short, while the interope-

rability is a plus. The computations performed by the SC and the RSE, as well
as the communication between them must be kept as simple as possible.

In the first scenario the user generates by himself the secret key/public key
pair (sk, pk) of the debit-token. In order to validate the payment instrument
during a withdrawal transaction, the issuing bank signs a certificate $\mathcal{C}_\mathcal{B}(pk)$ on
the public key of the token, in exchange for money. Figure 2 shows two possibilities to implement the payment transaction when the public key of the token is
explicitly certified by the issuing bank.

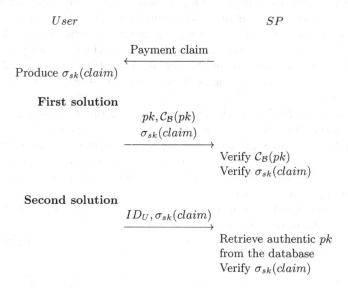

Fig. 2. Payment transaction with explicitly certified public keys.

There are two methods of forwarding the certified public key of the token
$\{pk, \mathcal{C}_\mathcal{B}(pk)\}$ to the service provider:

- During the payment transaction, the user sends both the public key of the
  token and its certificate to the service provider. In this case, beside the verification of the evidence produced by the user as a signature on the claim
  of the SP, $\sigma_{sk}(claim)$, the SP has to verify also the authenticity of the
  certified public key. Correspondingly, the duration of the payment transaction increases, due to both communication loading and computational effort.
  Thus, the functional requirement of the user cannot be satisfied.
- The service provider receives off-line the certified public keys of the valid
  tokens existing in the system, during a periodic updating of their RSE terminals. Each SP keeps a database containing the public keys of all the
  existing tokens in the system, or at least as many as possible. This database
  is indexed according to the identifiers of users. Every time a user passes a toll
  gate, she sends her identifier, which allows the service provider to retrieve

the appropriate public key of her token from the database. The user sends also the evidence produced on the payment claim with respect to the corresponding secret key of the token. In this case, the service provider verifies only the correctness of the received evidence.

Thus, both the communication and computational effort of the parties are reduced. However, in this case the cost of the database management is very high, especially when interoperability is a requirement, making this solution unacceptable.

The second scenario considers the possibility of using an *identity-based identification/signature scheme* in order to produce the evidence during the payment transaction. An issuing bank computes the public representation of a token, referred to as DT, and uses a redundancy function $red_{\mathcal{H}}$, which is a public knowledge in the system, to compute the public key pk of the token as $red_{\mathcal{H}}(DT)$. Using its secret information, the issuing bank computes the secret key sk of the token from the corresponding public key. During the payment transaction, the user has to send to the RSE only the public representation of the token DT, which allows the service provider to recompute the public key of the debit-token of the user as $red_{\mathcal{H}}(DT)$. This public key is implicitly certified by the issuing bank, since this is the only entity in the system that can compute the corresponding secret key of the debit-token, based on its secret information. If one assumes that a framing attack by the bank is ruled out, unless the bank would lose the trust of its clients, this scenario allows for a minimum of data communication and computation during the payment transaction.

The key transportation mechanism using implicitly certified public keys is presented in Figure 3.

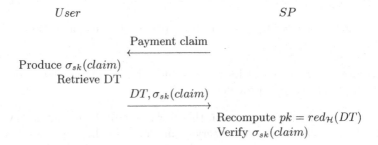

Fig. 3. Payment transaction with implicitly certified public keys.

3   GQ Debit-Tokens

This section firstly outlines the setup of the EFC system. Secondly, the form of the implicitly certified debit-tokens and their issuing protocol are presented, considering the identity-based version of the Guillou-Quisquater identification and signature scheme. Finally, the protocol of the payment transaction in the EFC system is described.

3.1 Setup of the Payment Scheme

The issuing bank chooses the primes p, q such that the composite modulus $n = pq$ is of a given length. The generation of p, q, n is performed in such a way that the factorization of n and the computation of RSA roots are intractable problems. $\mathbb{Z}_n = \{0, 1, 2, \ldots, n-1\}$ denotes the set of non-negative integers and $\mathbb{Z}_n^* = \{x \in \mathbb{Z}_n | \gcd(x, n) = 1\}$ denotes the set of positive integers x that are co-prime with the modulus n. All the arithmetical operations are performed in the RSA-group $(\mathbb{Z}_n^*, \cdot, 1)$, where the group operation is multiplication modulo n, and the unit of the group is denoted by 1. When the use of the RSA-group is clear, multiplication of two elements is denoted ab instead of $a \cdot b$. It is accepted that in the RSA-group there exist efficient polynomial-time algorithms for multiplication, inversion, exponentiation, selecting random elements, determining equality of elements, and testing group membership.

The issuing bank manages and generates the parameters of three cryptographic primitives: a Guillou-Quisquater (GQ) identification/signature scheme [7], an RSA signature scheme, and an RSA encryption scheme [12]. For the first scheme the bank randomly chooses an exponent v, such that $|v| \geq 160$, $\gcd(v, \lambda(n)) = 1$, with $\lambda(n) = lcm(p-1, q-1)$. $|v|$ denotes the bit-length of the parameter v. For the second scheme, the bank chooses the verification exponent $e = 3$ and computes the signature exponent d, such that $ed = 1 \bmod \lambda(n)$. For the third scheme, the bank chooses a small public exponent e_b and computes the corresponding secret exponent d_b, in such a way that $e_b \cdot d_b = 1 \bmod \lambda(n)$.

The issuing bank broadcasts the modulus n, the GQ system parameter v, the verification exponent e, and the public exponent e_b. It also chooses a collision-resistant hash function [9], with $|\mathcal{H}(\cdot)| < |v|$. This function is public knowledge in the system.

The issuing bank also obtain a certificate on its parameters (n, v), from the CA in the EFC system. This certificate allows every service provider to update its database in the RSE with the authentic GQ system parameters of each issuer in the system.

3.2 Issuing Implicitly Certified GQ Tokens

Let us assume that a user wants to obtain a validated debit-token, with the identification number id. This token has a threshold value val, an expiration date $date$, and it is linked to the authenticated pseudonym Π of the user. To this end, the user and the issuing bank carry out a two-stages protocol named $issue\_token$, using an anonymous channel on the Internet. The user is represented by her workstation (PC) and the bank is represented by a host mainframe, to which a Secure Application Module (SAM) is connected. The SAM stores the secret parameters of the bank: $p, q, 1/v \bmod \lambda(n), d$, and d_b.

In the first stage of the $issue\_token$ protocol, the user sends her authenticated pseudonym Π to the bank. The pseudonym of the user is a pair secret key/public key (s, π) in the framework of the GQ signature scheme, such that

$\pi s^v = 1 \bmod n$; its public key is certified by the bank through a blind signature protocol. The authenticated pseudonym of the user consists of the tuple $\Pi = \left(\pi, \{\xi_i\}_{i \notin R}, b\sigma_d(\pi)\right)$. All the details related to the issuing of authenticated pseudonyms to users are presented in Section 4. The bank verifies the authenticity of the pseudonym Π. If the pseudonym was never submitted before, the bank registers it in the pseudonym's database $PsDB$, and associates with it a serial number SN_Π. Otherwise, the corresponding serial number of the pseudonym is only retrieved from the $PsDB$.

The user generates a DES session key K, and she protects its secrecy with an RSA envelope $E = RSA_{e_b}(red_{PKCS}(K))$. The envelope is produced with the public exponent e_b of the bank, using the redundancy function proposed by the PKCS#1 standard. The user authenticates herself to the bank, producing a GQ signature (d_0, t_0) with the secret key s of her authenticated pseudonym on a message including the challenge c_0 received from the bank and the envelope E. Both the signature and the envelope are sent to the bank. If the verification of the authenticity of the user in the first stage of the protocol is successful, the bank sends back an "OK" message. The first stage of the *issue_token* protocol is presented in Figure 4.

The issuing bank computes the public key of the debit-token to be issued as $pk = red_{\mathcal{H}}(DT)$. The public representation of the token is computed as $DT = id\|SN_\Pi\| ID_B \|val\|date$. The redundancy function is $red_{\mathcal{H}}(x) = x, \mathcal{H}(x), \mathcal{H}(x,$

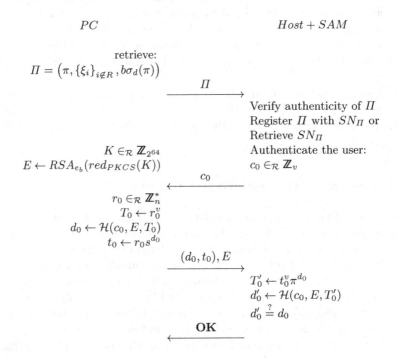

Fig. 4. The first stage of the *issue_token* protocol.

$\mathcal{H}(x)$),.... A collision resistant hash function $\mathcal{H}$ is iteratively applied to the public representation DT of the token, until the length of the public key pk is equal to the length of the modulus n, i.e., $|pk| = |n|$. The identification number id is chosen in such a way that $pk \in \mathbb{Z}_n^*$. The corresponding secret key sk of the token is computed by the SAM of the issuing bank as $sk = pk^{-1/v} \bmod n \in \mathbb{Z}_n^*$. Thus, the public key is implicitly certified by the issuing bank, since this is the only entity in the EFC system that can generate the corresponding secret key of the user's debit-token. This set-up characterizes an *identity-based* version of the GQ identification/signature scheme.

The SAM of the bank is used to recompute the session key K from the envelope E, such that $K = red^{-1}{}_{PKCS}(RSA_{d_b}(E))$. Afterwards, the session key is used by the SAM to encrypt the secret key sk of the token and its external representation DT, producing the cryptograms cr_1 and cr_2, respectively. The bank forwards the two cryptograms to the user. She uses K to decrypt them and to obtain the secret key sk of the debit token and its public representation DT. In this way the user verifies also the authenticity of the bank, since only the bank can recompute the correct session key K. The user recomputes pk from DT, and verifies that $pk \cdot sk^v = 1 \bmod n$. The user accepts the issued token as valid, sending back an "OK" message to the bank. The bank registers the issued token in relation with the pseudonym SN_Π of the anonymous user in the pseudonyms database $PsDB$. The second stage of the *issue_token* protocol is presented in Figure 5.

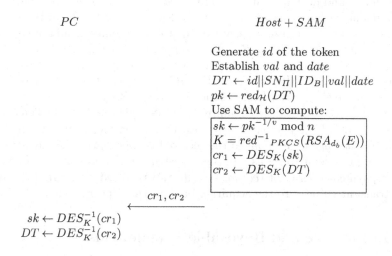

Fig. 5. The second stage of the issuing protocol for debit-tokens.

The secret key of the debit token is loaded in the smart card SC of the user, while the public representation of the token is loaded in the On-Board Unit (OBU) of the user.

3.3 Payment Protocol

When the SC is inserted in the OBU, an instruction "Start ZK Authentication" is submitted to the SC, which randomly generates $r_1 \in_{\mathcal{R}} \mathbb{Z}_n^*$ and computes the commitment $T_1 \leftarrow r_1^v \bmod n$. The SC returns T_1 to the OBU, which pre-computes the partial hash value $\mathcal{H}_1 \leftarrow \mathcal{H}(DT, T_1)$, where DT is the public representation of the debit-token to be used in the current payment protocol. The OBU stores the value $\mathcal{H}_1$, in order to be used in the following payment protocol.

The OBU of the user initiates a DSRC channel with the RSE of the SP and starts the current session in which the payment protocol is carried out. The RSE prepares a message $claim$, containing the details of the current transaction: the identity of the SP, the location and the type of the beacon, the current time and date, the amount to be charged, and a random challenge α of 32 bits. The message $claim$ is sent to the OBU.

The OBU sends back to the RSE the public representation DT of the user's token. Based on the information contained in DT, the RSE retrieves the public parameters (n, v) of the GQ scheme promoted by the issuing bank with identity ID_B. The RSE also verifies that the token is not expired, and re-computes the public key of the token as $pk \leftarrow red_{\mathcal{H}}(DT)$.

In parallel with the processing carried out by the RSE, the OBU issues the command "Compute hash" to the SC with the transaction details $claim$ and the partial hash value $\mathcal{H}_1$ as parameters. The SC computes the challenge $d_1 \leftarrow \mathcal{H}(claim, \mathcal{H}_1)$, decreases the value of its local account with the amount indicated in the $claim$, and decreases also the credit val assigned to that token with the same amount, i.e., $val \leftarrow val - amount$. Unless the user breaks in the tamper-resistance of the SC, the secret key s of the token becomes invalid immediately after its credit is zero. The OBU also recomputes the challenge d_1 in the same way as the SC did and sends the instruction "Compute ZK Authentication Message" to the SC. After receiving the SC's response, $t_1 \leftarrow r_1 s^{d_1} \bmod n$, the OBU sends the signature (d_1, t_1) of the user to the RSE.

The RSE recomputes the commitment $T_1' \leftarrow t_1^v pk^{d_1}$ and the challenge $d_1' \leftarrow \mathcal{H}(claim, \mathcal{H}(DT, T_1'))$. The payment transaction is considered finalized if the re-computed challenge d_1' is equal to the received challenge d_1. The payment protocol, using the debit token as a payment instrument, is presented in Figure 6.

The payment transcript $(claim, DT, (d_1, t_1))$ is stored in the RSE, in order to be transmitted later to the acquiring bank at the deposit stage.

4 Untraceable and Revocable Pseudonyms

The majority of the privacy-protecting payment systems in the literature [1,3, 5,6] intend to provide unconditional (information theoretic) untraceability for the payer. "Perfect" untraceability is justified for electronic cash, considering that metal coins have this feature. From the viewpoint of the cryptographer this feature is very challenging, but from a social and economical point of view, a certain degree of traceability is often preferred to permit law enforcement. Thus,

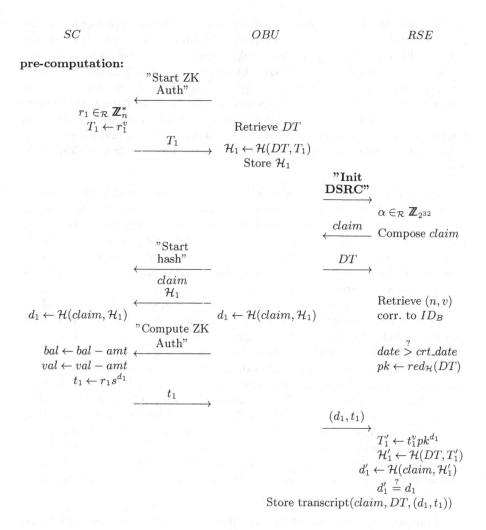

Fig. 6. The payment protocol.

"perfect" crimes, associated with unconditional untraceable electronic payment instruments, such as money laundering, blackmailing [13], and bank robberies [8], can be controlled. *Revocability* is the feature of an electronic payment instrument which allows it to become traceable with respect to the identity of the user, under certain conditions. This procedure is carried out by a *judge* or an *ombudsman*, playing the role of a *Trusted Third Party* (TTP). Revocable electronic money is proposed in several design solutions [8,14].

In the remainder of this section we introduce an original "cut-and-choose" protocol for issuing untraceable and revocable multi-term pseudonyms. Our solution allows the generation of a pseudonym, the secret key/public key of which can be issued in the framework of any signature scheme. Comparing to the original protocol introduced in [3], our protocol is simpler and the representation of the multi-term pseudonym is reasonably small. The number of havy operations is kept low, consisting of the computation of an RSA signature, a modular exponentiation with a small exponent ($e = 3$), and several modular reductions. However, we use tamper-resistant devices in order to protect the untraceability of the user. We rely on the assumption that the bank is not able to break in the tamper-resistance of its SAM in order to learn the secret information of the judge, which would allow it to trace abusively the payment transactions of its users.

$ID_U \in \mathbb{Z}_{2^{32}}$ denotes the secret identifier of the user, which was issued to her by the bank at the registration stage, and it is stored in her SC. During the *issue_pseudonym* protocol, she generates the secret key/public key of the pseudonym $(s, \pi) \in \mathbb{Z}_n^* \times \mathbb{Z}_n^*$, in the framework of the GQ scheme setup by the issuing bank (see Section 3.1). She asks the bank to certify the public key π of her pseudonym. On the one hand, her untraceability can be provided only if the bank uses a blind signing protocol [2] in order to certify this key. On the other hand, the bank requires that the pseudonym must be uniquely linked to the identity of the user (ID_U). This guarantees weak integrity for the bank, in the sense that if the user attempts to abuse a debit-token linked to this pseudonym, spending it over the treshold value accepted as a credit limit for the token, she can be identified after the fact, with the participation of the judge. This "over-spending" detection mechanism is based on the management of the pseudonyms database $PsDB$ and of the transcripts database TDB. The issuing bank manages the TDB, in which are stored all the transcripts $\{claim, DT, (d_1, t_1)\}$ of the payment transactions carried out by users that are clients of the issuing bank. In order to fulfill the two opposite requirements, both the user and the bank allow a judge (J) to observe the correctness of the protocol. The judge is a local trustee, agreed by both the bank and its clients, but it is not a requirement that the same judge is trusted by all the participants in the system.

In the sequel, it is assumed that the user is represented by her workstation (PC) in combination with a SC, while the bank is represented by a host mainframe and a SAM. The two partners are connected through an insecure Internet channel. In the *system initialization stage*, the judge loads the secret key K_J of a symmetric block cipher (triple DES, IDEA) both in the SCs to be issued to users and in the SAMs to be forwarded to the banks. At the registration stage of the user with the issuing bank, the bank loads the secret identifier $ID_U \in \mathbb{Z}_{2^{32}}$ in the SC.

Beside the pair (s, π), the pseudonym of the user also contains l terms, where l is a security parameter, which encode the identifier ID_U. The user chooses at random $s \in \mathbb{Z}_n^*$, $\rho \in \mathbb{Z}_n^*$, and computes $\pi \leftarrow s^{-v} \bmod n$, $M \leftarrow \rho^e \cdot red_{PKCS}(\mathcal{H}(\pi)) \bmod n$. She chooses l random blinding factors $\alpha_i \in \mathbb{Z}_{2^{32}}, \beta_i \in \mathbb{Z}_v$, and asks the SC to compute the terms $\xi_i = E_{K_J}(ID_U || \alpha_i)$. After receiving these terms, her workstation computes the commitments $\delta_i \leftarrow \mathcal{H}(\xi_i || \beta_i)$.

The user computes $B \leftarrow M \left(\prod_{i=1}^{l} \xi_i \right)$ mod n and sends it, together with the commitments $\{\delta_i\}_{i=1,l}$, to the bank.

The bank chooses at random $l/2$ indices and forms the set R [10]. For all the indices in this set, the user is required to open the corresponding commitments, providing the bank with the corresponding blinding coefficients $\Gamma = \{\alpha_i, \beta_i\}_{i \in R}$. The bank submits the user's identifier ID_U and the factors α_i, $i \in R$, to the SAM and asks it to compute $\xi_i' = E_{K_J}(ID_U || \alpha_i)$, $i \in R$. After receiving the values ξ_i', the bank verifies that $\delta_i \stackrel{?}{=} \mathcal{H}(\xi_i', \beta_i)$. If all the verifications hold true, then the bank is convinced that with high probability the right identity is encoded in a sufficient number of terms ξ_i. Every open commitment ξ is reduced from B, i.e., $B \leftarrow B \cdot \xi_i^{-1}$ mod n. Thus, B becomes, $B = M \cdot \left(\prod_{i \notin R} \xi_i \right)$ mod n. The bank asks the SAM to compute $\sigma' \leftarrow B^d$ mod n, and sends σ' to the user. Note that $\sigma' = \rho \cdot red^d_{PKCS}(\mathcal{H}(\pi)) \cdot \left(\prod_{i \notin R} \xi_i \right)^d$ mod n. She extracts ρ^{-1} from σ' in order to obtain the blind certificate: $b\sigma_d(\pi) = red^d_{PKCS}(\mathcal{H}(\pi)) \cdot \left(\prod_{i \notin R} \xi_i \right)^d$ mod n on the pseudonym. The user stores the authenticated pseudonym $s, \Pi = \left(\pi, \{\xi_i\}_{i \notin R}, b\sigma_d(\pi) \right)$ for later use in the issuing of the debit-token protocol (see Section 3).

Figure 7 describes the cut-and-choose protocol for the issuing of a multi-term pseudonym.

5   Conclusion

The identity-based version of the GQ identification/signature scheme was used in oder to build an interoperable Electronic Fee Collection system. The use of this scheme allows for an important reduction of the execution time of the payment transaction. The payment instruments used to produce evidence during the payment transaction are untraceable with respect to the identity of the user. Still, the untraceability of a payment instrument can be revoked, either as consequence of an "over-spending" by the user or following a legal misbehavior of the user in the system. Even that we did not elaborate on the implementability of the scheme, it is worth to mention that this scheme can be implemented using the Bull CP8 tamper-resistant devices running the TB98S IC-card operating system. This operating system is tailored to support the Guillou-Quisquater zero-knowledge authentication protocol as well as RSA processing.

References

1. S. Brands, *An efficient off-line electronic cash system based on the representation problem*, Report CS-R9323, Centrum voor Wiskunde en Informatica, March 1993.
2. D. Chaum, "Blind signatures for untraceable payments," *Advances in Cryptology, Proc. Crypto'82*, D. Chaum, R.L. Rivest and A.T. Sherman, Eds., Plenum Press, New York, 1983, pp. 199–203.

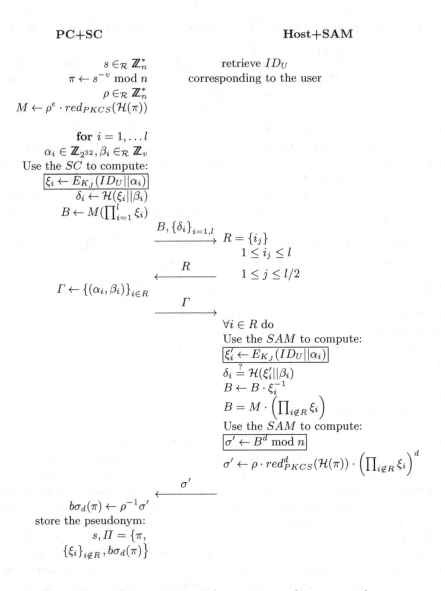

Fig. 7. Cut-and-choose protocol for issuing a multi-term pseudonym.

3. D. Chaum, A. Fiat and M. Naor, "Untraceable electronic cash," *Advances in Cryptology, Proc. Crypto'88, LNCS 403*, S. Goldwasser, Ed., Springer-Verlag, 1990, pp. 319–327.

4. *Dedicated Short-Range Communication (DSRC): Application Layer*, Road Traffic and Transport Telematics, RTTT-CEN/TC278

5. N. Ferguson, "Single-term off-line coins," *Advances in Cryptology, Proc. Eurocrypt'93, LNCS 765*, T. Helleseth, Ed., Springer-Verlag, 1994, pp. 318–328.

6. M. Franklin and M. Yung, "Secure and efficient off-line digital money," *Proc. ICALP'93, LNCS 700*, A. Lingas, R. Karlsson and S. Carlsson, Eds., Springer-Verlag, 1993, pp. 265–276.

7. L.C. Guillou, M. Ugon and J.-J. Quisquater, "The smart card: A standardized security device dedicated to public cryptology, " in *"Contemporary Cryptology: The Science of Information Integrity,"* G.J. Simmons, Ed., IEEE Press, 1991, pp. 561–613.

8. M. Jakobsson and M. Yung, "Revocable and versatile electronic money," *Proc. of the 3rd ACM Conference on Computer and Communications Security*, 1996, pp. 76–87.

9. B. Preneel, *Analysis and Design of Cryptographic Hash Functions*, PhD thesis, Katholieke Universiteit Leuven, ESAT Department, Leuven (Belgium), January 1993.

10. M.O. Rabin, "Digitalized signatures," *Foundations of Secure Computation*, R. De-Millo, D. Dobkin, A. Jones and R. Lipton, Eds., Academic Press, New York, 1978, pp. 155–168.

11. C. Radu, *Analysis and Design of Off-line Electronic Payment Systems*, PhD thesis, Katholieke Universiteit Leuven, ESAT Department, Leuven (Belgium), October 1997.

12. R.L. Rivest, A. Shamir and L. Adleman, "A method for obtaining digital signatures and public-key cryptosystems," *Communications ACM*, Vol. 21, February 1978, pp. 120–126.

13. S. von Solms and D. Naccache, "On blind signatures and perfect crimes," *Computers and Security*, No. 11, 1992, pp. 581–583.

14. M. Stadler, J-M. Piveteau and J. Camenisch, "Fair blind signatures," *Advances in Cryptology, Proc. Eurocrypt'95, LNCS 921*, L.C. Guillou and J.-J. Quisquater, Eds., Springer-Verlag, 1995, pp. 209–219.

The Banksys Signature Transport (BST) Protocol

Michel Dawirs and Joan Daemen

Proton World Int.l, Rue du Planeur 10, B-1130 Brussels
dawirs.m@protonworld.com, daemen.j@protonworld.com

Abstract. This document describes a new cryptographic protocol that allows the efficient authentication of an unlimited amount of data coming from an IC Card by an off-line terminal where the IC Card's cryptographic capability is limited to computing one-way functions and MACs. The authentication of the IC Card and its data are based on a Challenge-Response protocol using one-way functions. The protocol is especially suited for use in off-line electronic purse payments in an interoperable environment, where sharing of secret keys between different institutions is not allowed. It is also suited for off-line debit/credit payment applications. The protocol, when applied for purse payments or debit/credit allows transaction timings of the order of 1 second if implemented on currently mass-produced IC Cards.

Keywords. Electronic payment system, purse authentication, cryptographic protocols for IC cards, interoperable purse schemes.

1 Introduction

Interoperability between different Purse schemes is the new challenge for Purse Issuers. Several standards have been issued to achieve this goal. The European Draft Standard prEN1546 [EN1546] defines the Purse interface and transaction flow. However, Purse schemes which comply with prEN1546 are usually not interoperable. The most important reason is that in order to have interoperability between different schemes based on symmetric cryptography, the Purse Issuers must share their secret keys, something they are very reluctant to accept. As a consequence, the European Committee for Banking Standards (ECBS) has initiated the creation of a new standard [ECBS110] focused on interoperability of Purse schemes. This standard is based on EN1546 and EMV'96 [EMV96] and makes use of asymmetric techniques for data authentication. As a consequence, the transaction data are secured without the need of sharing secret keys.

We propose to base the data authentication on the BST protocol that makes use of one-way functions and Issuer-signed payment forms. The advantages of this solution compared with an active public key signature based solution such as proposed in [ECBS110] are twofold:

- The one-way function computations do not require a crypto-coprocessor in the IC Card;
- For parameters that result in comparable security, the execution of the BST protocol on currently available IC Cards is faster than RSA-based dynamic data authentication even if an IC Card with crypto-coprocessor is used for the latter.

J.-J. Quisquater and B. Schneier (Eds.): CARDIS 2000, LNCS 1820, pp. 41–51, 2000.
© Springer-Verlag Berlin Heidelberg 2000

2 One-Way Functions

The described protocols make use of so-called *one-way functions* [MOV97]. A one-way function converts an input and a diversification parameter to an output. This is written as:

$$Output \quad ^{Parameter} \quad Input$$

The protocol makes use of a one-way function that map an integer number of fixed-length blocks to a single-block output. The security of the protocol relies on the following cryptographic properties of the one-way functions used:

- pre-image resistance: given an output (and diversification parameter) it is infeasible to find a corresponding input;
- 2nd pre-image resistant: given an input, diversification parameter and corresponding output, it is infeasible to find another input for the same output (and diversification parameter).

Collision-resistance is **not** a requirement and for the block length it is advised to take 12 bytes.

3 Card Entity Authentication

Card authentication by the Terminal is based on a challenge-response mechanism: the IC Card proves the possession of a value, the *secret initial value (SIV)*, consistent with a previously sent *witness*, the *payment token (PT)*. The protocol assures that an eavesdropper has only a very low probability of success in an attempt to impersonate the Card with respect to a Terminal using the Card response. Figure 1 specifies how *PT* is derived from *SIV* according *to the payment token tree.*

SIV consists of w values $S_0[1..w]$. Every intermediate computation value $S_j[i]$ is computed from the value of the previous level $S_{(j-1)}[i]$ by the application of a one-way function diversified by the position in the payment token tree and a unique ID of the Payment token (ID_{PT}):

$$S_j[i] \quad ^{i,j,ID_{PT}} \quad S_{j\text{-}1}[i].$$

The Payment Token is derived from the final computation values $S_d[1..w]$ via an intermediate value α (the use of which will be explained later):

$$PT \quad ^{ID_{PT}} \quad ^{ID_{PT}} \quad \left(S_d[1], S_d[2], \ldots, S_d[w] \right).$$

In a first stage of the protocol the Card sends *PT* to the Terminal. In the second stage, the Terminal sends a Challenge to the Card. The Challenge specifies an intermediate level for every column of the payment token tree. A valid Card Response consists of the w intermediate values specified in the Challenge. Clearly, the Card knows *SIV* and can therefore compute any intermediate value.

Example: let $w = 8$ and $d = 7$. Let the Challenge specify following intermediate levels: $(7, 4, 3, 6, 4, 3, 1, 0)$. This results in Response: $S_7[1]$, $S_4[2]$, $S_3[3]$, $S_6[4]$, $S_4[5]$, $S_3[6]$, $S_1[7]$, $S_0[8]$.

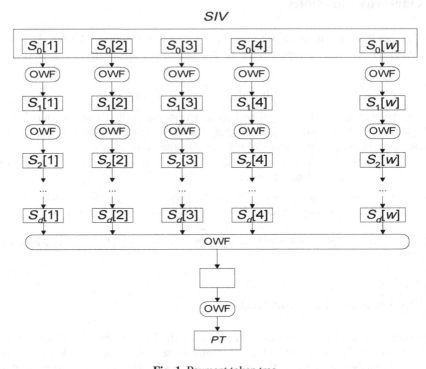

Fig. 1. Payment token tree.

The Terminal has received *PT* previously and can verify that the Response maps to *PT* as follows:

- for each of the received intermediate values, the terminal computes the final value $S_d[i]$.
- the final values $S_d[1..w]$ are used to compute *PT* (via α).

Obviously, the Card Response to Challenge $(0,0,0,0,0,0,0,0)$ would reveal the secret value *SIV* completely. An eavesdropper could use this value to construct the Response to any Challenge and therefore to successfully impersonate the Card. This is avoided by limiting the valid Challenges to a subset of all possible Challenges such that the Response to one Challenge does not allow to reconstruct the Response to any other one. This is done by imposing the following linear condition:

A Challenge is valid if the sum of the specified intermediate levels is equal to
$$wd\,/\,2\,.$$

The card verifies that that a Challenge is valid prior to generating the Response. It can easily be proven that a valid Challenge has a higher value than any other valid Challenge in at least one column of the payment token tree. Hence, using an observed Response to construct the Response to another Challenge requires the inversion of a one-way function and this is assumed to be infeasible.

If Challenges are generated in a uniform and unpredictable way, the probability of success in impersonation using an observed Response equals 1 divided by the total number of valid Challenges. This number depends on the depth and the width and can be calculated exactly using a recursive procedure. For a width $w=8$ and depth $d=7$, it is 1,012,664. This can be increased by augmenting width and/or depth, e.g., for $w=12$ and $d=10$, there are 4,577,127,763 valid challenges.

The above argument is only valid if for a given *PT* only a single Response is known to the eavesdropper. It is in fact essential for the security that:

A *PT*, its associated *SIV* and payment token tree are only used once.

This is similar to properties of the one-time digital signatures of e.g. Merkle [ME87]. It implies that the Card contains one *SIV* value per transaction to be conducted. To limit the storage, in practice the *SIV* values are derived from a common secret value by use of a diversified one-way function.

4 Transaction Data Authentication

4.1 With Respect to the Terminal

In the first stage of the Protocol, α is used by the Card as a key to MAC transaction data. This data and the corresponding MAC (denoted by S3 [EN1546]) are sent to the Terminal.

In the second stage of the protocol, the Challenge is sent to the Card that replies with the Response to the Terminal. The Terminal obtains α in the course of authenticating the Card and so can verify the validity of S3. Only the Card (possessing *SIV*) could have generated the MAC as α was private to the Card at the moment the MAC was presented and α maps to *PT* by a one-way function.

4.2 With Respect to the Card Issuer

After the Protocol has been conducted, α is revealed to the Terminal, and so the MAC S3 cannot be used to authenticate the data with respect to some third party. In Payment Transactions (electronic purse, debit/credit) it is important that the *Transaction Trace*, that remains in the Terminal after the transaction and is sent to the Card Issuer afterwards, contains a "proof" of the transaction verifiable by the Card Issuer.

For this purpose, an additional MAC (S6 [EN1546]) is computed in the first stage of the protocol with a secret key known by the Card Issuer. It is included in the data authenticated with S3, but only sent to the Terminal in the second stage of the protocol. It is included in the Transaction Trace and can be verified by the Card Issuer afterwards.

Note: Observe that the amount of authenticated transaction data is not limited by the protocol.

5   Acknowledgement and Cancellation of Purse Payment

For purse payments acknowledgement and cancellation can be performed with *transaction tokens* linked by one-way functions. The basic principle is that the authenticated data in the transaction trace include a so-called *witness token* T_{WITN}, generated in the following way:

$$T_{WITN} \quad \overset{ID,TN}{} \quad T_{CHAL} \quad \overset{ID,TN}{} \quad T_{ACKN} \quad \overset{ID,TN}{} \quad T_{CANC} \, .$$

ID and *TN* denote respectively the Terminal unique ID and unique Transaction Number. The Purse payment acknowledgement and cancellation can only be performed by the Terminal that actually conducted the payment transaction.

- Prior to the first stage, the Terminal presents T_{WITN} to the Card. The Card includes it in the data authenticated by S6 and S3.
- In the second stage, the *challenge token* T_{CHAL} is presented to the Card. The card verifies that it comes from the same entity as T_{WITN} by applying the one-way function. If so, it derives the Challenge from the challenge token T_{CHAL} and returns the appropriate Response.
- After the verification of the Response, the Terminal may send the *acknowledgement token* T_{ACKN} that can be verified by the Card.
- After the transaction, the Terminal may cancel it by sending a *cancellation token* T_{CANC}.

The authorisation of a cancellation requires the knowledge of T_{CANC} corresponding to the T_{WITN} in the Transaction Trace (and authenticated by S3 and S6).

6   Incremental Payments

In the basic BST protocol, there is a one-time authentication of data resulting in a transaction trace with a MAC S6 verifiable by the Card Issuer in the Terminal. For repeated electronic purse payments of small fixed amounts (e.g., payphones, photocopier,...) it is useful to have a mechanism to do incremental payments, resulting in only a single transaction trace. For this purpose a simple scheme using one-way function is used.

In the data authenticated by S6 and S3, the Card includes a so-called *initial tick token* TT_0.

A chain of tick tokens TT_i is computed in advance with:

$$TT_{i\ 1} \qquad TT_i$$

For every incremental payment, the Card supplies the subsequent tick token TT_i. For every Tick Token received, the Terminal:

- verifies that it maps to the previous tick token by applying the one-way function;
- if valid, updates the Transaction Trace with the most recent tick token TT_i and its index i.

The value associated with the Transaction Trace corresponds with the number of ticks performed, indicated by the tick token index i in the Transaction Trace. The Card Issuer can verify that it is valid by applying the one way function i times to retrieve TT_0 and verify S6 with this value.

7 Outline of a Payment Transaction

Figure 2 gives an overview of a payment transaction based on the BST protocol. In this figure the following conventions are used:

- a MAC computation on *data* using a *key* is denoted by:

$$\text{MAC}^{\ data}\ key$$

- the verification of a MAC or a one-way mapping is denoted by a question mark above the arrow.
- ✐ denotes the recording of information.
- ⟹ denotes an irreversible operation.

TD' denotes transaction data originating from the terminal, *TD"* transaction data originating from the IC Card

	IC Card		Terminal
1	⟹ TN_I ++ $S6\ ^{T_{\text{WITN}},TD}\ K_I$ $S3\ ^{T_{\text{WITN}},TD,S6}$	T_{WITN},TD'	⟹ TN_T ++
		$TD\ ,\langle PT\rangle,S3$	$\langle PT\rangle$ OK ?
2		T_{CHAL}	
	$T_{\text{CHAL}}\ ^?\ T_{\text{WITN}}$ ⟹ $\langle PT\rangle$ set to "used" $Response\ ^{T_{\text{CHAL}}}\ SIV$		
		$Response,S6$	$PT\ ^?\ ^{T_{\text{CHAL}}}\ Response$ $S3\ ^{T_{\text{WITN}},TD,S6?}\ K_R$ ✐ *Transaction Trace*
3	$T_{\text{ACKN}}\ ^?\ T_{\text{CHAL}}$	T_{ACKN}	
4		$TT_i(i=1,2,3,...)$	✐ replace $TT_{(i-1)}$ by TT_i in *Transaction Trace*
5	$T_{\text{CANC}}\ ^?\ T_{\text{ACKN}}$ ✐ Trace = (T_{ACKN},TN_I)	T_{CANC}	Invalidate *Transaction Trace*

Fig. 2. Outline of payment transaction conducted with the BST protocol.

8 Payment Token Authentication

In the protocol the Terminal uses *PT* to verify the response of the Card. As a consequence, a proof must be presented to the Terminal that the *PT* value originates from a Card issued by a genuine Card Issuer. This can be done by a simple certification of the payment token: *PT* is signed with the Card Issuer private key and the resulting signature can be verified by the Terminal. This signature on the payment token is sent along with the payment token in the first stage of the protocol as denoted by $\langle PT \rangle$.

Due to memory restrictions, it is not possible to store a signature for each token. By using authentication trees [ME87], many *PT* values may be signed by a single signature, called a *Payment Form*. An example of such an authentication tree is given in Figure 3. To authenticate *PT*(12) using a signature computed on *IM*, the values *PT*(13), *CV*(7) and *CV*(2) need to be sent along.

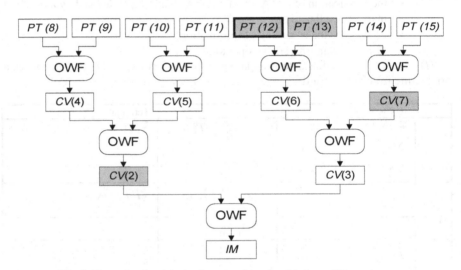

Fig. 3. Example of authentication tree: three-level balanced binary tree.

Pre-Calculation of Authentication Tree Nodes

PT values are the leaf nodes of the authentication trees. To allow the terminal to verify that a *PT* value maps to the imprint in a payment form, a number of nodes of the authentication tree need to be sent along. For authentication trees of realistic size (200-1000), the number of nodes is too large to store them all in the Card. Still, all nodes are needed in using the Payment Tokens. Leaf nodes need to be calculated during the life of the payment form. New authentication tree topologies and algorithms have been devised to allow for large trees with a reasonable amount of pre-calculation and storage. These are based on so-called binary Fibonacci Trees, that are defined recursively. An example of such a tree is given in Figure 4.

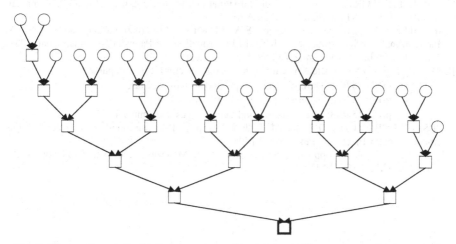

Fig. 4. Fibonacci tree of order 7. It is composed by joining a Fibonacci tree of order 6 at the right and a Fibonacci tree of order 5 at the left.

9 Payment Form Generation and Loading

The generation of a Payment Form consists of the generation of the *SIV* values of all payment tokens, the subsequent computation of the *PT* values themselves, their combination in the authentication trees to an imprint, and the signing of this imprint, combined with payment form specific data (such as expiration date) using the Card Issuer Private Key.

Payment forms can be loaded in the Card at personalisation time or loaded into IC Cards during on-line transactions (e.g. Purse load). Next to the payment form itself, it is essential that also the secret value from which the *SIV* are constructed be loaded in a secure way guaranteeing confidentiality.

10 Conclusions

A new signature transport protocol has been presented that is well suited for the use in IC Card-based electronic purse and debit/credit payment applications.

References

[ME89] R. C. MERKLE, "A certified digital signature", Advances in Cryptology - Crypto '89 (LNCS 435), 218-238, 1990
[ME87] R. C. MERKLE, "A digital signature based on a conventional encryption function", Advances in Cryptology - Crypto '87 (LNCS 293), 369-378, 1988

[LA79] L. LAMPORT, "Constructing digital signatures from a one-way function", Technical report, CSL-98, SRI International, Palo Alto, 1979

[EMV96] EMV '96, Europay International S.A., Master-Card International Incorporated, VISA International Service Association: IC Card Specification for Payment Systems, version 3.0, June 1996, including the Errata Version 1.0 (31 January, 1998)

[EN1546] prEN 1546 Identification card systems -Inter-sector electronic purse:
- prEN 1546-1: Definitions, concepts and structures, March 1995
- prEN 1546-2: Security architecture, January 1996
- prEN 1546-3: Data elements and interchanges, December 1996

[ECBS110] ECBS TCD 110-1, 2, 3, 4, 5, draft European Banking Standard for Interoperable financial sector Electronic Purse, April 1998

[MOV97] Handbook of Applied Cryptography, A. J. Menezes, P. C. van Oorschot, S. A. Vanstone, CRC Press, 1997

The OpenCard Framework

Reto Hermann, Dirk Husemann, and Peter Trommler

IBM Research Division, Zurich Research Laboratory,
Säumerstr. 4, CH-8803 Rüschlikon, Switzerland
{rhe,hud,trp}@zurich.ibm.com

Abstract. The increasing interest in conducting electronic business over the Internet requires authentication and secured transactions. The use of smart cards in an Internet context and especially in connection with Java has not been standardized. This paper presents the architecture of the OpenCard Framework, an industry initiative to standardize smart card middleware for Java. The reference implementation for the framework in the Java programming language is described. Related standardization efforts will be reviewed briefly.

Keywords: card service, card terminal, electronic commerce, framework, integrated circuit(s) card (ICC), ISO 7816, Java, middleware, smart card, OpenCard, OCF, PC/SC.

1 Introduction

The impact of the Internet on society, on our every-day life and work, is often compared to that of the invention and introduction of the telephone network around the beginning of the 20th century. In very much the same way that people started using the telephone for conducting business and for dealing with day-to-day issues we are adopting the Internet as the primary means of communication. The more we depend on Internet services—such as the World Wide Web, electronic mail, and Internet telephony—the more we are dependent on having some means of making our communications private, trusted, and authenticated.

With the ongoing globalization process, the mobility of people has steadily increased at all levels of both our business and private lives: companies have spread geographically across countries, continents, and the entire globe; changing market requirements lead to frequent reorganizations; traveling even to far-flung destinations is becoming ever more affordable even for private purposes. Despite the resulting substantial increase in mobility, people nevertheless expect to access their personal Internet services anytime, anywhere.

The network-centric computing paradigm—where resources are located throughout the Internet and secure access to them is ubiquitous—addresses this challenge of seamless service provision to an individual independent of location and time. Secure access relies on adequate communication protocols that use cryptographic secrets. Access ubiquity is achieved by letting service profiles and cryptographic secrets roam physically with the user and by having the service

J.-J. Quisquater and B. Schneier (Eds.): CARDIS 2000, LNCS 1820, pp. 52–70, 2000.

client implementations traverse the network to the user's point of access. Smart cards are an ideal device for the storage of a user's cryptographic secrets and service profile information: They are small and easy to carry, yet they offer sufficient tamper-proof storage and processing power to carry out cryptographic functions. The Java language and run-time environment serves as an ideal platform for implementing the service clients. It is this combination of network-loaded service client and user-provided smart card that enables a wide and exiting variety of Internet-based, pervasive applications.

However, today's development of smart card aware applications is anything but a simple task. Functionalities of smart cards and smart card terminals[1] vary widely between manufacturers and types. There are a number of reasons for this: Standardization of smart cards has been pursued by various standardization bodies including CEN [13], ETSI [22,23], and ISO [6,7,8,9,10,11,12] with the result that there is no single standard. The existing standards do not cover all aspects in sufficient detail, which has led to the development of industry specifications, most prominently the EMV specification [3] in the area of electronic payment systems. In addition, standardization is a slow process that can hardly keep up with the pace at which technological progress is achieved. This leads technology developers to define new specifications, such as the Java Card specification [14, 15,16], independently of standardization efforts.

Programming interfaces to smart cards and smart card terminals are typically vendor-dependent and of proprietary nature. Thus, smart card applications cannot be easily ported between different smart card platforms[2]. In addition, these interfaces tend to be at a conceptually low level, which makes it difficult to write applications against them.

The situation of developing smart card aware applications becomes even worse in the Internet setting where the user downloads a smart card aware application over the Internet: The application developer cannot foresee the environment in which the application will be executing; neither smart card nor card terminal are known in advance. This situation virtually prohibits deployment of smart card aware application in a ubiquitous, Internet-wide manner.

However, the situation is not beyond remedy and can be addressed by developing adequate middleware located between the smart card aware application and the smart card platform. Such a middleware should address the following objectives:

High-Level APIs [3]: Smart cards and card terminals offer diverse functionalities. With smart cards, the functionalities are accessible by exchanging pairs of Command and Response APDUs[4]; with card terminals, different interaction mechanisms exist. The middleware must hide the complexity of these

---

[1] The term *card terminal* is used here to refer to smart card acceptance devices, also known as card readers or card interface devices.

[2] The term *smart card platform* refers to the combination of card terminal, card/card operating system, and programming environment to access them.

[4] Application Protocol Data Unit.

exchanges and provide adequate abstractions at a high conceptual level that are easy to use. The interfaces to these abstractions must be standardized.

Card Terminal Transparency: Card terminals come in many different flavors, ranging from very simple ones to more sophisticated models that include perhaps a display, a PIN[5] pad, or even biometric[6] input devices. Where possible, the middleware must hide differences between these devices or try to compensate for lacking functionality (e.g. by offering a GUI[7] component in place of a missing card terminal display). The middleware must at least offer applications a way to determine which features a terminal supports.

Card/Card Operating System Transparency: Cards differ in the command set that they accept.[8] Often the same or similar functionality is available through slightly different command sets. The middleware must hide these differences where possible and at least let the applications discover the available functionalities.

Card Issuer Transparency: Card issuers determine the applications that reside on their cards and the way these applications are organized in the cards. They decide on the amount and the format of meta-information[9] in the card. The middleware must hide differences arising between card issuers.

Extensibility: Smart card technology has attracted considerable interest and is therefore continuously undergoing change. The middleware must be able to accommodate future technological advances.

In this paper we present the *OpenCard Framework* (OCF), a comprehensive smart card middleware that addresses these objectives. OCF comprises both an architecture and a reference implementation.

The paper is organized as follows: In Section 2 we provide an introduction to the architecture of the *OpenCard Framework*. In Section 3, the reference implementation of the OCF is briefly described and related to the architecture. We take a look at related work in Section 4 and conclude in Section 5 by summarizing the benefits of OCF and giving a brief outlook on future work.

2   Architecture

In this section we describe the architecture and key features of the *OpenCard Framework*. An overview of the general architecture is given and the main architectural components are described in more detail.

---

[5] Personal Identification Number.

[6] *Biometric identification* makes use of physical characteristics including finger print patterns, patterns of blood vessels in the retina, voice and facial characteristics to unambiguously identify persons.

[7] Graphical User Interface.

[8] The set of Command APDUs a card understands and the set of Response APDUs it generates constitute the interface to a card's operating system.

[9] Meta-information comprises information about the data and function contained in a smart card. The availability of meta-information is particularly important in the context of multi-application smart cards that can home several applications and in conjunction with post-issuance application deployment.

2.1 Overview

The core architecture of the *OpenCard Framework* consists of two components, the *CardTerminal* component and the *CardService* component—as shown in Figure 1.

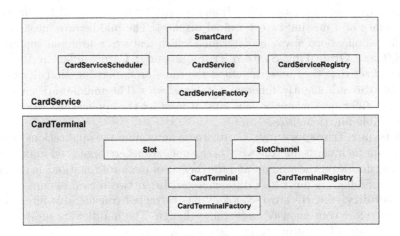

Fig. 1. *OpenCard Framework* Architecture. The *CardTerminal* and the *CardService* components are the two main constituents of OCF's architecture.

The *CardTerminal* component comprises all card terminal related classes; access to card terminals takes place through classes of this component.

The *CardService* component provides the necessary infrastructure to interact with a multitude of card operating systems (COS) and the functionalities offered by them. A particular card service usually implements a standard interface through which applications gain access to a specific smart card functionality. Examples of card services are:

FileSystemCardService: The *FileSystemCardService* component enables applications to access an ISO 7816-4 style file system [9] offered by a particular smart card.

SignatureCardService: The *SignatureCardService* component provides methods to generate and verify cryptographic signatures.

Both components of OCF, *CardTerminal* and *CardService*, are designed using the *abstract factory* pattern and the *singleton* pattern [1]. The objects dealing with the manufacturer-specific details are produced by a factory object supplied by the respective manufacturer. To determine which factory to use, OCF deploys a singleton called *registry*. A registry contains the configuration of an OCF component and creates the respective factory objects as needed.

Having described the overall structure of OCF, we shall discuss in the remainder of this section the *CardTerminal* component and the *CardService* component in more detail.

2.2 Card Terminals

There is a broad range of card terminals on the market with widely differing functionalities. Very simple card terminals merely provide basic card input–output (I/O) functionality via a single slot to insert the card. More sophisticated card terminals offer multiple slots or include a PIN pad and a display that can be used to perform card holder verification. Card terminals can attach to different I/O ports, such as serial port and PC Card bus. Card terminals come with proper driver software for selected computer operating systems. The *CardTerminal* component of OCF provides adequate abstractions for the details of the various card terminals.

The classes of the *CardTerminal* component, as illustrated in the lower part of Figure 1, serve a dual purpose: the most prominent function is to provide access to physical card terminals and inserted smart cards. This functionality is encapsulated in the `CardTerminal` class, the `Slot` class, and the `CardID` class.

In OCF a physical card terminal is represented by the `CardTerminal` class and the `Slot` class. The answer-to-reset (ATR)[10] is represented in OCF through the `CardID` class. OCF allows for both a static and dynamic configuration. With static configuration, the configuration of card terminals is known a priori at system startup time, whereas with dynamic configuration additional card terminals, such as PC Card-based terminals, can be added at run time.

The `CardTerminal` class is an abstract super class from which concrete implementations for particular card terminal types derive. Each `CardTerminal` object contains one or more `Slot` objects that represent the physical card slots of that card terminal. Access to a smart card that is inserted in a slot occurs through an exclusive gate object, the `SlotChannel` object: The `CardTerminal` class ensures that at any given point in time at most one `SlotChannel` object exists for a particular slot. Thus, once an object has obtained a `SlotChannel` object, no other object can gain access to the associated smart card until that `SlotChannel` object is released.

The `CardTerminal` class provides methods to check for card presence, to obtain a `SlotChannel` object, and to send and receive APDUs. For card terminals that offer additional functionality—such as a display, a PIN pad, a finger print reader, or other input–output facilities—OCF offers additional interfaces that a concrete `CardTerminal` sub-class can implement.

The second function of the *CardTerminal* component is a mechanism to add and remove card terminals (dynamically). The `CardTerminalFactory` class, and the `CardTerminalRegistry` object implement this function. Each card terminal manufacturer supporting OCF provides a `CardTerminalFactory` sub-class, which "knows" about a particular family of card terminals, and the respective

---

[10] The ATR is the initial information emitted by a smart card upon reset.

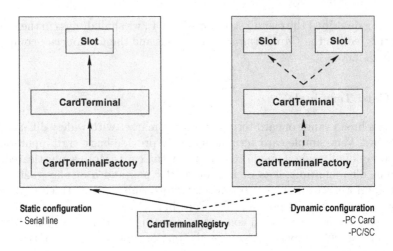

Fig. 2. Classes of the *CardTerminal* component. OCF represents a real card terminal through the `CardTerminal` class and the `Slot` class. Both static and dynamic configurations are possible with OCF.

`CardTerminal` sub-classes. The system-wide unique `CardTerminalRegistry` object keeps track of the installed card terminals—as illustrated in Figure 2. Furthermore, the `CardTerminalRegistry` object offers methods to register and unregister `CardTerminal` objects, and to enumerate all installed card terminals.

Both the `CardTerminalRegistry` object and `CardTerminal` classes generate events and notify other framework components (see Figure 3) when

- a card terminal is added to or removed from the system (`CardTerminalRegistry`), and
- a smart card is inserted into or removed from a card terminal (`CardTerminal`).

2.3   Card Services

The *CardService* component makes an abstraction from the different COSs that exist today. Rather than providing an abstraction of each individual COS, more generic services offered by smart cards have been identified. Thus, the component is called *CardService* instead of being called card operating system component.

At a lower level, interactions with a smart card occur by exchanging pairs of APDUs: The application sends a Command APDU to the smart card by passing it on to the device driver of the card reader, which forwards it to the smart card. In return, the card sends back a Response APDU, which the device driver hands back to the application.

The functionality of a smart card is determined by the set of Command and Response APDUs that it supports. Although standards for smart cards

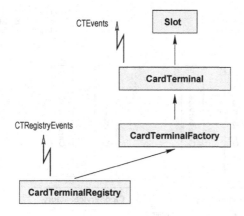

Fig. 3. Events of the *CardTerminal* component. The `CardTerminalRegistry` object generates `CTRegistryEvents` whenever a card terminal is registered or unregistered; likewise each `CardTerminal` object notifies interested parties of card insertion and removal through `CardTerminalEvents`.

exist, the functionality of the smart cards varies significantly (see Section 1). In other words, depending on the card vendor and the type of the card, different functions are available and the exact definition of the set of Command and Response APDUs may differ. In OCF the functions offered by these APDUs are aggregated into card services and made available through a specified API. As stated in Section 4 it is one of the goals of OCF to standardize the APIs of these card services. By design the framework allows the addition of new card services to accommodate new functionalities.

The *CardService* component comprises the abstract `CardService` class, the `CardServiceRegistry` class, the `CardServiceScheduler` class, and the `SmartCard` class (see Figure 4).

A concrete `CardService` sub-class implements a specific API and encapsulates the "know-how" of mapping it into a sequence of APDUs for a specific smart card. An example of a card service is the *FileSystemCardService* component: The classes and interfaces of the *FileSystemCardService* offer access to the file system on a smart card—provided that the particular card used supports the file system functionality and the card vendor has implemented a concrete `FileSystemCardService` sub-class for that card.

Similar to the `CardTerminalRegistry` object, the `CardServiceRegistry` object keeps track of the installed *CardService* components. When an application requests a specific card service for an inserted smart card, the `CardServiceRegistry` object obtains the ATR of that card and queries all `CardServiceFactory` objects available in the system. It provides both the requested card service class and the ATR as parameters to each `CardServiceFactory` object. Once one of the installed `CardServiceFactory` objects indicates that it

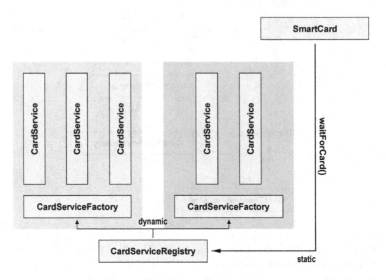

Fig. 4. Classes of the *CardService* component. Concrete `CardService` classes inheriting from the abstract `CardService` class implement a specific API representing specific smart card functionality (i.e., a `SignatureCardService` might offer access to the cryptographic signature functionality of a smart card). The `CardServiceRegistry` keeps track of the available `CardServiceFactory` classes in a system. A particular `CardServiceFactory` knows how to instantiate a set of card services for a particular smart card.

can produce the desired card service, the `CardServiceRegistry` object obtains the card service and returns it to the application.

Smart cards typically offer a single logical communications channel for interaction. ISO 7816-4 [9] defines the concept of logical channels as links to dedicated files (DF) where applications reside. The COS of smart cards supporting multiple channels would have to manage one context per channel comprising the state of the card and the communications. To our knowledge no smart cards available today actually support this multi-channel concept. As a consequence, only a single application is allowed access to the card at any point in time and the single available channel represents the crucial communications resource.

Provided a *CardService* component can deduce the state of a smart card based on past interactions with the card, multi-session capabilities can be emulated on a single logical channel by re-establishing the context associated with a session prior to resuming session operation. In the *OpenCard Framework*, the `CardServiceScheduler` class is a cooperative scheduling component that allows multiple instances of card services to gain access to a single smart card. Each `CardService` object has to allocate a `CardChannel` object from the `CardServiceScheduler` object to access the smart card and, once it has accomplished its task, release the `CardChannel` object again. We cannot employ a preemptive multitasking scheme for the following reasons: First, the state of a smart card depends on the type of card and, hence, must be dealt with in the type-specific card service component. Second, we wanted the scheduler to be an integral component of the framework core that is capable of scheduling card services from different implementors.

Figure 5 depicts two `CardServiceScheduler` objects, each of which is multiplexing access to one smart card (represented by its `SlotChannel` object). In the case of the right-hand `CardServiceScheduler` object, only one thread is accessing the smart card, but access occurs via two `CardService` objects; the left-hand `CardServiceScheduler` object arbitrates access to the smart card both among different `CardService` objects and among different threads.

The `SmartCard` class is the pivotal class of the framework for the application programmer. Most access to OCF takes place either through class methods of the `SmartCard` class or through instance methods of a `SmartCard` object. A `SmartCard` object can be obtained either through an event-driven (i.e., `SmartCard.getSmartCard()` class method) or through an application-driven programming model (i.e., `SmartCard.waitForCard()` class method)—OCF supports both programming paradigms.

An application using the event-driven programming model subscribes as a `CTListener` through the `addAsCTListener()` method of the `SmartCard` class. The application will then receive `CardTerminalEvents` from the re-

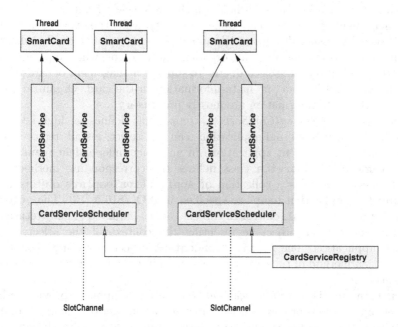

Fig. 5. Concurrent access to a smart card. The `CardServiceScheduler` provides concurrent access to a smart card (represented by its `SlotChannel`) both for multiple card services belonging to *one* thread and for multiple card services belonging to *multiple* threads.

gistered `CardTerminal` objects (see also Figure 3). Using the received `CardTerminalEvent` the application can instantiate a `SmartCard` object via the `SmartCard.getSmartCard()` class method.

With the application-driven programming model the application invokes the class method `waitForCard()` of the `SmartCard` class and passes along a `CardRequest` object. Through the `CardRequest` object the application can provide additional details regarding the behavior of the `waitForCard()` method; in particular, it can specify what kind of card it is looking for, into which card terminal the card should be inserted, whether to accept an already inserted card or wait for a new insertion, and which kind of `CardService` sub-class the card should support.

2.4   Card Application Management

Smart cards can offer multi-application capabilities whereby a single card can host several applications. Accordingly, smart card applications face situations where cards of the same or different types host diverse sets of applications. One might even have smart card applications that themselves install new or remove existing card-resident applications or suspend certain card-resident applications for some period of time. At the very least, smart card applications should have the capability of finding out which card-resident applications a particular card hosts and of presenting the card holder a choice to select from.

Management of card-resident applications is typically the responsibility of the card issuer. The issuer decides which applications are (planned to be) deployed with its cards, how applications are organized in the cards, when applications expire, how applications are selected, etc. To support management of card-resident applications, card issuers put meta-information in the card. Organization and format of the meta-information are mostly proprietary.

The *CardManagementCardService* component defines a high-level API through which card-external applications can list, select, install, remove, block, and unblock card-resident applications in an issuer independent manner. The `CardManagementCardService` class defines the corresponding methods. The `list()` method returns a collection of `ApplicationTemplate` objects modeled after the application template specified in ISO 7816-5 [10]. The `select()` method takes an `ApplicationID` object as a parameter and returns an `ApplicationContext` object representing the context of the selected card-resident application. The `ApplicationContext` object is an argument to the initialization method of the card service(s) used in conjunction with the selected application.

Furthermore, the *CardManagementCardService* component provides a hook that lets applications or card service implementations perform name resolution. In the context of the *FileSystemCardService* component name resolution can be used to map user-friendly file names to ISO file references (as specified in ISO-7816-4 [9]). The additional indirection can be used to present a logical file system structure to the application and to hide possible differences in the way issuers decide to organize the ISO file system in the card. The `getResolver()` method of the `CardManagementCardService` class returns a `Resolver` object through which names can be resolved into references and name-to-reference mappings can be added, deleted or modified.

3   Reference Implementation

The reference implementation of OCF is written entirely in Java and closely follows the architecture description in Section 2. The Java implementation consists of the two main packages `opencard.core` and `opencard.opt`, which in turn comprise several subpackages.

Opencard.core contains the basic infrastructure of OCF such as the abstract `CardTerminal` class and `CardService` class, the registries, and the `SmartCard` class. The application programmer can rely on the availability of the `opencard.core` classes. Opencard.opt on the other hand mainly contains packages that define a particular *CardService* API, such as the `opencard.opt.iso.fs` package, which defines the interfaces and classes of the *FileSystemCardService* component. Whether a particular *CardService* component is available for a particular smart card depends first of all on the functionality of the card itself and then on the availability of an appropriate *CardService* implementation.

3.1   Java Classes

All of the classes discussed in the architecture section have a counterpart in the Java reference implementation. Additional Java classes or interfaces are available where necessary or appropriate either to facilitate programming with OCF or to provide a seamless integration into the existing Java programming model. We shall concentrate on these additional concepts here.

In most packages of the *OpenCard Framework* reference implementation a number of exception classes have been defined to signal error conditions of various types and levels.

The `opencard.core.terminal` package defines a couple of supplementary interfaces and classes, including:

Pollable: The `Pollable` interface must be implemented by `CardTerminal` implementations if they do not generate events when a card is inserted into or removed from the card terminal.

VerifiedAPDUInterface: The `VerifiedAPDUInterface` can be implemented by `CardTerminal` sub-classes whose card terminals have the means to query the card holder for card holder verification data (for example, using an integrated display and PIN pad).

For the *CardService* component we have additional classes and interfaces to obtain card holder verifications from the user.

The `opencard.core` package contains two further sub-packages:

Opencard.core.event: This package contains OCF's event definitions, appropriate listener interfaces, and adapter classes as well as the OCFEventMulticaster—all modeled on the familiar Java AWT[11] event model.

Opencard.core.util: This package contains a number of utility classes for tracing, binary and hexadecimal string conversions, and packing and unpacking of ASN.1/BER-based TLV[12] structures (see also [18,19]). The Tracer class is used throughout OCF to help in debugging.

3.2   Standard Card Services

Apart from the SmartCard class, card services are the most visible parts of the *OpenCard Framework* and their APIs are the interfaces against which smart card applications are written. Establishing a number of standard interfaces for common functionalities provided by smart cards is thus crucial for widespread deployment of smart card aware applications and their portability, particularly in the Internet setting.

Card services and their interfaces are defined in sub-packages of the opencard.opt package. Currently, two *CardService* components are defined: a *FileSystemCardService* and a *SignatureCardService*. It is the intent to establish the interfaces of these services as the standard way of accessing the respective functionalities in smart cards.

The *FileSystemCardService* component belongs to the opencard.opt.iso.fs package and provides a set of interfaces and (abstract) classes that make the ISO file system functionality (as specified in ISO 7816-4 [9]) available to the programmer (see Figure 6). As with the rest of the framework, these classes and interfaces have been designed such that they fit seamlessly into the existing Java programming model. Thus, programmers familiar with the way Java deals with files and performs input–output will find the *FileSystemCardService* component easy to use.

The *SignatureCardService* component belongs to package opencard.opt.signature and offers methods to generate and verify cryptographic signatures. The cryptographic mechanism used for signature generation is RSA-based [20,21]. Methods to import public and private keys to the smart card are defined as well.

---

[11] Abstract Windowing Toolkit.
[12] Tag-Length-Value.

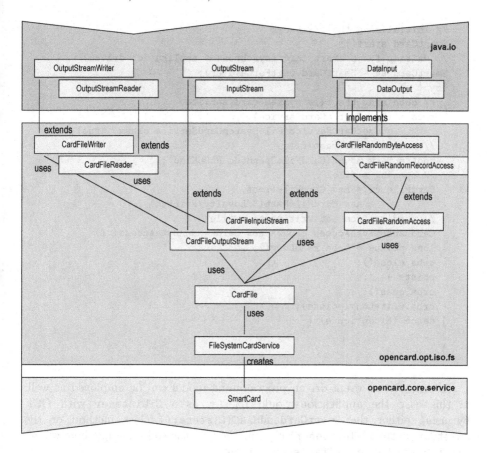

Fig. 6. *FileSystemCardService.* The **FileSystemCardService** offers access to the ISO 7816-4 file system functionality of a smart card. Wherever possible, OCF extends and implements classes and interfaces present in the **java.io** package.

3.3 Example Code

As stated in the beginning of this paper, having high-level APIs providing ease-of-use to the application programmer is one of the main objectives of OCF. The next code example illustrates the ease with which the ISO file system of a smart card can be accessed and files can be read and written.

```
...
// some declarations
FileSystemCardService fscs = null;
CardFile root = null;
CardRequest cr = new CardRequest(FileSystemCardService.class);
```

```
// initializing the framework
SmartCard.start();
// waiting for a smart card (synchronous application-driven)
SmartCard sc = SmartCard.waitForCard(cr);
try {
  // obtaining the file system card service
  fscs = (FileSystemCardService)
         sc.getCardService(FileSystemCardService.class, true);
  // mounting the root file
  root = fscs.mount(CardFileOpenMode.BLOCKING);
  // opening a file
  CardFile cf = new CardFile(root,
              new CardFilePath("/Loyalty/Points"));
  // reading from and writing to a file
  CardRandomByteAccess crba = new CardRandomByteAccess(cf);
  long points = crba.readLong();
  crba.close();
  points += 1;
  crba.open();
  crba.writeLong(points);
} catch (Exception e) {
  ...
}
```

Alternately, an event-driven programming model can be employed as well; in this case the application would register as a CTListener with OCF by using either the SmartCard.addAsCTListener() class method or the SmartCard.start(CTListener) class method. In the code example here we use the SmartCard.start(CTListener) variant.

```
...
FileSystemCardService fscs = null;
CardFile root = null;
...
public void init() {
   ...
   // initialize the framework and subscribe
   // as CTListener at the same time
   SmartCard.start(this);
   ...
}
```

Once OCF notices that a smart card is inserted, it retrieves the ATR of that card, instantiates a CardTerminalEvent for the retrieved ATR, and invokes the cardInserted() method of all registered CTListener objects. In the following code example our application's thread has previously invoked the wait() on the monitor object monitor; once OCF tells our application that a smart card has been inserted, our cardInserted() method notifies the waiting thread:

```
public void cardInserted(CardTerminalEvent ctEvent) {
  sc = SmartCard.getSmartCard(ctEvent);
  synchronized (monitor) {
     monitor.notify();
  }
}
```

After being notified of the card insertion event the application can then proceed and access the card in whatever manner is appropriate.

3.4 Configuration

Although configuration is an important issue for any framework providing access to system-external resources (such as card terminals and smart cards) we intentionally decided not to address configuration issues within the context of OCF.

The reason for this decision is that OCF can be deployed on a wide variety of platforms, ranging from PCs to Network Computers to set-top-boxes to smart phones and other platforms; in all likelihood, many of those platforms will not offer a file system that could be used to store configuration data. It is beyond the scope of OCF to define a sub-framework for configuration management. Instead we rely on the respective platform provider to offer some kind of configuration service that will set up system properties, and we use these system properties to obtain configuration information such as which card terminal factories and which card service factories are available.

4 Related Work

In this section we shall briefly review standardization efforts related to OCF. We shall discuss some features of PC/SC [17] and the CT-API [2], and point out how we integrated the two APIs with OCF.

4.1 PC/SC

The Interoperability Specification for ICCs[13] and Personal Computer Systems (PC/SC) [17] is an initiative to establish an industry standard for the use of smart cards with Personal Computers. The specification includes the physical characteristics of the smart card and an API. The PC/SC API is specified in a pseudo IDL[14] similar to COM,[15] and a reference implementation for the C programming language is given. Microsoft plans to integrate the PC/SC API into their software development tools for C, C++, Java, and Visual Basic [4],

---

[13] Integrated Circuit Cards.

[14] Interface Definition Language.

[15] COM denotes Microsoft's *Common Object Model.*

which makes the API language-independent. On the other hand, the advantage of OCF is that it is platform-independent, whereas PC/SC is available only for Windows platforms.

The architecture of PC/SC is quite similar to that of OCF. PC/SC also distinguishes between the card terminal component, called *Interface Device*, and a card service component. The card terminal component offers quite similar functionality as the corresponding component of OCF. Indeed, the card terminal component of PC/SC has been successfully integrated with OCF as a `CardTerminal` sub-class.

The architecture of the card service component of PC/SC offers interfaces for card services like a file system, for example, and clearly separates cryptographic functionality offered by the card for reasons of export restrictions. The card service component of PC/SC does not support the issuer independence provided by the *CardManagementCardService* component of OCF. In PC/SC the services offered by a smart card are accessed through an *ICC Service Provider* that implements the respective service interfaces. As opposed to the dynamic instantiation of a `CardService` by a `CardServiceFactory` in OCF the *ICC Service Provider* is a monolithic card specific component. Any new service or application that is added to the card by the issuer cannot be supported by the card-specific service provider. Thus, PC/SC cannot easily be used to support upcoming multi-application cards and especially Java Cards [14,15,16].

4.2   CT-API

In the context of smart cards and health care the European Union has proposed an interoperability specification for health card systems [2]. This specification contains a low-level API to access card terminals from within the C programming language, the so-called CT-API. On top of the CT-API a set of basic commands for dealing with the card terminal are defined. The card terminal commands are defined in the form of a byte array submitted to a low-level communication function of the CT-API. Several card terminals are available that support the CT-API. These card terminals have been successfully integrated into OCF by providing the respective glue-code using the Java Native Interface [5] to call the CT-API.

Unlike PC/SC and OCF, the health card specifications contain no high-level API specifications for card services.

5   Conclusion

In this paper we have presented the *OpenCard Framework* architecture and reference implementation. We have shown that OCF provides the developer of smart card applications with a set of building blocks that allow her to concentrate on the application logic instead of being concerned with how to communicate with smart cards. Furthermore, we believe that the *OpenCard Framework* offers significant advantages to application developers and service providers as well as to smart card and card terminal vendors:

Vendor Independence: Developers can choose cards and terminals from different suppliers and are no longer tied to one particular vendor.

Asset Protection: Extensibility of the architecture enables developers to participate in future developments of smart card technology at low cost by migrating at the level of the API.

Improved Time-To-Market: Developers profit from shorter development cycles by programming against a high-level API.

Lower Development Costs: Developers save the extra cost of porting their applications to different platforms and benefit from lower skill requirements to accomplish a given task.

Increased Clientele: Providers gain access to new market segments, thus reaching many more customers.

Improved Competition: Providers can compete in terms of functionality and are less vulnerable to the predominance of a single vendor.

Less Development Effort: Providers inherit functionality provided by the framework, which reduces their development efforts.

OCF's architecture and reference implementation provide both the blueprint and the shell for realizing the potential of smart card technology: An environment in which network computers, smart cards, service providers, and application developers all work in cooperation.

Our future work will focus on specialized card services (e.g., to support Java Cards or SQL[16]-like access to data on smart cards [12]), and we shall research the issues involved with running OCF on small-footprint platforms (e.g., embedded devices, PDAs, and so on).

6   Further Information

As of the spring of 1998, the *OpenCard Framework* Consortium—founded by Bull, Dallas Semiconductors, First Access, Gemplus, IBM, Netscape, NCI, Schlumberger, SCM Microsystems, Sun, UbiQ, and VISA—is actively pursuing the development of OCF itself and of *CardTerminal* components and *CardService* components for various card terminals and card services, respectively.

The OCF Consortium maintains a WWW site[17] where source code for the entire framework, Java class files, and documentation is available to the public. In addition, a mailing list exists for the discussion of technical issues.

Acknowledgments. We are indebted to numerous colleagues from Bull, Sun, Gemplus, IBM, and Schlumberger for their feedback and constructive criticism in the design and implementation phases—without their contributions, support, and enthusiasm, OCF would probably not have become an industry standard.

---

[16] Structured Query Language.

[17] Visit OCF's WWW site at http://www.opencard.org/.

References

1. Erich Gamma, Richard Helm, Ralph Johnson, John Vlissides, Design Pattern— Elements of Reusable Object-Oriented Software, Addison-Wesley Publishing Company, Reading, MA, 1994.
2. EU/G7 Healthcards—WG7, Interoperability of Healthcard Systems, Part 1: general Concepts, Berkshire, UK.
3. EMV '96: ICC Specifications, Version 3.0, Europay, MasterCard, Visa, June 30, 1996.
4. Microsoft Corporation, Windows NT Server: Smart Cards, White Paper, Redmond, WA, 1997.
5. Sun Microsystems, Java Native Interface Specification, Release 1.1, Mountain View, CA, 1997.
6. International Standard ISO 7816-1, Identification Cards, Integrated Circuit(s) Cards with Contacts, Part 1, Physical characteristics, ISO/IEC, 1987.
7. International Standard ISO 7816-2, Identification Cards, Integrated Circuit(s) Cards with Contacts, Part 2, Dimensions and locations of contacts, ISO/IEC, 1988.
8. International Standard ISO 7816-3, Identification Cards, Integrated Circuit(s) Cards with Contacts, Part 3, Electronic signals and transmission protocols, ISO/IEC, 1998.
9. International Standard ISO 7816-4, Identification Cards, Integrated Circuit(s) Cards with Contacts, Part 4, Interindustry commands for interchange, ISO/IEC, 1995.
10. International Standard ISO 7816-5, Identification Cards, Integrated Circuit(s) Cards with Contacts, Part 5, Numbering system and registration procedure for application identifiers, ISO/IEC, 1994.
11. International Standard ISO 7816-6, Identification Cards, Integrated Circuit(s) Cards with Contacts, Part 6, Interindustry data elements, ISO/IEC, 1997.
12. International Standard ISO 7816-7, Identification Cards, Integrated Circuit(s) Cards with Contacts, Part 7, Interindustry commands for Structured Card Query Language (SCQL), ISO/IEC, Working Draft, 1996.
13. CEN 726 (Parts 1–3), Identification card systems, Telecommunications integrated circuit(s) cards and terminals, European Committee for Standardization, 1995.
14. SUN Microsystems, Java Card 2.0 Programming Concepts, October 15, 1997, Revision 1.0.
15. SUN Microsystems, Java Card 2.0 Application Programming Interfaces, October 13, 1997, Revision 1.0.
16. SUN Microsystems, Java Card 2.0 Language Subset and Virtual Machine Specification, October 13, 1997, Revision 1.0.
17. Interoperability Specification for ICCs and Personal Computer Systems, Parts 1-8, CP8 Transac, HP, Microsoft, Schlumberger, Siemens-Nixdorf, Draft 0.9, December 1996.
18. Specification of Abstract Syntax Notation One (ASN.1), ITU Recommendation X.208, 1988.
19. Specification of basic encoding rules for Abstract Syntax Notation One (ASN.1), ITU Recommendation X.209, 1988.
20. R.L. Rivest, A. Shamir, and L. Adleman. A method for obtaining digital signatures and public-key cryptosystems. Communications of the ACM, 21(2):120-126, February 1978.

21. PKCS#1: RSA Encryption Standard, An RSA Laboratories Technical Note, Version 1.5, November 1993.
22. Digital cellular telecommunications system (Phase 2+): Specification of the Subscriber Identity Module - Mobile Equipment (SIM–ME) Interface, GSM Technical Specifications GSM 11.11, ETSI, June 1996.
23. Digital cellular telecommunications system (Phase 2+): Specification of the SIM Application Toolkit for the Subscriber Identity Module - Mobile Equipment (SIM–ME) Interface, GSM Technical Specifications GSM 11.14, ETSI, December 1996.

Smartcards - From Security Tokens to Intelligent Adjuncts

Boris Balacheff, Bruno Van Wilder, and David Chan

Hewlett-Packard Laboratories,
Filton road, Stoke Gifford
Bristol BS34 8QZ –UK–
boris_balacheff@hp.com

Abstract. Smartcards have traditionally been used as secure tokens in the corporate IT environment – for system logon, remote access, etc. With the increased programmability of smartcards, a new enhanced model of interaction between the smartcard and the corporate computing infrastructure is made possible. We define this new model of interaction as the Intelligent Adjunct model. It enables the use of smartcards to dynamically personalise the environment of the computing terminal and automate user-defined tasks (the terminal can be any computing device with a smartcard reader). In this paper, we describe various usage scenarios of a smartcard as an Intelligent Adjunct (IA) and we consider how such a model can be built using existing smartcards, specifically JavaCards. Various inadequacies of ISO standards are pointed out, an extension of the JavaCard API to support this new model is proposed, and a possible integration into the PC/SC infrastructure is described.

Keywords. Innovative technologies, Moving towards the pocket intelligence, Requirements for innovative cards, System Integration, PC/SC, Proactive.

1 Introduction

The objective of this paper is to show how user-programmable smartcards make it possible to push the smartcard usage model beyond its current limitations.

Smartcards are envisioned by some as the ultimate personal computer – one that can be carried in a wallet. With the increased processing power on the card, this vision is becoming less far-fetched. However, in today's corporate IT environment, smartcards are mainly used as secure tokens. As a step towards migrating greater functionality to the card, a new enhanced model of interaction between the smartcard and the corporate computing infrastructure is proposed. We call this the Intelligent Adjunct (IA) model. From the user's perspective, the Intelligent Adjunct model enables the use of smartcards to dynamically personalise the environment of the computing terminal and automate user-defined tasks. For example, a user can program a smartcard to take initiative all by itself: connect to a stock-market website to retrieve shares prices information, and possibly perform various investment tasks.

From the IT administration perspective, the Intelligent Adjunct model greatly simplifies the rollout of smartcard enabled applications as the application specific logic is captured in the smartcard and not the terminal.

J.-J. Quisquater and B. Schneier (Eds.): CARDIS 2000, LNCS 1820, pp. 71–84, 2000.
© Springer-Verlag Berlin Heidelberg 2000

One essential issue to remember here is security, and especially aspects like user input to the card, or card-initiated display on a machine's monitor. These security issues raised by the IA model will be discussed in a separate section.

2 Background Information on Existing Standards and Specifications

The world of smartcards is ruled by a series of standards and specifications. We present the main ones in this chapter to provide background information to some of the issues raised in this paper. It has to be said that considering the very fast evolution of smartcard technologies, most of the specifications change at a steady pace. We therefore stick to presenting each of them in a rather generic way.

2.1 ISO 7816. [1] this ISO standard defines the different aspects of smartcards: physical size, location and size of electrical contacts, electrical signals and protocols, commands, application identifiers, data elements.

2.2 The PC/SC Workgroup. [4] was created by a number of companies (Hewlett-Packard, Microsoft, IBM, Schlumberger, Bull, Gemplus, Siemens-Nixdorf, Sun, Toshiba, Verifone) in order to address critical technical issues related to the interfacing of smartcards to PCs.

The PC/SC architecture has a central Resource Manager (RM), which manages all registered readers and cards available on the system. An application wishing to use a smartcard service will contact the RM to check the availability of a card offering this service; the RM will then make a generic interface to the card's functionality available to the application.

2.3 GSM. [2] sets standards for communications between Mobile phones and Subscriber Identity Module (SIM) cards. GSM 11.14 was released in July 97' and specifies the "Pro-active technology", which enables a SIM card to initiate commands (a.k.a. GSM Phase 2+).

2.4 The JavaCard API. [3] as designed by Sun Microsystems is the onboard API for Java programming on the JavaCard. It is currently the standard followed by most JavaCard manufacturers. The Java Card API is a specification that claims to enable their Write Once, Run Anywhere ™ model for Java on smartcards and other devices with limited memory. Please note that our work does not rely on any one particular implementation of the JavaCard API.

2.5 OCF. [5] Like PC/SC, the Opencard Framework (OCF) is also a consortium of companies (e.g. Schlumberger, Gemplus, Netscape, IBM, Visa…) intending to make a uniform platform for using smartcards; their solution is essentially multi-platform, object-oriented and Java-based.

3 The Intelligent Adjunct Model

In the IA model, the smartcard is a general-purpose computing device that carries application logic. It carries out programmed tasks for the user with as much control over their execution as the terminal they are connected to would have. This model makes the Intelligent Adjunct an independent processor that will cooperate with a terminal to fulfill these tasks. Contrary to the usual model of the master/slave relationship between terminals and the usual smartcard, in the IA model smartcards and their terminals are peers: each of them can equally make use of the other's resources. Namely, the IA carries the logic to some personal applications that can access multiple Internet resources as well as local terminal resources.
(Note that we will now refer to a smartcard that implements Intelligent Adjunct Technology as an IA)

With this model, we envision a new range of services that can be made available to the end-users with unprecedented portability. Once all potential smartcard terminals are upgraded to enable this technology there will be no more limitations on what an IA can achieve, other than the limitation of the terminal's capabilities. We explain in *Part 6* how we intend to integrate the IA model into the PC/SC architecture.

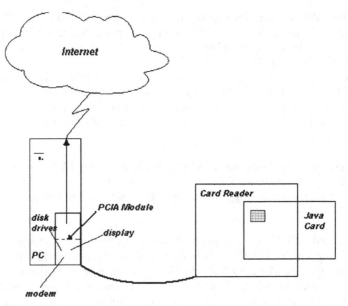

Fig. 1. Structural Model

Let us take the example of a Dial-up service. An IA could be programmed to control the dial-up procedure for a user's computer. It could contain fixed parameters as well as configurable ones, and modifiable scripts to carry out a number of tasks the user would normally do manually upon connection. In that way, a dial-up connection between the user's computer and his Internet Service Provider could be setup by the IA, and upon connection a number of things could be checked by the IA: new emails, specific emails, number of friends connected to the chat-rooms, last modified date of a given webpage... The IA could carry out any task that the user would normally do manually and systematically. And furthermore, once the IA model becomes more widespread, the user's IA will be able to do this from any terminal, without the terminal being configured to carry out these operations.

The only limiting aspect of this model is that of the trust of the terminal. We will discuss this issue later in this paper, and see how it impacts the type of tasks an IA can be expected to run.

Today's technology (JavaCards) addresses the issue with end-user programmability of smartcards. But given the very limited resources on the card and the severe restriction of the onboard virtual machine, more needs to be provided to make the paradigm useful.

The key features of the intelligent adjunct model are:
- to migrate the application logic to the smartcard
- to have card initiated actions
- to make terminal and network resources available to the smartcard
- to make sure this model can be integrated to existing infrastructures.

3.1 Card Driven

In the course of our work, the GSM Pro-active specification [2] became of obvious interest to us for smartcard/PC communications. Indeed we needed to find a way to allow smartcards to initiate commands, rather than answer the terminals requests. A more radical way to achieve this would be to modify both the ISO 7816 standard [1] and the PC/SC specifications [4] (maybe ISO T=2 and T=3 will allow it when they are specified). A reasonable option, for our prototype implementation, was therefore to make the GSM proactive technology available to JavaCards in general, so as to simulate two-way communications and still respect the ISO 7816 (T=0 and T=1).

It is appropriate to point out that the ISO 7816 standard for protocol T=0 was specified 10 years ago (1989) for the first generations of passive smartcards. It is therefore quite realistic that today's technology should need some higher-level communication protocols in order to be fully performant (ISO T=2,3 could be appropriate when defined).

3.2 Making External Resources Available to Smartcards

Another important development our IA model requires is to make off-card resources available to applets on the JavaCards.

For this purpose, the JavaCard API [3] needs to be extended to provide JavaCards programmers with the appropriate methods to access these resources. Also, a PC-side module needs to implement the way of providing these services to the applets. We will present the type of extension to this API that we believe would provide every card with basic access to network and PC resources, and discuss how they can be implemented both on and off the card.

3.3 Integrating with Existing Infrastructures

We have explained how essential it is for the IA model to take-off so that the services we want to provide JavaCards with are widely available. Currently the PC/SC architecture is the most widespread smartcard-interfacing infrastructure, but it does not allow a platform to provide services (access to network and PC-resources) to a smartcard. We therefore want to integrate the PC-side implementation of these services with the PC/SC stack.

The Smartcard Service Providers (SCSP - as defined in the PC/SC specifications) are only designed to provide smartcard functionalities to applications. To start with, we have implemented our PC Service Providers (PCSP which provides smartcards with PC services) as an independent module. We will also describe how we believe this could be smoothly integrated with the PC/SC architecture.

4 Card Initiated Actions

This chapter describes the proactive technology as defined by GSM, and presents the way we have adapted it to PC/SmartCards communications to enable smartcard initiated actions.

Proactive SIM (Subscriber Identity Module) is defined by GSM 11.14 as "a mechanism whereby the SIM can initiate actions to be taken by the Mobile Equipment (ME)". We are extending this definition by applying the concept of proactiveness to PC/SmartCards communications. In our model, the ME becomes some part of the PC/SC stack on the PC. Until we discuss the PC/SC stack issue, we shall call it the PCIA module. We will also leave the details of how we wrap it up into a procedure call to the next chapter.

The ISO 7816 standard establishes that a smartcard can only send messages in answer to a request. The proactive technology is described as follows:

> "The proactive SIM service provides a mechanism, which stays in the protocol of T=0, but adds a new status response word SW1. This status response has the same meaning as the normal ending ('90 00'), and can be used with most of the commands that allow the normal ending, but it also allows the SIM to say to the ME "I have some information to send to you". The ME then uses the FETCH function to find out what this information is. [...] The response code '91 XX' shall indicate to the ME that the previous command has been successfully executed by the SIM in the same way as '90 00' (i.e. "OK"), but additionally it shall indicate response data which contains a command from the SIM for a particular procedure.[...] The value 'XX' indicates the length of the response data. The ME shall use the FETCH command to obtain this data."
>
> [GSM 11.14 specifications, July 1997]

When we replace the ME by the PC Intelligent Adjunct module (PCIA module), this technology is quite straightforward to implement. A PCIA module/SC proactive communication will look like this:

1. PCIA module —   Any Command C1   →   SC
2. SC computes command C1, and sends result back if required
3. PCIA module ←   '91 XX' status   —   SC
4. PCIA module —   FETCH(XX)   →   SC
5. PCIA module ←   Command C2   —   SC
6. PCIA module processes command C2
7. PCIA module —   Command C2 Result   →   SC
8. PCIA module ←   Acknowledgment   —   SC

Now we need a way for the module to send a result back to the SC after Command 2 has been executed. The way this response is defined in the GSM standard is command specific. We will want to have a generic command for our module to send back such a response.

First we consider that the card, having initiated the command, knows the data type of the answer it is expecting. A PROCESSED_RESULT ISO command sent by the module will then carry the response data, which the card can interpret as long as the module uses the format expected for it. Another model would have been to make the card send the response data type it is expecting along with the command. But we believe that the implementation of the commands made available to the card should be standard enough to be compatible data-type wise.

As we are discussing the matter of today's single-threaded cards, such a PROCESSED_RESULT command has to be expected by the card before it accepts any other commands from the reader. We use the CARD_BUSY status (0x9300) for the applet on the card to answer any other request it could receive while waiting for the result of its proactive command (This return status is actually defined in TE9 as ST.BUSY, for the GSM SIM applications). This sequential model seems reasonable considering the available card technology. But an applet using off-card resources may want to carry out other tasks while its terminal processes a proactive command. This can be tackled by the implementation of a non-sequential proactive communication protocol (which would also require a "transaction" model for proactive communications), but we will not discuss these details in this paper.

We now have a means for a JavaCard to initiate commands and, once the appropriate API is defined, to access external resources. But still the proactive commands can be sent to the PCIA module only in response to a request, as specified by ISO.

We have therefore introduced the solution of having more than just one way to initiate a proactive command.

We shall use two possible return status bytes to initiate a proactive command cycle:
• The original '91 XX' when a command has just been properly executed
• A '93 XX' status when the command that has just been received cannot be executed before a proactive command is completed. 'XX' would still carry the length of the command to be fetched by the PCIA module.

Finally we will have to look carefully into how the response codes (especially error codes) are generated in a standard way. Indeed some error codes such as INS_NOT_SUPPORTED (0x6D00) should be able to support proactive extension: 6DXX. But for some others (e.g. 0x6F00 for ST.UNKNOWN_ERROR) it might not be appropriate to extend them to support the proactive response. This is still to be defined.

Here is an example of a basic PC application using a smartcard. This example will be re-discussed along with the development of our argument to illustrate the practical implications of our work.

Example: **CheckMail V0.0**

This application checks the number of new emails on a user's POP server, using a smartcard. This relies on the card storing a user login, password, and POP server name. Such a PC application would typically operate as follows:

- Request user login name, password, and POP server name from user smartcard
- Connect to POP server
- Retrieve new email information
- Disconnect from POP server
- Display information on screen

And now, let us look at what this example could look like using the IA technology technology:

Example: **CheckMail V1.0**

This applet is designed to establish a secure connection to a remote server, through the PCIA module, to check for new emails on that server. It does this on startup, and then offers one of two services:

Gives the number of emails on the remote server

Prints one of these emails with a given number

```
Main {
        C = ReceiveCommand()
        If C is known command Then SendStatus(93XX)
        Else SendStatus(6DXX)   // Command unknown

// Both of the above SendStatus initiate a proactive command.
// Now wait until the PCIA module sends a FETCH command to acquire the
// proactive command
        While ( (C = ReceiveCommand() ) != FETCH ) do {
                SendStatus(CARD_BUSY)
                C = ReceiveCommand()
        }
// Now send the command in answer to the fetch command received from the
// PCIA module. The user name and password to connect to the POP server
// are sent along with this command
        Send(Check New Mail Command(User login, password))

// Now wait for the module to send the result to the proactive command
        While ( (C = ReceiveCommand) != PROCESSED_RESULT ) do {
                SendStatus(CARD_BUSY)
        }
        Interpret the Result received
        // i.e. Store the number of new emails in a file
        // and get back to normal service mode
        While (1) do {
                // The following command receives x, the number of emails
                // to be retrieved and printed
                C = ReceiveCommand()
```

```
Switch (C) {
        Case 1: Send(Number of emails)
        Case 2: SendStatus(91XX)
                C = ReceiveCommand()
                While (C != FETCH) do {
                        SendStatus(SCARD_PROCESSING
                        C = ReceiveCommand()
                }
                Send(Retrieve and Print email number x)
        Case 3 : Send(Reset Card)
        // This will restart the applet and thus
        // check for new mail again
        }
    }
}
```

REMARKS:
- Note that in this applet, the proactive protocol could already be implemented as a procedure call, in a member method of our applet's class. The Main( ) would then be much simpler, using calls to that method.
- Of course the code XX should always be replaced by the size of the command to be fetched by the PCIA module.
- JavaCard programmers will notice that some SendStatus commands are missing, we just decided that a send(...) command would include the corresponding return status, to make this example clearer to people not familiar with this type of programs.

Remember that, here, we use the proactive technology hard-coded into an applet. The rest of this paper will develop the way in which we intend to make this functionality available as a procedure call to applets (in an API).

5   Making Terminal and Network Resources Available

We will now present the way we propose to make the terminal and network resources available to an IA.

This consists of two parts. Firstly the terminal side implementation, what we have called the PCIA module. Secondly the JavaCard side implementation, an extension to the JavaCard API to make new functionalities to the card's programs.

5.1   The PC-Side Implementation

What is it?

As far as the API extension package is concerned, the PCIA module will be required to execute two main types of commands. First will be commands that are "internal" to the PCIA module, which will require the module to manipulate temporary files and/or use some of the host machine's local resources. The other type will require the module to implement some network protocols and/or interfaces for the SC. In our prototype we chose to do the latter using COM objects (but other interface/library technologies can be envisaged).

<u>Two separate elements</u>
- The module-side implementation. Every proactive command initiated by a JavaCard will have a corresponding command in the PCIA module, which will carry out the appropriate task, and return a result to the card.
- The Library/COM objects which will actually implement the core functionalities of some of the commands.

> E.g. For a `GetLastModified(Http document)` command initiated by the card , the PCIA module might use a web browser's COM interface to actually perform the `HttpGET` command. The module-side implementation would then consist of using the COM object, retrieving the `LastModified` information from the HTTP header, formatting this information properly, and returning it to the card.

<u>A polling mechanism</u>

Our implementation of the PCIA module is a server-type application on the host machine that controls communications with the machine's card reader. Because we want the JavaCard applets to be able to initiate proactive commands even though no particular application as yet sent them a command, we've also included a polling mechanism in our PCIA module.

When a JavaCard is inserted in the host machine's reader, it will be spotted by the PCIA module, and a polling command will be sent to the card. The card can then either recognize it (if it is proactive enabled) and answer accordingly (91XX if it wants to start a proactive command, or a normal acknowledgement if it doesn't need to), or not recognize the polling command (if not proactive enabled) and therefore answer an INS_NOT_SUPPORTED return status.

<u>Clean execution</u>

Another feature of our implementation is that of clean execution. Our PCIA module implements the communications with the JavaCard for proactive commands, and it therefore has to deal with the context of these commands. As we will see in the next chapters the applet on the card cannot only access off-card resources, but it can also manipulate resources in the PCIA module environment itself. Essentially an applet will be able to command the module to retrieve a file over the network, save it in a temporary file and return the file Id to the applet. A subsequent proactive command might then ask the PCIA module to display one of its temporary files (created earlier on the initiative of that same applet) on the host machine's screen.

To make this work, we need to define the notion of **proactive session**: A session starts when an applet execution starts, and ends when it terminates. In this version of our prototype we have followed the rule that "No object persistency should be allowed on the PCIA module across sessions" (even if they are sessions of the same applet). We have implemented a temporary file management architecture which, for example, makes sure all temporary files in the PCIA module process are deleted when the applet that is responsible for them terminates (other applet selected or card is removed).

Of course this is not a final solution, as we end up having our PCIA module standing in between applications and the PC/SC stack, somehow implemented as a special Service Provider (in the PC/SC architecture sense).

5.2   The Application Programming Interface

Here we describe how we have chosen to provide JavaCards with the functionalities of the IA model, and which particular resources we believe are the important ones to make accessible to applets on these cards:

1. Off-host services

That is essentially network connections: use of HTTP, POP3, sockets, etc. These methods make the use of proactive technology transparent to the applet (and thus to the developer). Here are some of the categories we believe can be of interest.

2. Local Off-card resources

In this category we provide access to resources that are local to the PCIA module: printer, display, etc.

3. Internal commands.

These methods provide means of manipulating resources that are local to the PCIA module, and specific to the smartcard communication with the PC (copy temporary files....), as well as a proactive procedure call.

```
ourext.proactive.util.*
```

Including: `ourext.proactive.util.ProActive(Byte [ ])`
The ourext.proactive.util.ProActive method allows a developer to use proactive technology for other things than the methods included in our API extension. It also allows developers to add proactive capabilities to their PCIA module that will still be accessible in a standard way from the SC. This method is also used internally by most of the other API methods to carry out proactive initiation of commands.

These packages and their methods are intended to allow applets to be written for a JavaCard as though they were designed for a normal networked computer. The logic programmed into an applet will then be able to control part of any PC's local or networked resources.

To close this chapter we'll take a look at our CheckMail example applet again:

Example: **CheckMail V2.0**

This applet is still designed to establish a secure connection to a remote server, through the PCIA module, to check for new emails on that server. It does this on startup, and then offers one of two services. But this time the ProActive protocol is used as procedure call.

```
Main{
        Short SessionNumber;
        Byte Server[ ] = { /*initialised to the pop server name */}
        Byte UserName[ ] = {/*initialised to the user login name */}
        Byte Password[ ] = {/*initialised to the password */}
        Short NumberOfNewMailMessages
        SessionNum = pop3.Connect(Server,UserName,Password)
        NumberOfNewMailMessages = pop3.CheckNewMail()
        pop3.Disconnect(SessionNum);
        While (1) do {
                // The following command receives x, the number of emails
                // to be retrieved and printed
                C = ReceiveCommand()
                Switch (C) {
                        Case 1: Send(NumberOfNewMailMessages)
                        Case 2:
                                SessionNum=pop3.Connect(Server,UserName,Pa
                                ssword)
                                buffer=pop3.RetrieveMessage(x)
                                pop3.Disconnect(SessionNum)
                                util.Print(buffer)
                        Case 3 : Send(Reset Card)
                                // This would restart the applet and thus
                                // check for new mail again
                }
        }
}
```

6 Integrating This Technology to the PC/SC Architecture

The original structure of PC/SC more or less consists of the Resource Manager (RM) and the parts drawn above and below it (See Figure 2): above, the SmartCard Service Providers (SCSP), which interface towards the applications; below, the InterFace Devices (IFD) (with their device drivers), which interface to the smartcards. In this model the main communications take place between the applications and the cards, and are always initiated by the applications.

In our IA model, an extra communication path appears: the smartcard programs need to have access to off-card resources. In the description of our work we talked about the PCIA module as the terminal-side implementation that enables the proactive technology. Our PCIA module had two main roles:

• Manage the cards (insertion/removal/polling)
• Implement the proactive protocol, and interface proactive commands.

In the PC/SC model, we believe the PCIA module should be split in two parts. The proactive commands will be handled by the RM, which will forward them to the appropriate PC Service Provider (PCSP, a new type of service provider that we want to introduce to the PC/SC architecture). This PCSP will then interact with the resource in order to execute the card's request.

The PCSP:

What we call here a PCSP is basically any object that implement interfaces to the resources a card might want to access via proactive commands. The applet/PCSP communication will always happen via the RM. We recommend that these PCSPs should be implemented with the most standard interfaces possible, possibly as COM objects.

New Resource Manager functionalities:

Although the communication protocol between cards and the RM regarding proactive commands has not been fixed yet, it will definitely include some non-standard elements in the sense that a plain "passive card" application will be confused by it (an example is the 91XX return status as proposed by GSM). Therefore, it is necessary that the RM filters out these commands, so that the application still thinks it is talking to a "normal" passive card. To enable our model of the PC/SmartCards proactive communications, the RM will also be responsible for giving the card an opportunity to send commands, even if no commands have been sent to the card; i.e. the RM has to poll the cards.

When the RM receives a command from a card, it will also check which PCSP should handle this command, and have the command executed. Depending on the communication protocol used, these commands can happen as a "side effect" of a "normal" command; as stipulated before, the application that sent the normal command should not need to be aware of the fact it is talking to a proactive card.

The RM will probably also have to maintain some shared local resources, available to all PCSPs: an example of this is the temporary files to be passed between PCSPs. For example, an applet could require the http PCSP to retrieve an HTML document and later require the "printer PCSP" to print it. In that case, the RM would typically receive the first command, pass it onto the registered http PCSP, and receive the result of the HttpGet command. The RM would then save it into a local temporary file (linked to the context of what we called earlier a proactive communication session), and return the file Id to the applet. Then the applet can later issue a new command to have this particular file Id printed out. The RM would then forward the new command with the file corresponding to that file Id, onto the registered printer PCSP.

Note that a PCSP should ideally be provided by the manufacturers of the resource (e.g. Netscape will provide an http PCSP for interacting with Communicator).

Finally it is to be decided whether the API extension methods should be fully implemented by default, or whether the RM, or a specific PCSP, should just interface them so as to use any suitable resource available on the platform via another PCSP. An advantage of an API extension being that developers could use the same standard commands in their applets regardless of the implementation of these commands on the host-machine side.

7 Security Issues

Currently, the main reason for the existence of smartcards is security. When extending the possibilities of the cards with external resources, we also have to look at how this affects the security: for some of the external resources, access and usage can be suitably protected, while this can be very hard or impossible for other resources.

It is important to realize that conventional smartcard based systems face the same problem: they are indeed known to be very secure for whatever happens inside the card, but most usage scenarios also involve external servers and/or resources, which may then also be very security-sensitive. Most authentication protocols are a good illustration of this: the server checking the authentication data generated by the card also needs to be secure if we want the system to be reliable.

The security required by applications using IAs is left to the application developer. But when the cards go and access the resources themselves we will need a more generic security model, if possible with a fine granularity, so that the card can decide for itself which level of protection it wants.

We distinguish three kinds of resources a card may want to access via the PCSP: internal to the PCSP or RM, local (to the host machine), or external (networked).

Each of them has specific security features:

- Internal to the PCSP or RM: examples of this include displaying facilities, user input, local (temporary) file storage... The PCSP and the RM are normally system-level application modules on the host PC, and will thus enjoy the same level of security as other system components; their security level is thus as high (or as low) as that of the host PC.
- Local to the host machine: this mostly refers to peripherals attached to the host PC, like a printer, a modem... As for the internal resources, the security of the host machine limits the security level of the resource.
- External: when the card accesses resources somewhere on the network, cryptographic techniques can help to make the intermediate communication channel secure. In some cases, even the security level of the connection endpoint is unimportant: a networked file server could for example store encrypted files, which only the card can access.

Note that Denial-of-Service attacks have not been considered in this overview.

8 Conclusion – Looking into the Future

The Intelligent Adjunct is a new model of computing for smartcards, freeing them from their traditional security token role. The new computing capabilities of the

JavaCard technology have been the ideal platform to start implementing this concept, and we now hope that they will open doors to a completely new usage model for smartcards. End-users should be able to carry one smartcard around with their usual services (credit-card functionality, electronic wallet, etc.), but they should also be able to program or buy some configurable services that will be delivered by the card. A user can then carry around a number of personal applications that will be able to execute whenever he inserts his card into a terminal.

To enable this, using today's technology, we make card-initiated actions possible by using a solution based on the GSM proactive technology. We also design a way to make smartcard terminals offer services to the cards, and we propose to extend the functionality offered onboard the cards (by extending the JavaCard API for example). Finally we present a way to integrate this new model to the existing PC/SC architecture, in order to make the IA model available in a more widespread manner.

These solutions were designed for the purpose of prototyping the IA model. In the future some more performant solutions might be designed that will better serve the IA model, such as a more appropriate communication protocol than the proactive technology, and a proper integration of this new functionality to existing infrastructures.

References

1. ISO-7816. Identification Cards - Integrated Circuit(s) Cards with Contacts, Parts 1 to 7. http://www.iso.ch
2. Proactive SIM, GSM 11.14 specification, July 1997
3. JavaCard API. http://java.sun.com/products/javacard
4. PC/SC Workgroup specifications. http://www.smartcardsys.com
5. OpenCard framework. http://www.opencard.org

Formal Proof of Smart Card Applets Correctness

Jean-Louis Lanet and Antoine Requet

Gemplus Research Group,
Av du Pic de Bertagne,
13881 Gémenos Cedex France
{jean-louis.lanet,antoine.requet}@gemplus.com

Abstract. The new Gemplus smart card is based on the Java technology, embedding a virtual machine. The security policy uses mechanisms that are based on Java properties. This language provides segregation between applets. But due to the smart card constraints a byte code verifier can not be embedded. Moreover, in order to maximise the number of applets the byte code must be optimised. The security properties must be guaranteed despite of these optimisations. For this purpose, we propose an original manner to prove the equivalence between the interpreter of the JVM and our Java Card interpreter. It is based on the refinement and proof process of the B formal method.

Keywords. Java byte code, security, optimisation, formal specification.

1 Introduction

The use of Java for the next generation of smart cards offers the possibility to download executable code. This possibility increases the flexibility to update the contents of a smart card, but raises a risk of loading a hostile applet. Such an applet could access or modify part of the system. In order to ensure a safe execution, several conditions must be verified on the execution environment. Applet properties must be conscientiously checked.

Security in a smart card has several aspects. As applets often need to exchange information, some mechanism must be set up in order to avoid unauthorised information flow. Those mechanisms can be implemented within hardware devices (MMU) or in software. Java and its virtual machine provide by themself several properties that can ease the implementation of such a mechanisms. For example, the lack of pointer arithmetic associated with a strong check on the typing prevents an applet from forging an address and from scanning the memory space of the smart card bypassing the execution mechanisms. Such properties are enforced by a byte code verifier.

However, due to the size and performance limitation of smart cards, such a verifier cannot be embedded in the card. Alternative ways of ensuring that the executed byte code is valid must be used. A pragmatic approach is to use an off-line verifier, and to digitally sign verified applets. This approach has several advantages, for example, it only requires cryptographic mechanisms to be implemented within the card.

Another security aspect is linked to the modification of the Java virtual machine to better suit the smart card constraints. This optimisation allows to reduce the Java byte code size in order to load more applets into the smart card. So, it is necessary to

J.-J. Quisquater and B. Schneier (Eds.): CARDIS 2000, LNCS 1820, pp. 85–97, 2000.
© Springer-Verlag Berlin Heidelberg 2000

ensure that those optimisations do not weaken the type system, and do not introduce security holes. This is all the more difficult, as it is not possible to use the Java byte code verifier at this point. Those optimisations introduce two new problems :

- ensuring that the planned optimisations do not modify the byte code properties and that the transformed program is equivalent to the original one,
- validating the optimisation process, making sure that the optimisations are correctly applied.

The next paragraph describes the different transformations and optimisation processes. Then we describe the different approaches to formally specify the interpreter. In the fourth paragraph, we express the different properties which must be verified. After a brief introduction to the B Method we present our approach.

2   Definition of the Problem

Two different operations are performed before a Java applet can be loaded into the card : the conversion and the optimisations. The goal of the transformations is to translate the Java byte code into Java Card byte code, while the optimisation process tries to minimise the size of the code and improve its performance. Both the size of the code and the required run time memory are optimised although reducing the run time memory is more important. There are several levels of optimisation.

The first one consists in reducing the size of the frame by adjusting the variable locations and using the overlay technique. This technique tries to assign the same memory location to variable that are not used in the same time. The second level deals with local optimisations like peephole, inlining and constant propagation. If the inlining increases the size of the EEPROM in the other hand it can reduce the RAM utilisation which is of paramount importance. The transformer can be split into several modules :

- the analyser, that performs the data flow analysis in order to derive the static type for each memory location. Several information are obtained by this function :
  - the type of each element of the operand stack at each program step, i.e. the stack types,
  - the type of each local variable at each program step, i.e. the frame types,
- the converter, that translates the Java instructions into Java Card instructions. The translations are always one to one mapping.
- the data optimiser. This module modifies the frame in order to adjust local variables in term of their size and use (overlay),
- the local optimiser. It performs some peephole transformations and the inlining (if necessary) of private methods.

In this paper, we are interested in formally specifying transformations (conversion and data optimisation) and in proving that they preserve the security properties of the byte code. We consider that the data flow analysis has been done and that the static type system can be trusted. The formal specifications of the Analyser and the Local Optimiser will be done in a further work.

Currently, the Java Card byte code is proprietary which allows to modify the JVM implementations to optimise memory accesses by specialising instructions. In the current model, only a few instructions are modified. They deal with the field and local variable access. The conversion process replaces one instruction by another one without modifying the method call convention.

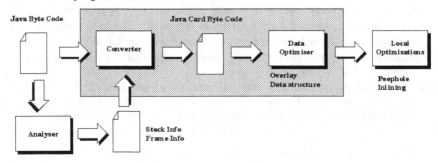

Fig. 1. The Complete Transformation Scheme.

The technique described here is to prove that the byte code interpreter of the smart card is a valid refinement of the Java interpreter. For this purpose we formalise the operational semantics of the instructions and the static constraints of the Java byte code. We express by invariants how to refine it into a Java Card interpreter. We use the B Method to state and prove the different invariants between the two interpreters.

3   Related Work

In our approach we formally specify a part of the Java virtual machine. The semantics of the Java virtual machine has been described by [Qia-97]. In this approach the author considers a subset of the byte code and tries to demonstrate the run time type correctness from the static typing. He provides an operational semantics of the Java byte code and a static inference system. This approach is very close to ours.

Another approach different from ours is described in [Coh-97]. The author gives a formal model of a subset of the Java virtual machine called defensive JVM. The run time checks imply a type safe execution. Our approach is different in the way that we use a static type inference to guarantee run time type errors.

Our approach is partially inspired by the works of [Sta-98] and [Fre-98]. Both of them define a subset of the JVM to prove some properties. Stata et al. define a part of the byte code verifier to focus on the verification of the subroutine whereas Freud et al. verify the correctness of object creation and initialisation.

4   Byte Code Properties

4.1   The Java Card Subset of Java

Due to the physical limitations of smart cards, some features of Java are too expensive to be implemented. Several restrictions have been imposed on the use of Java such as:

- no support for multidimensional arrays and floating point numbers,
- no multithreading,
- no garbage collection mechanism,
- no dynamic loading of class files.

4.2 Verifications Needed

The byte code verifier enforces static constraints on the Java byte code. These constraints rule out type errors (e.g. dereferencing an integer), access control violations (e.g., accessing a private method from outside its class), object initialisation failures (e.g., accessing a newly allocated object before its constructor has been called) and some other dynamic errors. [Yel-96] describes the byte code verifier in an informal manner. Given its importance for security, the current description of the verifier is not sufficient, and we think that an extension to this description using a formal technique of the to-be-checked properties would prove to be useful.

As seen previously, the Java byte code is compiled into a specialised byte code interpreted by the smart card JVM. This byte code is then loaded into the smart card. As the performed optimisations modify the type system of the byte code, several properties must be checked again after the optimisation process. Moreover, after the optimisation process, new checks have to be done in order to verify that the applet respects some specific smart card properties such as correct memory access and restricted loops.

5 The B Method

The B Method is a formal method for software engineering developed by J.R.Abrial [Abr-96]. It is a *model oriented* approach to software construction. This method is based on the set theory and the first order logic. The basic concept is the *abstract machine* which is used to encapsulate the data describing the state of the system. Invariants can be expressed on the state of the machine which can only be accessed by the specified operations.

The abstract machine is refined by adding specification details. Several steps can be used before reaching the implementation level where the specification is detailed enough to generate code. The refinements and the implementation have other invariants which express relations between the states of the different refinements.

The proof process is a mean to check the coherence among the mathematical model, the abstract machine and the refinements. This way, it is possible to prove that the implementation is correct according to its specification. The tool *AtelierB* generates the proof obligations (PO) of the specification according to the mathematical model. A theorem prover is provided to discharge automatically the proof obligations and an interactive theorem prover allows the user to intervene in the proof.

6 The Model

6.1 Model Representation

As explained in [Gol-97] and due to the fact that the optimisations performed do not alter the method call convention, we do not need to model the complete JVM. We only need to model a subset of the JVM interpreter corresponding to a method. We specify our interpreter in terms of a state machine and transition rules. The transitions define how the execution of an instruction changes the state of the machine under some pre-conditions.

To verify the feasibility of this approach we consider only a subset of the instructions of the JVM. We use the same subset as [Fre-98]. This subset contains simple operations on stack manipulation (*OP_PUSH0*, *OP_POP*), stack operation (*OP_INC*), data transfer (*OP_STORE*, *OP_LOAD*), object manipulation (*OP_NEW*, *OP_INIT*, *OP_USE*), control (*OP_IF*) and return instruction (*OP_HALT*). In the next step we will extend the set to the complete set of the Java Card instructions.

The following machine gives a partial description of the state of our JVM. A method is defined as a pair of sequences. One of them represents the method opcodes and the second the parameters used by the opcodes. Apart from the typing invariants we state that all the domains are equal since all the information have to be available for each method instruction.

INVARIANT

$opcodes \quad \in$ **seq** $(OPCODES\_JVM0) \quad \wedge$

$parameters \in$ **seq** $(PARAMETERS) \quad \wedge$

$types\_stacks \in$ **seq** $(TYPING\_STACK)) \quad \wedge$

$types\_frames \in$ **seq** $(NATURAL \leftrightarrow\!\!\!\!+ TYPING\_INFO) \wedge$

dom$(opcodes) \quad =$ **dom**$(parameters) \wedge$

dom$(types\_stacks) =$ **dom**$(opcodes) \wedge$

dom$(types\_frames) =$ **dom**$(opcodes) \wedge$

size$(opcodes) > 0$

The variables *types_stacks* and *types_frames* are the result of the type inference. They provide typing information about the stack and the frame for each instruction. For verifying our type system we define the type *TYPING_STACK* which is a sequence of primitive types representing the type of elements stored in an operand stack. For each instruction the *type_frame* variable represents a partial map from local variable numbers to types. We give hereafter an example to illustrate the information provided by the type inference. Note that there are several possible *type_frame* variables corresponding to this program.

Table 1. Type Inference Information for a Method.

instructions	type_stack	type_frame
push 0	[ ]	{ }
store 1	[Byte]	{ }
push 0	[ ]	{1|->Byte}
Inc	[Byte]	{1|->Byte}
store 3	[Integer]	{1|->Byte}
load 3	[ ]	{1|->Byte, 3|->Integer}
load 1	[Integer]	{1|->Byte}
Halt	[Integer, Integer]	{ }

6.2 The Static Constraints

In this machine we define the static constraints of our system. As most of the transformations deal with type definition we have to ensure that the refinement of the JVM is correctly typed. In the following machine we express a part of the static constraints that must always be verified. We give only a subset of the constraints related to the instructions *OP_PUSH0, OP_IF* and *OP_STORE*.

The first theorem deals with the instruction *OP_PUSH0*. At this method line, if the instruction is *OP_PUSH0* and the program counter is valid, then it must imply that the next instruction is also in the domain of the method. It states that a byte has been added on top of the stack for the next instruction. Such instruction has no parameter.

$$
\begin{aligned}
&\forall pc.(pc \in \mathbf{dom}(opcodes) \land \\
&\quad opcodes(pc) = OP\_PUSH0 \\
&\quad \Rightarrow \\
&\quad \mathbf{size}(parameters(pc)) = 0 \land \\
&\quad pc{+}1 \in \mathbf{dom}(opcodes) \land \\
&\quad types\_stacks(pc{+}1) = Byte \rightarrow types\_stacks(pc) \land \\
&\quad types\_frames(pc{+}1) \subseteq types\_frames(pc))
\end{aligned}
$$

In the previous theorem, the last rule express that the typing information of the local variables at the next instruction can be a subset of the one for the current instruction. In the following example, there is a jump (instruction 7) to the instruction 4 and the contents of the local variable 1 differs according the path used to reach this instruction. Depending on the incoming path, this variable can get different types (Byte or ObjectRef). So, it cannot be defined in *type_frame* (4) although it is included in *type_frame* (3).

Table 2. Example of Typing Information that cannot be determined.

	instructions	type_frame
1	push 0	{ }
2	store 1	{ }
3	push 0	{1|-> Byte}
4	**new Object**	{ }
5	init Object	{ }
6	store 1	{ }
7	if 4	{1|-> ObjectRef}

The instruction OP_IF requires several theorems. Those linked with object initialisation are not presented here. The following theorem checks the correctness of the frame and stack typing and that the target of the jump (*pc+parameters(pc)(1)*) is included in the method.

$$
\begin{aligned}
&\forall pc.(pc \in \mathbf{dom}(opcodes) \land \\
&\quad opcodes(pc) = OP\_IF \\
&\quad \Rightarrow \\
&\quad \mathbf{size}(parameters(pc)) = 1 \land \\
&\quad \mathbf{head}(types\_stacks(pc)) \in INTEGERS\_T \land \\
&\quad pc{+}1 \in \mathbf{dom}(opcodes) \land \\
&\quad types\_stacks(pc{+}1) = types\_stacks(pc) \downarrow 1 \land \\
&\quad types\_frames(pc{+}1) \subseteq types\_frames(pc) \land \\
&\quad pc{+}parameters(pc)(1) \in \mathbf{dom}(opcodes) \land \\
&\quad types\_stacks(pc{+}parameters(pc)(1)) = types\_stacks(pc) \downarrow 1 \land \\
&\quad types\_frames(pc{+}parameters(pc)(1)) \subseteq types\_frames(pc))
\end{aligned}
$$

The typing rule for the *OP_STORE* instruction ensures that the top element of the operand stack belongs to a correct type and the same type is stored in the local variable indexed by *parameters*(*pc*)(1). It also makes sure that this index is an index in the *types_frames* domain.

The B following operator ($\Leftleftarrow$) allows us to overload the partial map *types_frames(pc)* by the couple {*parameters*(*pc*)(1)↦**head**(*types_stacks*(*pc*)). The last rule express the possibility that the type may not be determined, as explained previously.

$$
\begin{aligned}
&\forall pc.(pc \in \mathbf{dom}(opcodes) \wedge \\
&\quad opcodes(pc) = OP\_STORE \\
&\quad \Rightarrow \\
&\quad \mathbf{size}(parameters(pc)) = 1 \wedge \\
&\quad pc{+}1 \in \mathbf{dom}(opcodes) \wedge \\
&\quad \mathbf{size}\,(types\_stacks(pc)) > 0 \wedge \\
&\quad types\_stacks(pc{+}1) = types\_stacks(pc) \downarrow 1 \wedge \\
&\quad parameters(pc)(1) \in \mathbf{dom}(types\_frames(pc{+}1)) \wedge \\
&\quad types\_frames(pc{+}1) \subseteq (types\_frames(pc) \Leftleftarrow \{ parameters(pc)(1) \mapsto \\
&\quad \mathbf{head}(types\_stacks(pc)) \}))
\end{aligned}
$$

6.3 The Operational Semantics

We define the state machine of our interpreter by a tuple (*current_instruction, frame, stack*). Each instruction is modelled by an operation that transforms the machine state. Hereafter we show a part of the refinement machine of our abstract machine.

```
REFINEMENT
    jvm_refl
REFINES
    jvm_base
VARIABLES
    opcodes,  parameters,  types_stacks,  types_frames,  max_stack,  stack,  frame,
    current_instruction
INVARIANT
    stack ∈ seq(INTEGER ) ∧
    frame ∈ NATURAL ⇸ INTEGER ∧
    current_instruction ∈ dom(opcodes) ∧
    size(stack) = size(types_stacks(current_instruction)) ∧
    (∀pc.(pc∈dom(opcodes)
        ⇒(dom(types_frames(pc)) ⊆ dom(frame))))
```

We use variables, definitions and invariants to specify the state :
- *current_instruction* indicates the method line to be executed, the invariant states that *current_instruction* $\in$ **dom**(*opcodes*),
- *frame*, is a partial map from the frame position to their values, *frame* $\in$ *NATURAL* $\nrightarrow$ *INTEGER*,
- *stack* represents the operand stack, modelled by a sequence: *stack* $\in$ **seq** (*INTEGER*).

The operational semantic of the interpreter is described by B operations. We give hereafter some operations corresponding to the previously described opcodes.

```
OPERATIONS

op_push0 =
  SELECT
      opcodes(current_instruction)=OP_PUSH0
  THEN
      current_instruction := current_instruction + 1 ||
      stack := 0 → stack
  END;

op_if =
  SELECT
      opcodes(current_instruction)=OP_IF
  THEN
      current_instruction :∈ {(current_instruction + 1),
         current_instruction+parameters(current_instruction)(1)} ||
      stack := stack ↓ 1
  END;

op_store =
  SELECT
      opcodes(current_instruction)=OP_STORE
  THEN
      frame:= frame ⩤ {(parameters(current_instruction)(1)↦head(stack))} ||
      current_instruction := current_instruction + 1 ||
      stack := stack ↓ 1
  END;
```

6.4 Specification of the Optimisation

Within the Java VM, all local variables and parameters are stored using four bytes in the frame. This means, for example, that three bytes of memory are lost for a byte variable. This can increase performance on a 32 bit machine where memory consumption is not a problem, but on a smart card the memory is the most valuable resource to spare. The first performed optimisation consists in using the smallest number of bytes to store a local variable. Moreover the references on a smart card are two bytes wide, which can lead to the spare of a couple of byte.

In order to allow such optimisation, the instruction set of the virtual machine is specialised. In our example, the instructions *store* and *load* are replaced by the instructions *store_byte, store_short, store_integer, store_ref, load_byte, load_short, load_integer* and *load_ref*. Those instructions perform the same operations, excepted that they allow to manipulate one, two or four bytes variables, and address the frame in byte units instead of variable numbers.

The second optimisation that can be performed is the *overlay* optimisation. It consists in allocating the same location in memory for two different variables when they are used at different point in the program. This can also be used to allocate a variable at different positions for different instructions. Such optimisations that can be performed in the table 3:

Table 3. Example of Optimisations

Instructions	Unoptimised frame	Optimised frame	optimised frame (overlay)
1 push 0	{}	{}	{}
2 store 1	{}	{}	{}
3 nop	{ 4 |-> Byte }	{ 1 |-> Byte}	{ 1 |-> Byte}
4 load 1	{ 4 |-> Byte }	{ 1 |-> Byte}	{ 1 |-> Byte}
5 inc	{}	{}	{}
6 new Object	{}	{}	{}
7 init Object	{}	{}	{}
8 store 2	{}	{}	{}
...	{ 8 |-> ObjectRef }	{ 3 |-> ObjectRef }	{ 2 |-> ObjectRef }

Applying this optimisation to the frame can reduce the memory needed for the applet. But it can introduce errors leading to type confusion. The use of formal methods can help to ensure that those optimisations do not introduce errors or security holes. In the next refinement we specify what is allowed for reallocating the variables.

We represent the new location of the variable as a partial injection, mapping the number of the variables used in the previous example to their real position in the frame : *optimised_locations*. This variable uses a sequence since it must be defined for each instruction of the method.

$optimised\_locations \in \mathbf{seq}(\ NATURAL \nrightarrowtail NATURAL) \land$
$\mathbf{size}(optimised\_locations) = \mathbf{size}(opcodes) \qquad\qquad \land$
$\mathbf{dom}(optimised\_locations(pc)) = \mathbf{dom}(types\_frames(pc)))$

The invariant ensures that no local variables overlap each other. The following invariant checks that if the type of the local variable is an integer all the four bytes used cannot be allocated to another variable.

$\forall(pc,ii).(pc \in \mathbf{dom}(opcodes) \land$
$ii \in \mathbf{dom}(types\_frames(pc)) \land$
$Type(types\_frames(pc)(ii)) = Integer$
$\Rightarrow$
$optimised\_locations(pc)(ii) \geq PrivateDataSize + 4 \qquad \land$
$optimised\_locations(pc)(ii) - 1 \notin \mathbf{ran}(optimised\_locations(pc)) \land$
$optimised\_locations(pc)(ii) - 2 \notin \mathbf{ran}(optimised\_locations(pc)) \land$
$optimised\_locations(pc)(ii) - 3 \notin \mathbf{ran}(optimised\_locations(pc)))$

The following invariant ensures that the variables are allocated at the same position for each instruction where they can be used.

$\forall(pc,ii).(pc \in \mathbf{dom}(opcodes) \land$
$pc + 1 \in \mathbf{dom}(opcodes) \land$
$ii \in \mathbf{dom}(types\_frames(pc)) \land$
$ii \in \mathbf{dom}(types\_frames(pc+1)) \land$
$types\_frames(pc)(ii) = types\_frames(pc+1)(ii)$
$\Rightarrow$
$optimised\_locations(pc)(ii) = optimised\_locations(pc+1)(ii))$

Another allocation constraint is generated by the if opcode : a variable accessible after the branch must be allocated at the same place as it was previously allocated.

$\forall(pc,ii).(pc \in \mathbf{dom}(opcodes) \land$
$opcodes(pc) = OP\_IF \land$
$ii \in \mathbf{dom}(types\_frames(pc)) \land$
$ii \in \mathbf{dom}(types\_frames(pc+parameters(pc)(1)))$
$\Rightarrow$
$optimised\_locations(pc+parameters(pc)(1))(ii) = optimised\_locations(pc)(ii))$

Although those rules are valid for the considered instruction set, the complete Java byte code requires more care, since some instructions can access directly local variables. Moreover, the exception handling and subroutines calls introduce new constraints.

6.5   The Refinement into the Java Card Interpreter

Until now the refinements were used in order to define the interpreter of the JVM by adding successively new details to enrich the specification. The next refinement transforms the JVM specification into the Java Card specification. We use the notion of gluing invariants to specify the conversion. The gluing invariant expresses how to match the variables of the current refinement with the variable of the previous level. The matching is implicit if the variables have the same name or explicit by expressing the relation between them with an invariant.

We define new variables for the method, the frame. We have to define the relation between the old and the new definition of those variables using the notion of gluing invariants. The next invariant specifies the conversion of the if instruction. It is translated without any change like most of the considered instructions.

$\forall pc.(pc \in \mathbf{dom}(opcodes) \land$
$opcodes(pc)=OP\_IF$
$\Rightarrow$
$pc \in \mathbf{dom}(opcodes\_ref2) \land$
$opcodes\_ref2(pc)=REF2\_IF \land$
$parameters\_ref2(pc)=parameters(pc))$

We also define the new set of opcodes of our Java Card interpreter. Some byte code have been added like those manipulating the local variables (e.g. *REF2_STORE_SHORT*).

The instructions manipulating the frame need a specific invariant. The opcode must be translated into its specialised opcode according to the type contained in the frame. The opcode operand (*parameters_ref2(pc)*) has to be adjusted to the new position of the variable in the frame.

$$\forall(pc,yy,zz).(pc \in \mathbf{dom}(opcodes) \wedge$$
$$opcodes(pc)=OP\_LOAD \wedge$$
$$yy=opcodes\_ref2(pc) \wedge$$
$$zz= types\_frames(pc)(parameters(pc)(1))$$
$$\Rightarrow$$
$$pc \in \mathbf{dom}(opcodes\_ref2) \wedge$$
$$((zz=Integer) \Leftrightarrow (yy=REF2\_LOAD\_INTEGER)) \wedge$$
$$((zz=Short) \Leftrightarrow (yy=REF2\_LOAD\_SHORT)) \wedge$$
$$((zz=Byte) \Leftrightarrow (yy=REF2\_LOAD\_BYTE)) \wedge$$
$$((zz \in \{ObjectRef, UninitialisedObjectRef\}) \Leftrightarrow (yy=REF2\_LOAD\_REF)) \wedge$$
$$parameters\_ref2(pc)= \{ (1\mapsto optimised\_locations(pc)(parameters(pc)(1))))$$

The next invariant expresses the relation between the frame and the new optimised frame *(frame_ref2)*. It states that every known variable has the same value in the new frame as in the old one. In order to reduce the complexity of the model, we choose to model the access to the frame variables by using only one location in the frame. Consequently, the following invariant need only one access to the frame to store any kind of variables.

$$\forall ii.(ii \in \mathbf{dom}(frame) \wedge ii \in \mathbf{dom}(types\_frames(current\_instruction))$$
$$\Rightarrow$$
$$frame\_ref2(optimised\_locations(current\_instruction)(ii)) = frame(ii))$$

Now we can express the operational semantics of our Java Card interpreter which must be a valid refinement of the Java interpreter despite the conversion. The operation corresponding to the store opcodes has the same behaviour whatever the store opcode considered due to the previous hypothesis.

```
op_store =
   SELECT
opcodes_ref2(current_instruction) ∈ {REF2_STORE_BYTE,
REF2_STORE_SHORT, REF2_STORE_INTEGER, REF2_STORE_REF}
   THEN
   frame_ref2 := frame_ref2 ⋐ { (parameters_ref2(current_instruction)(1) ↦
head(stack_ref2) ) } ||
   current_instruction := current_instruction + 1 ||
   stack_ref2 := stack_ref2 ↓ 1
   END;
```

6.6 The Proof of the Specification

The AtelierB generated 645 proof obligations, including 260 non obvious PO. Obvious PO are automatically proved by the theorem prover. Using the strongest force, the theorem prover discharged about 60% of the non obvious PO. The remaining PO have been proved manually using the interactive prover. We encountered several times the same kind of PO, so in order the make the proof generic we added extra rules.

For example, most of the proofs need to instanciate the static constraints corresponding to the current instruction. This can be done, of course, manually but adding the following rule allowed us to prove several PO with the same demonstration.

```
THEORY prhh IS
      binhyp(opcodes(current_instruction$1) = x) &
      binhyp(current_instruction$1 : dom(opcodes)) &
      binhyp(!pc.(pc : dom(opcodes) & opcodes(pc) = x => y))
      =>
      [pc:=current_instruction$1] y
END
```

Finally the whole specification has been proved as shown in the following table. However the manual proof still represents a considerable effort even for this reduced model.

COMPONENT	TC	GOP	Obv	nPO	nUn	%Pr	BOC
constants	OK	OK	1	0	0	100	-
jvm_base	OK	OK	27	86	0	100	-
jvm_ref1	OK	OK	134	44	0	100	-
jvm_ref2	OK	OK	477	124	0	100	-
method_base	OK	OK	2	4	0	100	-
opcodes_base	OK	OK	1	0	0	100	-
opcodes_constraints	OK	OK	1	0	0	100	-
opcodes_jcvm	OK	OK	1	0	0	100	-
types_base	OK	OK	1	0	0	100	-
typing_info	OK	OK	0	2	0	100	-
TOTAL	OK	OK	645	260	0	100	-

7. Conclusions

Byte code verification is an important part of the Java platform. We believe that properties verification is a key point process in the security policy needing the use of formal methods to ensure a high confidence in the optimisation process. However, difficulty arises when this verification is adapted to platforms such as smart cards. The traditional approach using the Java byte code verifier is unusable when the VM is modified. In our approach we replace the use of a dedicated byte code verifier with the formal proof of the transformations.

In this paper, we have presented an original technique to express a formal proof of a part of the optimisation process included into the Gemplus RAD. We gave a part of the formal description of the operational semantics and the static constraints of two interpreters of a subset of Java byte code. By specifying rigorously the transformation process through gluing invariants, we proved on a subset of opcode that we do not modify the type system properties.

We expect to extend this approach to the entire set of Java Card instructions in order to prove our converter and data optimiser. The next step will be to use the gluing invariants to specify the converter itself and automatically generate the code of the transformer. As we use a formal model, we can experiment several optimisation algorithms.

Future works include the specification of two other entities : the peephole optimiser and the type inference system. For the peephole optimiser, we will probably use the specification of the Java Card interpreter as a starting point.

References

[Abr-96]   J.R. Abrial The B Book. Assigning Programs to Meanings. Cambridge University Press, 1996

[Coh-97] Cohen, Defensive Java Virtual Machine
http://www.cli.com/software/djvm

[Fre-98]   S. N. Freud, J. C. Mitchell, A type System for Object Initialization In the Java Byte Code Language http://theory.standford.edu/~freunds

[Gol-97]   A. Golberg, A Specification of Java Loading and Bytecode Verification Kestrel Institute, Dec-97 http://www.kestrel.edu/HTML/people/goldberg/

[Har-98]   P. Hartel, M. Butler, M. Levy, The operational semantics of a Java Secure Processor.

[Qia-97]   Qian A formal specification of Java Virtual Machine Instruction. Technical Report (abstract), Universitat Bremen, 1997 http://www.informatik.uni-bremen.de/~qian/abs-fsjvm.html

[Sta-98]   R.Stata, M.Abadi, A Type System for Byte Code Subroutines Proc. 25th ACM Symposium on Principles of Programming Language, Jan-98

[Yel-96]   Franck Yellin, Tim Lindholm , The Java Virtual Machine Specification, ed. Addison Wesley, 1996

Smart Card Payment over Internet with Privacy Protection

Pui-Nang Chan, Samuel T. Chanson, Ricci Ieong, and James Pang

Department of Computer Science
Hong Kong University of Science and Technology
chanson@cs.ust.hk

Abstract. The world woke up to the existence of the Internet in the early 90's and Internet usage has grown very rapidly since then. Payment over the Internet, especially for low cost products and services, is becoming popular. Although many secure payment standards, like SET, are available, they are either ineffective for large volume micro-payment or indifferent to the cardholders' privacy. In this paper, we propose a solution based on the smart card technology such as the Java™ Card™ on secure micro-payment over the Internet. One of the special properties of our solution is the identity of the purchaser can remain anonymous both to the merchant and the bank. The design and correctness of the proposed scheme are discussed here.

1 Introduction

As the number of people surfing the Internet increases, web-based shopping has grown tremendously. The International Data Corporation estimates the amount of web-based commerce will reach more than US$400 billion by 2002. In the past few years, many researchers have tried to develop technologies to make on-line business practical. Solutions on security and anonymity protocols have been proposed. In this paper, a new smart card over the Internet payment system based on some of the available solutions is proposed. First we describe the basic technologies on which the project is based.

One of the popular security protocols is SSL[1] by Netscape Communications Corporation. SSL provides private connection, authentication, and reliable connection. After several years of testing in the real word, it may be one of best security protocols available and is widely supported. Besides Netscape's products, common web servers and browsers also provide SSL, like Apache-SSL[2] and Microsoft Internet Information Server (IIS)[3]. Although not all of them can give 128bit encryption due to the US export law, the protocol standard is open. The specification [4] and the code, such as SSLeay[5], can be obtained through the Internet, and 128bit SSL implementation is readily available.

Besides security, anonymity is another interesting issue for payment systems. Many people do not want their purchasing habits to be known by others. Therefore cash-like or coin-like on-line payments schemes have been developed. eCash™ [6] and blind signature [7,8] are the technologies for payment and signing without revealing user identity. Also, anonymity proxy server [9-11] technology can provide anonymous web surfing.

J.-J. Quisquater and B. Schneier (Eds.): CARDIS 2000, LNCS 1820, pp. 98–104, 2000.
© Springer-Verlag Berlin Heidelberg 2000

The emergence of Java Card [12] allows programmers to add their own programs and execute them on the card. The smart card is a secure, non-duplicable storage device. Java Card technology also provides flexible and sophisticated solution on security. For example it can run random-challenge response protocol for authentication.

Payment protocol over the Internet is also available. SET [13] is developed by MasterCard International and Visa International for credit card payment. But credit card is intended for payment involving larger amounts (dollars instead of cents). It may not be suitable for micro-payment, which is expected to be the most popular kind of payment over the Internet.

In this paper, we propose a new solution for secure payment over the Internet with privacy protection using smart cards. In the following section, the system design is discussed. Section 3 presents some correctness argument. A brief discussion of various practical issues is given in Section 4 followed by the conclusions in Section 5.

2 System Design

Overview of the System

Our design assumes the existence of some infrastructure components, namely SSL [1] and anonymity proxy server [9-11]. SSL is in widespread use and there is no reason to come up with a new encryption protocol. Also, if anonymity is needed during the communication process, an anonymity proxy server can be used.

As mentioned, our concerns are security, privacy and efficiency. To provide security, both prevention and detection methods are used. All the important information is encrypted. If a fraud is detected in any transaction, the protocol will try to prevent the defrauder from gaining any profit.

Privacy is protected by ensuring the anonymity of the purchaser. Electronic coins are used. The protocol prevents the bank from knowing the identity as well as the purchasing habit of the cardholder. Although each coin has a serial number needed for the detection of forgery, the bank does not know who owns the coins. The anonymity of the cardholder can also be maintained when paying or receiving goods/service from the merchant. The cardholder can do the transaction over a SSL channel and via an anonymity proxy server. S/he may also pick up the goods, if desired, by presenting a receipt that will be stored in her/his smart card during the transaction.

Functionary of the Card

We assume the card has enough space to store the electronic coins. Basic functions like public key and private key encryption and signature should be supported. The transactions on the client's side are executed by the processor chip on the card, rather than on the computer attached because the cardholder may also be an attacker. Some possible replay attacks and their defense will be discussed in a later section.

In our design, each card is associated with a private key that is stored on the card. This key is accessible only by the program onboard the card. The public key is kept in the bank's database. Each card also has a unique card identity number. The bank can thus pair up the card's identity number with its public key. In this way, the bank can send encrypted information to the card that can decrypt it with its private key. The card also stores the bank's public key so it can send encrypted information to the bank.

Electronic Coins

The coin is just a unique random number with the bank's signature. The random number should be unique because the bank can then check whether the coin has been used before to detect forgery.

Protocol

There are two parts to the protocol. The first deals with downloading electronic coins from the bank. The other handles purchasing with the coins. Downloading electronic coins is done with blind signature [7-8]. The card first downloads one (or more) unique random number R from the bank. The bank does not know the identity of the user at this stage. The user can connect to the bank from an anonymity proxy server. The user then blinds (transforms) the random number R to R' and sends it with the card's identity number to the bank. The bank withdraws money from the cardholder's account and blindly signs R' (in other words, it signs R indirectly). It then encrypts it with the card's public key and sends this back to the card. The card can decrypt it with its private key and calculate the signature of R. Finally, the card stores the pair of unique numbers (the random number R and the bank's signature) for use as an electronic coin. In the whole process, the bank does not know which coins the cardholder got since it sees R' rather than R. Also, the cardholder cannot duplicate the coin to another card because only one card has the private key that can decrypt the electronic coin.

Authentication of the cardholder can be done by certificate checking in SSL or the user keying in a password under SSL. This certificate and password can also be stored on the card to make it more convenient to the cardholder.

When the cardholder purchases goods/service over the Internet, he or she should first establish a SSL connection to the merchant. The user can check the identity of the web site in the SSL by reading its certificate. If the cardholder purchases services/goods that can be delivered electronically, and wants to hide his/her identity from the merchant, s/he can make use of an anonymity proxy server for communication. After the connection is established, the cardholder can send the order with the encrypted and password-locked coins. The coins are transformed shown as in figure 2.

The merchant then forwards these encrypted and password-locked coins to the bank for verification. If the coins are valid, the merchant will send a receipt to the cardholder. The cardholder should then instruct the card to send the coins' password to the merchant, so that the merchant can require the bank to deposit them into his account. Upon confirmation from the bank that the password is good and the merchant's account has been credited, the merchant should deliver the goods/service according to the order; otherwise the cardholder can sue the merchant with the receipt.

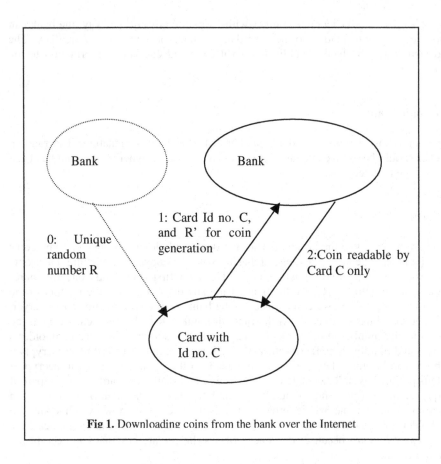

Fig 1. Downloading coins from the bank over the Internet

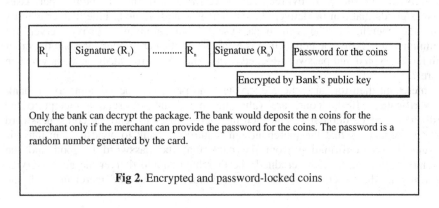

Only the bank can decrypt the package. The bank would deposit the n coins for the merchant only if the merchant can provide the password for the coins. The password is a random number generated by the card.

Fig 2. Encrypted and password-locked coins

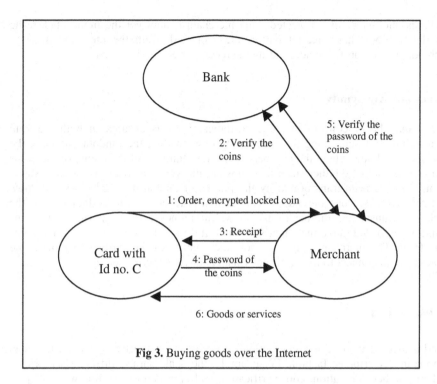

Fig 3. Buying goods over the Internet

The coins sent to the bank will be expired and can no longer be used again, even before the merchant provided the password of the coins. Therefore, the merchant can believe the cardholder has no incentive to keep the password from him as the cardholder will have lost the coin anyway, and will not receive the goods/service. The bank can verify that the transaction is not yet completed for missing password. The merchant has nothing to gain by withholding the password sent by the purchaser, as his account will not be credited.

3 Arguments on Correctness

Security

Security is the most important issue in a payment protocol. From the bank's point of view, it is concerned about forged coins. But this can be checked as each coin has a unique random number that acts like the serial number of a bank note. When two coins have the same serial number, the bank detects forgery. Also it is difficult to forge a coin. All coins are downloaded in encrypted form and only one card can read them.

The merchant is protected since it will get confirmation of the validity of the coin from the bank. If he acts honestly and sends the receipt, he can expect the cardholder to give him the key to unlock the coin. This is because the cardholder cannot get back the coins from the bank (i.e. the bank expires the coins on receiving them).

The cardholder is also protected - the merchant cannot get the money before he gets the receipt. Therefore, all parties are protected. Both the merchant and the cardholder cannot profit by not sending the receipt or electronic coins.

Privacy and Anonymity

Privacy may be of concern to some customers. This is ensured in both the coin downloading and purchasing transactions. In downloading the random numbers, the bank does not know where the numbers (i.e. serial numbers of the coins) of the coins went (it does not care either since the coins are not yet signed). In the signing stage, the number has been transformed by the purchaser and so the bank does not know what the purchaser has purchased (cannot associate coin with cardholder). In the purchasing transaction, the bank only knows the money associated with some coins should be deposited into a merchant's account. It does not know which card the coins came from. The merchant may not know the identity of the cardholder either. The cardholder can connect to the merchant via an anonymity proxy server.

4 Discussion

Speed is also an issue. Some encryption operations are required. However, they can be done in a distributed fashion. For example, the bank can use different servers for random number generation, coin verification and coin deposit. In this way, all jobs can be done quickly.

The keys are also important. The key pairs should be renewed or changed after a period of time. Therefore the card should be expired after a period of time to change the bank's public key and the card's private and public keys. The key for signing coins for the bank can be updated periodically without affecting the cardholders. This is because the validation and issuance of the coins are done by the bank; it can change the signing key at any time. It is required only to store the information on which random numbers are signed by which keys.

In the implementation, distinct random numbers cannot be generated indefinitely. However, when a coin is used (deposited by a merchant), its serial number, i.e., the random number, can be reused. The bank can sign the random number with a different key. In this way, forged coins (copy of the old coins) can still be detected because they would be signed with the old private key.

5 Conclusions

The system we have proposed is practical and useful. The implementation is not difficult because some of the functions make use of existing infrastructure - SSL does the encryption and anonymity proxy server supports the privacy in communications. This can free up much manpower for testing and smart card program design. The scheme is useful since not all people can get a credit card or are willing to have one. Paying cash is still the most common way to purchase goods and services. With this scheme, people have the flexibility of purchasing over the Internet which removes space and time boundaries. The bank has lower overhead compared to processing the credit cardholder's bill with many low value payments. The merchant is protected by receiving cash-like electronic money. Sophisticated software and hardware are not required by either the merchant or the purchaser. The core of the system is built on top of current infrastructure like the Internet and SSL. For small and medium size enterprises (SMEs), this model can help them to start selling on line with little setup cost.

References

[1]   Secure Socket Layer (SSL). http://www.netscape.com/newsref/std/SSL.html
[2]   Apache-SSL. http://www.apache-ssl.org
[3]   Microsoft Internet Information Sever. http://www.microsoft.com
[4]   Secure Socket Layer (SSL) specification
       http://home.netscape.com/eng/ssl3/index.html
[5]   SSLeay. http://www.psy.uq.oz.au/~ftp/Crypto/
[6]   eCash. http://www.digicash.com
[7]   D. Chaum. Blind Signatures for Untraceable Payments, Advances in Cryptology Proceedings of Crypto 82, 1983, pp. 199-203
[8]   D. Chaum. Security without identification: Transaction system to make big brother obsolete, Communications of ACM, vol. 28, 1985, pp. 1030-1044
[9]   The anonymizer. http://www.anonymizer.com/
[10]   M.G. Reed, P.F. Syverson, D.M. Goldschlag. Proxies for Anonymous Routing, Proc. 12th Annual Computer Security Applications Conference, San Diego, CA, IEEE CS Press, December, 1996, pp. 95-104
[11]   P.F. Syverson, D.M. Goldschlag, M.G. Reed. Anonymous Connections and Onion Routing, Proc. 1997 IEEE Symposium on Security and Privacy, Oakland, CA, IEEE CS Press, May, 1997, pp. 44-54
[12]   Java Card. http://java.sun.com/products/javacard/index.html
[13]   Secure Electronic Transaction (SET) LLC. http://www.setco.org/

Developing Smart Card-Based Applications Using Java Card⋆

Jean-Jacques Vandewalle and Eric Vétillard

Gemplus Research Lab
E-mail: {jeanjac,eric}@research.gemplus.com

Abstract. In this paper we describe a methodology for developing smart card-based applications which accounts for both internal and external software production: on-card and client programs. This development methodology is based on the application of distributed object-oriented principles to Java Card. We design a model in which a card application is viewed as a remote object accessed through method invocations handled by a proxy object executing on the terminal. With a simple example, we show how this model enhances the development of smart card-based applications by allowing Java programmers to rapidly design and develop on-card and off-card programs without worrying about the specific smart card features. This scheme has been implemented as the core technology in the Gemplus Java Card application development environment *GemXpresso RAD*.

Keywords. Java Card software production, Smart card-based application design, Object-oriented framework.

1   Background and Objectives

In this section we review the emergent and promising open smart card development platform based on the Java Card specification. We give an overview of the processes involved in the creation of a Java Card-based application. We outline the limits of the Java Card specification as a model for the interaction between Java Card applets and the outside world. We then show how this limit has brought us to define a development methodology based on distributed object-oriented principles applied to Java Cards.

1.1   Java Card Brings Objects to Smart Cards

During the past twenty years smart cards have evolved from simple dedicated devices (phone cards, French "Carte Bleue") to open computing platforms [11,

---

⋆ Java and Java Card are trademarks of Sun Microsystems Inc. GemXpresso RAD is a trademark of Gemplus. All other product names mentioned herein are the trademarks of their respective owners.

J.-J. Quisquater and B. Schneier (Eds.): CARDIS 2000, LNCS 1820, pp. 105–124, 2000.

7,9]. Research was focusing on providing programmable smart cards to enable programmers to write themselves card applications on top of a card virtual machine executing the code in a portable and secure environment [1,4]. With the advent of Java Card [16], promoted by Sun and the Java Card Forum, smart card technology has been made accessible to a wide body of programmers, most of them new to smart card programming.

A Java Card is simply defined as a smart card that is capable of running Java programs. Java Card brings the object-oriented programming model that is enforced by the usage of the Java programming language. Object orientation brings to card programming the same advantages that it brings elsewhere, by encouraging the development of code in small and self-contained units. This approach brings modularity, encapsulation and information hiding to card applications. This leads to more independence between objects, and a restriction of the interactions between objects to well-defined interfaces.

Nevertheless, the Java Card object-oriented approach only addresses "on-card" software production. A complete smart card application also includes the "off-card" software (the application running on a host/terminal as a client program of a smart card applet). The Java Card standard has kept the traditional communication model between a smart card and its clients, which is well-suited for the resolution of legacy problems, linked to the continued use of existing card applications standards. As such, it does not propose a standard object-oriented way to define a high-level interface between a card applet and its client program.

In typical smart card-based applications the communication between the card application and the client is defined by commands (to card) and responses (from card) embedded in Application Program Data Units (APDUs). In Java Card, a card application communicates with the outside world through an instance of the class `javacard.framework.Applet` that provides a method to process APDUs.

1.2   More Object Orientation

The Java Card specification describes a limited version of the Java language and platform well dedicated to smart cards and legacy applications. Defining the communication between the card application and the outside world as exchanges of APDUs forces programmers to design a proprietary protocol for every application they write. Both the client program and the card applet have to implement a significant amount of tedious code to encode and decode the information exchanged accordingly with the protocol defined. This approach is cumbersome to program, and it forces the developer to focus on the definition of a smart-card dedicated low-level protocol rather than on the object design of the whole application.

In this paper we propose a development methodology which allows the card and client programmers not to worry about the protocol between the card and the host. This methodology is based on the representation of the client/server architecture made by the host and the card as a distributed object system. The Java Card is considered as a server running an application that is described by an *interface*. The card applet is a class that implements this interface. The client

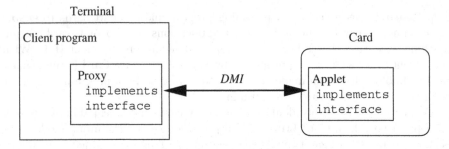

Fig. 1. Distributed object-oriented smart card-based application

program communicates with the card applet accordingly to the *remote object* interface. The interface is a kind of contract that binds a server to its clients. The server guarantees that it will respond, as expected, to the methods defined in the interface.

For the communication between client programs and card applet we have defined a protocol called *Direct Method Invocation* (DMI), which encapsulates client requests to the card applets. The DMI protocol links the card to the host and defines the way in which the card applet and the client program communicate. The protocol is handled by the Java Card operating system, making the card applet source code enterely independent of it. On the client side the protocol is handled by a *proxy* program which is automatically generated from the interface. The proxy represents the remote object (the card applet) on the client side by offering to the client program the interface implemented by the applet. The proxy implements the card applet interface but it contains the code required to invoke the card applet methods using the DMI protocol (*cf.* Fig. 1).

1.3   Outline of the Paper

Section 2 explains in detail how to develop a Java Card-based applications using the protocol-oriented approach defined by the Java Card specification. A card applet and a client program will be provided on the basis of an application built around a simple "counter"[1]. Section 3 illustrates our approach with the same example. The design patterns, the processes and the tools implied in our architecture are described. Finally, we outline some perspectives to enhance our model in two directions: security and reference passing between cards and clients.

2   Developing Java Card-Based Applications

This section describes how to develop an application with a Java Card. The two main tasks are to implement a Java Card applet, and to implement a client

---

[1] A lightweight version of an electronic purse, since it can be incremented or decremented by an amount, but does not perform any security control.

application that communicates with the Java Card applet when the smart card is inserted into a card reader. But, before to detail those implementations, it is necessary to examine how communication with smart cards is realized, and how communication is handled in the Java Card API. Following documents can usefully complement the content of this section: [17], [14], [5], and [6].

2.1 Communicating with a Smart Card

To communicate with a smart card you need to write an application that sends commands to a smart card connected to your host through a reader. From the host to the reader, and from the reader to the smart card data (commands and responses) are transported using protocols. The communication protocols between smart cards and readers are defined by an ISO standard [10, part 3] as $T=0$ (character protocol) or $T=1$ (block-chaining protocol). The problem is that there is no standardized protocol between the host and the reader. To permit the description of card commands independently of host-reader and reader-card protocols a format has been standardized [10, parts 3 and 4]. This format defines the command message sent from the client application, and the response message returned by the card to the client application as *Application Protocol Data Units* (APDUs). Each manufacturer provides a driver to transport APDUs with its proprietary host-reader protocol (*cf.* Fig. 2).

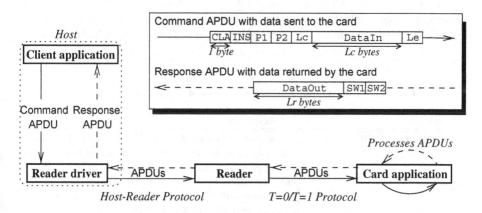

Fig. 2. Communication with Application Protocol Data Units

The meaning of the APDU message bytes can be set by a standard, by a manufacturer, or by a designer regarding the application requirements. Some command APDUs are standardized by various standards according to the capabilities provided by smart card applications. For example, ISO 7816-4 defines commands for file management, ISO 7816-7 defines commands for database management, and EMV defines commands for general-purpose payment management. Off-the-shelf smart cards sold by manufacturers and proprietary smart cards deployed by national organisms or consortiums define also their own command APDUs for their application's needs.

In fact, to communicate with a smart card from a client application the following steps must be followed:

1. Have knowledge of the card command set, in fact the list of command APDUs that smart cards can process, the possible values for their parameters, and the format of data.
2. Build the command APDUs sent to smart cards regarding the application data retrieved from local variables, databases, user inputs, *etc.*
3. Use a driver to transport APDUs from the host to the smart card through a reader.
4. Decode the response APDUs regarding the format of data returned by the card and analyze the different possible values of the status bytes.

2.2 Handling Communication in Java Card Applets

Principles. Java Card does not specify how a card applet has to be loaded or initialized, or how the terminal may obtain information about a smart card. The Java Card specification is a standard for programmers, whose goal is to guarantee the interoperability of Java Card applications at the source code level. To support this level of integration, a Java Card applet is defined as a `javacard.framework.Applet` object with a set of methods (*cf.* Table 1) enabling the applet to communicate through `javacard.framework.APDU` objects.

Table 1. Main methods of the class `javacard.framework.Applet`

Method	Description
`void install(APDU apdu)`	Static method called by the JCRE during the final stage of applet installation. Allocates and initializes the applet. A command APDU can serve to provide initialization parameters to this method, and a response APDU can returned information on the processing of this method.
`void deselect()`	Called by the JCRE when the applet is deselected (*i.e.* when another applet is selected). Contains code that must be executed at the end of each session with the applet.
`boolean select()`	Called by the JCRE when the applet is selected. Contains code that must be executed at the beginning of each new session with the applet.
`void process(APDU apdu)`	Main method, which receives and processes all the APDUs for the applet, while it is selected.

Processing the APDU Object. The argument used in an applet's `install` and `process` methods is an `APDU` object. This object is used to encapsulate the command and response APDUs exchanged by the card with both the T=0 and T=1 protocols. The `APDU` object is handled as a buffer in which the application can first read the command APDU received, and then can write the response to be sent back (*cf.* Fig. 3).

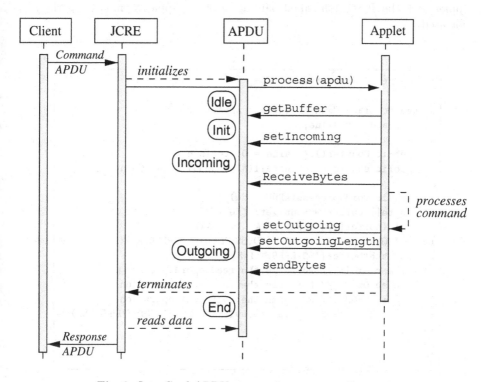

Fig. 3. Java Card APDUs processing sequence diagram

The "End" state is reached by setting the response APDU's status bytes. Three cases may occur:

1. If the `process` or `install` method executes and finishes normally, then the JCRE sends the status code 0x9000 (normal completion) as the status bytes of the response APDU.
2. If the `process` or `install` method throws an `ISOException`, then the JCRE sends the reason for that exception as the status bytes of the response APDU.
3. If any other exception has been thrown, the behaviour of the underlying operating system is undefined. In fact, the JCRE may decide to mute the card, block the applet, or perform any number of operations to ensure the future security of the applet or the card itself.

2.3 Writing a Java Card Applet

Applet Design. This section is intended to illustrate the Java Card development process with a simple "counter" card applet, which stores an `int` value that can be read, and can be incremented and decremented by a given amount (*cf.* Fig. 4). The counter is installed in the card by calling the constructor of the applet, which sets the counter with an initial value to 0 and registers this applet with the JCRE (the `APDU` parameter of the applet's `install` method is not used).

```
1   import javacard.framework.*;
2
3   public class Counter extends Applet {
4     private int value;
5
6     public Counter() { value = 0; register(); }
7     public static void install(APDU apdu) { new Counter(); }
8
9     public void process(APDU apdu) {
10     byte[] buffer = apdu.getBuffer();
11     if (buffer[ISO.OFFSET_CLA] != 0xAA)
12       ISOException.throwIt(ISO.SW_CLA_NOT_SUPPORTED);
13     switch(buffer[ISO.OFFSET_INS]) {
14     case 0x01: // Performs the read operation
15     case 0x02: // Performs the increment operation
16     case 0x03: // Performs the decrement operation
17     default: ISOException.throwIt(ISO.SW_INS_NOT_SUPPORTED);
18     }
19   }
20 }
```

Fig. 4. Java Card `Counter` class source code

Applet Operations and APDUs. Other operations are handled by the applet's `process` method, which decodes them with their arguments and returns results according to the APDU mapping described in Table 2.

Implementation of the Applet Operations. The source code of the decrement operation (*cf.* Fig. 5) illustrates what has to be implemented to realize a processing on APDU data. First it is necessary to retrieve the incoming data from the APDU buffer (line 3). As data are in a byte array, it is necessary to format them accordingly to the type used within the Java applet; in our example, an `int` must be retrieved in the 4 bytes of the command APDU data (lines 6 to

Table 2. APDUs mapping for the "counter" operations

Operation	APDU
int read()	Command: AA 01 XX XX 00 04
	Response: RV3 RV2 RV1 RV0 90 00
int increment(int)	Command: AA 02 XX XX 04 AM3 AM2 AM1 AM0 04
	Response: RV3 RV2 RV1 RV0 90 00
int decrement(int)	Command: AA 03 XX XX 04 AM3 AM2 AM1 AM0 04
	Response: RV3 RV2 RV1 RV0 90 00

9). Then, the processing can be performed with the applet's instance variables and the incoming data (line 12). To send back data to the outside world, they must be stored in the APDU buffer as bytes (lines 13 to 17).

```
1   case 0x03: // Performs the decrement operation
2   {
3     byte byteRead = (byte)(apdu.setIncomingAndReceive());
4     if (byteRead != 4) ISOException.throwIt(ISO.SW_WRONG_LENGTH);
6     int amount = (buffer[ISO.OFFSET_CDATA]<<24) |
7       (buffer[ISO.OFFSET_CDATA+1]<<16) |
8       (buffer[ISO.OFFSET_CDATA+2]<<8) |
9       buffer[ISO.OFFSET_CDATA+3];
10    if (amout<0 || value-amount<0)
11      ISOException.throwIt((short)0x6910);
12    value -= amount;
13    buffer[0]=(byte)(value>>24);
14    buffer[1]=(byte)(value>>16);
15    buffer[2]=(byte)(value>>8);
16    buffer[3]=(byte)(value);
17    apdu.setOutgoingAndSend((short)0, (short)4);
18  }
```

Fig. 5. Counter "decrement" operation source code

If a protocol error occurs, a standardized status word can be returned in a response APDU by throwing an ISOException with a constant value provided by the class ISO (lines 4 and 5). For an application error (for example, an illegal negative value, lines 10 and 11), the developer can return a response APDU with a specific status word value to signal this error to the client application.

2.4   Writing a Java Card-Based Client Application

As we have seen while developing the Java Card "counter" applet, the communication between a card applet and the outside world is encapsulated in APDU data structures. Thus, writing a client application that runs with a card applet consists in developing code, which deals with the command APDUs accepted and the response APDUs returned by the card applet method `process`. A client application is a front-end for a card applet, which must perform the following tasks when communicating with the card applet:

- To select the card applet using its AID. This selection is performed by sending a "SELECT APDU" command.
- To prepare command APDUs compliant with the ones accepted by the applet's method `process`. The data sent with the command APDU can be retrieved from various sources (application data, user interface, database, *etc.*) and must be converted to match with the format defined for the APDU's `DataIn` field of bytes (*cf.* Table 2 for the format of data sent with "counter" command APDUs).
- To use a reader driver library to send command APDUs to the card applet and to get back response APDUs from the card applet
- To decode response APDUs according to the format of the data returned in the APDU `DataOut` field of bytes (*cf.* Table 2 for the format of data returned by the "counter" response APDUs). The client application must also check if the status bytes in the response APDU indicate an error.

The overall design of a Java Card-based application (*cf.* Fig. 6) shows that the main tasks of both the client application and the card applet are to process command and response APDUs to exchange information. The JCRE is the main

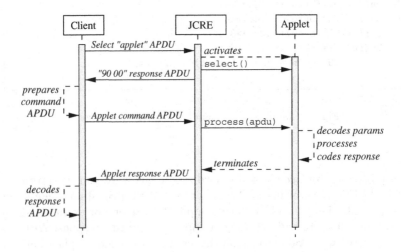

Fig. 6. Java Card-based client application sequence diagram

server process to activate the card applet selected. It also provides the incoming command APDUs to the card applet's method process, and sends back the outgoing response APDUs to the client application.

2.5   Summary

Developing a Java Card-based application requires first to implement a Java Card applet with the Java Card API. The applet code is essentially a code manipulating card communication packets which are APDU data structures. Then, the Java Card applet is compiled using a regular Java compiler. The output is converted in order to produce a byte code, which can suitably be downloaded on a Java Card, and run on the JCVM. Applet conversion and installation are not discussed in this article because they are yet to be standardized, and because we focus here on the whole Java Card-based application development methodology rather than on the tools implied. Finally, it is necessary to implement the client part of the Java Card application that is the code requesting operations to the Java Card applet. This code communicates with the Java Card applet with APDU data structures which must conform to those "understood" by the Java Card applet method process.

3   Developing GemXpresso-Based Applications

In this section, a development methodology[2] is defined in order to help Java programmers to include Java Cards into the information systems they develop. This methodology is based on the definition of a distributed object system dedicated to Java Card in which a client application accesses a Java Card applet through an object *interface*. It is not an alternative to the Java Card specification since it is built over it, and allows Java Card applets to operate with both modes.

3.1   Distributed Object Programming with Java Card

Java Card applets are objects residing in a different machine (a smart card) from the terminal application. In Java Card, terminal and card programs form a client-server system where communication is defined by exchanges of low-level communication packets (APDUs). By applying distributed programming techniques [3] – namely, Remote Procedure Call (RPC) – and object methodology to Java Card, GemXpresso provides a development methodology which allows developers to abstract their design and code from communication protocol considerations.

---

[2] This methodology is herein referred by the word *GemXpresso* since it has been first implemented in the Gemplus GemXpresso RAD product.

Remote Procedure Calling. In client-server programming model, the Remote Procedure Call (RPC) mechanism has been introduced in order to abstract the communication interface to the level of a procedure call [13,15]. Request messages are regarded as procedure calls from a caller (the client), and reply messages are regarded are return values from the callee (the server) which executes the procedure body. Like a regular or local procedure call, an RPC is a synchronous operation requiring the requesting program to be suspended until the results of the remote procedure are returned. The interesting feature of RPC is that it is a protocol that one program can use to request a service from a program located in another computer without having to understand communication details. Instead of working directly with communication packets, the programmer has the illusion of calling a local procedure, when in fact the arguments of the call are packaged up and shipped off to the remote target of the call. Generally, RPC systems encode arguments and return values using a language-neutral and machine-independent data representation. In distributed object-oriented systems object interfaces provide a means for client and server to agree on exactly which server's methods can be invoked through RPC. Each interface contains the definitions for the methods and their parameters expressed in an Interface Definition Language (IDL).

When a client invokes a remote method, the call is handled by a client stub running on the client host (*cf.* Fig. 7). The client stub converts the method's parameters into a form suitable for transmission (a process called *marshaling*)

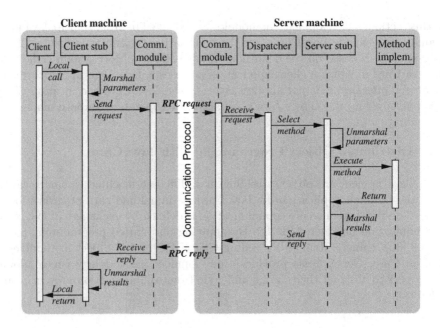

Fig. 7. Typical RPC modules

and causes one or more communication packets to be sent to the server. At the server, a server stub *unmarshals* the parameters, putting them in the correct format for that system, and invokes the requested method. The method executes, then sends any results back via the same path, that is, through the stubs. Once complete, the called method returns from the client stub back to its caller like an ordinary method call. Throughout this process, remote calls are embodied in RPC protocol's messages (containing the marshaled parameters and results) which are transported on top of communication protocols.

Creating a distributed application with RPC-based systems, then, requires specifying all interactions between clients and servers in one or more interfaces. These interfaces are used to produce stubs, which in turn are combined with the actual application code. Whatever the distributed application is doing, RPC runtime routines provide a foundation for interaction between its components. Therefore, RPC-based systems make the developer's work easier by hiding the cumbersome task of communication management thanks to:

- The computed generation of client and server stubs from the interface. Generated codes are specific to the client and server languages and platforms.
- The integration in client and server machines of RPC runtime libraries, which handles the communication (transmission and reception of RPC request and reply messages) and the binding of client and server.

Java Card Applets as Remote Objects. The development methodology promoted by GemXpresso extends the Java Card concept (a card that can be programmed in the object-oriented Java language) to a distributed object-based system where communication between card applets and client applications is abstracted from low-level protocols. The main characteristics of this approach is that it relies on an RPC-based system dedicated to smart cards. A GemXpresso card applet is a server object, which is developped without any concern about communication protocols; it just has to be defined by a Java interface. For the client application, card applets are like remote objects in a distributed system; it invokes applet methods through a client stub handling the communication interface. GemXpresso is built on the following facilities which support the infrastructure for building such distributed applications (*cf.* Fig. 8):

- A card applet must be defined by a Java interface. An interface specifies the methods provided by a card applet that are visible to the card applet's clients.
- The card applet interface definition is used as a basis on which to construct the client stub of the client (called `proxy`) and to provide applet description to the JCRE. The provided information will be used by the proxy and the JCRE (some kinds of client and server stubs) for the marshaling and unmarshaling processes of the method invocations.
- An RPC-like communication protocol, called Direct Method Invocation (DMI), is used for transporting method calls and return results as request and reply messages exchanged between the terminal application and the smart card.

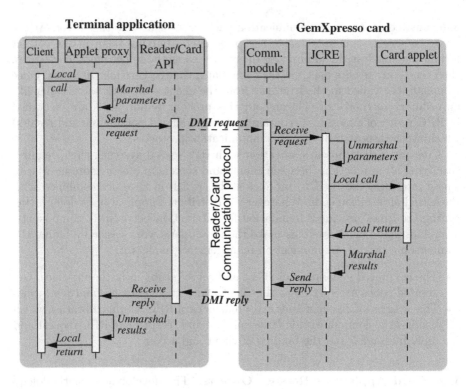

Fig. 8. GemXpresso DMI modules

The following sections show the GemXpresso development methodology in action, using the "Counter" card applet. The card applet design and implementation is described in section 3.2. Section 3.3 describes how to use the generated applet proxy to build a client application.

3.2   Writing a GemXpresso Applet

Card Applet Design. The first step in creating a GemXpresso card applet is to define an interface describing the methods that are available remotely. This interface defines the entry points for the card applet with a list of methods that will be available to client program through DMI. For example, the ICounter interface (*cf.* Fig. 9) defines three methods with their parameter and return types, and the exceptions they may throw. Those are method signatures that will be used by DMI to marshal and unmarshal method invocations from client applications to the implementation of ICounter. As a card applet interface is used to describe what is handled by the DMI protocol, the DMI's characteristics impact on what can be described in the applet interface. Current limitations are outlined below:

```
1   import javacard.framework.*;
2
3   public interface ICounter {
4     public int read();
5     public int increment(int amount) throws UserException;
6     public int decrement(int amount) throws UserException;
7   }
```

Fig. 9. GemXpresso ICounter interface source code

- Parameter and return types: byte, boolean, short, int, and unidimensional arrays of the previous basic types (void is available for methods which do not return a result).
- Exception types: those defined in the Java Card specification.

Card Applet Implementation. In Java Card the javacard.framework.Applet class is the basic class which must be extended by a card applet to implement its processing of APDUs and its interactions with the JCRE. In GemXpresso, an interface is used to represent the contract which binds an applet to its clients. Thus, a card applet must be declared as an implementation of this interface. The processing of APDUs and the interactions with the JCRE do not need to be explicit since they are taken in charge by the DMI mechanism provided with the JCRE. Moreover, GemXpresso card applets do not have to implement the method install, the invocation of one of the constructors is sufficient for instantiating and installing the applet object in the card. These features enable the programmer to implement an applet like an ordinary Java class without considerations about the communication of data between the card applet and the client applications (*cf.* Fig. 10).

In order to keep an upward compatibility with Java Card a GemXpresso card applet also extends the class Applet. The methods of Applet keep the same semantics and can be overridden to work with the JCRE like an ordinary Java Card applet.

Card Applet Installation. A GemXpresso applet, like any Java Card applet, needs to be loaded and installed on a card, before it can be used. However, it needs a few specific features:

- The card's JCRE must support the DMI protocol. As of today, this means that these applets can only be installed on GemXpresso cards.
- The applet's code need to be complemented with some additional data, that describes precisely the declared interface (including the declared parameter types and the thrown exceptions).

```
1  import javacard.framework.*;
2
3  public class Counter extends Applet implements ICounter {
4    private int value;
5
6    public Counter() { value = 0; register(); }
7
8    public int read() { return value; }
9
10   public int decrement(int amount) throws UserException {
11     if (amount<0 || value-amount<0) throw new UserException((short)1);
12     value -= amount; return value;
13   }
14
15   public int increment(int amount) throws UserException {
16     if (amount<0) throw new UserException((short)1);
17     value += amount; return value;
18   }
19 }
```

Fig. 10. GemXpresso Counter class source code

Once the GemXpresso applet has been loaded and linked, it is installed by simply invoking one of its declared constructors. Each constructor needs to call the register method in its body in order to register the applet instance to the JCRE.

3.3 Writing a GemXpresso-Based Application

Application Design. The writing of a GemXpresso-based application is centered around a software component called a *proxy*. The proxy enables the client application to access to the smart card applet *via* a local object implementing the same interface as the card applet. It realizes all the exchanges of the DMI request messages corresponding to the effective method calls coming from the client application. This kind of DMI message is called a DMI's invoke message. The returned result (a return value or an exception) from the card applet is transported by a DMI reply message, which is filtered by the proxy in order to be engineered as a regular returned result for the client application. In order to initialize the DMI communication with a card applet, the client application just needs to perform the following steps:

- Establish a connection to the smart card thanks to a client API (like the Gemplus Java Client API).
- Create the proxy object corresponding to the card applet.

- Request the proxy to bind with its corresponding card applet, that is to select it *via* a "SELECT APDU" command. In fact, this command is also integrated in the DMI protocol as a DMI's `select` message.

If the previous steps complete successfully, the application program can make local method invocations to the proxy in order to send requests to the card applet (*cf.* Fig. 11).

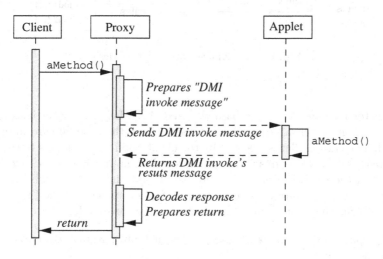

Fig. 11. GemXpresso client application sequence diagram

The Applet Proxy. With GemXpresso, a Java Card proxy is generated from the card applet interface by a software component called a *proxy generator*[3]. The proxy is a piece of code that takes in charge the communication between the client application and the card applet. This "Proxy" design pattern (*cf.* [8, pp. 207–217], [2, pp. 263–275], and [12]) is the foundation of RPC-based distributed system in which the client invokes methods on a local object (the *proxy*), which represents the original object (the card applet) on the client-side. The proxy is used by the client like the original applet since both the proxy and the applet are implementations of the same interface (*cf.* Fig. 12).

The GemXpresso proxy encapsulates and maintains the binding with the card applet. For that, it needs a reference to the object representing the GemXpresso card on the client side. It obtains this reference as the input parameter in its

---

[3] Currently, this tool is integrated in the *GemXpresso RAD* development environment.

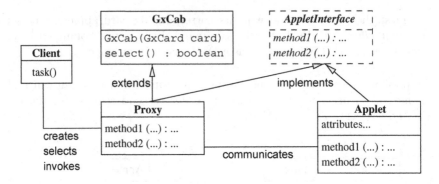

Fig. 12. GemXpresso applet proxy design

constructor inherited from the base class GxCab[4]. Thus, a proxy is instantiated by every client application in which the services of the original card applet are needed. The card applet is selected by the client application thanks to the other inherited proxy's method `select`. If the original applet has been successfully selected in the card, the proxy is ready to process the method calls originated from the client. The proxy implementation of every applet's method is a routine that performs the actual communication with the card applet:

1. It prepares a DMI `invoke` message with the input parameter values provided by the client.
2. It sends this message to the GemXpresso card, which decodes the message to invoke locally the method on the card applet. The value or the exception resulting from the method execution is returned to the proxy as a DMI response message.
3. It decodes the response message and returns the return value or the exception to the client like a result from a local call.

Application implementation. From the client application point of view, the code needed to communicate with the card applet is totally encapsulated in the proxy. Programmers just have to write the code to invoke methods in order to request a service from the card applet. In a GemXpresso client application, invoking a decrement operation on our "Counter" card applet can be written as shown in Figure 13.

In the above code sample, we get a problem (lines 3 and 5) because `select()` is not a method from ICounter[5]. Now, working with an object of the type

---

[4] `Gxcab` stands for GemXpresso *Card Applet Bridge* in the package `com.gemplus.gcr.toolkit.gemxpresso` provided as part of the Gemplus Java Smart Card Development Kit Client API.

[5] The method `select` is only defined in `javacard.framework.Applet` and in `GxCab`.

```
1  // We assume that we already have a "card" object
2  // Create the card applet proxy with the generated class GxCabCounter
3  ICounter counter = new GxCabCounter( card );
4  // Select the applet
5  if ( counter.select() == true ) {
6   // Use counter to communicate with the card
7   System.out.println( "Balance = " + counter.read() );
8   System.out.println( "New balance = " + counter.decrement(10) );
9  }
```

Fig. 13. GemXpresso client application implementation

ICounter to represent the card applet in the client code is a good design practice, since that enforces the fact that the client code strictly manipulate the card applet in conformity with its definition (*i.e.*, its interface). In order to solve the previous problem (and have clean client code), we recommend to make every applet's interface inherits from an interface IApplet that would provide the select() method[6].

4   Conclusion

We have described a methodology for the design and implementation of new card applications, based on the Java Card framework. This methodology allows the card programmer to use standard distributed computing patterns to design together its Java Card applet, and the application that uses it from the terminal. The technology is centered around remote procedure calls, between the terminal and the card. The methodology of a Java Card application development process with GemXpresso is here summarized by the following features:

- A design-by-interface approach, which demands programmers to decouple the applet interface from its implementation.
- A card operating system, which keeps track of the applet interface (that can be stored in a kind of repository) regarding the interface description provided with the applet loadable file.
- A generator, which automates the proxy's code generation.
- A card operating system, which can take in charge the DMI communication message on behalf of the applets.

---

[6] Currently, this interface is provided in a proprietary card library accompanying the GemXpresso's Java Card libraries. It would be better if such a generic applet interface was defined in the classes of the Java Card API specification...

The main advantage of the GemXpresso approach is that it enables programmers to focus on the applet's functionality rather than on the applet's communication means. Hence, it enhanced the Java Card programming techniques with the following elements:

- A clear definition of the services provided by the card applet.
- A "pure" Java way of programming card applets that does not require programmers to have knowledge of smart card specific features like APDU messages.
- The automated generation of tedious code (the formatting of communication messages) that is often difficult to test.
- The reduced memory footprint taken by the applets in the smart card, since their implementation does not contain code related to the exchange of messages (such a code is present once in the card: it is the communication module implemented in the JCRE).

Furthermore, the GemXpresso's features do not require to change the general Java Card architecture; but need some additional software components in the overall system. We have described here the first work performed on GemXpresso with the DMI protocol. This initial GemXpresso framework needs to be improved. In particular, it needs to be integrated with the latest standards, such as Java Card 2.1 [18] and the Open Card Framework[7]. There is no doubt that such an integration will be possible in conformity with these standards.

References

1. BIGET, P., GEORGE, P., AND VANDEWALLE, J.-J. How Smart-Cards Can Take Benefits From Object-Oriented Technologies. In *2nd International Conference on Smart Card Research and Advanced Applications* (CWI, Amsterdam, The Netherlands, Sept. 1996), P. H. Hartel, P. Paradinas, and J.-J. Quisquater, Eds., pp. 175–194.
2. BUSCHMAN, F., MEUNIER, R., ROHNERT, H., SOMMERLAD, P., AND STAL, M. *Pattern-Oriented Software Architecture - A System of Patterns*. John Wiley & Sons, 1996.
3. COULOURIS, G., DOLLIMORE, J., AND KINDBERG, T. *Distributed Systems: Concepts and Design*. Addison-Wesley, 1994.
   [http://www.dcs.qmw.ac.uk/research/distrib/book.html#guide].
4. DE JONG FRZ, E. K. How to make a Java Card. In *CardTech/SecurTech 1997 Conference* (Orlando, Florida, USA, May 1997), pp. 89–102.
5. DI GIORGIO, R. S. Smart Cards: A primer. *JavaWorld 2*, 12 (Dec. 1997).
   [http://www.javaworld.com/javaworld/jw-12-1997/jw-12-javadev.html].
6. DI GIORGIO, R. S. Understanding Java Card 2.0. *JavaWorld 3*, 3 (Mar. 1998).
   [http://www.javaworld.com/javaworld/jw-03-1998/jw-03-javadev.html].
7. DREIFUS, H., AND MONK, J. T. *Smart cards - A guide to building and managing smart card applications*. John Wiley & Sons, 1998.

---

[7] See the paper of Reto Hermann *et al* in these proceedings.

8. GAMMA, E., HELM, R., JOHNSON, R., AND VLISSIDES, J. *Design Patterns - Elements of Reusable Object-Oriented Software.* Addison-Wesley, 1994.

9. GUTHERY, S. B., AND JURGENSEN, T. M. *Smart Card Developer's Kit.* Macmillan Technical Publishing, 1998.
   [http://www.scdk.com/].

10. INTERNATIONAL ORGANIZATION FOR STANDARDIZATION. *International Standard ISO/IEC 7816: Integrated circuit(s) cards with contacts, parts 1 to 9*, 1987-1998.

11. RANKL, W., AND EFFING, W. *Smart Card Handbook.* John Wiley & Sons, 1997.

12. ROHNERT, H. The Proxy Design Pattern Revisited. In *Pattern Languages of Program Design*, J. M. Vlissides, J. O. Coplien, and N. L. Kerth, Eds., vol. 2. Addison-Wesley, 1996, ch. 7, pp. 105–118.

13. ROSENBERRY, W., KENNEY, D., AND FISHER, G. *Understanding DCE.* O'Reilly & Associates, Oct. 1992.
   [http://www.ora.com/catalog/udce/].

14. SIDDALINGAIAH, M. The Java card. *The developer.com Journal* (Oct. 1997).
   [http://www.developer.com/journal/techfocus/n_tech_javacard.html].

15. SUN MICROSYSTEMS, INC. *Network Programmming Guide*, Mar. 1990. Manual set for SunOS 4.1.x.

16. SUN MICROSYSTEMS, INC. *Java Card 2.0 Language Subset and Virtual Machine Specification, Programming Concepts, and Application Programming Interfaces*, Oct. 1997.
   [http://java.sun.com/products/javacard/].

17. SUN MICROSYSTEMS, INC. *Java Card Applet Developer's Guide*, July 1998.
   [http://java.sun.com/products/javacard/JCADG.html].

18. SUN MICROSYSTEMS, INC. *Java Card 2.1 Virtual Machine, Runtime Environment, and Application Programming Interface Specifications*, Public Review ed., Feb. 1999.
   [http://java.sun.com/products/javacard/javacard21.html].

The Performance of Modern Block Ciphers in JAVA

Rüdiger Weis[1]⋆ and Stefan Lucks[2]⋆⋆

[1] Praktische Informatik IV
University of Mannheim, 68131 Mannheim, Germany
rweis@pi4.informatik.uni-mannheim.de
[2] Theoretische Informatik
University of Mannheim, 68131 Mannheim, Germany
lucks@th.informatik.uni-mannheim.de

Abstract. This paper explores the question of how fast modern block ciphers can be realized as machine-independent Java implementations. The ciphers we considered include well-known proven ones such as DES and IDEA and recent candidates for the proposed DES-successor AES.

Keywords: performance, block cipher, JAVA.

1 Introduction

Apart from its security, the efficiency of a block cipher is what mainly interests application developers. Typically, block ciphers first run the *key schedule*, and then start encrypting.

For the performance, two numbers are of importance: the *latency* and the *throughput*. Given key and plaintext, the latency is the time one has to wait until the first ciphertext block is known. The throughput is the speed at which huge plaintexts can be encrypted, ignoring the key schedule. (Depending on the actual application, either the latency or the throughput may be of greater importance.)

Essentially, the latency allows to estimate the speed at encrypting small plaintexts, and the throughput stands for the speed at encrypting large plaintext. In our experiments, we actually measure the speed (in kilobytes per second) at encrypting small plaintexts (of 1 kilobyte) and the speed at encrypting large plaintexts (of 100 kilobytes).

In this paper we concentrate on the *speed of encryption*. We found great no differences to the speed of decryption, though the key schedule time for decryption can differ somewhat from that of its encryption counterpart.

Our machine–independent approach is mainly of interest to application developers who need efficient encryption but don't need to push a given machine to its performance limits.

⋆ Supported by the Landesgraduiertenförderung Baden-Würtemberg.
⋆⋆ Supported by Deutsche Forschungsgemeinschaft (DFG) grant KR 1521/3-1.

J.-J. Quisquater and B. Schneier (Eds.): CARDIS 2000, LNCS 1820, pp. 125–133, 2000.
Springer-Verlag Berlin Heidelberg 2000

Java is a new portable, object–oriented programming language with many interesting security features (e.g. sandbox paradigm, bytecode verification). Initially, Java was designed for settop boxes. Today, Java is highly portable and can be used in different environments like phones, computer networks, and, of course, in smartcards.

The design of block ciphers may involve certain bit–fiddling operations best done in hardware or in assembler. If one restricts oneself to a certain high–level language, as we restrict ourselves to Java, this affects on the performance of the ciphers. For practical purposes, it can be important that a cipher is *fast enough*, such that a portable implementation can be used and no additional low–level optimization is necessary. We are interested in the efficiency of such a portable high–level implementation, exploring various different block ciphers.

Our measurements are done on a conventional PC, not on a smartcard. Nevertheless, we believe the results to be of interest to smartcard developers, too. Java Smartcards are on their way, and the inherent advantages and limitations of the Java programming language are of relevance for these.

The Java Security API [SUN97] from SUN is a widely known cryptographic package in Java. It is still under construction and provides standard interfaces for different cryptographic protocols. Other packages are from RSA [RSA98] and Microsoft [Wiew96]. A freeware alternative to these packages without export restrictions is the Cryptix library [Cryt97], which we use for our tests.

Publications exploring the performance of ciphers are surprisingly rare in the literature. Some years ago, Roe published benchmark results [Roe94] followed by an update [Roe95] one year later. More recently, Schneier and Whiting counted the number of machine cycles some cryptographic operations needed on a Pentium [ScWh97]. They concentrate on low–level optimizations for a specific machine. This certainly is of great interest to application developers who need to write an application as fast as possible on that specific machine (and possibly also on similar machines). But it does not help much to answer the question we consider in this paper.

In Section 2 we present our results for a couple of well–known and widely used ciphers, Section 3 deals with other, lesser known ciphers. In Section 4, we present our results for some very recent candidate algorithms for the DES successor AES. In Section 5 we describe our testing environment. In Section 6 we give some conclusions. Finally, in the Appendix we visualize our results.

For the sake of better comparison, we include the performance we measured for DES and Triple–DES in all tables and figures.

2   Proven Ciphers

In this section we concentrate on established ciphers, published at least a couple of years ago, carefully examined by the cryptographic community and widely used today. The block size of all ciphers considered in this section is 64 bit.

2.1 DES–Family

The famous DES [FIPS46] encryption algorithm, which was originally designed for confidential, non–classified data, is used in many applications today (e.g. electronic banking). Internally, the DES is based on the so–called Feistel structure, repeating a simple round function a couple of times (in the case of DES, exactly 16 times). The DES developers had to design DES to be cheaply implementable in hardware, considering the state of hardware design in the seventies.

Due to its key size of only 56 bits, DES has to be considered weak. The key length for symmetrical algorithms today should be at least 75–90 bit [Blea96].

In the financial services business we find a strong preference for DES–based systems. Since DES has been cracked by brute force attacks [DESC97], we suggest to use Triple–DES [SiBa97] or DESX [Roga96] in this application field.

Note that Triple–DES performs poorly and makes poor use of its 168 key bits. Recently, the effective key length of Triple–DES was found to be no more than 108 bits [Luck98a]. This, of course, is still prohibitive for brute force attacks. A cheaper method to avoid brute force attacks on DES is based on whitening. With one key–dependent permutation both before and after the DES encryption, the so–called DESX [KiRo96] cipher is much more resistant against keysearch attacks than single DES.

We did not yet implement and measure DESX. Our implementation of Triple–DES is not optimized, i.e., both the initial permutation and its inverse are evaluated for each of the three DES steps.

2.2 IDEA

The IDEA block cipher [Lai92] has a strong mathematical foundation and possesses good resistance against differential cryptanalysis [Lai91]. The key length of 128 bit protects against brute–force attacks. Many cryptographers think that IDEA is the strongest public algorithm [Schn96]. IDEA was the preferred cipher in the PGP–Versions (Pretty Good Privacy) prior to version 2.63.

IDEA uses three algebraic operations: bit–wise XOR, addition modulo 2^{16} and multiplication modulo $2^{16} + 1$. On small machines such as smartcards, the efficiency of IDEA greatly depends on the time such a multiplication requires.

2.3 Blowfish and CAST

In spite of their having been developed independently, the basic structure of the block ciphers Blowfish [Schn94] and CAST [Adam97b] is very similar.

We concentrate on the CAST variant CAST-128 [Adam97a] proposed for standardization. While the size of a Blowfish key is variable (though limited to no more than 448 bit), a CAST-128 key has the fixed size of 128 bit.

CAST is designed with resistance to differential cryptanalysis, linear cryptanalysis and related–key cryptanalysis in mind. CAST possesses a number of other desirable cryptographic advantages compared to DES, e.g. no complementation property and the absence of weak and semi–weak keys. No such strong results regarding known cryptanalytic techniques have been published for Blow-fish. On the other hand, no attacks of any practical relevance are known for either CAST or Blowfish.

Both CAST and Blowfish appear to be much faster than DES. Note though, that an implementation of either cipher needs 4 kilobytes of memory for the S–boxes. The CAST S–boxes are fixed and can be stored in ROM, while the Blowfish S–boxes are key–dependent and hence need to be stored in RAM. For smartcards, this is a significant disadvantage – memory, and especially RAM, is expensive on a smartcard.

The Blowfish key schedule is more involved than the CAST key schedule, hence for small blocks, CAST is much faster than Blowfish. For large blocks, our measurements indicate that Blowfish is faster than CAST. This has some-thing to do with the CAST-128 round function using key–dependent rotations, XOR–operations and additions/subtractions, while Blowfish only uses XOR and addition.

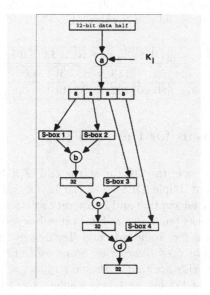

Fig. 1. Generalized CAST–Round, using operations a, b, c and d [Adam97b].

2.4   SAFER

SAFER [Mass94] is a freely available block cipher which does *not* depend on the Feistel structure. It was designed with small processors (i.e., eight–bit micropro-cessors) in mind and thus is of special interest with respect to smartcards. We concentrate on the SAFER variant SAFER-SK 128/R 13 with an improved key schedule, 128 key bits, and 13 rounds. This variant is proposed for OpenPGP [OPGP97] standardization (e.g. [GeWe98]).

2.5 Results

Cipher	DES	Blowfish	CAST	IDEA	SAFER	Triple–DES
100k packetsize	85.33	170.67	146.29	85.33	56.89	25.60
1k packetsize	80.46	39.38	146.29	80.38	51.20	25.60

3   Others

In this section, we explore the performance of the ciphers Square [DKR97], RC2 [Rive97,KRRR98] and LOKI91 [BKPS93]. Both Square and RC2 were published not long ago. The LOKI91 cipher is not recommendable for high–security applications [Knud93b]. We included LOKI91 in this test because it is the predecessor of the LOKI97 AES proposal (see Section 4).

Cipher	DES	Square	RC2	LOKI91	Triple–DES
100k packetsize	85.33	113.78	85.33	128.00	25.60
1k packetsize	80.46	102.40	80.46	128.00	25.60

4   Some Proposals for the AES

Due to its 56–bit key size, the DES is at the end of its useful life. DES–based ciphers like DESX and Triple–DES solve the key–length problem, but DES is designed for hardware encryption and is not very software efficient. Also, a block cipher with larger blocks (such as 128 bits) often has security advantages. Thus the National Institute for Standards and Technology has issued a call for a DES successor, the *Advanced Encryption Standard* (AES). Some of the essential requirements for the AES are that it should support key sizes of 128, 192, and 256 bits, a block size of 128 bit, and, nevertheless, be at least as fast and secure as Triple–DES.

Cipher	DES	DEAL	LOKI97	Rijndael	Serpent	Twofish	Triple–DES
100k packetsize	85.33	24.38	51.20	191.31	72.10	46.42	25.60
1k packetsize	80.46	23.63	47.26	179.86	58.00	39.97	25.60

Remark

For both LOKI97 [Brow98] and DEAL [Knud98], cryptanalytic weaknesses have already been found [RiKn98,Luck98b].

5   Testing Environment

The test was performed on a PC with an Intel Pentium 200 MMX CPU under Linux 2.0.33. The main memory size was 64 megabytes, and we used the SUN Java implementation JDK 1.1.5.

All Java classes were compiled with compiler–optimization *disabled* since otherwise some of the self–tests failed. For the same reason, no just–in–time compiler was used. No native routines were used although some are shipped with the current version of Cryptix and would give an important speedup.

The test measured the encryption speeds of various algorithms depending on different plaintext sizes in ECB mode. Particularly, 1024 and 102400 byte plaintexts were used.

6   Conclusions

The AES contest will bring us fast and secure ciphers for 128bit blocksize. For 64bit blocksize there are some possible choices. Blowfish and CAST are both free and offer fine performance and security. Their memory requirements may be prohibitive for many smartcard implementations, though. As a hardware–oriented design, the old DES is surprisingly fast. While a key size of 56 bit of must be considered insecure today, Triple–DES and DESX are reasonably good choices for block ciphers.

While the Java programming language is better at supporting machine–independent software development, compared to competitors such as C and C++, it does not support machine–oriented optimizations very well. As our results indicate, most modern block ciphers do not require such optimizations for reasonable efficiency.

Acknowledge

The authors would like to express thanks to Sascha Kettler of the Cryptix Development Team for his assistance in developing and performing the tests.

References

[Adam97a]   Adams, C., "RFC2144, The CAST-128 Encryption Algorithm", May 1997.

[Adam97b]   Adams, C, "Constructing Symmetric Ciphers Using the CAST Design Procedure", in: Designs, Codes and Cryptography, v.12, n. 3, Nov 1997, pp. 71–104.

[BAK98b]   Biham, E., Anderson, R., Knudsen, L, "Serpent: A New Blockcipher Proposal", AES submission, 1998.
            http://www.cl.cam.ac.uk/~rja14/serpent.html

[Brow98]   Brown, L., "Design of LOKI97", draft AES submission, 1998.

[BKPS93]   Brown, L., Pieprzyk, J., Seberry, J., "Improving Resistance to Differential Cryptoanalysis and the Redesign of LOKI", Advances in Cryptology – ASIACRYPT '91 Proceedings, LNCS Springer Verlag, 1993, pp. 36–50.

[DKR97]   Daemenen, J., Knudsen, L., Rijmen, "The Block Cipher Square", Fast
            Software Encryption, 4th International Workshop Proccedings, LNCS
            Springer Verlag, 1997, pp. 149–165 .
[Blea96]   Blaze, M., Diffie, W., Rivest, R., Schneier, B., Shimomura, T., Thomp-
            son, E., Wiener, M., "Minimal Key Lengths for Symmetric Ciphers to
            Provide Adequate Commercial Security", a report by an ad hoc group of
            cryptographers and computer scientists , January 1996.
[Cryt97]   Cryptix - Cryptografic Extensions for Java, 1997,
            http://www.systemics.com/software/cryptix-java/
[DESC97]   RSA–Challenge'97. http://www.rsa.com/des/
[FIPS46]   National Bureau of Standards, NBS FIPS PUB 46, "Data Encryption
            Standard", January 1977.
[GeWe98]   Geyer, W., Weis, R., "A Secure, Accountable, and Collaborative White-
            board", Proc. of IDMS'98, Oslo, Springer LNCS 1983, 1998.
[KiRo96]   Kilian, J., Rogaway, P., "How to protect DES against exhaustive key
            search", Proc. of Crypto'96, Advances in Cryptology, Berlin, Springer,
            1996.
[Knud93a]   Knudsen, L., "Cryptoanalysis of LOKI", Advances in Cryptology – ASI-
            ACRYPT '91, LNCS Springer Verlag, 1993, pp. 22–35.
[Knud93b]   Knudsen, L., "Cryptoanalysis of LOKI91", Advances in Cryptology –
            AUSCRYPT '92, LNCS Springer Verlag, 1993, pp. 196–208.
[Knud95]   Knudsen, L., "A Key–Schedule Weakness in SAFER K-64", Advances in
            Cryptology – Crypto '95, LNCS Springer Verlag, 1995, pp. 274–286.
[Knud98]   Knudsen, L., "DEAL: A 128-bit Block Cipher",
            http://www.ii.uib.no/~larsr/newblock.html
[KRRR98]   Knudsen, L., Rijmen, V., Rivest, R., Robshaw, M., "On Design and Se-
            curity of RC2", Fast Software Encryption, 5th International Workshop
            Proceedings, LNCS Springer Verlag, 1998, pp. 206–221.
[Lai91]   X. Lai, "Markov Ciphers and Differential Cryptoanalyis", Proc. of EURO-
            CRYPT'91, Advances in Cryptology, Springer, 1991.
[Lai92]   X. Lai, "On the Design and Security of Blockciphers", ETH Series in
            Information Processing, v. 1, Hartmut–Gorre–Verlag, Konstanz, 1992.
[Luck98a]   Lucks, S., "Attacking Triple Encryption", to Proc. Fast Software Encryp-
            tion 5, 1998, (ed. S. Vaudenay), LNCS, Springer, 1998.
[Luck98b]   Lucks, S., "On the Security of the 128-bit Block Cipher DEAL", Univer-
            stität Mannheim, Fakultät für Mathematik und Informatik, 1998.
            http://th.informatik.uni-mannheim.de/m/lucks/papers/deal.ps.gz
[Mass94]   Massey, L.J., "SAFER K-64: A Byte-Orientated Blockciphering Algo-
            rithm", Fast Software Encryption, Cambridge Security Workshop Pro-
            ceedings, LNCS Springer Verlag, 1994, pp. 1–17.
[OPGP97]   Callas, J., Donnerhacke, L., Finnley, H., "OP Formats - OpenPGP Mes-
            sage Format", Internet Draft, November 1997.
[Rive92]   Rivest, R., "RFC 1321", MD5 Message Digest Algorithm, April 1992.
[RiKn98]   Rijmen, V., Knudsen, L., "Weaknesses in LOKI97",
            ftp://ftp.esat.kuleuven.ac.be/pub/COSIC/rijmen/loki97.ps.gz
[Rive97]   Rivest, R., "A Description of the RC2(r) Encryption Algorithm", Inter-
            net–Draft, working in progress, June 1997.
[Roe94]   Roe, M., "Performance of Symmetric Ciphers and One–way Hash Func-
            tions" Fast Software Encryption, Cambridge Security Workshop Proceed-
            ings, LNCS Springer Verlag, 1994, pp. 83–86.

[Roe95]   Roe, M., "Performance of Block Ciphers and Hash Functions – One Year
             later", Fast Software Encryption, 4th International Workshop Proceed-
             ings, LNCS 809, Springer Verlag, 1994, pp. 359–362.

[Roga96]   Rogaway, P., "The Security of DESX", CryptoBytes, Volume 2, No. 2,
             RSA Laboratories, Redwood City, CA, USA, Summer 1996.

[RSA98]   RSA inc., http://www.rsa.com/rsa/products/jsafe
             or outside USA: http://www.baltimore.ie/jcrypto.htm

[Schn94]   Schneier, B., "Description of a New Variable-Length Key, 64-Bit Block
             Cipher", Proc. of Cambridge Security Workshop on Fast Software En-
             cryption, LNCS 809, Springer, 1994, pp. 191–204.

[Schn96]   Schneier, B., "Applied Cryptography Second Edition", John Wiley & Sons,
             New York, NY, 1996.

[ScWh97]   Schneier, B., Whiting, D., "Fast Software Encryption: Designing Encryp-
             tion for Optimal Speed on the Intel Pentium Processor", Fast Software En-
             cryption, 4th International Workshop Proceedings, LNCS Springer Verlag,
             1997, pp. 242–259.

[SiBa97]   Simpson, W. A., Baldwin, R., "The ESP DES-XEX3-CBC Transform",
             Internet–Draft, July 1997.

[SUN97]   Java Security, 19.11.1997, http://www.javasoft.com/security/

[Wiew96]   E. Wiewall, Secure Your applications with the Microsoft CryptoAPI, in
             Microsoft Developer Network News, 5/96,3/4, 1, 1996.

[Weis98]   Weis, R., "Modern Blockciphers" (in German), in: "Kryptographie",
             Weka–Fachzeitschriften–Verlag, Poing, 1998.

A   Appendix

In this Appendix we visualize the results previously given in tables. Note that
(s) stands for the speed at encrypting *small* plaintext packets of 1 kilobyte, while
(b) represents encrypting *big* plaintexts packets of 100 kilobytes with the same
key.

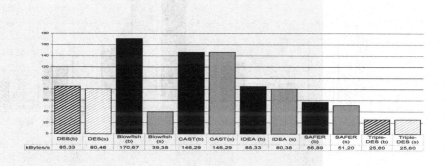

Fig. 2. Proven ciphers: DES, Blowfish, CAST, SAFER, and Triple–DES

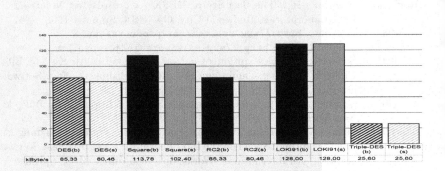

kByte/s	DES(b)	DES(s)	Square(b)	Square(s)	RC2(b)	RC2(s)	LOKI91(b)	LOKI91(s)	Triple-DES (b)	Triple-DES (s)
	85,33	80,46	113,78	102,40	85,33	80,46	128,00	128,00	25,60	25,60

Fig. 3. Other ciphers

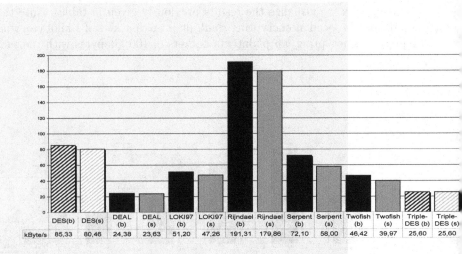

kByte/s	DES(b)	DES(s)	DEAL (b)	DEAL (s)	LOKI97 (b)	LOKI97 (s)	Rijndael (b)	Rijndael (s)	Serpent (b)	Serpent (s)	Twofish (b)	Twofish (s)	Triple-DES (b)	Triple-DES (s)
	85,33	80,46	24,38	23,63	51,20	47,26	191,31	179,86	72,10	58,00	46,42	39,97	25,60	25,60

Fig. 4. Some proposals for the AES

Recoverable Persistent Memory for SmartCard

Didier Donsez[1], Gilles Grimaud[2], and Sylvain Lecomte[2]

[1] Laboratoire d'Informatique et de Mathématiques Appliquées de Valenciennes
Université de Valenciennes, Le Mont Houy BP 311
59304 Valenciennes Cedex France,
E-mail: donsez@univ-valenciennes.fr
[2] RD2P - Recherche et Développement Dossier Portable
CHR Calmette - rue du Pr. J. Leclercq
59037 Lille Cédex - France
Tel: +333 20 44 60 46 - Fax: +333 20 44 60 45
E-mail: {grimaud, lecomte}@lifl.fr

Abstract. Smartcard is well adapted to store confidential data and to provide secure services in a mobile and distributed environment. But many cases of smartcard application failure can corrupt data in smartcard persistent memory. In this paper, we propose a recoverable persistent memory to maintain data consistency in a smartcard. Then, we adapt and compare two recovery algorithms used in Database Management Systems (shadow paging and before-image logging) to the smartcard memory features. At last, we present a prototype, which demonstrates the feasibility of these algorithms in a smartcard.

Keywords. Recovery, Persistent Memory, Transaction, Smartcard

1 Problems of Failure in SmartCard

Smartcard is well adapted to store confidential data and to provide secure services in a mobile and distributed environment[Cor96]. So, the range of their applications is continuously growing (electronic commerce, medicine, phone card, etc). These applications are more and more designed as distributed applications [Lec97][Lec98]. The computation of the application is spread over several computers on a network. The smartcard is one of these computers when it is slotted into a terminal.

However, as in distributed systems, failures should have been considered. We distinguish the node failure in which a node (smartcard or other) crash and the communication failure between nodes. In the smartcard context, the communication failure is mainly the failure of the link between the smartcard and the other nodes of the distributed application. This can be caused by the failure of the terminal and by the wireless link when the smartcard is plugged in a mobile terminal such as cellular phone. The second kind of failure is the node crash and especially the smartcard crash. Since the card user (a human being) can unplugged the card from the terminal before the application completion and the terminal supply electricity power to the card, the smartcard is suddenly powered

J.-J. Quisquater and B. Schneier (Eds.): CARDIS 2000, LNCS 1820, pp. 134–140, 2000.

off and all the RAM contents is suddenly lose. A second cause of smartcard crash is an execution error due to a bad argument or to a programmation error in the application.

Communication and node failures can introduce incoherence in the smartcard (and in the other nodes) data. Smartcard can complete the computation (for example to credit an electronic purse) and valid updates of its data after the communication failure even if the other nodes decided to discard their part of the computation (for example to debit a bank account). The smartcard crash may cause also an incoherence in the data since a part of updates may be in RAM and lost by the crash.

The developer should have to handle these problems. The communication failure can be resolve by distributed validation protocols such as the two-phase commit protocol [Gra93]. A simple way to manage the incoherence of the data during a smartcard crash is to restore the previous state of data, i.e. the state of the data at the beginning of the computation.

In this paper, we do not study the problem of distributed application, but only the recovery failure of the data in case of a smartcard crash. The recovery is based on the transactional execution model briefly present in section 2. Section 3 describes the adaptation of two recovery algorithms to the smartcard memory context. Section 4 presents briefly the demonstrator and section 5 concludes.

2   Transactional Model and Recovery Persistent Memory

A simple way to manage failure is to make atomic all updates done by an application (distributed or centralized). Atomicity of updates done by a group of code lines is a part of a larger concept, the concept of transaction [Gra93]. A transaction is a group of actions (i.e. code lines). The transaction completes in two ways: the *Commit* in which all effects (i.e. updates) is durable either the *Abort* in which all effects are discarded. So, the transaction guaranties the ACID properties (Atomicity, Coherence, Isolation and Durability). Atomicity means that all or none of the modifications are validated. Consistency says that a transaction takes data in a coherent state and returns it in a coherent state. Isolation isolates the effect on the transaction until the commit so concurrent transactions can not seen the uncommitted updates. Durability enforces that effects of the transaction are accessible even in case of failure (media...).

In the smartcard context, the natural group of actions for which Atomicity and Durability must be guarantied is the APDU command (Application Protocol Data Unit)[Iso95]. But the transactional model can be used to execute atomicaly a group of actions over several APDU commands or several cards sessions (i.e. the card is plugged several times in different terminals before the commitment of a transaction) [Lec97]. On the other hand, a command APDU may be composed of several transactions.

New models and platforms for application development hide the difference between volatile (RAM) and non-volatile memories (Hard Disks...) by supplying Recoverable Persistent Memory (RPM)[Atk83][Sat93]. RPM provides mechanisms to allow the atomicity, since it can undo updates or make them persistent at commit time. Many works have focused on RPM in Operating Systems (OS) and in Database Management Systems (DBMS) [Sin92][Whi94]. The main techniques are described by [Ber87]. These techniques suppose that the non-volatile memories are magnetic media such as hard disks or tapes to guaranty the properties of Atomicity and Durability.

To store persistently data, DBMS and OS consider mainly block devices such as hard disks or tapes to make persistent data. These media can not be addressed directly by the CPU so data are loaded by bulk in the buffers in RAM. However some recovery algorithms [Cop89][Tec97] consider special hardware such as UPS-RAM (Uninterruptible Power Supply RAM) to improve the performance of logging operations by maintaining safe the logging buffers.

3   Recovery Manager in SmartCard

Smartcard persistent memories provide different features than magnetic media. Indeed, smartcard manufacturers use mainly the 3 following technologies to implant persistent memory in SmartCard: EEPROM, FeRAM, and FlashRAM. With these technologies, CPU can address (i.e. read and write) directly memory cells.

But in case of Flash-RAM, a quite long erasing operation (100 ms) must precede writing operation. So the Memory Manager (MM) must emulate a paginated memory with a page size close to 8 to 16 words. MM imposes to write in non-volatile memory only through a RAM cache[Bel66] so it translates logical addresses of data toward RAM or non-volatile memory addresses. But this needs a translation table residing in RAM and sometimes in non-volatile memory. Caching in RAM extends also smartcard's life duration since writing operations damage EEPROM media (manufacturers guaranty only 10000 writing operations in an EEPROM cells)[Cas95].

Taking into account these features, we adapt two recovery algorithms designed for Database Management Systems to the smartcard persistent recoverable memory manager. The two algorithms are the "Shadow Pages" algorithm and the " Before-Image Logging " algorithm. The following sections present efficient and simple RPM over EEPROM and FlashRAM technologies. Nevertheless, we do not consider the After-Images Logging which is very equivalent to the Shadow page algorithm in the smartcard context.

3.1   Adaptation of the Shadow Pages Algorithm

The shadow page algorithm preserves the original state of data. Each write operation into a page is performed on a copy of this page, named "shadow page". In order of that, the algorithm uses a translation table. With FlashRAM, this table is loaded in RAM from non-volatile memory at the beginning of the transaction. All writing operations are performed in shadow pages allocated from the list of free pages. The translation table maps toward the shadow pages. To commit atomically all updates, the translation table is written in a shadow copy. So the previous state of the translation table is preserve. If the failure occurs before the commit phase of the transaction, the original table is reloaded so current updates are discarded. If the failure occurs during the commit phase of the transaction, the MM reloads the latest persistent copy of the table which is not corrupted (i.e. all write operations of the table are completed or not before the failure). With EEPROM, the translation table stays in persistent memory. To map the shadow page of an update page, the translation table is updated in a shadow copy. Shadow page algorithm is shown in fig. 1.

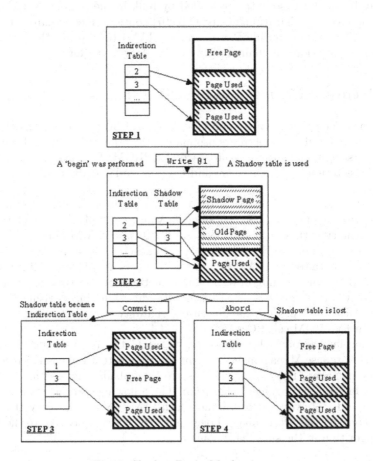

Fig. 1. Shadow Pages Machanism

This algorithm is easy to implant but it has major drawbacks. Firstly, only one transaction is running at a time (i.e. batch processing model) because the translation table can not be shared between several simultaneous transactions. Secondly, with FlashRAM, the translation table takes a great part of the RAM so this reduces the cache performance.

3.2   Adaptation of the Before-Image Logging Algorithm

This algorithm does not need a persistent translation table. It uses only a small in-RAM table (12 bytes) for the needs of the caching mechanism (if it is enabled). The Before-Image Logging algorithm keeps the original data values in a distinct area of the non-volatile memory called Before-Image Log. The log is a file that contains log records. Before performing a writing operation, the original value is saved in a new log record. The log record contains also an incremental sequence number, the value identifier (i.e. the address of a page if whole pages are logging or the offset and the size in case of sub-page logging). If a failure occurs before and during the commit phase, the MM plays forward the log to replace the new (uncommitted) values by the original (committed) values saved in the log. With EEPROM technology, sub-page logging is possible (if the caching mechanism is enable). Sub-page logging consist in saving only the updated parts of the page in a log record. Indeed before each cache replacement, the updated page (which is in the RAM cache) is compared with the non-volatile page to detect updated words and to log these original corresponding values. The operation called "Diffing" is used for Client-Server OO-DBMS Recovery [Sin92][Whi95]. With Flash-RAM technology, the Diffing allows only whole page logging since erasing operation deletes the state of a whole page before writing.Before image log file is shown in fig 2.

The Before-Image Logging presents several advantages. Firstly, no huge translation table is required. Therefore, cache size is maximal and this improves performances by reducing the number of cache replacements. This reduces also the number of log records if the Diffing is used. Secondly, several transactions can access concurrently to the persistent memory. Thirdly, the MM can easily rollback over multiple checkpoints and can provide recovery mechanisms to implement extended transaction models [Elm92] such as nested-transactions [Mos85]. However, the two former features require a complex (for the smartcard) recycling (compression) of the log.

4   Implementation of a Prototype

We develop a demonstrator to evaluate performances of these recovery algorithms (Shadow Pages, Before-Image Logging with and without Diffing) for the two following non-volatile memory : EEPROM and FlashRAM. These algorithms are benchmarked with several configuration of memory (varying size of RAM and varying size of persistent memory) and several application workloads. The presentation of these benchmarks and these results are not presented in this paper. A part of the demonstrator is also integrated on GemXpresso, the GEMPLUS's JavaCard [SUN97] compliant smartcard. This card is also used in a distributed platform to participate in the secure completion of distributed applications.

5   Conclusion and Perspectives

In this paper, we first present the failures, which can make incoherent data stored in a smartcard. Then to recover these failures, we propose mechanisms based

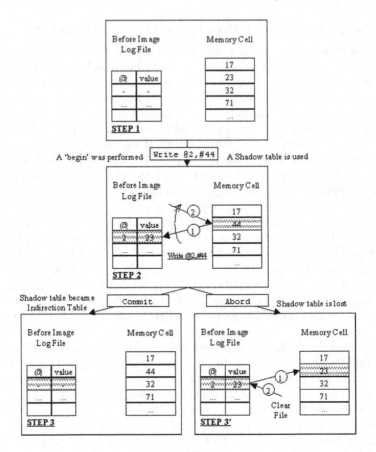

Fig. 2. Before image log file

on the transactional model. We propose to implement Recoverable Persistent Memory in smartcards. RPM hide the difference between volatile (RAM) and non-volatile memories (FlashRAM, EEPROM, ...) and guaranty the atomicity and durability of a group of code lines. We adapt and implement DBMS recovery algorithms to the smartcard memory context. These algorithms are the " Shadow Pages " one and the " Before-Image Logging " one.

However, smartcards will be completely integrated when they will be able to participate to distributed transactions[Lec98]. This assumes that ACID properties are guaranties by every node of the distributed transaction. The ACID properties in distributed transactions oblige the card to participate to a distributed validation protocol such as the two phases commit protocol specified by X/Open and OMG. In another hand, the smartcard can execute several transactions simultaneity. The Isolation property must be guaranty by the card. We work on concurrency control mechanisms such as the two-phase locking which provides a coherent sharing of data.

References

Atk83.   Malcom Atkinson, Ken Chishlom, Paul Cockshott, Richard Marshall, " Algorithms for a Persistent Heap ", Software, Practice and Experience, 13(3) :259-271, March 1983.

Bel66.   Belady, "A study of Replacement Algorithms for Virtual Storage Computers", IBM Systems Journal 5, 1966, pp78-101.

Ber87.   P.A. Bernstein, V. Hadzilacos, N. Goodman, "Concurrency Control and Recovery in Database Systems", Addison-Wesley, Reading , MA, 1987.

Cas95.   Esprit program EP8670, " CASCADE: Operating System ", European project ESP8670 , April 1995.

Cor96.   V. Cordonnier, " The future of SmartCards : Technology and Application ", In proceedings IFIP World Conference on Mobile Communication, Camberra, September 1996.

Elm92.   A.K. Elmagarmid, " Database Transaction Models for Advanced Applications ", Morgan Kaufmann Publishers, 1992

Gra93.   Jim Gray, Andreas Reuter, " Transaction Processing : Concepts and Technics ", Morgan Kaufmann Publishers, 1993.

Iso95.   International Standard Organisation (ISO), " Identification cards, integrated circuit cards with contacts : Part 4 inter-industry command for interchange ", International Standard ISO/IEC 7816-4, 1995

Lec97.   Sylvain Lecomte, Didier Donsez, "Intégration d'un Gestionnaire de Transaction dans les cartes à microprocesseur " , Proceeding of NOTERE, Nouvelles Technologies de la Répartition, Pau, France, 4-6 Novembre 1997, pp. 347-362

Lec98.   Sylvain Lecomte, " COST-STIC : Cartes Orientées Services Transactionnels et Systèmes Transactionnels Intégrant des Cartes",PhD Dissertation, University of Lille I, Villeneuve d'Ascq, France, November 1998.

Mos85.   J.E.B. Moss, "Nested Transactions: An Approach to Reliable Distributed Computing", Boston, MIT Press, 1985.

Tec97.   Wee Teck Ng, Peter M. Chen, "Integrating Reliable Memory in Databases", VLDB'97, Proceedings of 23th International Conference on Very Large Data Bases, August 25-29, 1997, Athens, Greece. Morgan Kaufmann 1997, ISBN 1-55860-470-7, pp76-85.

Cop89.   George P. Copeland, Tom Keller, Ravi Krishnamurthy, Marc Smith, "The Case For Safe RAM", VLDB 1989, pp327-335

Sat93.   M. Satyanarayanan, H.H . Mashburn, P. Kumar, D.C. Steere, J.J. Kistler, " Lightweight Recoverable Virtual Memory ", Proc of 1993 Symposium on Operating System Principles, pp 146-160, December 1993.

Sin92.   V. Singhal, S.V. Kaddak, P.R. Wilson, "Texas: An Efficient, Portable Persistent Store", Proc. of the Fifth Intl Workshop on Persistent Object System, San Miniato, Italy, September 1992.

SUN97.   Sun Microsystems, "JavaCard 2.0 Language subset and Virtual Machine Specification", Rev 1.0 final, October 1997.

Whi94.   S.J. White, D.J. DeWitt, "QuickStore : A High Performance Mapped Object Store", Proc. of the 1994 ACM SIGMOD Conf. Minneapolis, Minnnesota, May 1994.

Whi95.   Seth J. White, David J. DeWitt "Implementing Crash Recovery in QuickStore: A Performance Study" In proceedings of the 1995 ACM SIGMOD Conference, pp 187-198

Pirate Card Rejection

David M. Goldschlag and David W. Kravitz

Divx, 570 Herndon Parkway, Herndon, Virginia, 20170, USA
+1 703-708-4000 (voice), +1 703-708-4025 (fax)
{david.goldschlag, david.kravitz}@divx.com

Abstract. Renewable security cards provide the primary security protection in conditional access (CA) systems. Since the legitimate cards are intended to be inexpensive to produce, easy to distribute, and user-installable via externally accessible slots, sales of counterfeit cards may offer the pirate a profitable business. However, since the legitimate infrastructure is likely to be backed by a significant operating budget, it is reasonable to design that infrastructure to detect and reject counterfeit cards. Such an infrastructure would require customers of the pirate to use pirated hosts as well as pirated cards. This secondary security layer increases the pirate's cost of doing business, and may therefore reduce the amount of piracy. This paper presents a protocol that the legitimate infrastructure can use to detect and reject content decrypted by counterfeit cards.

1 Introduction

Many conditional access (CA) systems use a renewable security device such as a smartcard in conjunction with a non-renewable host like a TV to control access to chargeable content. The primary security in these systems is the smartcard, since it is the only element (aside from content) that is under the ongoing control of the CA provider. For example, the CA provider can change the algorithms and secrets used to protect content, and provide his customers with new smartcards that work with the new system.

Many renewable CA systems also place a *verifier* function on the host, to enable it to detect and reject pirated smartcards. This verifier function serves a secondary security role, since it can help prevent the use of pirated smartcards. Of course, pirated hosts could skip this detection/rejection step, and therefore use pirated smartcards, but pirated hosts are harder to manufacture and distribute than smartcards. So the verifier increases the cost of piracy. The goal of the verifier is to leverage off of the cost and complexity of the legitimate infrastructure to reduce the potential size of the pirate's market. If that market is small enough, the pirate cannot amortize the expense needed to compromise legitimate smartcards and build counterfeit ones.

In this paper, we describe a strong type of verifier, which we call *pirate card rejection*. Our pirate card rejection protocol has four significant features that distinguish it from other verifiers:

- It is immune to a *combo card* or *conduit card* attack. In this attack, the counterfeit card lives between the host and the legitimate card, with the goal of using the legitimate card to respond to verification challenges, while using the counterfeit card to enable free access to pay-content.

J.-J. Quisquater and B. Schneier (Eds.): CARDIS 2000, LNCS 1820, pp. 141–149, 2000.

- It does not impose constraints on card latency.
- It does not require the host to be aware of the billing policy. Many verification schemes require the host to be aware of the billing policy, to coordinate its challenges with the granularity of billing. For example, if pay-movies are billed for the whole movie independently of how much is watched, when the host tunes to a new pay-movie, the verifier may require that the host receive authorization from the legitimate card before displaying the movie. Notice that the card then charges for the entire movie, so it does not matter if the pirated card does the subsequent decryption. In contrast, in our protocol, the host and the card participate in the pirate card rejection protocol, and the host does not need to understand the billing policy. (Of course, the card may request the host to display menus and queries, requiring the user to accept a charge.)
- It does not constrain the service provider's billing policy. In many verification schemes, the frequency of challenges limit the granularity of billing, and because of computational constraints, challenges cannot occur continuously. In practice a single challenge may enable decryption and trigger billing for the entire movie. In contrast, our protocol efficiently authenticates the entire stream in real-time, so the billing policy is orthogonal to pirate card rejection. In fact, billing can even be done based upon the amount of content decrypted.

This paper is organized in the following way: Section 0 presents an overview of the solution, including attack assumptions, and the system architecture. Section 0 presents the protocol, and section 0 presents analysis. Section 0 presents concluding remarks.

2 Overview of Solution

Pirate card rejection is really a misnomer for this and other verification schemes, since it is impossible for a host to distinguish between a legitimate card and a counterfeit version or clone of such a card. The strategy is therefore as follows: The host learns the identity (i.e., the public keys) of a small number of cards (perhaps a single card) with which it is allowed to communicate, perhaps via certificates signed by some authority. The host will then reject content delivered by other cards. The protocol enables the host to verify that the expected card is doing the decryption. Notice that it is insufficient for a card to merely identify itself and then do decryption, since a pirate card could sit between the host and the legitimate card and direct challenges from the host to the legitimate card, while doing the decryption (for free) by itself.

2.1 Attack Assumptions

The effectiveness of pirate card rejection therefore depends upon the following assumption:
- The pirate cannot cost-effectively sell counterfeit cards based on each customer's legitimate card. We assume the pirate can recover secrets from any card. But we assume that the cost of this attack is prohibitive to do for

each customer. In particular, the pirate will compromise a small number of cards, and sell counterfeit cards based on those secrets (i.e., their private keys).

We assign trust in the following way:

- The host is trusted to follow the pirate card rejection protocol and to reject data decrypted by the card if the protocol fails.

We make the following assumptions about the strength of the attacker:

- The counterfeit card cannot *change* the (encrypted) data before the host receives it (from the broadcast, for example). This attack is similar to building a pirated host.

- The pirate cannot expect his customers to tamper with the internals of the TV or other host devices (the *screwdriver attack*).

- The customer of the pirate can attack the CA card interface in any way he chooses: for example, by replacing the legitimate card with a pirated card or by inserting a pirated card between the host and the legitimate card.

We assume that the pirate *cannot* obtain private keys used by the backend key management system that are not embedded in devices that he has access to, such as CA cards or the hosts themselves. Unlike other verifiers, we do not make the assumption that the pirate cannot *see* the (encrypted) data before the host receives it.

2.2 Operating Environment

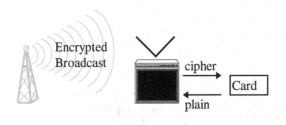

Fig. 1. CA Data Flow

In this paper, we assume that the renewable device does content decryption in addition to conditional access (Fig. 1. CA Data Flow). We layer our pirate card rejection protocol on top of this device. Our pirate card rejection protocol also works with the usual CA approach, where the renewable smartcard does not decrypt content directly. Instead the smartcard provides a stream of changing keys to the host, and the host uses those keys to decrypt the content. This usual approach to CA is fundamentally flawed, since universal keys (those that can be used by anyone to decrypt content) are sent to a non-renewable device. The pirate can recover and redistribute the low density keying material., providing *continuous* pirated service without ever compromising a single smartcard [this is John McCormac's Jugular Attack]. The security of this architecture depends more on the difficulty of inserting keys into the non-renewable host than on the difficulty of recovering keys from the renewable smartcard. This makes the primary security dependent on the non-renewable device, and the secondary security dependent on the renewable device. In the long run, this smartcard architecture makes the CA provider's renewal strategy irrelevant and makes increases in smartcard security futile.

The primary security of a CA system should depend on the renewable components. Secondary security may then rely upon non-renewable components too. Pirate card rejection provides a secondary layer of security, once the primary layer that protects universal keys is compromised. We therefore advocate a renewable security module that does content decryption within the renewable device.

The data sent back to the host can be further protected in a variety of ways. Although, with some effort the pirate may access the decrypted content, the density of that data makes it much more expensive to redistribute than keying material.

For the rest of this paper, when we refer to smartcards, we mean ISO 7816 smartcards. When we refer to cards, we mean any renewable security module, be it a smartcard, an NRSS Part A or Part B card, or some other device. The NRSS Part B card is similar to a PCMCIA card, while the NRSS Part A has the smartcard form factor along with the high speed ports that permit on-the-card content decryption. Both PCMCIA and NRSS Part A products that do high speed decryption on the card exist [DVB, SCM Microsystems, SGS Thomson, VLSI, Divx].

3 The Protocol

The protocol assumes the following minimum system capabilities: There is no non-volatile memory (NVM) on the host, but NVM is available on the card. The host cannot authenticate itself. The host and card are bound to each other through a certificate which pairs the particular host with a particular card's public key. Host H uses the certified public key of card C during session-key negotiation. The card C and host H count the number of packets that they see, and can coordinate when they start counting, so that their counts remain synchronized. The secret value RANDOM enables setting an authenticated challenge, authenticating the response, and authenticating delivery of an updated value of RANDOM.

The host is trusted enough to follow the protocol, which includes the responsibility to refuse decrypted content from the card if the protocol fails or if the host has not sent encrypted content to the card. Although the host responds to challenges, it is actually the correct functioning of the certified card which is being verified by the host. This architecture uses the card as the response-verifier to accumulate an activity profile in its NVM, thus tracking potential piracy. If enough failures are detected (i.e., because of a pirated card), the legitimate card will refuse to participate in the protocol. The host will then refuse to process data, thereby rejecting the pirated card. The CA system may support mechanisms implementing the policies under which the card is to be reactivated, so the customer may become a paying customer again. These mechanisms may range from a service visit by CA personnel to the other extreme of autonomous reset after an appropriate suspension of service by the card. The protocol has three phases:

1. H→C: Session-key negotiation; C→H: Use session key to encrypt and authenticate RANDOM value and to authenticate status. H verifies, returning to phase 1 if necessary.

2. H→C: Response, authenticated by the same host which negotiated the session. If out of packet sync, host H can request re-sync. C verifies.

3. C→H: Use current RANDOM value to encrypt and authenticate a freshly generated RANDOM value, and to authenticate status. H verifies, and returns to phase 2 if successful, and to phase 1 if unsuccessful.

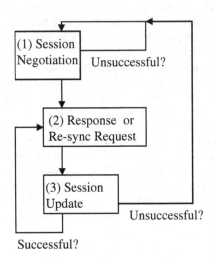

Fig. 2. Protocol Phases

Each instance of the phase 2 - phase 3 repeating loop, as shown in Figure 2, covers an interval composed of three (non-overlapping) subintervals of packets, as shown in Figure 3. Assume that the host and card count all the packets they see. The time-out interval is chosen to be of constant length just long enough to handle re-transmissions of the response due to (non-malicious) communication failure. As part of phase 1, the card and host share secrets which define the challenge interval. One of these secrets is the index of the packet on which the challenge will occur. Phase 2 begins once the card decrypts the challenged packet and sends the corresponding plaintext back to the host. At that point, the host and the card each compute the response, which combines the plaintext and ciphertext corresponding to that packet. The card and host must compute the response before the end of the response interval, and the host must send the response to the card during the time-out interval. The card verifies the correctness of the response, and thus determines whether the response was generated by the host. In phase 3, if the card is satisfied with the response, it sends new secrets to the host, which enables repeating the challenge-response loop beginning at phase 2.

Details of phase 1: Session-key negotiation consists of H sending to C, g^{Hrand} and its NACK PENALTY FLAG value. This flag value on the host is 0 unless it is currently set to 1 in volatile memory, which occurs as a result of successful verification by H of the session negotiation. The flag is reset to 0 only upon loss of the volatile memory. Hrand is randomly generated by H. The Diffie-Hellman value is computed as $DH=(g^{Hrand})^C$ or $DH=(g^C)^{Hrand}$, by C and H respectively, where (C, g^C) is the certified key pair of card C. Both the card C and the host H produce a set of secrets from the negotiated DH value, by using the key derivation function $DHj=Hash(j,DH,j)$[1]. The card chooses a random number, RANDOM, and sends it to the host encrypted and authenticated using the DHj's. Both the card and the host produce a set of secret salts, $Saltj=Hash(j,RANDOM,j)$. Updated values of RANDOM are encrypted and authenticated using the Saltj's (within phase 3)[2].

---

[1] j appears both as prefix and suffix arguments of the hash to thwart successful use of the hash property: Hash(a,c) can be derived from Hash(a,b) for some c≠b, where a is a secret value.

[2] Throughout all three phases, encryption of a value m is achieved by transmitting m⊕key, where key is one of the DHj or Saltj. Also, authentication of a value m' is achieved by

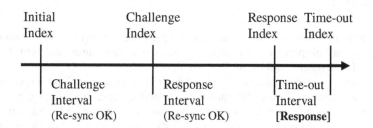

Fig. 3. Challenge Response Cycle

Challenge and response intervals are derived from one of the Saltj's. The Status in phase 1 indicates the initial index value and whether a negative acknowledgment (NACK) was accumulated as a result of the NACK PENALTY FLAG value received by C. NACK requests (where NACK PENALTY FLAG is set to 1) are considered redundant (and only accumulated once by the card) if no intervening data is sent to the card. This can be implemented by having the card set a flag after processing session-key data, and reset the flag upon receipt of other data. If this flag is set, a NACK is not accumulated in response to the received value of the NACK PENALTY FLAG.

The host H checks the NACK field of the Status for validity. The card C will refuse to participate in session negotiation in phase 1 (or session update in phase 3) if the total number of NACKs accumulated exceeds a pre-determined threshold.

Details of phase 2: The [plaintext,ciphertext] pair designated by the challenge index is authenticated by H. Alternatively, a packet re-synch request is authenticated by H, if necessary. Re-synch requests are not honored by the card C during the time-out interval, i.e., the card will accumulate a NACK because the card increments its NACK counter at the onset of the time-out interval and decrements it only if the correct authenticated response is received by the card and received by the end of the time-out interval. Note that these NACKs are accumulated in addition to any NACKs accumulated during phase 1 in response to the NACK PENALTY FLAG.

Details of phase 3: At the end of the time-out interval, or in response to an authenticated re-synch request, the card updates RANDOM and indicates the Status which includes the new initial index value and whether a NACK was accumulated as a result of a missing or improper response to the last challenge.

Note that purposeful shutdown to avoid accumulation of NACKs should impose enough user inconvenience or diminishment of the viewing experience so as to serve as an effective deterrent.

---

transmitting Hash(m',key')⊕key'', where each key' or key'' is one of the DHj or Saltj. Note that this authentication mechanism preserves the secrecy of any part of m' which needs to remain secret.

4 Analysis

In this section we briefly analyze the protocol presented in section 0 by demonstrating the attacks on sub-protocols and concomitant countermeasures, the introduction of which leads to construction of the final protocol.

If the verifier function is constructed so as to be separable in that no specific use is made of the content during the card-to-host binding operation, then the legitimate card, which possesses secret information unknown to the pirated card, will interact normally with the host with respect to the verifier functionality while the pirated card will handle the content decryption so that the extent of content access cannot be logged by the legitimate card.

If we counter the separability threat by involving the content plaintext within the response function, then it might seem that by thus imposing a requirement that the host and the card both see the same plaintext, the legitimate card is forced to use (and log use of) the correct key. However, the pirated card can fool the legitimate card into using an unassociated "free" key (such as a premium channel subscription key) while still recovering the true plaintext, if appropriately modified ciphertext is generated by the pirated card (from the true ciphertext) and delivered to the legitimate card. Specifically, the pirated card would recover the true plaintext (by using knowledge of the legitimately associated key) and then re-encrypt it using the free key.

The incorporation of both plaintext and ciphertext into the responses thwarts the modified ciphertext attack by forcing the pirated card to allow the legitimate card to decrypt the information packets containing the challenged data by using the correct key, unless the pirate's customer is willing to allow the video corresponding to challenged data portions to be garbled because the ciphertext is decrypted using a free key.

The encumbrance upon the pirate's customer can be made more significant by hiding appropriate aspects of the verifier function processing. We can introduce common packet counting between the host and the card and hide the randomly chosen index of the challenged packet in an attempt to exacerbate the corrupted video effect associated with use of a free key (if the card responds to challenges) or increase the extent of use of the true key by the legitimate card in order to allow viewing of the true plaintext (if the host responds to challenges). The pirated card cannot determine the index of a challenged packet until it witnesses a response to that challenge. In fact, once the pirated card does witness the response, it can confine the video corruption or true-key usage to the challenged data if it had buffered the packets and thus suspended delivery to the verifier of the responses. More specifically, if the card is the responder, the pirated card can deliver the true plaintext to the host except for the challenged data packets, while if the host is the responder, the pirated card can have the legitimate card use a free key to decrypt the non-challenged data.

If we hide the content of the responses so that even after witnessing a response the pirated card cannot determine the challenged packet index, the effect of video corruption or true key usage is extended to N packets for each challenge, where N is an upper bound on the response time which measures the number of content packets which are communicated from the occurrence of the challenged packet until the response is communicated.

The N packets-per-challenge penalty may not serve as a sufficient deterrent for the pirate's customer, in which case the delay before responding can be randomized. This delay is secretly established between the host and the card. This may be thought of as first randomly choosing the duration of the "challenge window" (which begins when the challenge is sent and ends when the response may be transmitted) and then randomly choosing a point within to designate as the challenged packet index. The pirated card can still shut down the host in order to have it "reset" and forget the status of outstanding transactions, unless the host is implemented using non-volatile memory. In particular, the pirated card can stop relaying content to the legitimate card after the legitimate card establishes a challenge with the host. This will result in one free challenge cycle of content play, which will result in no penalty beyond shutdown in the absence of non-volatile memory on the host.

5 Conclusion

The pirate card rejection protocol presented in this paper is a strong verifier function that lets the legitimate host detect and reject cards with which it is not permitted to communicate. To overcome this protocol, the pirate must either compromise individual customer's cards (which is prohibitively expensive), must manufacture and distribute pirated hosts (which is not the pirate's desired business), or must require his customers to tamper with the internals of their TVs (the *screwdriver attack*).

The protocol provides a secondary level of security in conditional access systems. Even if the pirate is able to recover the decryption keys (the hiding of which is the responsibility of the renewable security module), the pirate must provide his customers with devices that enable them to use those keys.

The protocol efficiently authenticates all the data moving between the host and the card. This makes the protocol especially well suited for CA systems in which decryption is done on the renewable CA modules. Such a CA system keeps the decryption keys within the renewable security perimeter, and thereby protects those keys better than in smartcard-based CA systems.

Note that the random duration of the challenge interval serves to spread the effect of the challenges, while the random duration of the response interval serves to penalize piracy through billing or shutdown independently of communications latency limits.

The protocol is designed to be orthogonal from the billing policy. Unlike other verifier functions, the host TV does not need to be aware of the billing policy. In addition, the frequency of challenges does not limit the granularity of billing—the service provider can *bill by the foot* of movie watched, for example. This separation of concerns places fewer constraints on the evolution of the CA system and the services it provides.

Acknowledgments

We appreciate discussions with Carmi Bogot, Mark Buer, Miles Circo, David DeLand, Randy Eye, David Schlacht, and Rob Schumann.

References

1. *Diffie-Hellman* - W. Diffie and M.E. Hellman, "New Directions in Cryptography," IEEE Transactions on Information Theory, v. IT-22, no. 6, Nov. 1976, pp. 644-654.
2. *Hash* - S.G. Akl, "On the Security of Compressed Encodings," Advances in Cryptology: Proceedings of Crypto 83, Plenum Press, 1984, pp. 209-230.
3. *Authentication* - via Diffie-Hellman and Hash as we do in paper, or Fiat-Shamir type: A. Fiat and A. Shamir, "How to Prove Yourself: Practical Solutions to Identification and Signature Problems," Advances in Cryptology - CRYPTO '86 Proceedings, Springer-Verlag, 1987, pp. 186-194.
4. EIA-679, National Renewable Security Standard (NRSS) Parts A and B, March 1998.
5. 'Open Verifier' Functionality in Consumer Electronics Devices, GD-T204, Release B, News Data Systems, Ltd.
6. ISO 7816 Identification Cards, Integrated Circuit Cards with Contact, 1987.
7. Technical Specification of DVB Simulcrypt, DVB Document A028, May 1997.
8. C. Hofter, "Security in Simulcrypt Protocols—Encryption and Authentication (inp009a)," 11th Simulcrypt Technical Group Meeting, EBU, Geneva, July 23-24, 1997.

Secure Authentication with Multiple Parallel Keys

John Kelsey and Bruce Schneier

Counterpane Systems
101 E. Minnehaha Pkwy
Minneapolis, MN 55419
{kelsey,schneier}@counterpane.com

Abstract. Many authentication tokens, most notably smart cards, cannot implement conventional digital signature algorithms for performance reasons. Simple solutions involving symmetric cryptography put the global shared secret in every verification device. We propose a more robust solution using Multiple Parallel Keys: use n symmetric keys to authenticate, and give each verification device only one of them.

1   Introduction

Public key cryptography provides a powerful tool for authenticating tokens. The token manufacturer can create a digital signature on a trusted machine and load it onto the token. These signatures can be later verified on a much less trusted machine. However, in many systems, performance requirements prevent the use of public-key cryptography: the token does not have a powerful enough processor, the time constraints don't allow for time-consuming public-key operations, the bandwidth requirements don't allow passing of a digitally signed message, etc. In these systems, a common solution is to embed a global shared secret into both the signing machine and all the verifying machines. This shared secret is used to sign a bit string using a Message Authentication Code (MAC) algorithm [BCK96], which is stored on the token. The verifying machine uses the same shared secret to verify the MAC. Unfortunately, this leaves the security of the whole system depending on the tamper-resistance of all those low-cost verifying devices, which are typically not kept under particularly high security.

A typical example is a smart card used as an access token: to a building, public-transportation system, vending machine, parking lot, etc. The tokens can be created by the system operator in high-security conditions, but the verification devices will generally be in public places, often isolated, and hence susceptible to theft. Putting the system-wide authentication secret inside one of those verification devices is a considerable security risk.

However, if the verifying machines are somewhat expensive to compromise, either because they're kept under reasonable physical security or because they have reasonably good tamper-resistance properties, we can assume that while an attacker can compromise *some* verifying machines he cannot compromise an arbitrarily high number of them. This is the basis for our solution.

J.-J. Quisquater and B. Schneier (Eds.): CARDIS 2000, LNCS 1820, pp. 150–156, 2000.

1.1   An Outline of Our Proposed Solution

Our proposed solution uses many low-trust-level symmetric keys in each MAC signature. The low-trust verifiers each get one key while the signer gets many keys. Therefor, compromising a few verifiers leaves an attacker unable to forge signatures with any degree of confidence. He can forge signatures to some small subset of the whole set of verifiers, but most verifiers will simply refuse to accept his signatures. And the attacker has no way of knowing which verifiers he can successfully fool before he tries.

1.2   An Illustrative Example

Consider the problem of detecting counterfeit hundred dollar bills by verifying that their serial numbers are valid. (We ignore the intractable cryptographic problem of detecting "replayed" hundred dollar bills.) We want to put readers to detect these counterfeit bills in bank offices all over the world. Let us also suppose that there is insufficient time to verify signatures for each hundred dollar bill, and that serial numbers need to remain reasonably short.

A natural solution would be to use a triple-DES [NBS77] key to form a MAC, and then use the MAC to determine several digits of the serial number. This calculation would take place at the mint where the bills are printed. Each reader would then hold that triple-DES key, and an attacker who compromised one reader would be able to defeat all other readers' security. This would require that the readers be kept under extremely tight security, and use the best tamper-resistance technology available.

Our solution works differently. Consider a hundred dollar bill with a 20 decimal digit serial number. The first 10 digits are a never-repeated sequence number, the second 10 digits are a checksum. There are 10 different secret triple-DES keys; each is used to MAC the first 10 digits, and the 64-bit resulting MAC is reduced modulo 10 to get a check digit. (This leaves slightly nonuniform probabilities in each check digit, but the non uniformity is so small it has no practical importance.) Each reader machine is given one of the keys, but the mint (which is presumably quite well guarded) is given all ten. Each serial number has the right 10 checksum digits, but an attacker has no way of recovering the triple-DES keys used or predicting correct values for other serial numbers.

Consider an attacker who compromises a reader machine, and who has the technology to print convincing hundred dollar bills. He can now put out hundred dollar bills, but 9/10 of banks who receive them will identify them as counterfeit and refuse to accept them. Most obviously, this will make these counterfeit bills much less valuable. Just as importantly, any back-end auditing mechanism should be able to detect that a particular hundred dollar bill (or particular user) is regularly being denied validity, and is more likely to be caught counterfeiting.

1.3   Comments on the Example

Note that an attacker who compromises enough of the reader machines can create counterfeit serial numbers with no difficulty at all. Hence, our solution does not provide any security when readers are trivial or very cheap to compromise, but it does provide some security when readers are relatively expensive to compromise.

Also note that the size of the checksums and numbers of keys in the above example are probably too small for real security. The example is meant to help explain an idea, not as a proposed anti counterfeiting defense, though a reasonable one might be adapted from it.

1.4   Guide to the Rest of This Paper

In the remainder of this paper, we consider Multiple Parallel Keys in some detail, then discuss several applications for the idea, and then consider some extensions to the basic idea. We close with some conclusions about Multiple Parallel Keys, and a brief list of still-open questions.

2   Multiple Parallel Keys

As discussed briefly above, the idea of Multiple Parallel Keys is to have many symmetric keys used for signing something, and the same set of keys used for verifying it. Since all the keys involved are symmetric, they must be kept secret. However, any one key is only of a little value to an attacker, since it doesn't allow him to successfully forge signatures to many recipients. In economic terms, the marginal value to the attacker of the first key compromised is rather low; the value of a set of k compromised keys, where n = the number of keys in the system and $k <= n$, is the value of being able to forge signatures so that k/n verifiers accept them as valid.

When compromising a single verifier's key is within an attacker's abilities, but compromising many such keys is not, then we can make use of Multiple Parallel Keys to build a system with acceptable security, without the use of public-key cryptography.

2.1   Global Shared Secrets

In principle, there is still a global shared secret in our proposal: The signer has the whole global shared secret, and the n parts of that secret are split up among many verifiers[1]. The difference between our system and a standard system using a global shared secret is that compromise of a small number of verifiers does not render the system completely insecure. Instead, the level of security (in terms of the likelihood that an attacker will be able to successfully forge a signature to a random receiver) falls as the number of compromised verifiers increases.

---

[1] In some ways, this conceptualization is very similar to secret-sharing techniques, although the security properties are different.

2.2 Structure of the Signatures

A signature is formed by n different MACs, each capable of providing an acceptably low probability of forgery by an attacker who doesn't know its key. Let:

$K_i = $ global key i.
$C_i = $ checksum $i = MAC_{K_i}(Message)$.

Then, the signature is:
$$C_0, C_1, ..., C_{n-1}.$$

As an example, if each checksum is 32 bits long and $n = 16$, then we get a 512-bit signature.

2.3 Key Compromise and Other Attacks

Consider a verifier using key K_i. If K_i has *not* been compromised, then the signature is exactly as secure as one underlying MAC, C_i. If K_i is compromised, then the signature has no security. If the probability of generating a correct MAC, C_i, without knowledge of the key, K_i, is P, then an attacker who has compromised k/n keys has probability $k/n + (1 - k/n)P$ of having his signature accepted. The system is acceptably secure if that probability is never high enough to develop a useful attack, so long as k is low enough that the attacker might actually be able to manage to compromise k keys.

2.4 Security and Performance Tradeoffs

There are three parameters that can be traded off against one another in this system: Signature size, probability of a non-compromised key's MAC being forged, and n. The system is more usable, and performance is generally better, when signature size is as small as possible. The larger n we use, the more key compromises our system can survive. The probability of an attacker forging a MAC when he doesn't know the key is usually a function of how many bits of the MAC are used. These all trade off; with $n = 10$ and $P = 2^{-16}$, we get 160-bit signatures; with $n = 20$, we get 320-bit signatures.

2.5 Where Should This Be Used ?

This system can be used when the following conditions hold:

1. Key compromises on the signer side are very rare and difficult for an attacker to get.
2. Key compromises on the verifier side, while possible to get, are neither easy nor cheap to get.
3. Public key operations are not practical for this system.
4. An attack isn't really successful when the attacker has a small (e.g., $1/n$) chance of getting a verifier to accept an invalid signature.

5. It's not free to try a signature and fail; there must be some cost, whether in dollars, reputation capital, or risk of arrest.

In systems such as these, using Multiple Parallel Keys is a superior alternative to using simple global shared secrets.

3   A Simple Payment System

In this section we discuss a simple payment system, suitably mainly for low-value payments and micro payments, that uses Multiple Parallel Keys. The system uses N systemwide parallel keys, $k_{0..N-1}$.

3.1   Coins

Each coin is made up of the following components, known to the Bank and the Spender to whom the coin is initially issued:

1. A coin header consisting of version, denomination, and a unique 64-bit coin ID.
2. A sequence of secret keys for this coin, $ck_{-1..N-1}$. ck_{-1} is a random secret key for this coin; $ck_j = e_{k_j}(\text{coin header})$, for $j = 0..N-1$.

3.2   Withdrawal

In withdrawal of a coin, the Bank issues the user all of the above information over a secure link for each coin, after properly validating the user and his request to withdraw some coins.

3.3   Spending

The following is the spending protocol:

1. The Spender sends the coin header.
2. The Merchant returns a random challenge, R_0, and its ID, $ID_{merchant}$, along with $0 <= j < N$.
3. The Spender computes and sends t_j, s_j.
    1. $t_j = Low32(e_{ck_{-1}}(j, ID_{merchant}))$
    2. $s_j = e_{ck_j}(\text{coin header}, ID_{merchant}, R_0, t_j)$
4. The Merchant verifies the checksum s_j. If it is valid, he accepts the coin.

3.4   Redeeming Coins

To redeem the coins, the merchant sends up all the information used above. The bank verifies both the s_j and t_j blocks, and if the merchant ID is right for both, and this coin isn't a multiple spend, it credits the merchant's account. Note that an attempt by the merchant to respend a coin is doomed to failure, since upon depositing that coin, the merchant ID in s_j and t_j will no longer match.

3.5   Attacks and Caveats

Forgery. To get a key that will trick 1/16 of the merchants, a single merchant device must be compromised, and its key learned by the attacker. This leaves 15/16 of the merchants unwilling to accept coins.

Furthermore, if the unsuccessful counterfeiter is prosecuted whenever he fails, attempting to pass a forged coin would become very risky.

Merchant Respending. A merchant cannot respend the coins, because his attack will be detected, since t_j's merchant ID value will not match the s_j merchant ID value.

Double Spending. The Spender can't double spend without getting caught as soon as the coin is deposited a second time, since s_j, t_j will agree on the merchant ID.

4   Other Systems

The concept of Multiple Parallel Secrets is applicable in several other systems, which will be described more fully in the final version of the paper:

- Distributed commands to satellite system receivers.
- Distributed keys for copy-protected software.
- Identification cards.

5   Other Applications

The full paper will discuss at least one other application that can use this system.

6   Extensions

In the full paper, we will discuss some possible extensions to this system.

7   Open Problems

The primary problem for using Multiple Parallel Keys in a real-world system is balancing checksum size, number of keys, and probability of successfully fooling a single verifier machine. Determining the right point is clearly a hard problem, and we currently have only vague guidelines for it. A better method of making this tradeoff would be very useful.

A more fundamental question is whether, with increasing computer hardware performance, Multiple Parallel Keys will be of much use at all in the future.

8   Conclusions

We have presented a way to use Multiple Parallel Keys to substitute for a single global shared secret in certain systems, with substantial security advantages. This system provides considerable performance and component costs over public-key systems, and is uniquely suited for many real-world applications of secure tokens (like smart cards).

References

[BCK96]   M. Bellare, R. Canetti, and H. Karwczyk, "Keying Hash Functions for Message Authentication," *Advances in Cryptology — CRYPTO '96 Proceedings*, Springer-Verlag, 1996, pp. 1–15.

[NBS77]   National Bureau of Standards, NBS FIPS PUB 46, "Data Encryption Standard," National Bureau of Standards, U.S. Department of Commerce, Jan 1977.

[Sch96]   B. Schneier, *Applied Cryptography, Second Edition*, John Wiley & Sons, 1996.

Relaxing Tamper-Resistance Requirements for Smart Cards by Using (Auto-)Proxy Signatures

Marc Girault

France Telecom, CNET
42, rue des Coutures
B.P. 6243
14066 CAEN Cedex, FRANCE
marc.girault@cnet.francetelecom.fr

Abstract. We address the problem of relaxing tamper-resistance requirements for smart cards by deriving short-term asymmetric keys from a long-term asymmetric signature key, while increasing as few as possible the amount of memory necessary to store them. This leads us to consider (auto-)proxy signatures in the sense of Mambo, Usada and Okamoto [MUO], and to provide a generic and secure method for constructing such schemes. Then we give six different schemes generated this way, among which all the proxy signature schemes known to date appear as particular cases, and compare them in terms of efficiency, flexibility and transparency.

Keywords. Smart cards, tamper-resistance, short-term keys, digital signatures, proxy signatures.

1 Introduction

Tamper-resistance is a highly critical property of smart cards. (Secret) keys, including PINs (Personal Identification Number), manufacturer keys, issuer keys, application keys etc. cannot be stored in such cards if high confidence in their resistance to " physical " attacks is not achieved.

Much progress has been made in this area for the last ten years, and some largely spread cards (e.g. french banking cards) have been attributed a high level evaluation certificate (called E3 strengthened, in a scale going from E1 to E6). But, in the same period, evidence was given that other types of cards could be (relatively) easily be penetrated, and their secret keys revealed to the outside world.

Tamper-resistance is both hardware and software issues. For instance, protecting a PIN from " direct " observation with an electron microscope is useless if the internal program which makes the card mute after three fake trials can be bypassed. As a consequence, tamper-resistance can be achieved only by a joint work of chip designers and code programmers. Clearly, they are the " key people " for progress in this topic.

Nevertheless, another approach is possible, which is complementary to the previous one. It simply consists to decrease the damages a key discovery can cause, by severely restricting its conditions of use. Mainly, the key can be limited to a very short period of time (such keys are often called " short-term " keys) and/or limited to

J.J. Quisquater and B. Schneier (Eds.): CARDIS 2000, LNCS 1820, pp. 157–166, 2000.
© Springer-Verlag Berlin Heidelberg 2000

a very particular utilization. The two approaches converge when, e.g., extraction of secret keys is considered as practically unfeasible in a few hours and only one-day keys are stored in this card.

Hence the following scenario may be of interest : first of all, Alice generates an asymmetric signature key pair (X, Y) where X is the secret (or private) key and Y the public one. Then she gets a certificate $\text{Cert}(Y, M)$ from the Certification Authority (CA) she is affiliated to, i.e. a digital signature by this CA of her public key and other parameters M including at least her identity, and very likely a period of validity, CA's identity, a certificate serial number etc. : $\text{Cert}(Y, M) = S(Y, M)$. (Actually, $\text{Cert}(Y, M)$ may be a *chain* of certificates rather than one certificate only, but it is of no importance here.) Of course, the delivery of a certificate by the CA is not a frequent act, and the period of validity is consequently rather long (let us say one year, at least one month).

We call (X, Y) the *long-term key pair* (or, briefly, the *long-term key*) of Alice. Because (X, Y) is a long-term key, it has to be highly protected : we suggest that it is stored in a very secure device (e.g. a smart card whose security has been evaluated at a high level) and/or that this device stays in a non-public place (typically Alice's home or office), rather than being transported here and there.

Now, every morning, Alice requests her secure device to carry out a key generation algorithm, which generates a key pair (x, y) whose validity is restricted to (let us say) the current day. We do not describe yet the way the restriction conditions of this key will be recognized by the outside world, since this issue is the main one of the rest of the paper. Neither, we do not make any assumption on the usage of this key pair, which may be a priori encipherment, authentication, signature or anything else.

The day key is then stored in a (PIN-protected or not, depending on the context) smart card, along with a message m, which describes the validity conditions of this key (i.e. m is the equivalent for the day key of M for the long-term key), and which includes the current day. This smart card must be reasonably tamper-resistant, but not necessarily at the same level than the secure device. It stays in Alice's pocket, so that she can use it at any time and at any place throughout this day.

Suppose now that Alice's card is stolen or lost. Then the damage is relatively low, perhaps even null. Indeed if tamper-resistance is such that, almost certainly, the key cannot be physically extracted in a few hours, then the enemy will not have the time to perform a fraud with it (once extracted, the key will be already obsolete). Even if such a guarantee does not exist, Alice may find moderately important that an enemy can use her key for a maximum of one day. For example, she is a post(wo)man, and this key allows her to enter the buildings of a restricted area.

The examples could be multiplied, showing that a key which is restricted to a very limited time and/or a very limited usage needs not be given the same physical protection as a long-term and/or general usage key.

Of course, computing and storing the day key are not enough. The card must also contain the " validity conditions " message m and a proof that it reflects Alice's willingness. So the question we address in this paper can be summarized by : " How to generate day keys[1] conveniently ? "[2].

---

[1] Throughout the paper, we will indifferently use the terms " short-term key " and " day key ". They both stand for (more generally) " restricted-usage keys ".

In section 2, we observe that our problematic is roughly equivalent to the so-called "proxy signatures" one. In section 3, we present state-of-the-art-based solutions (namely those using certificate-based schemes and those using identity-based schemes), and point out their advantages and their drawbacks. In section 4, which is the main contribution of this paper, we propose a generic approach which can be applied to a great number of existing signature schemes. We observe that the schemes produced that way are secure, if the underlying signature scheme is secure. We show that proxy signature schemes known up to now are particular cases of these schemes. Finally, we conclude in section 5.

2   Relationship with "Proxy Signatures"

2.1   What Are Proxy Signatures ?

In 1996, Mambo, Usada and Okamoto addressed the problem of efficiently delegating the signature capability. In a paper published in *IEICE Trans. Fundamentals* [MUO], they classify such delegations into three types : full delegation (Alice simply gives her secret key X to a proxy signer) ; delegation by warrant (Alice expresses the delegation conditions to the proxy signer by the way of a specific signature) ; and the partial delegation (Alice creates a proxy signature key from her own secret key, along with some parameter allowing to derive the proxy public verification key from Alice's one).

The delegation by warrant perfectly solves the problem in terms of security, but has two drawbacks : first, "efficiency" is (implicitly claimed to be) not achieved since there is at least one more signature to store, transmit and verify ; second, "transparency" is not achieved in that verification procedures are not the same, depending whether the signature was computed by the original signer or by the proxy signer. This is why the partial delegation, which achieves transparency and a better efficiency is preferred by the authors of [MOU], who propose two main schemes, based on the discrete logarithm problem and on integer factorization.

2.2   Some Comments on Proxy Signatures

We observe that the schemes proposed in [MUO] achieve both more and less than what is claimed by the authors.

"More" because their (first) scheme outputs a new key pair (x,y) where y is a modular exponential of x, but does not compel a particular way of using this key. Since such a key pair can be used for other purposes than signature only, this scheme actually achieves a delegation for various cryptographic capabilities. For example, Alice can delegate the power of deciphering the messages sent to her for some period of time. We will say that this scheme satisfies "flexibility" property (even if it does not claim so).

---

[2] Note that some other research on the same subject has been performed at the same time by G. Hachez and J.J. Quisquater.

" Less " because delegation of anything can definitely not be achieved if the delegation conditions are unknown to the verifier. In MUO scheme, there is (strangely) the willingness of not attaching any message to the proxy key, preventing such conditions from being stated by the original signer and known by the verifier. Kim, Park and Won pointed out the problem and proposed a solution at *ICICS'97* Conference [KPW], which was in fact already present in [MOU] -but only to show the similarity between their scheme and Schnorr's signature one [Sc] !

" Less " also because, as the secret key x is computed (hence known) by Alice, first a secure channel is needed to provide the proxy signer with x, second there is no possibility of distinguishing between Alice's signatures and the proxy signer's ones - which may cause problems in the event of a dispute. (Actually, a so-called proxy-protected proxy signature scheme is proposed to solve this problem, but it fixes only the second flaw and lacks both efficiency and transparency ; a better solution, using blinding techniques, is proposed by Petersen and Horster in [PH].)

2.3 (Auto-)Proxy Signatures Versus Day Keys

Now, it appears that the property of deriving day keys from long-term keys is only a particular case of delegation, the case when the delegation is given by Alice to herself, or " self-delegation ". (Note however that full delegation cannot be used in our context : a long-term key and a short-term key must not be the same). Conversely, since the requirements for self-delegation are as tough as for delegation in MOU sense, it appears that the *same* schemes can be used for proxy signatures (either delegation by warrant or partial delegation) and for day keys. Note that this observation is implicit in [PH].

In order not to add a new term to an already long list, we will therefore qualify our schemes as being " proxy signature schemes ", or rather " auto-proxy signature schemes ", since the drawback mentioned at the end of subsection 2.2 actually makes already known proxy signature schemes only usable for self-delegation.

In summary, our goal is now to specify auto-proxy signature schemes which are efficient, flexible and transparent. Note that the scheme described in [KPW] seems to be the first step in this direction.

3 State-of-the-Art-Based Auto-Proxy Signature Schemes

3.1 Certificate-Based Solutions

The trivial solution of self-delegation problem consists in Alice's secure device producing with her long-term key a " self-certificate " of the pair (y,m) : $S_A(y,m)$. In such a case, the card must store the seven following elements :

$$\{Y, M, Cert(Y, M), y, m, S_A(y,m), x\}$$

The advantage of this solution, due to its generic description, is that it can work with *any* signature scheme S and *any* key y (whatever its usage is).

Its main drawback is the (great) size of the key material to be stored. Indeed the expansion length, which is the difference between the length of the above key material and the length of the long-term key material (i.e. $\{Y, M, Cert(Y, M), X\}$), may be as long as (about) 2000 bits. This is a very undesirable expansion, since each bit of the data memory of smart cards (which often contains between 1 and 8 Kbytes) is precious.

Another drawback occurs when the day key is itself a signature key. Even if y and Y are used with the same signature scheme, the verification procedure is not the same, depending upon whether Alice signed with her long-term key or with a day key (there is one more signature to check in the latter case). It would be convenient that signing with the long-term key appears only as a particular case of signing with a day key -i.e. that the scheme be " transparent ".

Note that this solution corresponds to the so-called " delegation by warrant / bearer proxy " in [MUO] taxonomy. From now on, all the proposed solutions are related to the " partial delegation " in this taxonomy.

3.2 Identity-Based Solutions

The " identity-based " concept is due to Shamir [Sh]. Briefly speaking, it consists to choose Alice's identity as her public key. The private key is derived from her identity by the means of a trapdoor one-way function, which is held by a trusted authority. More generally, the public key can be any message m (or its hashed value) chosen by Alice, e.g. the " validity conditions " message defined in the introduction.

The most popular trapdoor one-way function is based on factorization and is defined as : $y = f(x) = x^e \pmod n$, where n is composite, and its prime factors p and q held secret by the trusted authority. It is well known that it provides a digital signature scheme because, if we choose y equal to the message m to sign (more precisely a redundant or hashed version of this message), then x can be considered as a signature of m by the entity who holds the factors of n.

We therefore can solve the short-term key problem as follows : let (X, Y), with $X = (p, q)$ and $Y = (n, e)$, be the long-term signature key and let (x,y) be the day key, with y equal to m and x such that $y = x^e \pmod n$. Then such a day key can be used for authentication/signature purposes by using the adequate zero-knowledge-based protocol. More precisely, if $e = 2$, then the signature scheme is Rabin's one [R] and the day key is a Fiat-Shamir's one [FS]. If $e = 2^t$, then the signature scheme is a variation of Rabin's one and the day key is a Ong-Schnorr's one [OS]. If e is coprime with $(p\text{-}1)(q\text{-}1)$, then the signature scheme is RSA [RSA] and the day key is a Guillou-Quisquater's one [GQ].

In each case, the key material to be stored in the card is reduced to :

$$\{Y, M, Cert(Y, M), m, x\}$$

and is therefore very compact.

Compared to the certificate-based solution used with exactly the same algorithms, both the public key and its " self-certificate " are saved, i.e. 2048 bits if the size of n is 1024 bits. From this point of view, it is the best possible solution.

Nonetheless, it may not be the most convenient one for the following two reasons. First, in case the day key is used to produce signatures, we have the problem that the long-term key and the day key use completely different algorithms, which violates the transparency requirement in the most flagrant manner. Second, the day key cannot be used for encipherment because keys generated that way are not known to be usable for that purpose.

We are therefore led to find other solutions, which still save a significant number of memory bits, while offering more flexibility and more transparency.

4 A Paradigm for Efficient / Flexible / Transparent (Auto-)Proxy Signature Schemes

4.1 A Generic Construction of (Auto-)Proxy Schemes

We present here a generic construction of day keys which is simultaneously efficient (many memory bits are saved), flexible (the day keys generated can be used for various purposes) and transparent (from verification point of view, the use of the long-term key only appears as a particular case). Actually, this construction is more or less latent in [MUO], but in a rather non-explicit and quite restricted manner. It is also closely related to the concept of self-certified public key, as introduced by the author in [G] and extended by Horster, Michels and Petersen in [HMP].

Let S be a signature algorithm and (X, Y) be a key pair for S, where $Y = f(X)$, f a one-way function. We assume that S has the following properties : each signature generated by S has the form (r, s) and the verification equation has the form : $f(s) = \phi(Y, r, m)$, where ϕ is a publicly known function. Many popular signature algorithms (but not RSA neither DSS [DSS]), satisfy these properties.

Then this signature algorithm can be used to generate a day key (x, y) by simply computing the signature (r, s) of m and choosing :

$$\boxed{\begin{aligned} x &= s \\ y &= f(s) \end{aligned}}$$

We claim that this method for generating day keys is secure, because such a key cannot be computed by anybody but Alice (unless the underlying signature scheme is existentially forgeable) and discovery of the secret part x of this key does not reveal anything about the long-term secret key X (unless the underlying signature scheme is vulnerable to a known-message attack).

Second, we achieve efficiency, since the key material to be stored in the smart card is only :

$$\{Y, M, Cert(Y, M), r, m, x\}$$

which is still a significant reduction over the certificate-based solution (even if less drastic than the identity-based solution), since we roughly save the size of the self-certificate (generally, r is the same size as y).

Third we achieve flexibility when f is modular exponentiation, since keys of this form can be used for various purposes.

Finally, we achieve transparency in case the day key is used for producing signatures, since it clearly appears from our set-up than the day key has exactly the same form as the long-term key.

Let us now give some concrete examples generated by this generic method.

4.2 Specific New (Auto-)Proxy Schemes

Here are six specific (auto-)proxy schemes. All the proxy signature schemes known to date (and to us) appear as particular cases and are mentioned where appropriate. As a consequence, all the others can be viewed as new proxy signature schemes.

In the following, p and q are prime numbers, respectively 1024 and 160-bit long for illustration, n is a 1024-bit composite number, and h is a 160-bit collision-free hash-function. When both p and q are involved, q is a divisor of p-1. In the first four examples, f is exponentiation modulo p (and g is a primitive element modulo p), in the fifth example f is exponentiation modulo n (and g is a maximum-order element modulo n), and in the last example, f is power function modulo n. Note that, when f is modular exponentiation (modulo p or n), flexibility is always achieved, since generated day keys can be chosen to be encipherment keys (using e.g. El-Gamal encipherment scheme [E] or other Diffie-Hellman-based [DH] schemes), signature keys or authentication keys (using e.g. the underlying signature scheme).

Efficiency is evaluated by measuring the key material expansion length (that is the difference between the length of $\{Y, M, Cert(Y, M), r, m, x\}$ and the one of $\{Y, M, Cert(Y, M), X\}$) and comparing it to the expansion length of a certificate-based solution using the same signature scheme. We first give the difference between these two expansion lengths (the " gain "), then the expansion lengths themselves. For convenience, the length of m is fixed to 512 bits. With this assumption, the key material expansion length is equal to 1536 bits for all schemes but one.

4.2.1 El-Gamal-Based Scheme [E]

$$Y = g^X \,(\mathrm{mod}\ p)$$
$$r = g^k \,(\mathrm{mod}\ p)$$
$$x = Xr + kh(m) \,\mathrm{mod}(p\quad 1)$$
$$y = Y^r r^{h(m)} \,(\mathrm{mod}\ p)$$

Remarks :
0) If $m = 1$, this is the first Mambo-Usada-Okamoto scheme (version 2) [MUO].
1) Efficiency : 2048 bits are saved (1536 instead of 3584).
2) Flexibility : the day key can be used for any purpose.
3) Transparency : if $r = 1$, the day key is equal to (X, Y).

4.2.2 Nyberg-Rueppel-Based Scheme [NR]

$$Y = g^X \,(\mathrm{mod}\ p)$$
$$r = mg^k \,(\mathrm{mod}\ p)$$
$$x = k + Xr \,(\mathrm{mod}\ q)$$
$$y = m^{\,1} rY^r \,(\mathrm{mod}\ p)$$

Remarks :
- 0) If $m = 1$, this is (again) the first Mambo-Usada-Okamoto scheme (version 2).
- 1) Efficiency : 1184 bits are saved (1536 instead of 2720).
- 2) Flexibility : the day key can be used for any purpose.
- 3) Transparency : if (e.g.) $r = 1$ and $m = 1$, the day key is equal to (X, Y).

4.2.3 Yen-Laih-Based Scheme [YL]

$$Y = g^X \pmod p$$
$$r = g^k \pmod p$$
$$x = Xh(m) + kr \pmod q$$
$$y = Y^{h(m)} r^r \pmod p$$

Remarks :
- 0) If $h(m)$ is replaced by 1, this is the first Mambo-Usada-Okamoto scheme (version 1).
- 1) Efficiency : 1184 bits are saved (1536 instead of 2720).
- 2) Flexibility : the day key can be used for any purpose.
- 3) Transparency : since r and m cannot be computed such that $y = Y$, it should be agreed that, when e.g. $r = 0$, then the day key is equal to the long-term key.

4.2.4 Schnorr-Based Scheme [Sc]

$$Y = g^X \pmod p$$
$$r = g^k \pmod p$$
$$c = h(r, m)$$
$$x = k + Xc \pmod q$$
$$y = r Y^c \pmod p$$

Remarks :
- 0) This is exactly the Kim-Park-Won scheme [KPW] (but affiliation to Schnorr's scheme is not explicitly made in the paper) ; if m is restricted to Alice's identity, this is also the Petersen-Horster scheme [PH].
- 1) Efficiency : 320 bits are saved (1536 instead of 1856).
- 2) Flexibility : the day key can be used for any purpose.
- 3) Transparency : since r and m cannot be computed such that $y = Y$, it should be agreed that, when e.g. $r = 0$, then the day key is equal to the long-term key.

4.2.5 Girault-Poupard-Stern-Based Scheme [G,PS]

$$Y = g^X \pmod n$$
$$r = g^k \pmod n$$
$$c = h(r, m)$$
$$x = k + Xc$$
$$y = r Y^c \pmod n$$

Remarks :
1) Efficiency : 320 bits are saved (1936 instead of 2256) if we take X 160-bit long and k 400-bit long.
2) Flexibility : the day key can be used for any purpose.
3) Transparency : since r and m cannot be computed such that $y = Y$, it should be agreed that, when e.g. $r = 0$, then the day key is equal to the long-term key.
4) In this scheme, the secret day key is longer than the secret long-term secret key (240 bit longer), and so is the signature computed with this key.

4.2.6 Guillou-Quisquater or Ong-Schnorr-Based Scheme [GQ,OS]

$$Y = X^e \pmod{n}$$
$$r = k^e \pmod{n}$$
$$c = h(r,m)$$
$$x = kX^c \pmod{n}$$
$$y = rY^c \pmod{n}$$

Remarks :
0) This scheme is vaguely related to the second scheme of [MUO], which is based on the (completely unpractical) one-key Fiat-Shamir signature scheme.
1) Efficiency : 1184 bits are saved (1536 instead of 2720).
0) 2) Flexibility : the day key can be used only for signature   and authentication.
2) Transparency : since r and c cannot be computed such that $y = Y$, it should be agreed that, when e.g. $r = 0$, the day key is equal to the long-term key.

5   Conclusion

As a way of relaxing tamper-resistance requirements for smart cards, we have investigated the possibility of deriving short-term asymmetric keys from a long-term asymmetric signature key. We have observed that we were faced to a particular case of the delegation problem, and therefore reduced to specifying proxy signature schemes in the [MUO] sense, that we preferred to call " auto-proxy signature schemes ". This led us to design a wide range of such schemes : first, those based on certificate-based and identity-based schemes ; second (and our contribution actually stands here), those according to a general paradigm, which allowed us to generate six different schemes (but there could be many other ones), whose security is the one of the underlying signature scheme, and among which all proxy signature schemes known to date appear as particular cases.

Acknowledgements. The author would like to thank J.J. Quisquater for fruitful discussions and H. Petersen for drawing his attention to the [PH] reference.

References

[DH]   W. Diffie and M. Hellman. New directions in cryptography. In *IEEE Transactions on Information Theory*, Vol. IT-22, pages 644-654, Nov. 1976.

[DSS]   Digital Signature Standard. In *FIPS 186*, US Department of Commerce/NIST, 1994.

[E]   T. El Gamal. A public key cryptosystem and a signature scheme based on discrete logarithms. In *Advances in Cryptology - CRYPTO '84*, LNCS 196, Springer-Verlag, pages 10-18, 1985.

[FS]   A. Fiat and A. Shamir. How to prove yourself : Practical solutions to identification and signature problems. In *Advances in Cryptology - CRYPTO '86*, LNCS 263, Springer-Verlag, pages 186-194, 1987.

[G]   M. Girault. Self-certified public keys. In *Advances in Cryptology - EUROCRYPT '91*, LNCS 547, Springer-Verlag, pages 490-497, 1991.

[GQ]   L.C. Guillou and J.J. Quisquater. A practical zero-knowledge protocol fitted to security microprocessors minimizing both transmission and memory. In *Advances in Cryptology - EUROCRYPT '91*, LNCS 330, Springer-Verlag, pages 123-128, 1988.

[HMP]   P. Horster, M. Michels and H. Petersen. Meta-Message recovery and meta blind signature schemes based on the discrete logarithm problem and their applications. In *Advances in Cryptology - ASIACRYPT '94*, LNCS 917, Springer-Verlag, pages 224-237, 1994.

[KMW]   S. Kim, S. Park and D. Won. Proxy signatures, revisited. In *ICICS '97*, LNCS 1334, Springer-Verlag, pages 223-232, 1997.

[MUO]   M. Mambo, K. Usada and E. Okamoto. Proxy signatures : delegation of the power to sign messages. In *IEICE Trans. Fundamentals*, Vol. E79-A, n°9, pages 1338-1354, 1996.

[NR]   K. Nyberg and R. Rueppel. A new signature scheme based on the DSA giving message recovery. In *Proceedings of 1st ACM Conference on Computer and Communications Security*, ACM Press, pages 58-61, 1993.

[OS]   H. Ong and C. Schnorr. Fast signature generation with a Fiat Shamir-like scheme. In *Advances in Cryptology - EUROCRYPT '90*, LNCS 473, Springer-Verlag, pages 432-440, 1991.

[PH]   H. Petersen and P. Horster. Self-certified public keys – Concepts and applications. In *Proc. of Communications and Multimedia Security '97*, Chapman & Hall, pages 102-116, 1997.

[PS]   G. Poupard and J. Stern. A practical and provably secure design for " on the fly " authentication and signature generation. In *Advances in Cryptology - EUROCRYPT '98*, LNCS 1403, Springer-Verlag, pages 422-436, 1998.

[R]   M.O. Rabin. Digitalized signatures and public-key functions as intractable as factorization. In *MIT/LCS/TR-212*, MIT Lab. for Computer Science, 1979.

[RSA]   R.L. Rivest, A. Shamir and L. Adleman. A method for obtaining digital signatures and public-key cryptosystems. In *CACM*, Vol. 21, n°2, pages 120-126, Feb. 1991.

[Sc]   C.P. Schnorr. Efficient identification and signature for smart cards. In *Advances in Cryptology - CRYPTO '89*, LNCS 435, Springer-Verlag, pages 239-252, 1991.

[Sh]   A. Shamir. Identity-based cryptosystems and signature schemes. In *Advances in Cryptology - CRYPTO '84*, LNCS 196, Springer-Verlag, pages 47-53, 1985.

[YL]   S.M. Yen and C.S. Laih. New digital signature scheme based on discrete logarithm. In *Electronics Letters*, Vol. 29, n°12, pages 1120-1121, 1993.

A Practical Implementation of the Timing Attack

Jean-François Dhem[*1], François Koeune[3], Philippe-Alexandre Leroux[3],
Patrick Mestré[*2], Jean-Jacques Quisquater[3], and Jean-Louis Willems[3]

[1] Belgacom Multimedia & Infohighways,
Bld E. Jacqmain 177, B-1030 Brussels, Belgium.
dhem@belbone.be
[2] Europay International,
198A Chaussée de Tervuren, B-1410 Waterloo, Belgium.
pme@europay.com
[3] Université catholique de Louvain, UCL Crypto Group,
Laboratoire de microélectronique (DICE),
Place du Levant 3, B-1348 Louvain-la-Neuve, Belgium.
{fkoeune,leroux,jjq,willems}@dice.ucl.ac.be
http://www.dice.ucl.ac.be/crypto

Abstract. When the running time of a cryptographic algorithm is non-constant, timing measurements can leak information about the secret key. This idea, first publicly introduced by Kocher, is developed here to attack an earlier version of the CASCADE smart card[1]. We propose several improvements on Kocher's ideas, leading to a practical implementation that is able to break a 512-bit key in few hours, provided we are able to collect 300 000 timing measurements (128-bit keys can be recovered in few seconds using a personal computer and less than 10 000 samples). We therefore show that the timing attack represents an important threat against cryptosystems, which must be very seriously taken into account.

Keywords: timing attack, cryptanalysis, RSA, smart card.

1 Introduction

Implementations of cryptographic algorithms often perform computations in non-constant time, due to performance optimizations. If such operations involve secret parameters, these timing variations can leak some information and, provided enough knowledge of the implementation is at hand, a careful statistical analysis could even lead to the total recovery of these secret parameters (fig. 1).

This idea was first presented by Kocher [Koc96], who laid the foundations of the basic ideas exploited in this paper. However, the results of Kocher were quite

---

[*] Work done when both of these persons were research assistant at the UCL Crypto Group.

[1] Later modified to resist against it.

J.-J. Quisquater and B. Schneier (Eds.): CARDIS 2000, LNCS 1820, pp. 167–182, 2000.

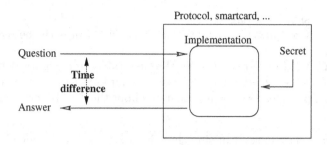

Fig. 1. The timing attack principle.

theoretical[2] and we found them rather difficult to exploit in practice. This paper presents an effective and efficient attack of a cryptographic algorithm running on a smart card. The first practical timing attack to our knowledge was described at the rump session of CRYPTO'97 by Lenoir. Our paper, however, develops quite different ideas.

Another problem of the attack presented by Kocher is that the attacker needs a very detailed knowledge of the implementation of the system he is attacking, as he has to be able to compute the partial timings due to the known part of the key. As for this paper, the knowledge needed is very limited, which makes the attack quite general and easy to carry out.

Last but not least, some completely new ideas, such as the attack of the square rather than the multiply, are presented.

We begin by presenting the model we are attacking and the characteristics it must present to be vulnerable. We then describe the attack that was carried out, as well as its results and possible improvements. Finally, we describe some countermeasures that would allow to defeat it.

We try to present both a formal and an intuitive view of the timing attack, our goal being to make the principle of the attack easy to understand, but also to provide a detailed enough description to allow the reader to implement it without encountering major problems.

2   The General Framework

We here give the characteristics that the system must present to be vulnerable, and briefly formalize the model in which our attack will be drawn. Given a message m as input, an algorithm A performs a computation (that we call a signature) using a secret key k. We note:

M, the set of messages,
K, the set of keys,

---

[2] Kocher identified several targets for the timing attack and ran simulations to determine what the success rate would be for an attack of the modular multiplication, but did apparently not carry out the attack itself.

S, the set of signed messages,
$A : M \times K \to S : (m, k) \to A(m, k)$, the signature of m with the secret key k,
$B = \{0, 1\}$,
$T : M \times K \to \mathcal{R} : m \to t = T(m, k)$, the time taken to compute $A(m, k)$.
$O : M \to B : m \to O(m)$, an oracle, based on our knowledge of the implementation, that provides us some information about the details of the computation of $A(m, k)$.

Remark: It may look surprising that the oracle does not depend on the key k, although the computation of $A(m, k)$ does, but this is precisely the idea of this paper: typically, we want to build a decision criterion (formalized by the oracle) that will be meaningful or not, *depending on the actual value of some bit of the key.* By observing the meaningfulness of our criterion, we will deduce the bit value.

The scenario of our attack is the following: Eve disposes of a sample of messages and, for each of them, the time needed to compute the signature of the message with the key k. Her goal is to recover k, which can thus be considered as an unknown parameter rather than as a variable. To simplify our notations, we will thus simply note $T(m)$ instead of $T(m, k)$.

To attack the bit i of the key k, Eve will use an oracle O to build two subsets of messages $M_1, M_2 \subseteq M$. We will denote the corresponding timings by the functions:

$$F_1 : M_1 \to \mathcal{R} : m \to F_1(m) = T(m)$$

$$F_2 : M_2 \to \mathcal{R} : m \to F_2(m) = T(m)$$

Suppose these two functions have the following properties:

$$\begin{cases} \text{If } k_i = 0, \text{ then } & F_1 \text{ is a random variable } v_1^0 \\ & F_2 \text{ is a random variable } v_2^0 \\ \\ \text{If } k_i = 1, \text{ then } & F_1 \text{ is a random variable } v_1^1 \\ & F_2 \text{ is a random variable } v_2^1 \end{cases}$$

and suppose that, for a parameter of these random variables $\phi(v)$ (e.g. the mean or the variance) we have:

$$\phi(v_1^0) = \phi(v_2^0) \quad \text{and} \quad \phi(v_1^1) > \phi(v_2^1)$$

then with the following statistical test:

$$H_0 : \phi(F_1) \overset{?}{=} \phi(F_2)$$
$$H_1 : \phi(F_1) \overset{?}{>} \phi(F_2)$$

we deduce that if H_0 is accepted with error probability α, then $i = 1$ with error probability α.

In other words, this means that Eve is able to construct two samples of messages and two functions whose statistical behaviours will depend on the actual value of the bit i. By observing the relative behaviours of the two functions, Eve will be able to determine, with a certain error probability, the value of the bit i. Of course, couples of ciphertexts / decryption timings, with the same properties, could also be used.

3   Towards a Practical Attack

3.1   The Implementation

We have attacked an RSA computation (without CRT), performed in an earlier version of the cryptographic library we developed for the CASCADE [Cas] smart card. It is interesting to note that this implementation was already naively protected against a timing attack, but that this protection turned out to be insufficient; we will come back on this later (section 9).

The computation in the smart card was: $m^k \bmod n$.

The algorithm is the left to right square and multiply (fig. 3.1).

$$
\begin{aligned}
&x = m \\
&\textbf{for} \ \ i = n - 2 \ \textbf{downto} \ \ 0 \\
&\quad x = x^2 \\
&\quad \textbf{if} \ (k_j == 1) \ \textbf{then} \\
&\quad\quad x = x \cdot m \\
&\textbf{endfor} \\
&\textbf{return} \ \ x
\end{aligned}
$$

Fig. 2. Square and multiply

Both the multiplication and the square are done using the Montgomery algorithm. The time for a Montgomery multiplication is constant, independently of the factors, except that, if the intermediary result of the multiplication is greater than the modulus, then an additional subtraction (called a reduction) has to be performed.

3.2   A First Attempt: Attacking the Multiply

The most obvious way to take advantage of this knowledge is to aim our attack at the *multiply* step of the square and multiply. The idea is the following:

We start by attacking k_2, the second bit[3] (MSB first) of the secret key. Performing the Montgomery algorithm step-by-step, we see that, if that bit is 1, then the value $m \cdot m^2$ will have to be computed during the square and multiply.

Now, for some messages m (those for which the intermediary result of the multiplication will be greater than the modulus), an additional reduction will

---

[3] We can of course suppose that the first bit of the key is always 1.

have to be performed during this multiplication, while, for other messages, that reduction step will not be necessary. So, we are able to divide our set of samples in two subsets: one for which the computation of $m \cdot m^2$ will induce a reduction and another for which it will not. If the value of k_2 is really 1, then we can expect the computation times for the messages from the first set to be slightly higher than the corresponding times for the second set.

On the other hand, if the actual value of k_2 is 0, then the operation $m \cdot m^2$ will not be performed. In this case, our "separation criterion" will be meaningless: there is indeed no reason for which a m inducing a reduction for the operation $m \cdot m^2$, would also induce a reduction for $m^2 \cdot m^2$, or for any other operation. Therefore, the separation in two subsets should look random, and we should not observe any significant difference in the computation times.

Let us rewrite this a little more formally:

The algorithm $A(m, k)$ could be split into $L(m, k)$ and $R(m, k)$ where $L(m, k)$ is the computation due to the additional reduction at the multiplication phase for bit k_2 and $R(m, k)$ the remaining computations. This gives for the computation times: $T(m) = T^L(m) + T^R(m)$, where $T^L(m)$, $T^R(m)$ are the times to compute $L(m, k)$ and $R(m, k)$ respectively.

The oracle O is:

$$O : m \rightarrow \begin{cases} 1 \text{ if } m \cdot m^2 \text{ is done with a reduction,} \\ 0 \text{ if } m \cdot m^2 \text{ is done without a reduction.} \end{cases}$$

As in section 2, define

$$\begin{aligned} M_1 &= \{m \in M : O(m) = 1\}, \\ M_2 &= \{m \in M : O(m) = 0\}, \\ F_1 &: M_1 \rightarrow R : m \rightarrow F_1(m) = T(m), \\ F_2 &: M_2 \rightarrow R : m \rightarrow F_2(m) = T(m). \end{aligned}$$

We have

$$\begin{cases} F_1 = T^R & \text{if } k_2 = 0 \\ F_1 = T^R + T^L & \text{if } k_2 = 1 \end{cases}$$

while,

$$F_2 = T^R$$

independently of the value of k_2.

Now, analyzing the mean as parameter ϕ, and testing:

$$H_0 : \phi(F_1) \overset{?}{=} \phi(F_2)$$
$$H_1 : \phi(F_1) \overset{?}{\neq} \phi(F_2)$$

should reveal the value of k_2.

Once this value is known, we can simulate the computation up to the multiplication due to bit k_3, attack it in the same way as described above, and so on for the next bits.

3.3   Problems

Using the previous attack, we were able to recover 128-bit keys by observing samples of 50 000 timings.

However, this method is not fully satisfying. Mainly two problems arise: Firstly, the operations we observe are multiplications by a constant value m, and these operations seem to be much more correlated than expected. Rather surprisingly, we observed that, while the probability for an additional reduction to be necessary when the two factors and the modulus are random is about 0.17, this probability will, when the modulus and one factor are fixed, vary between 0 and 0.5, depending on modulus and factor (see figure 3). So, although it seems difficult to explain theoretically, our selection criterion seems to be highly biased.

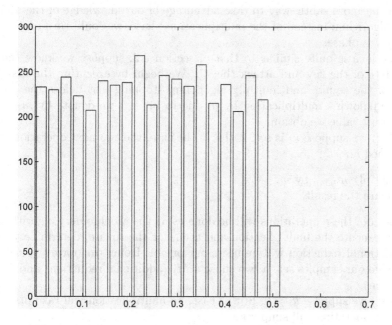

Fig. 3. With fixed modulus, probability for an additional reduction to take place when multiplying by a constant factor. The test has been carried out with 4 500 factors and, for each of them, with 20 000 multiplications.

Secondly, the decision we have to make is of the type: "are these two samples different *or not*". That is, we have to decide, on the basis of a finite set of measures, whether the differences we observe between the two sets is significant or not. Statistics can be of some help, but not as much as could be expected. As we said before, Montgomery multiplication by a constant seems to be a biased operation, so that the two subsets we build *always* appear different, even if the corresponding bit is 0. The answer to the statistical tests we tried is *always* positive, at a very high level of confidence. So, the question we have to ask is rather: "are these two samples 'very' different, or simply different ?".

Luckily, statistics can though be used to answer that question: we can simply decide that our two subsets are very different when the observed value for the statistic is 'very high', and that they are simply different when the value is 'not so high'. The problem will now be to decide what "very high" and "not so high" mean[4], and we will have to tune up some swap value for each key we attack. Some heuristics can help us in this tuning operation, but we will not describe them here, as there is a more efficient approach:

Aiming our attack at the *square* operation solves both of these problems.

3.4   Attacking the Square

There is a more subtle way to take advantage of our knowledge of the Montgomery algorithm: instead of the multiplication phase, we could turn ourselves to the *square* phase.

The idea is quite similar to that of section 3.2: suppose we know the first $i - 1$ bits of the key and attack the ith. We begin by executing the first $i - 1$ steps of the square and multiply algorithm, stopping just before the possible - but unknown - multiplication by m due to bit k_i ; we denote by m_{temp} the temporary value we obtain.

First, we suppose k_i is set. If this is the case, the two next operations to be performed are

1. multiply m_{temp} by m,
2. square the result,

and both of these operations will be done using the Montgomery algorithm. We simply execute the multiplication and then, for the square, determine whether an additional reduction will be necessary or not. Doing this for every message, we divide our samples set in two subsets M_1 (additional reduction) and M_2 (no reduction).

Next, we suppose $k_i = 0$. In this case, no multiplication will take place, and the next operation will simply be

$$m_{temp}^2.$$

Once again, we divide the samples set in two subsets M_3 and M_4, depending on whether this square requires a reduction or not.

Clearly, only one of these separations makes sense, depending on the actual value of k_i. All we have to do now is to compare the separations: if the timing

---

[4] For example, attacking a 128-bit key using 50 000 samples and the χ^2 test, a typical observed value for the statistic was about 4300, which is much, much higher than $\chi^2_{0.95}$. We can however decide that values above 4320 correspond to "very different", while values beyond 4320 correspond to "simply different". This may look tedious on a theoretical point of view, but works well in practice and allowed us to recover the secret key.

difference between M_1 and M_2 is more important than that between M_3 and M_4, then conclude $k_i = 1$, otherwise, conclude $k_i = 0$.

Back to formalization, to attack bit k_i knowing bits $k_0, \ldots, k_{i-1}$, we split the algorithm $A(m, k)$ into $L(m, k)$, which is the computations due to the additional reduction at the square phase at step $i + 1$, and $R(m, k)$, the remaining computations.

Compute

$$m_{temp} = (m^b)^2 \qquad \text{where } b = k_0 k_1 \ldots k_{i-1}.$$

We need two oracles,

$$O_1 : m \to \begin{cases} 1 \text{ if } (m_{temp} \cdot m)^2 \text{ is done with a reduction,} \\ 0 \text{ if } (m_{temp} \cdot m)^2 \text{ is done without a reduction,} \end{cases}$$

$$O_2 : m \to \begin{cases} 1 \text{ if } (m_{temp})^2 \text{ is done with a reduction,} \\ 0 \text{ if } (m_{temp})^2 \text{ is done without a reduction.} \end{cases}$$

Define

$$\begin{aligned}
M_1 &= \{m \in M : O_1(m) = 1, \} \\
M_2 &= \{m \in M : O_1(m) = 0, \} \\
M_3 &= \{m \in M : O_2(m) = 1, \} \\
M_4 &= \{m \in M : O_2(m) = 0, \} \\
F_k &: M_k \to R : m \to F_k(m) = T(m), \qquad \text{for } 1 \leq k \leq 4.
\end{aligned}$$

If $k_i = 1$, we have

$$\begin{cases} F_1 = T^R + T^L \\ F_2 = T^R \\ F_3 = F_4 \qquad (= T^R + T^L \cdot O_1, \text{ but this is not important}) \end{cases}$$

and thus $\mu(F_1) > \mu(F_2)$, while $\mu(F_3) = \mu(F_4)$.

On the other hand, if $k_i = 0$, we have

$$\begin{cases} F_1 = F_2 \\ F_3 = T^R + T^L \\ F_4 = T^R \end{cases}$$

and thus $\mu(F_3) > \mu(F_4)$, while $\mu(F_1) = \mu(F_2)$.

Testing which of these conditions is true should reveal the value of k_i.

Remark: The last bit cannot be revealed by this attack and must thus be guessed.

This attack does not suffer from the problems mentioned in previous section:

– Firstly, the operation we are observing (i.e. the square) does not involve a constant factor, and its behaviour appears to be much less biased than for the multiplication.

- Secondly, we do not have anymore to decide whether a separation makes sense or not: we have now to compare two separations and decide which is the most significant. We are thus relieved of the difficult task to tune up an appropriate swap value for a given key.

Using this attack, we were able to recover 128-bit keys with 20 000 timings. Some keys were disclosed with only 12 000 timings.

4   Statistics

We have not yet said very much about the statistics we have to use to compare samples, and that is mainly because they were not very useful in practice. We tried several of the tools that statistics offer to compare two samples, such as the Chi-square, Student, Hotteling, and even a test from non-parametric statistics, the Wald-Wolfowitz [Sie56] test. None of them offered really efficient results. Chi-square and Student provided criteria upon which a right decision could be made, but a simple comparison of the means of the two populations allowed the same decision, with a similar, if not better, success rate.

There is, however, a possible use for statistics: as the Chi-square test, for example, does not seem to yield the same errors as the means comparison, it can be used to provide us with some sort of level of confidence in the goodness of our choices. When both tests agree on the value of some bit, it is more probably right than when they disagree, and this can help us to detect erroneous deductions. We implemented this in practice, and it appeared to be of some help, but did not produce any significant breakthrough in efficiency.

The reason for this uselessness of statistics is probably the one we mentioned before, that is, Montgomery multiplications with constant modulus are not independent events, and our decision criteria are thus biased[5]. Perhaps a better understanding of *why* this bias appears would allow to derive an useful statistical test? Up to now, however, they seems to be limited to a role of confirmation.

5   Error-Detection

One remarkable property of our attack is that it has an error-detection property. This is easy to understand on an intuitive point of view: remember that the attack basically consists in simulating the computations until some point, then build two decision criteria, with only one of them making sense, depending on the searched value, and finally decide the bit value by observing which criterion actually makes sense. Also note that each step of the attack relies on the previous ones (we need the previous bit values to simulate the computation).

Now, suppose we made an erroneous decision for the value of bit k_i. In the following step, we will not correctly simulate the computations, so that the value

---

[5] This is also true for square, even it is at a much less extend than for multiplication by a constant factor.

m_{temp} we will obtain will not be the one involved in step $i + 1$. Our attempts to decide whether the Montgomery multiplications will involve an additional reduction or not will thus not make sense, and the criteria we will build will *both* be meaningless. This remains true for the following bits.

In practice, this translates to abnormally close values for the two separations: while, as long as the choices were right, the two separations were generally[6] easy to distinguish, one of them being clearly more significant than the other, they appear much more similar (and both bad) after an erroneous choice has been made. This fact is well illustrated in figure 4, showing the attack of a 512-bit key on the basis of 350 000 observations. The decision criterion is simply the difference between the mean times for the two subsets, and the graph shows the absolute value of $diff_1$ (the difference between M_1 and M_2) minus $diff_2$ (difference between M_3 and M_4). Clearly, an error has occurred near bit 149.

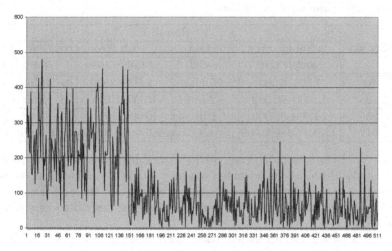

Fig. 4. Detection of an error for a 512-bit key

Once an error has been detected, it is not difficult to take back, make a different choice for the last chosen bit, and go ahead a few steps to see if things go better; if they do not, then we go back two steps, change the bit value, and so on.

In practice, this error-correction scheme allowed us to reduce significantly the amount of measures needed. Samples of 10 000 timings, for example, were sufficient to recover 128-bit keys, and some of them were revealed with as few as 6 000 timings.

---

[6] There are however some tedious cases, were the two criteria are uneasy to differentiate although no error has been made. That is why it is better to wait until several contiguous low values are observed before to conclude to an error.

6   Practical Results

Our attack was first implemented in Visual C++ 4.2 on a 200 MHz PentiumPro PC under Windows NT.

Timings were collected using an emulator of the CASCADE smart card, that was able to monitor the number of cycles between two points. This seems to be quite a realistic scenario: the amount of measures required for a real attack of the electronic device would probably be slightly larger, to filter out additional noise, but we believe it should not grow too much.

With about 10 000 samples (couples messages, time for modular exponentiation), we were able to break 128-bit keys, at a rate of about 4 bits/s. The speed for a 512-bit key was of a little more than 1 bit/minute and approximately 350 000 samples were needed. The implementation was not optimized for speed.

Our results summarize as follows:

Key size	Result				
	without error correction		with error correction	
	sample size	speed	sample size	speed
64	1 500–6 500	> 20 bits/s	1 500–4 500	> 20 bits/s
128	12 000–20 000	2 bits/s	6 000–10 000	4 bits/s
256	70 000–80 000	1 bit/4s	40 000–50 000	1 bit/2s
512	±350 000–400 000	1 bit/65s	200 000 – 300 000	1 bit/37s

However, these results correspond to a very high success rate: the error-correction algorithm we implemented was very simple and allowed us to correct errors only if they occur for a very small percentage of the bits. Experiments showed that the sample size grows very fast with the desired success rate (see e.g. figure 5).

A more sophisticated algorithm, that would for example explore several choices when a possible error is detected, handle the case of two successive errors, ..., would probably resist to a higher error rate, thus allowing to reduce drastically the amount of measures needed. As most of the computational effort consists in simulating the exponentiation steps for a large amount of data, the attack would also be very easy to parallelize.

7   Remarks about the Attack

Accuracy of measures. The timing variation we are basing our attack on is very small regarding the total computation. For example, a 512-bit exponentiation on the CASCADE chip takes about 7 400 000 cpu cycles, and the variation we are trying to detect is only 422 cycles long!

The accuracy in measures is therefore of great importance. As the rounding effect induced by less accurate measures can be considered as noise, a greater amount of measures would still make the attack possible, but the sample size would rapidly grow.

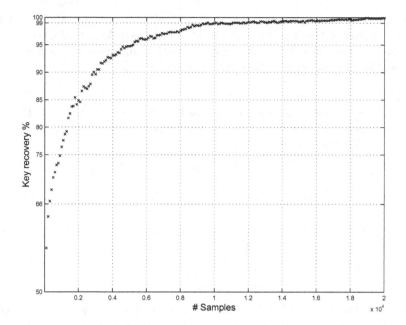

Fig. 5. Sample size / success rate dependence

Choice of Messages. It is worth noting that we simply need to be able to determine the value of $O(m)$ for each message: we do not have to *build* messages for which the oracle will have a given value. This is important because many protocols will not accept to sign arbitrary message, but will require for these to have a specific format (e.g. to exhibit some redundancy). As long as we are able to trace the transformations preceding the modular exponentiation, the attack can be carried out.

Knowledge of the Implementation. We also insist on the fact that we do not need too many details about the implementation of the cryptographic algorithm itself. All we have to know is that the exponentiation is square-and-multiply with Montgomery multiplication. It is amazing to note that one of the authors began with the timing-attack program before the CASCADE library was available for him. He thus decided to build his own exponentiation routine as a first target. When he finally received the CASCADE library, he discovered that his attack program did not need any modification to work against it.

Possible Improvements. Even if the number of samples at disposal in not sufficient to discover the complete key, the attack is likely to reveal a part of it : we observed that samples twice as small as the required size for complete recovery could reveal 3/4 of the key before the first error occurs (as we have seen, nothing significant is produced afterwards). Therefore, any method allowing Eve to guess a part of the key before carrying out the attack or to deduce the last bits once the first ones are know can dramatically improve performances.

Consider for example the frequent case where:

- the public exponent $e = 3$,
- the secret exponent k is calculated such that $k \cdot e = 1 \mod (p-1)(q-1)$ (the important point is that we do not use the $lcm(p-1, q-1)$),
- p and q have the same l-bit length.

We have:

$$k \cdot 3 - s(p-1)(q-1) = 1, \quad \text{with} \quad s = 1 \text{ or } 2,$$

$$k \cdot 3 = \begin{cases} 1 + 1[n - (p+q) + 1] \\ 1 + 2[n - (p+q) + 1] \end{cases}$$

$$k = \begin{cases} [n - (p+q) + 2]/3 \\ [2n - 2(p+q) + 2]/3 \end{cases}$$

Because the length of n is twice the length of p and q, there is a great probability that the $l-3$ most significant bits (depending on the length of the propagation of a possible carry due to the subtraction by $p+q$) of the key k are the $l-3$ first bits of $n/3$. Eve can thus start the attack at the first unknown bit.

8 Other Targets and Further Research

The attack could easily be extended against some variants of the square and multiply algorithm. The implementation of RSAREF, for example, processes the bits two by two, performing two square followed by a multiplication by 1, m, m^2 or m^3, depending on whether the bits are 00, 01, 10 or 11. The attack could quite easily be adapted to this case.

Other cryptosystems involving a modular exponentiation are of course subject to the same attack. Consider for example the Diffie-Hellman key exchange protocol: to build a common secret parameter, Alice and Bob exchange the values g^x and g^y, where g is public and x, y are secret values, known only by Alice and Bob, respectively, but often kept constant. The common parameter, that only Alice and Bob can compute, is obtained by computing $(g^y)^x$ or $(g^x)^y$.

Now, suppose Alice wants to discover Bob's secret parameter y. She chooses several random values $x_1, \ldots, x_N$, sends the values g^{x_i} (e.g. pretending to be someone different each time) and collects the corresponding response times (which can be, for example if Bob is a smart card, measured with very good accuracy). Clearly, the conditions of our attack are fulfilled. As a typical value for a Diffie-Hellman key size is 160 bits, a few thousand exchanges would suffice to discover the secret key.

Other protocol could probably be attacked in the same way. It must however be noted that the basis of the exponentiation (i.e., the parameter x in x^k) has to be known for the attack to be carried out as described here. Therefore, systems such as DSS, ... seem less vulnerable, although a more detailed study should have to be carried out.

One important weakness of our attack is that it cannot be carried out against systems using the Chinese Remainder Theorem for modular exponentiation. Kocher [Koc96] proposes some leads for a timing attack of the CRT, but it is not known whether such an attack would be practicable.

When developing the attack, we faced many difficulties on building a rigorous mathematical model explaining *why* things work. In fact, we encountered more than once the strange situation of building a model which should reveal some information, implementing it, and discovering that the system behaves differently than expected, *although the information is well revealed*. It seems that other researchers interested in the timing attack have faced the same problems with theory. A complete theoretical model would of course be useful, although we believe it is a real challenge.

9   Countermeasures

Three countermeasures come to mind when we try to protect ourselves against the above attack.

The first one is to modify the Montgomery algorithm so that an additional subtraction is always carried out, even if its result is simply discarded afterwards. This modification is easy to carry out, does not decrease performance very much and clearly defeats the attack. One must however be very careful when implementing it and make sure to remove *all* time variation. For example, it later turned out that the CASCADE implementation we were attacking was using this countermeasure, but in a too naive way: additional subtraction was always carried out, which hid most time variation, but the difference between discarding and copying its result still induced a difference of some clock cycles (422 in 512-bit version). This countermeasure did not prevent the attack to be carried out, it simply made it a bit more difficult. Experiments showed that, with this naive protection removed, the attack would have been efficient with ten times less samples.

Even with a careful implementation, it cannot be guaranteed that this would make the system immune to *any* type of timing attack, only against those which exploit the reduction of the multiplication algorithm.

Another countermeasure, suggested by [Koc96], would be to use some blinding: before computing the modular exponentiation, choose a random pair[7] (v_i, v_f) such that $v_f^{-1} = v_i^e$; multiply the message by v_i (mod n) and multiply back the output by v_f (mod n) to obtain the searched result. As Eve can no more simulate the internal computations, she can hardly exploit her knowledge of the timing measurements.

It is worth noting that the attack is quite general, in the sense that it was not directed against the peculiar case of a Montgomery multiplication, but against

---

[7] [Koc96] proposes a way to generate such pairs at a reasonable cost.

the fact that this algorithm is constant-time, except for a potential final reduction. This means that the use of other modular multiplication schemes, such as the standard versions of the Barrett or Quisquater algorithms, would not protect the system against our timing attack.

However, Dhem [Dhe98] recently proposed an improvement of these multiplications schemes, allowing several modular multiplications to be chained with only *one* extra reduction being performed after the last multiplication. This scheme seems to be especially interesting here, as it would suppress our attack's main target.

An often proposed countermeasure is simply to add random delays to the algorithm, in order to hide time variation. We insist on the fact that this countermeasure is inefficient, as it is equivalent to adding white noise to a source. Such noise can easily be filtered out for a linear increase in sample size.

10   Conclusion

This paper shows that the timing attack represents a practical, important threat against cryptosystems implementations, namely in the case of a smart card, where the attacker can quite easily collect large amount of message decryptions and measure time with high precision.

It is also shown that a very good understanding on the way the timing attack works is necessary in order to be able to implement efficient countermeasures. The implementation we broke, for example, possessed some protection means, which turned out to be insufficient.

It is important to note that the attack is quite general, in the sense that it does not require a very detailed knowledge of the implementation: all we have to know, besides some general hardware characteristics such as the word size, is that the modular exponentiation is done using the square and multiply and Montgomery algorithm. Computation details, timings necessary for specific operations, . . . , are not necessary. This is an important improvement on Kocher's attack.

As shown in previous section, the attack is also general in the sense that it could have been directed against other classical modular multiplication schemes, if they are used in there standard form and not with Dhem's improvement.

In view of these results, the design of the CASCADE smart card has been modified to make it immune against the timing attack. It is however our belief that few smart cards take care of this, and that similar attacks could be successfully conducted against many of them.

Acknowledgements. The authors wish to thank Gael Hachez for useful comments and technical help, and HP Labs, Bristol, UK for the grant of the PCs which were used to carry out the attack.

References

[Cas]   Cascade (Chip Architecture for Smart CArds and portable intelligent DEvices). Project funded by the European Community, see http://www.dice.ucl.ac.be/crypto/cascade.

[Dhe98]   J.F. Dhem. *Design of an efficient public-key cryptographic library for RISC-based smart cards*. PhD thesis, Université catholique de Louvain - UCL Crypto Group - Laboratoire de microélectronique (DICE), May 1998.

[Koc96]   P. Kocher. Timing attacks on implementations of Diffie-Hellman, RSA, DSS, and other systems. In N. Koblitz, editor, *Advances in Cryptology - CRYPTO '96, Santa Barbara, California*, volume 1109 of *LNCS*, pages 104–113. Springer, 1996.

[Ler98]   P.-A. Leroux. Timing cryptanalysis : Breaking security protocols by measuring transaction times. Master's thesis, Université catholique de Louvain - UCL Crypto Group, June 1998.

[RSA78]   R.L. Rivest, A. Shamir, and L. Adleman. A method for obtaining digital signatures and public-key cryptosystems. In *Proc. Communications of the ACM*, volume 21, pages 120–126. ACM, February 1978.

[Sie56]   S. Siegel. *Nonparametric Statistics*. McGraw-Hill, 1956.

[Wil98]   J.-L. Willems. Timing attack of secured devices (in French). Master's thesis, Université catholique de Louvain - UCL Crypto Group, June 1998.

Techniques for Low Cost Authentication and Message Authentication *

Henri Gilbert

France Télécom
CNET DTL-SSR
38-40 Rue du Général Leclerc
92131 Issy les Moulineaux, France
henri.gilbert@cnet.francetelecom.fr

Abstract. Unconditional security techniques may represent an advantageous alternative to computational security techniques for smart card systems providing authentication or message authentication when the number of authentications needed during the lifetime of each key is limited. In this paper we propose simple algorithms based on modulo 2 scalar products among binary vectors which are easy to implement in so-called synchronous cards, require a reasonable amount of secret key bits (typically 10 to 20 bits per authentication), and provide provably secure authentication and message authentication. Applications mainly include low cost prepaid cards for telephone, parking meters, transportation, automatic vending machines, etc.

Keywords. information authentication, payment systems, prepaid cards, telephone cards, unconditional security, synchronous cards.

1 Introduction

Almost all existing applications of cryptology are based on computational security, except a few military or diplomatic applications based on unconditional security techniques, e.g. the well known one time pad for encryption, or authentication codes for message integrity [1]. In commercial applications, keys need to be short enough to be easy to manage, and on the other hand cryptologic algorithms are generally expected to provide security against an adversary capable to collect a large number of related inputs and outputs. In other words, cryptologic algorithms generally need to remain secure far beyond the "unicity distance" [2], and thus cannot provide unconditional security; their security is based upon computational intractability assumptions.

However in low cost devices requiring some integrity protection by means of authentication or message authentication as for instance prepaid telephone cards, prepaid cards for transportation, automatic vending machines, parking meters, etc., the number of times a device performs an authentication before being thrown or reloaded is very limited. In such applications, the maximum number of runs of the

---

* The authentication and message authentication techniques presented in this paper are subject to a France Télécom patent.

J.J. Quisquater and B. Schneier (Eds.): CARDIS 2000, LNCS 1820, pp. 183–192, 2000.
© Springer-Verlag Berlin Heidelberg 2000

algorithm is often very low (100 is a typical order of magnitude), and even with reasonable limits on the keylength (say one to a few kilobits) it may become sufficient to require that the algorithm be secure under the unicity distance.

In this paper, we show how to take advantage from such unusual security requirements. We propose authentication and message authentication algorithms which differ from the usual computationally secure secret-key designs by the following distinctive properties :

- much less complex algorithms, well fit for low cost cards with severe processing limitations, in particular so-called *synchronous cards*[1].
- longer (but not huge) keys : 1000 bits is a typical order of magnitude, instead of 64 to 128 ;
- provision of unconditional security, instead of computational security.

Although the unconditional security properties of authentication and message authentication protocols presented in this paper are not totally unrelated to those of so-called authentication codes [1], the problematic and the requirements are here quite different. As a matter of fact, we investigate protocols in which the same secret key must inherently be reused for several authentications or message authentications in order to prevent replay attacks, whereas in authentication codes a one time use of secret keys is usually considered. A detailed analysis of the specific requirements of the applications considered in this paper is provided in Section 2 hereafter.

In contrast to previous attempts to design practical unconditionally secure algorithms (see in particular [3] for an encryption algorithm proposal), our concern is even more to minimise the algorithm complexity than to achieve provable security.

The constructions proposed here show that in the context of information authentication, unconditional security techniques may provide both advantages.

This paper is organised as follows : in Section 2 we summarise the requirements of the intended applications, in particular low cost cards based payment systems, with respect to the structure of the authentication protocols, the security provided by the authentication or message authentication algorithms, and the preferred basic operations involved in the cryptologic computations. In Sections 3 and 4 we propose explicit constructions meeting the requirements of Section 2.

2 Requirements for the Intended Applications

2.1 Structure of the Authentication Protocols

The authentication techniques described in this paper are primarily intended for protecting payment or access control systems for telecommunications, transportation or distribution services, in particular systems based on low-cost pre-paid cards, or

---

[1] Synchronous cards are very low cost cards with some wired logic, capable to perform a few elementary operations at each pulse received from an external clock. In Europe most existing telephone cards are synchronous cards. The processing capabilities of synchronous cards are far from being sufficient to implement usual secret key ciphers, e.g. DES. The design of computationally secure algorithms for such cards is a very challenging task.

any other kind of physically protected devices distributed to the users. In such systems, the cards (or devices) are involved in transactions with an application. In the cryptologic protocols performed during these transactions, the application usually represents the *verifier,* whereas the device represents the *prover.* Authentication or message authentication are based on secret key techniques : each card shares an individual *secret key* K with the application[2].

We assume that the cards or devices are capable to enforce, by physical protection methods, a ***maximum number of authentications*** (or message authentications), denote by Cmax, for the life time of the card key K. This can be done for instance by updating inside a card a *counter value* c, initially set to 0 at key installation, and incremented by 1 at each authentication. When the counter value Cmax is reached, the card is blocked, and cannot longer be used. In the particular case of a reloadable card, the card can however be unblocked and the counter c reset to 0 when new personalisation parameters (new card number, new key value K, etc.) are written in the card.

The main purposes of authentication and message authentication protocols are :
- for both protocols, to prevent that a fraudster (for instance the owner of a valid card) be able to produce fake cards behaving in the same way as a valid card.
- for message authentication protocols, to prevent that a fraudster be able to misuse a valid card by altering some data in the card-application exchanges. For instance, when payment is managed inside a pre-paid card, an application may need to receive an authenticated value of the credit left in the card after each charging instruction. For message authentication, we will focus in the sequel on the particular case of authenticating data contained inside the card.

Of course, these protocols must prevent replay attacks. In the context of this paper we expect the authentication and message authentication protocols to provide protection against replay even to a *'memoryless' verifier*, possessing no knowledge of the history of the previous transactions (e.g. previous authentication exchanges, current counter value of a given card, etc.). This is motivated by practical considerations : the systems considered are often decentralised, or at least cannot perform a systematic interrogation and update of a central data base at each transaction. This 'memoryless verifier' requirement has a crucial impact upon the authentication and message authentication algorithms. It is not compatible with the following types of solutions : the use of 'one time passwords' for authentication ; the mere use of authentication codes for message authentication ; the use of 'one-time' or 'tree' identification/signature schemes (as for instance the schemes proposed in [4] and [5]). In order to take this requirement into account, we assume a classical challenge-response structure for the authentication (resp message authentication) protocols. The structure of these protocols is depicted in figure 1. In order to authenticate (resp

---

[2] In some decentralised applications, it may be convenient to derive the value of K from the serial number SN of the card and an application master key MK, using a pseudo random generator G :
$$K = G(MK, SN)$$
Thus K only needs to be securely stored in the cards, and can be reconstructed at any time from MK by the security modules of the system. In some other applications, the key K associated with a given card may be simply drawn at random, and securely stored in the card and in one or more authentication centers in the system.

authenticate the value D of a d-bit data word contained inside the card), the verifier sends a randomly generated r-bit challenge R to the card, and checks the m-bit response S deduced by the card from the key K, the random challenge R and, in the case of message authentication, the data D. The current counter value c may also (for some schemes) be involved in the computation of S ; if this is the case, the response must contain the c value.

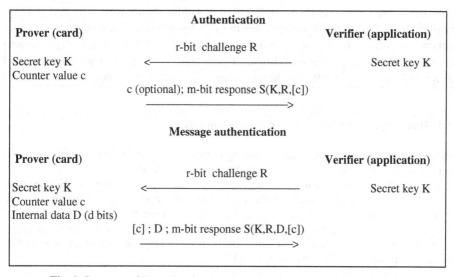

Fig. 1. Structure of the authentication and message authentication protocols

2.2 Security Requirements on the Algorithms

The security requirements on the authentication algorithm have to express that even the owner of a card must be unable to exploit the previous authentication exchanges he may have observed or triggered to predict authentication responses to new challenges without the card being involved. We state them as follows :

Based on the observation of a number $c \leq Cmax$ of authentication responses S^j, j=1 to c, corresponding to c known or even chosen challenges R^j, j = 1 to c, it must be impossible to a cheater to provide a correct response (c', S) to a new challenge R with a success probability better than $1/2^m$ for a non-negligible fraction of the R values.

The security requirements on the **message** authentication algorithm are slightly more complex : a cheater receiving a challenge R from the application and wanting to authenticate a data value D, for instance the owner of a card, must be unable to exploit previous **message** authentication exchanges, and also additional authentication exchanges he might be able to trigger in the card once knowing the challenge R, in order to provide a correct response to R authenticating D without D being present in the card[3]. We state them as follows :

> Based on the observation of a number $c \le Cmax$ of authentication responses S^j, $j=1$ to c, corresponding to c known or even chosen challenges R^j , j = 1 to c and data D^j, j= 1 to c, it must be impossible to a cheater wanting to authenticate a data value D to provide a correct response (c', S) to R with a probability better than $1/2^m$ except for a negligible fraction of the R values. This must still hold even if the cheater is able to obtain, once knowing R, up to Cmax-c additional (j, D^j, R^j, S^j), $c < j \le Cmax$ counter-data-challenge-response 4-uples where the D^j may be any chosen values different from D, and the R^j may be any values chosen by the cheater.

2.3 Basic Operations Involved in the Computations

In the intended applications, the computing capabilities of the provers device may be very low, in particular when the provers device is a synchronous card.

In order to take this requirement into account, the explicit constructions proposed in Sections 3 and 4 are based on the mere use of modulo 2 dot-products and modulo 2 additions. If $x = (x_1,...,x_k)$ and $y = (y_1,...,y_k)$ are two k-bit words, the dot-product of x and y (resp the modulo 2 addition of x and y), denoted by x.y (resp x+y), is the binary value of scalar product of x and y (respectively the sum of x and y) in the the k-dimensional GF(2) vector space $\{0,1\}^k$:

$$x.y = (\sum_{i=1}^{k} x_i.y_i) \bmod 2 \quad ; \quad x+y = (x_1+y_1 \bmod 2, ..., x_k+y_k \bmod 2)$$

Scalar products and modulo 2 additions are extremely well fit for implementation on synchronous cards, even for relatively large values of k. For instance, the computation of a scalar product is quite easy to perform in k elementary steps of one clock pulse, where step i consists in computing the logical AND of the bits x_i and y_i and accumulating it (by means of an XOR) in a one-bit cell initially set to zero.

3 Authentication

The proposed authentication method is depicted below. The random challenge is a r-bit word R. The prover's secret key is an m x r binary matrix $K=(K_{ij})_{i=1..m,j=1..r}$.

---

[3] For instance assume a payment system where cards manage an internal credit counter, and where the credit of a card can be decreased (never increased) by means of a special instruction. Assume the application wants to make sure that an instruction to decrease the credit of a card from 10$ to 3$ has been correctly performed in the card, by means of message authentication. Further assume that the owner of the card prevents the decrease instruction from being transmitted to the card, decreases instead by himself the credit in his card from 10$ to 9$ and then from 9$ to 8$, and collects from his card responses authenticating the 9$ and 8$ values. It must be impossible to such a cheater to reconstruct the correct response authenticating the 3$ value from the collected authentication values for 9$ and 8$, in order to make a fraudulous benefit of 8-3 = 5$.

Depending upon the application, the m.r bits of K are either drawn at random (as independant unbiased bits) or generated as the output of a pseudo random generator, as explained in a note to Section 2. The response is the m-bit vector $S=(S_i)_{i=1..m}$ given by the matrix vector product of K and R over GF(2) : S=K.R.

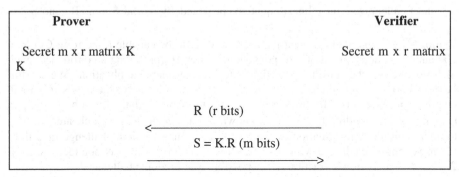

Prover	**Verifier**
Secret m x r matrix K	Secret m x r matrix K

R (r bits)

S = K.R (m bits)

Fig. 2. The proposed authentication method

The complexity of the above computation is very low. It bounded over by m binary XORs and m binary AND operations for each of the r bits of the R challenge. For reasonable values of m, the computations can be easily performed on a synchronous card.

The security of the above method results from the following proposition :

Proposition 1. After $c \leq Cmax$ authentications, the probability over the value of a new random challenge R that a cheater possessing the c previous challenge-response pairs (R^j , S^j) be able to predict any information on the new response S to the challenge R (i.e. be able to predict S with a probability better than $1/2^m$) is bounded over by the quantity $\dfrac{2^{Cmax}}{2^r}$.

Proof : The single situation where the chater may be capable to predict some information is when R belongs to the GF(2)-subspace spanned by $R^1,..,R^c$. The cardinal of the set of unfavourable R values is thus bounded over by the quantity 2^{Cmax}, whereas R is randomly drawn from the $\{0,1\}^r$ space, of cardinal 2^r. As a matter of fact :

-    when $R \in < R^1,.., R^c >$, there exist c binary coefficients $\varepsilon_1, , \varepsilon_c$ such that

$$R = \sum_{j=1}^{c} \varepsilon_j R^j .$$ Since for any fixed value of K S is a GF(2)-linear function of R, this implies $S = \sum_{j=1}^{c} \varepsilon_j S^j$. In this unfavourable case, the cheater knows the correct S response.

- when $R \notin < R^1,..,R^c >$, then for all the $S = (S_1,..,S_m)$ candidate responses in $\{0,1\}^m$, the number of K keys compatible with the $(R^1,S^1) , , (R^c,S^c)$ and (R,S) challenge response pairs is the same (and is equal to exactly $1/2^m$ of the number of keys compatible with the $(R^1, S^1), \ldots, (R^c, S^c)$ challenge response pairs), because for each $i = 1$ to m value, the linear equation $S_i = \sum_{j=1}^{r} K_{ij}.R_j$ in the r unknonw $(K_{ij})_{j=1..r}$ is independent from the c linear equations provided by R^1 and $S_i^1, \ldots, R^c$ and S_i^c.

Example : Assume that we want the user's device to be capable to perform Cmax = 100 authentications, and that a response-length m = 16 (providing a confidence level of 1-1/65536) can be considered sufficient for the considered application. We can for instance chose a random challenge size r of 128, which leads for the key K to a total length n = 2048 bits. In this example, the probability that after observing the responses corresponding to $c \leq$ Cmax known or chosen challenges, a cheater be able to infer from it any information on the response to a new random challenge (and thus to answer the R challenge with a probability better than $1/2^{16}$) is bounded over by $2^{r-Cmax} = 2^{-28}$ - a negligible fraction of the possible new random challenges[4].

4 Message Authentication

The construction we propose here is an application, in the context of replay immune message authentication against a "memoryless verifier", of the idea that the well known one-time pad is helpful in message authentication, because it allows for repeatedly using the same authentication code with a constant authentication key in an unconditionally secure way, which was developed in general terms by Carter and Wegman [7] and applied to LFSR-based constructions by Hugo Krawczyk in [6]. It also has some connection with an unconditionally secure authentication method proposed in [8]- but the reuse of the same authentication key for several messages, which is an essential feature of the scheme discussed here, is not addressed in [8].

The random challenge is an r-bit word R. The message to be authenticated is a d-bit word D. The n-bit key consists of two parts : a m .(r+d) binary matrix K and a m.Cmax binary matrix K'. The m-bit column vectors of K' will be denoted by K'[1] to K'[Cmax]. Depending upon the application, the n=m.(r+d+Cmax) bits of the (K, K') key are either drawn at random, as independent unbiased bits, or generated as the output of a pseudo random generator, as explained in a note to Section 2.

The message authentication is depicted in figure 2. The message authentication code S corresponding to the counter value c, the random challenge value R, and the data value D is the m-bit vector given by

$$S = K.(R\|D) \oplus K'[c]$$

where $R\|D$ denotes the concatenation of the R and D words.

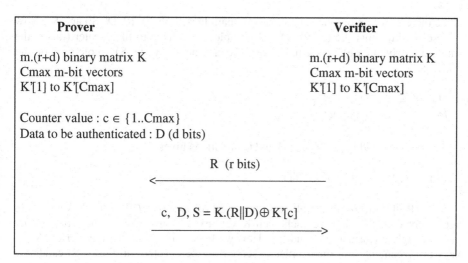

Fig. 3. The proposed message authentication method

The complexity of the computations is very low. It bounded over by m binary XORs and m binary AND operations for each of the r+d bits of the R∥D challenge and data word. For reasonable values of m, such computations can be easily performed on a synchronous card.

The security of the above method results from the following proposition :

Proposition 2. After $c \leq$ Cmax message authentications, the probability over the value of a new random challenge R that a cheater wanting to authenticate a data value D be able to predict any correct (i.e. consistent with R and D) response (c',S) with a probability larger than $1/2^m$ is bounded over by $Cmax/2^r$, even if the cheater is capable to obtain :
- the c previous (j, R^j, D^j, S^j) counter-data-challenge-response 4-uples ;
- up to Cmax-c subsequent (j, R^j, D^j, S^j) counter-data-challenge-response 4-uples, where D^j may be any values <u>different from D</u>, and the R^j any value chosen by the cheater ;

Proof : The single unfavourable case is when R belongs to the set of the c first random challenge values $R^1,...,R^c$: this occurs for at most Cmax values out of the 2^r possible R values.

Outside from this unfavourable situation, R differs from the R^1 to R^c values available to the cheater, and D differs from the D^j, j > c values, so for each of the (j, R^j, D^j, S^j) 4-uples available to the cheater the $R^j\|D^j$ word differs from R∥D.

This implies that for all other R values, for any (c', S) $\in$ {1..Cmax}x{0,1}^{m} candidate response, the information on the key K contained in the observed 4-uples does not provide the cheater with any information as whether the (c', R, D, S) 4-uple is correct or not.

As a matter of fact, due to the use of the K' one-time key, none of the available (j, R^j, D^j, S^j) j≠c' 4-uples provides the cheater with any information on K : for any K value there exists an unique $K'[j]$ value compatible with the (j, R^j, D^j, S^j) and K. Now for j=c', assume that the $(c', R^{c'}, D^{c'}, S^{c'})$ 4-uple is available to the cheater (this is the single non-trivial case).This 4-uple and the candidate (c', R, D, S) 4-uple provide the relations

(1) $S^{c'} = K . R^{c'} \| D^{c'} \oplus K'[c']$
(2) $S = K . R \| D \oplus K'[c']$

The modulo 2 addition of the (1) and (2) relations gives :

(1') $S^{c'} \oplus S = K.(R^{c'} \| D^{c'} \oplus R \| D)$

Since $R^{c'} \| D^{c'}$ differs from $R \| D$ (as stated above) exactly $1/2^m$ of the K keys are in agreement with (1'), and for each such K key, exactly one $K'[c']$ value, provided by (1), is in agreement with (1) and (2). Thus we have shown that the number of (K,K') keys in agreement with the 4-uples observed by the cheater and the (c',S) candidate response does not depend upon the S value.

Remarks

1. The particular case d = 0 (which means in practice that no data are involved in the computations) provides an alternative to the construction of Section 3 for mere authentication.
2. The construction of this Section can be generalised, using the concept of universal family of universal hashing [5][7]. It can easily be shown that if the K linear mapping is replaced by any family of r+d bits to m bits universal functions indexed by a key, the security result of Proposition 2 is still valid. Some of the resulting constructions might be slightly more effective in terms of key length, but not much more in practice (because the mx(r+d) bits overhead is not large as compared with the information theoretic bound m x Cmax), and probably at the expense of an increase of the algorithm complexity.

Example : Assume that we want the user's device to be capable to perform Cmax = 100 authentications, and that a response-length m = 16 (providing a confidence level of 1-1/65536) can be considered sufficient for the considered application. Let us further assume a size d=16 bits for the internal data D we want to authenticate, and a size r = 24 bits for the random challenges R. We are led to a key length n = m.(Cmax + r + d) = 2240 bits for the key (K,K') key. The probability over a random challenge R that a cheater be able to correctly authenticate a given data value D with a probability better than $1/2^{16}$ without D being present in the card is bounded over by $Cmax/2^r \approx 2^{-17}$- a negligible fraction of the possible new random challenges.

---

[5] A set H of n-bit to m-bit functions is called a universal family of hash functions if
$\forall (x,x') \in \{0,1\}^n \times \{0,1\}^n (x \neq x') \Rightarrow (\forall y,y' \in \{0,1\}^m \times \{0,1\}^m \ Pr_{h \in H} \{h(x)=y \text{ and } h(x')=y'\}= 1/2^{2m})$

5 Conclusions

The constructions described in Sections 3 and 4 are only based on binary additions and binary dot-products. They require extremely limited computing capabilities and keys of moderate length   (approximately 2000 bits for 100 authentications with an authentication response size m = 16 bits, which is close to the mxCmax = 1600 bits information theoretic bound for perfect authentication), and are, as shown in Section particularly adapted for an implementation on synchronous smart cards. Thus they represent a cost-effective solution for the protection of low cost cards, e.g. pre-paid telephone cards.

These constructions are in principle also applicable when more powerful devices (e.g. IC-cards equipped with an 8-bit microprocessor) are available to the provers and verifiers. In this case however,   secret-key algorithms, e.g. triple DES, are cost effective, and the single remaining merit of the methods we suggest here is to provide some provable security, at the expense of limiting the number of algorithm runs. The simplicity of the algorithms is less crucial here,   and variants of the above constructions based on universal families of hash functions rather than the key-dependent GF(2)-linear mappings used in this paper might deserve some investigation. It might also make sense in this different context to design hybrid algorithms offering provable unconditional security for a sufficient number of computations and computational security for any larger number of computations.

References

[DH]   W. Diffie and M. Hellman. New directions in cryptography. In *IEEE Transactions on Information Theory*, Vol. IT-22, pages 644-654, Nov. 1976.

[DSS]   Digital Signature Standard. In *FIPS 186*, US Department of Commerce/NIST, 1994.

[1]   G. J. Simmons, "A survey of Information Authentication",in *Contemporary Cryptology, The science of information integrity*, ed. G.J. Simmons, IEEE Press, New York, 1992.

[2]   C.E. Shannon, "Communication theory of secrecy systems", *Bell Syst. Tech. J.*, vol.28, pp 656-715, Oct. 1949.

[3]   U.M. Maurer, "A provably-secure strongly-randomized cipher", in *Advances in Cryptology - EUROCRYPT'90*, Lecture notes in Computer Science, vol.473, Springer-Verlag, pp361-373.

[4]   L. Lamport,   "Constructing Digital Signatures from One-Way Functions", *Technical Report SRI* intl. CSL-98, 1979.

[5]   R. Merkle, "A certified digital signature", in *Advances in Cryptology - CRYPTO'89*, Lecture notes in Computer Science, vol.435, Springer-Verlag, pp.218-238.

[6]   H. Krawczyk, "LFSR-based Hashing and Authentication", in *Advances in Cryptology - CRYPTO'94*, Lecture notes in Computer Science, vol.839, Springer-Verlag, pp129-139.

[7]   M.N Wegman and J.L Carter, Universal hash functions, *JCSS*, 18(2), pp 143-154.

[8]   Y. Desmedt, "Unconditionally secure authentication schemes and practical and theoretical consequences", in *Advances in Cryptology - CRYPTO'85*, Lecture notes in Computer Science, vol.218, Springer-Verlag, pp 42-55.

Enhancing SESAMEV4 with Smart Cards

Mark Looi[1], Paul Ashley[1], Loo Tang Seet[1], Richard Au[1], Gary Gaskell[1],
and Mark Vandenwauver[2]

[1] Information Security Research Centre
School of Data Communications
Queensland University of Technology
GPO Box 2434, Brisbane, Queensland 4001, Australia
{m.looi,p.ashley,w.au,g.gaskell}@ qut.edu.au
lt.seet@student.qut.edu.au

[2] ESAT/COSIC
Kardinaal Mercierlaan 94
3001 Heverlee, BELGIUM
mark.vandenwauver@esat.kuleuven.ac.be

Abstract. SESAMEV4 is a security architecture that supports role based access control with single sign-on facilities for heterogenous distributed network environments. Several vulnerabilities are identified in SESAMEV4's user authentication process. This paper proposes four options for enhancing this user authentication process by integrating smart cards into SESAMEV4. The proposals are shown to successfully increase the level of security of SESAMEV4 and will be shown to correctly operate with existing SESAMEV4 applications and servers, with no modifications required to the applications or servers.

1 Introduction

As the use of networked computing systems within organisations becomes more and more widespread, so does the desire to simplify the user authentication process while retaining or increasing the level of security provided. With this increase in networked computer systems, we have seen a general corresponding decrease in ease of use. Users are generally required to manage several computer accounts, with potentially different usernames and passwords, and with different file systems and network resources available.

Along with this, there has been an increase in the level of security required. Attackers are becoming more sophisticated, with greater access to attacking tools, and with greater access to networked systems. Simply put, attackers have now more opportunity to break into systems, and as such, added security measures are essential.

There have been several systems proposed to address these issues. One of these systems is an architecture proposed to meet the security requirements of large organisations with a diverse range of networked systems, and with a large and distributed body of employees. This system is SESAMEV4, the Secure European System for Applications in a Multi-vendor Environment [Kaijser, 1993] [Kaijser *et al*, 1994].

J.-J. Quisquater and B. Schneier (Eds.): CARDIS 2000, LNCS 1820, pp. 193–202, 2000.
© Springer-Verlag Berlin Heidelberg 2000

SESAMEV4 is a role based, single sign-on system, which has strong security requirements and features. However, SESAMEV4 user authentication is still based around the concept of a username or stored authenticating information (a private key stored on a local filesystem). As we discuss later, these schemes are vulnerable to certain types of attacks.

To increase the level of security further, we investigated methods by which we could incorporate smart cards into SESAMEV4. The primary consideration in our research work was that of security. This paper will report on the results of the research work, the various designs considered, and on progress towards the actual implementation of selected designs.

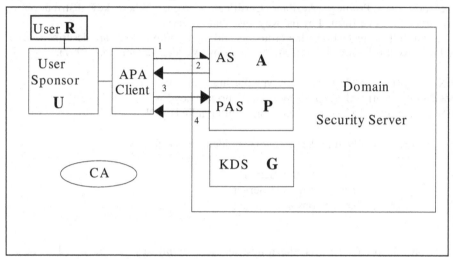

Fig. 1. The SESAME Architecture

2   Weaknesses of the Existing SESAMEV4 User Authentication

The existing SESAMEV4 architecture (shown in Figure 1) supports two user authentication models. The first model is a username and password authentication scheme based around the Kerberos V5 [Kohl & Neumann, 1993] model. The second and more secure model is based on public key cryptography and is referred to as "strong authentication".

A typical SESAMEV4 based network consists of users, client applications, server applications and the SESAMEV4 domain security server. The human and system entities are registered in and can be authenticated to the SESAMEV4 system. These entities are referred to as "principals". Principals can act in an active or in a passive role. Active principals, called initiators, request access. These active principals are often client applications. Passive principals, called targets, are accessed. These passive principals are often server applications. These basic SESAMEV4 components are described in [Ashley & Vandenwauver, 1998].

The SESAMEV4 core consists of three online authorities and one database. These are commonly located on the same machine, the domain security server. The three authorities are the Authentication Server (AS), the Privilege Attribute Server (PAS) and the Key Distribution Server (KDS).

The Authentication Server is responsible for performing authentication of the user. This authentication processes suffers from several weaknesses, and it is this authentication process that the research work reported in this paper attempts to address.

In SESAMEV4, a principal's access rights are referred to as "privileges". These are managed by the Privilege Attribute Server, and are conveyed to other servers in the form of a Privilege Attribute Certificate (PAC). Where key distribution is required, this is performed by the Key Distribution Server.

In the following sections, the protocols and modified protocols are described. The notation used is based on that from the paper by (Vandenwauver *et al*, 1997).

$ENC(K_{AB})(m)$: Message m encrypted using symmetric key K_{AB}
$SIGN(PK_A^{-1})(m)$: Message m signed with private key PK_A^{-1}
$ENC(PK_A)(m)$: Message m encrypted with public key PK_A

The entities involved in the protocols are identified as follows:

A   : Authentication Server
G   : Key Distribution Server
U   : User Sponsor
R   : User

Before the protocol starts, the following (long term) keys are assumed to be in place:

LK_{APG} : A long term symmetric key shared between A, P and G
LK_R : A long term symmetric key derived from user R's password
PK_A : Public key of A, known by the other participants
PK_A^{-1} : Private key of A, known only by A
DC_A : Directory Certificate of the public key of A

The following key is generated during a run of the protocol (a basic key is also known as a session key):

BK_{UPG} : Key generated by A for use between U and P

Various other attributes include:

RL_x : Requested Lifetime of a ticket
T_s, T_e : Start and end time of a ticket
t_I : Timestamp placed by i
r_I : Non-repeating number (nonce) generated by i

2.1 Weaknesses of the Password Authentication Model

The SESAMEV4 password authentication model draws heavily from Kerberos V5 [Kohl & Neumann, 1993]. This password authentication model is based on symmetric key cryptography. Under this model, all long term keys of principals must be stored on the domain security server, and known to the Authentication Server.

When a user intends to gain access to the system, the user executes the User Sponsor program **ses_login**. The user supplies the username, password and optional role name to the User Sponsor program. The User Sponsor sends an Authentication Server Request message to the Authentication Server. The message is equal to the KRB-AS-REQ message of Kerberos V5 with the optional pre-authentication enforced. By sending the encrypted timestamp, the authentication server will be able to verify if the local user has typed in the correct password.

$$R, G, RL_U, r_U, ENC(LK_R)(t_U)$$

This message authenticates the user, and identifies the target key distribution server and the requested lifetime of the basic key. The message also includes a nonce to prevent replay.

The Authentication Server then replies with a Authentication Server Reply message (KRB-AS-REP). This message contains a new session key (BK_{UPG}) encrypted with the key LK_R. The Kerberos Ticket Granting Ticket (TGT) is not relevant for the security of the authentication phase and will therefore not be discussed. The message takes the form:

$$ENC(LK_R)(BK_{UPG}, T_s, T_e, r_u, G), TGT$$

The User Sponsor program can decrypt this token with LK_R to retrieve the basic key BK_{UPG} that will be used in the rest of the protocol. As shown LK_R is only used in these first two steps of the protocol. Our smart card implementation will protect LK_R from being divulged. The later parts of the SESAMEV4 process are not relevant to the enhancements reported in this paper and are not discussed further.

This stage is equal to the authentication model of Kerberos V5. The original Kerberos (V4) was analyzed by Bellovin and Merritt in [Bellovin & Merritt, 1990] and some of those limitations are still present in the SESAMEV4 password authentication model. The model remains susceptible to offline password guessing attacks. The session key generated by the Authentication Server is returned to the client encrypted under the user's secret key LK_R. This secret key LK_R is derived from the user's password using a publicly known algorithm (a one-way function with a seed value). Therefore, if an attacker were to obtain the encrypted response from the SESAMEV4 Authentication Server, the attacker would be able to conduct an offline password guessing attack in order to decrypt the session key. This might succeed as the encrypted packet also contains recognizable data such as the time of day and the name of the network service requested.

Because of the limited password key space (printable characters) and the tendency of users to select easily remembered (and thus, easily guessed) passwords, this offline password guessing attack leads to a vulnerability in the SESAMEV4 authentication. It is also susceptible to other types of attacks. These include theft of the password through non-technical means, and through host based attack methods. Non-technical attacks are such as watching a user enter their password, and obtaining the password through the carelessness or negligence of the user (for example, if the user had their password written down and kept in a desk drawer, or if the user had divulged their password to colleagues).

It is also possible to attack the SESAMEV4 password authentication model by compromising the client computer and replacing the SESAMEV4 login program with a Trojan horse program. An attacker who has compromised the client computer can thus obtain the secret key. In addition, a successful attack against the Authentication Server would reveal the secret keys of all the users, resulting in the attacker being able to impersonate any of the users.

2.2 Weaknesses of the Strong Authentication Model

The strong authentication model uses public-key cryptography. In this model, the user's private key PK_R^{-1} is stored on the local (client) computer, and is protected by the client computer's operating system access controls. As such, host based attacks against the client computer leave the user's private key vulnerable to theft. The Authentication Server only stores users' public keys (PK_R). Therefore, attacks against the Authentication Server will not reveal the users' private keys.

The authentication protocol has the following messages. The phase starts with the user executing the User Sponsor program **strong_login**. The user supplies the username (and optional rolename) to the User Sponsor program. The user's public key is certified by a central certification authority. The User Sponsor sends to the Authentication Server:

$$U, DC_R, G, r_U, RL_U, SIGN(PK_R^{-1})(A, r_U, t_U)$$

This message contains the user's identity and certificate and authenticates the user to the Authentication Server. It also identifies the key distribution server, contains a random challenge, and a requested lifetime of the basic key. The Authentication Server verifies the signature on the authenticator using the user's public key (PK_R) found within the certificate DC_R. If the certificate is valid, the client's signature is verified, the timestamp t_U and nonce r_U are fresh and not replayed, and the client's authentication has been successful. The Authentication Server then replies with a message containing a session key, a ticket granting ticket, and an authenticator (to allow the user to authenticate the Authentication Server). This message has the form:

$$ENC(PK_R)(BK_{UPG}, r_U, T_s, T_e, G), TGT, A, DC_A, SIGN(PK_A^{-1})(U, r_U, r_A, t_A)$$

The User Sponsor obtains the new session key BK_{UPG} by decrypting the first part with the user's private key PK_R^{-1}. It then verifies the Authentication Server's authenticator in the same way as described in the previous paragraph.

At the end of a successful procedure the User Sponsor and the Authentication Server will be **mutually** authenticated. The rest of the SESAMEV4 process is not relevant to this paper and will therefore be omitted.

3   Issues of Trust

As with every security architecture, the SESAME V4 implementation relies on some basic assumptions of trust. It is impossible to construct a security architecture without trusting someone or something. Good solutions will be able to move the trust from unreliable components to more reliable ones.

In the password authentication model the Authentication Server is unconditionally trusted. Because it knows the long term keys LK_R of each user it can listen in on every user's communication and it can even impersonate anyone.

In the strong authentication model the Authentication Server does not need to be trusted. However the user is required to maintain a trusted copy of the certification authority's public key. This key is used to verify the certificates received. Successful host based attacks against the client computer could result in the attacker being able to replace the certification authority's public key with a false key.

4   Smart Card Enhancements

Research was conducted into how smart cards could be integrated into SESAMEV4 in order to address the problems and weaknesses identified above. Because of the necessity to ensure easy integration into existing SESAMEV4 servers, it was decided that the only changes to be made were to be on the client side. No changes to SESAMEV4 servers were considered in this project. Note though that it is of course necessary to make changes to the SESAMEV4 user enrolment program, to add in facilities to issue a smart card to the user when the user is enrolled.

The key features of smart cards which we deemed to be useful for this project are:

- the facility to store data in a secure manner;
- the ability to perform cryptographic computations on the smart card;
- the facility to restrict use of the smart card to users who have presented the smart card with the correct personal identification number (PIN).

In [Gaskell & Looi, 1995] methods of integrating smart cards into Kerberos were described. This paper extends the research reported there and applies the work to the distributed computing concept of SESAMEV4. This paper explores four proposals for integrating smart cards into SESAMEV4. The first two proposals relate to the password authentication model of SESAMEV4 and the last two proposals relate to the strong authentication model of SESAMEV4.

4.1   Enhancements to the Password Authentication Model

Two proposed enhancements for integrating smart cards into the password authentication model of SESAMEV4 are described in this section. These enhancements aim to address the limitations described in section 2.1.

Storing the User's Secret Key on the Smart Card

This proposal changes the user's secret key LK_R from being a value derived from the user's password to being a random symmetric key chosen at user enrolment time and stored at both the server and the user's smart card. We propose to have this secret key LK_R protected from being read unless the smart card has been presented with a valid PIN by the card holder.

When the user attempts to login to the system, instead of supplying a password to the SESAMEV4 password login program (**ses_login**), the user enters a PIN into the smart card, thereby enabling the user's secret key LK_R to be read from the smart card. The **ses_login** program will then read the secret key from the smart card and proceed in the usual manner.

This enhancement allows a much larger keyspace to be used for the secret key. Instead of being restricted to the set of printable characters, the full keyspace can now be used by the randomly selected secret key. In addition, there is no longer a password to be guessed. The secret key is randomly generated and protected on the smart card. Finally, this enhancement requires the user to have possession of the smart card, adding a "something you have" authentication factor to the "something you know" (the user's PIN or previously the user's password).

The secret key LK_R is still vulnerable to being obtained through a host based attack however. This is addressed in the next proposal.

Decryption of Session Key by the Smart Card

In this proposal, the fundamental change is that the secret key never leaves the smart card. All user authentication elements of the previous proposal remain in effect. However, the **ses_login** program is modified to send the encrypted session key, which it receives from the Authentication Server, to the smart card. The smart card then makes use of the user's secret key LK_R to decrypt the session key. The decrypted session key is then sent back from the smart card to the client.

It is important to note that in this proposal, the session key is still vulnerable to theft through a host based attack. However, the vulnerability is limited to the session, or to be more precise, to the period of time before that session key expires. A solution to this problem is suggested in section 7.

4.2   Enhancements to the Strong Authentication Model

Again, two proposed enhancements to the strong authentication model of SESAMEV4 are suggested. These two enhancements are based around the same ideas as the enhancements suggested for the password authentication model of SESAMEV4. These enhancements aim to address the limitations described in section 2.2.

Storing Keys on the Smart Card

In this proposal, the smart card is used to securely store the user's private key. Again, this proposal requires the keys to be protected from being read until the smart card has been presented with a valid PIN.

The modifications required to SESAMEV4 are confined to the SESAMEV4 strong authentication client program **strong_login**. Instead of reading the user's private key from disk storage space on the client, **strong_login** reads this key from the activated smart card. This prevents host attacks from being able to obtain or modify these keys before the session commences. However, this proposal is still vulnerable to the user's private key being stolen during the login process (when the key is resident in the client), and the session key being stolen at any time during that session.

Decryption of Session Key by the Smart Card

Just like the second proposal of the password authentication scheme, this proposal ensures that the user's private key never leaves the smart card. A smart card capable of the appropriate public key cryptographic algorithm has to be used. The encrypted session key is sent to the smart card, where it is decrypted using the user's private key. The session key is then returned to the client where it remains vulnerable to a host based attack.

5 Changes to the Protocol

Using the smart card implies making changes to the protocols outlined in section 2. As an example we illustrate these changes for the case that the password authentication model is used and the decryption is performed on the smart card (see Figure 2).

1. t_U — the User Sponsor sends a timestamp to the smart card.

2. $ENC(LK_R)(t_U)$ — the smart card encrypts the timestamp with the long term key

3. $R, G, RL_U, r_U, ENC(LK_R)(t_U)$ — the User Sponsor sends the same message as in section 2.1

4. $ENC(LK_R)(BK_{UPG}, T_s, T_e, r_U, G), TGT$ — the Authentication Server replies with the usual message

5. $ENC(LK_R)(BK_{UPG}, T_s, T_e, r_U, G)$ — the encrypted session key is sent to the smart card

6. $BK_{UPG}, T_s, T_e, r_U, G$ — the smart card returns the content of the key package

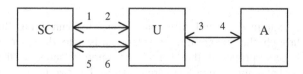

Fig. 2. The modified SESAMEV4 password authentication

6 Implementation and Verification

These enhancements are currently being implemented. Testing to ensure proper operation with regards to anticipated security improvements and proper interaction with existing SESAMEV4 applications and servers are undertaken. These tests are performed in a cross-platform environment, including Linux based and Solaris based systems.

A development platform consisting of Pentium based PCs running Red Hat Linux 5.1 and SESAMEV4 has been selected. ISO standard smart cards and smart card readers are being used for the trial implementation. The development is based around Philips PE-122 smart card readers. Smart cards being used for both the password based and the strong authentication models are the Philips DX smart card and the Gemplus GPK4000 smart card.

The first enhancement with the user's secret (symmetric) key being stored on a smart card is now operational using a Philips DX card. The enhancement to the strong authentication process involving storing the user's private key on the smart card has also been completed and is fully operational using the Gemplus GPK4000 card and the Philips DX Plus card.

Current development work is based around the enhancement to the strong authentication process involving performing public key cryptographic computation on the smart card. This is well advanced and is in the final stages of testing.

7 Further Improvements

As explained in section 3 the implication of trust is extremely important. It is possible to shift the trust completely to the smart card by moving the certification authority's public key onto it. We can even go further and let the smart card perform all the certificate verifications. This will imply a big change to the protocols and therefore needs to be examined carefully before starting its implementation process.

Another possible improvement is to move the session keys onto the smart card and let the card perform all en- and decryptions. This would eliminate the host based attack but would require significant processing power from the smart card's CPU and a high bandwidth for the communication between the smart card and the client computer.

8 Conclusion

This paper has examined several different options for enhancing the security in SESAMEV4 through the integration of smart cards into the user authentication process. It has been proposed that significant improvements to the security of SESAMEV4 user authentication process are possible. The two features of smart cards that allow for the improved security are secure data storage and on-board cryptographic processing.

References

Ashley P., Vandenwauver M., 1998, Practical Intranet Security: Overview of the State of the Art and Available Technologies, Kluwer Academic Publishers, 1998.

Bellovin, S., Meritt, M., 1990, Limitations of the Kerberos Authentication System, Computer Communications Review, vol 20, no 5, pages 119-132, 1990

Gaskell, G., Looi, M., 1995, Integrating Smart Cards into Authentication Systems, In Cryptography: Policy and Algorithms Conference, LNCS-1029, pages 270-281, Springer, Berlin, 1995

Kaijser, P., 1993, SESAMEV4 The European Solution to Security for Open Systems. In Proceedings of the 10th World Conference on Computer Security, Audit and Control COMPSEC, pages 289-297, London, UK, October 1993

Kaijser, P., Parker, T., Pinkas, D., 1994, SESAMEV4: The Solution to Security for Open Distributed Systems. Computer Communications, 17(7):501-518, July 1994

Kohl, J., Neumann, C., 1993, The Kerberos Network Authentication Service V5, Internet RFC 1510, 1993

Steiner, J., Neuman, C., Schiller, J., 1988, Kerberos: An Authentication Service for Open Network Systems. In Proceedings of the 1988 Usenix Winter Conference, pages 191-202, Texas, USA, February 1988

Vandenwauver, M, Govaerts, R., Vandewalle, J., 1997, Security of Client Server Systems, In Proceedings of 2nd International Small Systems Security Conference, IFIP, 1997

How to Say "YES" with Smart Cards

Yair Frankel and Moti Yung

CertCo, N.Y., NY, moti@certco.com
{yfrankel,moti}@cs.columbia.edu

Abstract. The advance of smart card technology will enable ubiquity (wide distribution) of services, due to increased portability and security provided by the devices. In this work we demonstrate that in the ubiquitous environment certain architectural considerations are needed to assure secure and fast services. Specifically, we demonstrate problems that may arise when employing a service that combines "cryptographic integrity calculation" together with its counterpart "cryptographic integrity verification" (due to operational requirements and possible symmetries) when the underlying technology is based on efficient symmetric ciphers (rather than public-key). We suggest a general architectural solution which assures that both calculations and verifications (or checks) are performed correctly and securely. Examples of the services above include: distributed notaries, distributed time-stamping etc.

1 Introduction

With advances in smart card technology, the notion of distributed "autonomous" cryptographic services may become a reality. These portable and highly available services may change many of the commercial and business procedures and transactions. Here, we investigate the employment of a service that combines "cryptographic integrity calculation" together with its counterpart "cryptographic integrity verification" using secure smart cards. We suggest a general architectural solution which assures that both calculations and verifications (or checks) are performed correctly and securely using symmetric cipher technology.

Public key technology is especially inefficient on the scalability of security which can be measured by the change of the "performance -over- security ratio" as the security requirement increases. Therefore, to achieve a large scalability of security (i.e., increased security while not paying a performance penalty which is unacceptable), one prefers to use "symmetric key" (private key) technology as much as possible, rather than employ the costly "public key" technology. To exemplify this note the following: the performance -over- security ratio in moving to iterated-DES (e.g., 3-DES) from a single DES operation is much higher than when moving to 2048-bit RSA from 1024-bit RSA. This ratio difference seems crucial in smart card environments where a smart cards computational power may be limited (or may grow in a much slower rate than that of a general purpose processor).

Let us concentrate on cryptographic services which provide integrity and in particular (as a working example) on a time-stamping service. The notion of

J.-J. Quisquater and B. Schneier (Eds.): CARDIS 2000, LNCS 1820, pp. 203–212, 2000.
© Springer-Verlag Berlin Heidelberg 2000

time-stamping is important, a digital service providing time-stamping using global information and linking was suggested by Haber and Stornetta [11]. The main problem that they identified and ingeniously solved is how to secure and protect against a time-stamping server who is willing to stamp current documents as past documents (the problem amounts to: "Who will guard the guards themselves?").

Using smart card with access to global time (e.g., having a tamper proof accurate clock or access to authenticated and secure time server) gives a different mechanism which may achieve time-stamping. This mechanism provides the possibility of widely available distribution of service without relying on availability of past documents while easily guaranteeing a very refined time-stamping clock (to easily distinguish actual "real" time of various actions). Finally, in such a mechanism, checking is not tedious and is done without history linking.

1.1   The Immediate Approach and Its Problems

To achieve integrity computation we may want to resort to a MAC computation encapsulated in hardware. Signature "generation" becomes the application of the MAC on the message internally in the smartcard using a private key. Whereas "verification" takes as input the message signature pair, then computes a new MAC of the messages with the same private key and outputs YES if the newly computed MAC is the same as the inputed "signature". This process can be viewed as a "private signature" [7,6].

In the working environment above, actual access to the service provider is needed for verification. Thus, the model is similar to "undeniable signature" [4,5], where verification is possible with the participation of the verification device only (due to the MAC key being hidden in the device). The above scenario assumes that the parties are indeed the actual players as specified (honest parties).

In our working environment there are users and judges, where users obtain a time-stamping service and judges decides on validity of integrity checks. A primary difference is that we may assume that parties may not be honest.

Now assume that the above procedure is indeed used for time-stamping and its verification. The time-stamping applies a MAC over the current time and the document and outputs the current time and the stamp. The verification, given a document, time and a stamp checks for validity of the stamp. Now, observe what happens once we get rid of the "trusted access" assumption:

- In this case the verification procedure answers YES/NO as above. Therefore, when the device is spoofed, the verifying party may have been interacting with an untrusted device. This device may then give an arbitrary answer (either NO when the time-stamp is valid, or YES which gives "false assurance").

The above problem arises since the user gets no "evidence" for the given answer. Thus we try to assure the user that the device is trustworthy. For this, we can require the verification to provide evidence such as "produce the MAC" of the time/message pair rather than feeding the MAC as an input to test for equality.

— But in this case, it is not difficult to see how an "untrusted user" can fool the system. Namely, a verification process in which a time-stamp server produces a MAC using an expired date may be **abused** in order to "back date" documents!

We conclude that we have to assure that attacks by spoofed devices and untrusted users are both foiled. We notice that, when participants are not trusted, we have to provide evidence and at the same time we are in a situation where breaking the symmetry between the actual integrity calculation and its verification is needed. We cannot "rely" fully on the device and we have to assure proper verification by users and judges. This is the major problem we deal with.

Remark: Note that another problem that may arise is "assuring proper *integrity calculation*." Namely, assuring that at the time of calculation, the device is not spoofed. To this end we may apply two (or more) independent devices in parallel (at the same time– assuming a "time granularity" which is not too refined, so that the actual chosen time will be identical). We note that a mechanism to check a result based on "cryptographic program checking" [10] is also possible (for certain multiplicative domains).

1.2   Model Variations

There are a number of settings and aspects to consider, let us review them:

Public vs. Private Operations: The integrity calculation and verification can be directed either to any user (namely, be public), or to a specific user (namely, be private).

Users vs. Judges: The verification by users are authentication, while judges need to have a non-repudiation property (like a digital signature) since they have to verify without generating new signature; however in a tamper-proof model the difference is not so large. On the other hand, we may be in a model where we want to hide certain aspects from the judges (e.g., content of messages, keys, etc.)– yet they have to perform their task. In short, the information given/available to users and judges may differ.

Implicit vs. Explicit Authentication: The channel may be required, in addition to the calculated value, to include also an explicit authenticator of the channel/ token. Alternatively, the calculated value (time stamp) already "contains" implicitly the required authentication (which may be public or private as noted above).

Given the last issue, we note that the more implicit the authentication mechanism is, the less constraints are put on the channel of communication between the parties. In other words, if the mechanism has implicit authentication (self-authenticated message that assures to be coming from a source) no additional channel authentication is required between the parties. Thus, the operation is more efficient and more users can play as parties to the exchange (e.g. even parties without certain authentication keys, such as judges).

2   Time-Stamping with Hardware

We suggest (1) an integrity calculation mechanism (generating a time-stamp is our example) and (2) an integrity verification mechanism (checking a time-stamp). Both mechanisms employ a number of cryptographic primitives.

We employ a strong cryptographic *message authentication code (MAC)* function which can be thought of as a keyed hash function (and can be constructed from block ciphers or from any other pseudorandom functions). A MAC function takes two inputs, a message M and a private key k, and its purpose is to provide for assurance of the source and integrity of a message. Hence from tuple $S = \langle M, MAC_k(M) \rangle$, an adversary is unable to modify S in any way without it being noticed by someone holding the secret k.

We also employ the recent *perfectly one-way hash functions*[2,3]. These are hash functions in which computing collisions is intractable and furthermore the input is hidden **perfectly** (similar to semantic security[12] for encryption). That is, for perfectly one way hash function $V(\cdot)$ it is not computationally feasible to find x_1, x_2 such that $V(x_1) = V(x_2)$ and moreover no additional information is revealed about input x given $V(x)$ than what is known a-priori about the distribution that x is drawn from. A perfectly one way hash function is a randomized function, and for notation we write $\langle CHECK_1, CHECK_2 \rangle = V(x)$ where $CHECK_1$ is the random string which is given as output but is also used in calculating $CHECK_2$. The constructions in [3] employ efficient primitives which in practice are typically based on symmetric key technology.

The timestamp token is a tamper-resistant devices which incorporates a secure hardware clock or has another mechanism to find the correct time (e.g., global time reading). The integration of tamperproof token into cryptographic applications has been investigated in several papers (e.g., [1,14]). The IFIPS140 document [8] discusses some of the requirements for such a secure module.

2.1   System Setup and Notation

The following notation is used throughout the paper. $MAC_k(\cdot)$ denotes a cryptographic MAC function keyed with key k. $H(\cdot)$ denotes a publicly available cryptographically secure hash function (concretely e.g., SHA, MD5 [9,13]) and $V(\cdot)$ (see [2,3] for constructions) denotes a perfectly one way hash function. Furthermore let $||$ denote string concatenation.

We have three types of entities in our system: users, judges and a time-stamping token. During system setup a secret key k is generated privately by the token and stored secret internally (and/or transported to a multitude of devices). This key will be the key for the "private signature" system.

During the initiation of user u we perform a one-time setup (over an authenticated and private channel), consisting of obtaining from the token $K_u = MAC_k(R||u||T||L)$ where R is a large random string (we may derive R pseudorandomly from u's name and a version number, if we want K_u to be reproduceable at the device), T is the token's current time and L is the length of the string. As will be seen in Section 2.2 this is nothing more than a stamping operation on a random document. The goal is that all communication between a user/judge and the token will be performed over an authentication and private channel with keys derived from K_u.

2.2   The Process

Next we discuss our primary working example which is time-stamping.

Here we assume that the smartcard token has access to a clock. Using smart card with access to global time (e.g., having a tamper proof accurate clock/ time-reader) provides a time-stamping service without relying on availability of past documents while easily guaranteeing a very refined time-stamping clock (to easily distinguish actual time). In such a mechanism checking is not tedious and is done without history linking checks.

There are two issues to be dealt with in a time-stamping with hardware which is tamperproof.

1. **Verifiability**–*assuring correctness of integrity check:* The user requires assurance that the private signature is correct.
2. **Oblivious Verifiability**– *Verifiability by a judge without possession of the private signature:* A judge is able to verify that a user possess a timestamp of a document without access to the document.

Three routines are now developed to produce a hardware based time-stamping mechanism.

The *stamping* which produces a private signature of a document bounded by the token's time using a private MAC function. Since we have a secure token we only require each document to be signed with a trusted time rather than relying on the token maintaining a publicly verifiable data structure to prove linking and ordering of time-stamping transactions.

The *user verification* routine based on the production of a check string which can only be produced upon knowledge of the private signature of the document but, for security against back-dating, the check string itself does not reveal any information about the private signature of the document-time binding. The basic idea is that the user and token can both produce the checkstring based on information they each have: the user has available the private signature to produce the checkstring and the token can reproduce the private signature, since it does not maintain old private signatures, and then produce the check string. The check string is also bound to the current time of the verification.

The *judge verification* routine simply demonstrates to the judge that both the token and user can produce the same check string. Since the checkstring can only be generated with knowledge of the private signature, for the user to produce the same check string as the token, requires that the user has knowledge of the private signature for the document-time binding.

Next, we describe the procedures at length. Then we will claim what they achieve.

Stamping Routine:

Similar to [11] the user submits D, the document or a cryptographic hash of the document.

The stamping operation performed by the smartcard is as follows.

1. Input "STAMP" $||D||N$ where N is the author-name.
2. Read and store clock-time: T.
3. Set $S = D||N||T||L$ where L is the length of S and compute $G = H(S)$.
4. Obtain $SIG = MAC_k(G)$.
5. Output: the timestamp tuple $\langle T, SIG \rangle$.

Under the private signature model, the signature is transmitted over a secure (private and authenticated) channel using (a key derived from) K_u as the private key. SIG can be thought of as the signature of S. The user may now maintain T and SIG.

We observe that without the device it is not possible to generate a time-stamp for "hashed input" G which has not previously been timestamped by observing that if it were possible then the cryptographically secure MAC primitive would be insecure (i.e., allowing someone to forge the source or integrity of a message input). A strong MAC derived from a pseudorandom function, is existentially unforgeable even after chosen message attack.

Hence for an adversary to have a timestamp for a document/time pair which has not previously been signed the adversary must find a new input S' such that $H(S') = G = H(S)$ which is not computationally feasible due to the security definition of the collision-intractable hash function H.

The only other possibility to generate the signature is via other protocols, but we will later show that these protocols only produce information that perfectly conceals the signature.

User Verification Routine:

We desire the user to be able to verify a token without obtaining new information which will compromise the system. For example, we do not want the user to be able to query the token for a new document/time tuple and obtain sufficient information to generate the timestamp for the new document and time tuple. Hence we have two simultaneous fundamental goals:

1. *Assuring correctness of integrity check* for the user (assurance to the user); and
2. *Preventing back-dating* by the user (assurance to the device).

Let us next see the user verification process. The token performs the following operation for a public verification process:

1. Get input: "VERIFY $||S'$ where $S' = D'||N'||T'||L'$ and L' is the length of S'.
2. Compute $SIG' = MAC_k(H(S'))$ as in steps 3-4 in the stamping procedure.
3. Read current time stored in $TIME$.
4. Compute internally $CHECK = \langle CHECK_1, CHECK_2 \rangle = V(SIG', TIME)$ with publicly known perfectly one way hash function $V(\cdot)$.
5. Output: $\langle TIME, CHECK \rangle$.
   This is what the token is performing at (public) verification. Let us see how to complete the process:

Public Verification Action:
This additional process is public and should be implemented independently of the card. It applies V' which is V on the chosen random string $CHECK_1$. To verify SIG the user can now verify that the time is prompt and if $CHECK \overset{?}{=} V'(CHECK_1, SIG, TIME)$. If they match it is accepted as the signature.

Let us first note that the verification process performed by the token reveals no useful information to an adversary. Observe that due to the definition of perfectly one way hash which states that it reveals no additional information about SIG' (or, similarly, k) given $CHECK, TIME$ and forces the adversary to "know" SIG' in order for the check to be meaningful. Hence, the verification process reveals nothing useful to an adversary.

Privaten Verification Action:
The other option, *private verification*, is now considered. To perform this option the following computation can only be performed by the token and the user:

4'. $CHECK = \langle CHECK_1, E_{D(K_u)}(CHECK_2) \rangle$ where $\langle CHECK_1, CHECK_2 \rangle = V(SIG', TIME)$ is computed internally with publicly known perfectly one way function $V(\cdot)$ and $D(K_u)$ is a string (key) derived from the shared key K_u and is used as a key (seed) to a pseudorandom function E. (V' is modified similarly to include and employ the derived private shared key).

The above procedure assures to the user of the correctness of the time stamp due to the collision intractability of the hash and, as explained above, at the same time does not reveal new timestamps to the adversary. Thus, both assurances to the user and the device are achieved.

Judge Verification Routine:

The user now wants to prove to the judge that it has the signature of the document at a particular time but does not want to give the signature to the judge (to avoid enabling the judge to be able to impersonate the user). But the judge wants assurance that the user actually does have the signature by having the user prove that both the user and the token can produce the same signature pair. The trick is that $CHECK$ generated during user verification can be publicly produced by both the user and the token and, moreover, revealing check does not compromise the security of the signature SIG or the secret MAC key k.

The judge verification process is based upon the user verification process. Let us next see the verification process that the judge performs.

1. Judge sends to token "VERIFY" $||S'$ where $S' = D'||N'||T'||L'$ where L' is the length of S'.
2. Judge obtains as output from the token: $\langle TIME, CHECK \rangle$.
3. Depending on type (i.e., public vs. private) of verification:
   judge transmits to the user $TIME, CHECK_1'$ and obtains
   - (public verification:)
     $CHECK' = \langle CHECK_1', CHECK_2' \rangle = V(TIME, SIG)$ where SIG is "private signature" for S' and $CHECK_1'$ is used as the random string for $V(\cdot)$.
   - (private verification:)
     $CHECK' = \langle CHECK_1', E_{D(K_u)}(CHECK_2') \rangle$ where $\langle CHECK_1', CHECK_2' \rangle = V(TIME, SIG)$ and where SIG is "private signature" for S' and $CHECK_1'$ is used as the random strong for $V(\cdot)$.
4. If time is prompt and $CHECK \overset{?}{=} CHECK'$ then accept else reject.

As before we note that $CHECK$ and $CHECK'$ do not reveal useful information about SIG or k. If the user was able to obtain on its own a $CHECK'$ which is equal to $CHECK$ then the user would be able to compute a collision or circumvent the MAC primitive (under adaptive chosen message attacks). This contradicts the security definitions of V and MAC.

Note that the judge is trusted to send to the user the $CHECK_1$ random string component. We can strengthen this by not assuming the judge to be necessarily honest. This is done by actually producing an authenticator which is the value $MAC_{K_u}(TIME, CHECK_1)$ which uses (part of) the common key (using a MAC which is secure against adaptive chosen message attacks) to authenticate the string that the potentially misbehaving judge presents to the user. The authenticator assures that the string handed by the judge was, in fact, originated at the device. (Note that we have a number of uses of the shared key K_u in our protocols, it is understood that each use is done with a different portion of the shared string!)

The result is that the judge does not learn the signature (it is well concealed by the hash function), yet it is assured that the two parties hold the signature. This oblivious verifiability may have other uses.

If we do not want the judge to learn the document, we may hand an encrypted document (which is encrypted and MACed under (other portions of) K_u). The judge then passes to the token the encrypted document and the user name. The device can decrypt and verify MAC of the document and continue as above. This assures an **oblivious blind verification** (where the judge is only assured that the parties indeed posses a signature on the unknown document).

3 Outcome and Properties

Let us next review the major aspects of the design.

First, notice the asymmetry between the stamping which uses an internal secure inaccessible clock and the verification produces output based on the input clock. The stamping never reads any untrusted time. Also, stamping produces signature SIG, while checking cannot be used to get signature at validation time since V is a perfect-hash which in effect gives a pseudo-random output thus the outcome cannot be used to get SIG. It is important that the checking produces only partial information related to the actual signature and that the signature is hard to get from it. So, it cannot be used to "back-date" documents. This means that asymmetry in the design and separation of functions are important.

While relying on the same key the operations have to be independent. Having a signature does not imply possible check forgery (as the checking device is physically only given document information) and having a check does not give a signature (thus, cannot be used for forgery).

Next, note that a signature string is not given to the checking mechanism, checking is done solely on the input which is the document (not the SIG) as the calculation starts from a document and signature is internally produced in the checking mechanism. No SIG input is given— since otherwise signing can be spoofed since a device which only computes V is easy to produce. Similarly, the fact that checking needs the signature secret keys is important as well: a device that just says OK is not enough as it is easy to manufacture without knowing the signature key, whereas our mechanism is not easy to forge by producing a device without such knowledge. The principle here is the need to rely every action on the actual key used in the operation and bind each and every operation to this internal key (to avoid spoofing).

In conclusion, what was needed is:

- key-binding of every operation; while
- assuring asymmetry and independence of these various operation.
- In addition, to complete the design, care must be taken to design properly the authenticated and/or secure channels between the various entities.

We claim that a physically protected stamping mechanism and corresponding verification mechanism provide for the entire functionality of secure time-stamping service and achieve increased functionality (due to the protected environment and protected availability of clock). This functionality include: ubiquity (wide distribution) of service providers, autonomy of separate devices, no reliance on previous documents and other events, and provision of quite a refined notion of time.

The design relied upon underlying cryptographic technology, physical security technology, and (internal or external reliable) clock technology. These components are all available and operational.

References

1. M. Abadi and M. Burrows and C. Kaufman and B. Lampson, *Authentication and Delegation with Smart-Cards*, DEC Systems Research Center, 67, October 1990.
2. R. Canetti. *Towards realizing random oracles: Hash functions which hide all partial information.* In Advances in Cryptology. Proc. of Crypto'97, pages 455–469, 1997.
3. R. Canetti, D. Micciancio, and O. Reingold, *Perfectly one-way probabilistic hash functions,* In Proceedings of the Thirtieth Annual ACM Symposium on the Theory of Computing (STOC 98). pp. 131-140. 1998.
4. D. Chaum and H. Van Antwerpen, "Undeniable signatures", *Advances in Cryptology- Crypto '89 (LNCS 435)*, pp. 212-216, 1990.
5. D. Chaum, "Zero-knowledge undeniable signatures", *Advances in Cryptology-Eurocrypt '90 (LNCS 473)*, pp. 458-464, 1991.
6. G. Davida and B. Matt, *Arbitration in tamper proof devices (If DES $\equiv$ RSA then what's the difference between true signatures and arbitrated signature schemes?),* Advances in Cryptology-Crypto '87 (LNCS 293), pp. 216-222, 1987.
7. Y. Desmedt and J. -J. Quisquater, *Public key systems based on the difficulty of tampering (Is there a difference between DES and RSA?, Advances in Cryptology-Crypto '86 (LNCS 263)*, pp. 111-117, 1987.
8. Security requirements for cryptographic modules (FIPS PUB 140-1). Technical Report FIPS 140-1, National Institute of Standards and Technology, Gaithersburg, MD, 1994.
9. Secure Hash Standard (FIPS PUB 180-1). Technical Report FIPS 180-1, National Institute of Standards and Technology, Gaithersburg, MD, 1995.
10. Y. Frankel, P. Gemmell and M. Yung, *Witness Based Cryptographic Program Checking and Robust Function Sharing.* In Proceedings of the Twenty eighth Annual ACM Symposium on the Theory of Computing (STOC 96). 1996. pp. 499-508.
11. S. Haber and W.S. Stornetta, *How to Time-Stamp a Digital Document,* Journal of Cryptography, v. 3 n. 2, 1991, Springer International,, pp. 99-112.
12. S. Goldwasser and S. Micali, *Probabilistic encryption,* JCSS, Vol 28, No 2, pp. 270-299, 1984.
13. R. Rivest, *The MD5 Message Digest Algorithm,* IETF RFC 1321, April 1992.
14. B. Yee, *Using Secure Coprocessors,* Ph. D. thesis, Carnagie Mellon University, Computer Science Tech. Report CMU-CS-94-149, May 1994.

An Efficient Verifiable Encryption Scheme for Encryption of Discrete Logarithms

Feng Bao

Information Security Group
Kent Ridge Digital Labs
21 Heng Mui Keng Terrace
Singapore 119613
baofeng@krdl.org.sg

Abstract. A verifiable encryption scheme (VES) is useful for many cryptographic protocols. A VES may be either for (encryption of) discrete logarithms or for (encryption of) e-th roots. So far, all the VESs for discrete logarithms are inefficient, but there exists an efficient VES for e-th roots. In this paper, we presents an efficient VES for discrete logarithms and prove its security.

1 Introduction

A verifiable encryption scheme (VES) can be informally described like this: a party E encrypts a message m with party K's public key meanwhile generate a certificate for proving that m is a discrete logarithm (or e-th root) of a given value(public), without disclosing m. After E hands the ciphertext and the certificate to party V, V verifies the certificate. If the verification is passed, V is convinced that the ciphertext is indeed the encryption of the m. In other words, if K later decrypts the ciphertext, the output must be the discrete logarithm (or e-th root) of the given value.

VESs have good applications in fair exchange protocols [1], [2] and also in other cryptographic protocols [4], [8], [10].

[10] presents two VESs, one for encryption of discrete logarithms one for encryption of eth-roots. [1] presents a very general VES for encryption of pre-image of any homomorphic one-way function.

The two VESs of [10] all take ElGamal PKC as the encryption scheme while the VES of [1] can take any encryption scheme since in the generation/verification of the certificate, the encryption is taken as a one-way function. This is a great advantage since RSA and ECC can be used as the PKC in this VES.

However, the complexity of the VES in [1] is large since it uses cut-and-choose method. The VES for discrete logarithms of [10] is also based on cut-and-choose method. The complexities of generating/verifying certificates in the two VESs are more or less same: the time complexity is more than one hundred times of that of an encryption, and the size of a certificate is as large as several K-Bytes. But the VES for discrete logarithms of [10] has an advantage in decryption over

J.-J. Quisquater and B. Schneier (Eds.): CARDIS 2000, LNCS 1820, pp. 213–220, 2000.
© Springer-Verlag Berlin Heidelberg 2000

the VES in [1]: the former needs only one decrypting action while the latter requires dozens of decrypting actions. This is the main costing of the VES in [1].

The second VES of [10] is dozens times more efficient than the above two schemes in both computation complexity and in size of the certificate. But this scheme can't be used for encryption of discrete logarithms. It is for the encryption of e-th roots.

A very important application of VES is to encrypt signatures: to encrypt a signature and prove that what being encrypted is indeed a desired signature while not disclosing it. However, the second VES of [10] can't be used to encrypt discrete logarithm-based signatures. It can only be used to encrypt the signature of Guillou-Quisquater scheme.

In this paper we present an efficient VES for the encryption of discrete logarithms. It can be used to encrypt any discrete logarithm-based signatures, including ECC-based signatures. To our knowledge this is the first efficient VES for discrete logarithms. Its efficiency is similar to that of the VES for eth-roots in [10].

2   The Scheme

2.1   The Principle

Let G_1 and G_2 be two groups of large orders and g_1 and g_2 be two generators of G_1 and G_2, respectively. Suppose g_1^x is a one-way function but g_2^x is a trapdoor one-way function(public key encryption). Then by proving the equality of discrete logarithms(PEDL), we can prove that a ciphertext is indeed an encryption of a discrete logarithm.

Two techniques help here. The first is the new trapdoor one-way function proposed in [9], where the function of x is in the form of g^x mod n. The second is the proof of equality of discrete logarithms where the computations of exponents are conducted in $\mathbf{Z}$(instead of in $\mathbf{Z}_q$), as done in [6] and [10].

One thing worth mentioning here is that in our setting, the order of G_1 is publicly known while the order of G_2 is secret. Hence, by PEDL, we actually prove the equality of discrete logarithms modulo the order of G_1. But that is enough for our goal.

2.2   Okamoto-Uchiyama Trapdoor One-Way Function

The System Let $n = p^2q(p, q$ primes) and g be an element of $\mathbf{Z}_n$ such that $(g \bmod p^2)$ is a primitive element in $\mathbf{Z}_{p^2}^*$. A randomly chosen g in $\mathbf{Z}_n$ satisfies it except for a negligible probability $1/p$. Then n, g and $|p|$ are published.

Trapdoor One-Way Function The function g^x mod n is a trapdoor one-way function from $\mathbf{Z}_p$ to $\mathbf{Z}_p$. The trapdoor information is the factorization of n. Suppose p is known. Let $C = g^x$ mod n. x can be computed by

$$x = \frac{(C^{p-1} \bmod p^2) - 1}{(g^{p-1} \bmod p^2) - 1} \bmod p \tag{1}$$

The proof is like this: $g^{p(p-1)} = 1 \bmod p^2$ means $(g^{p-1})^p = 1 \bmod p$, i.e., $g^{p-1} = 1 \bmod p$. Let $(g^{p-1} \bmod p^2) = kp + 1$ $(k < p)$, then $C^{p-1} = (kp+1)^x = xkp + 1 \bmod p^2$. Hence, (1) holds.

It is easy to see that reversing this one-way function is as hard as factorizing n: randomly choose an X(larger than p), compute $C = g^X \bmod n$, reverse C getting x, we have $X = x \bmod p$. With large probability, $p = \gcd(n, X - x)$. Although factorization of $n = p^2 q$ has not been known whether same difficult as factorization of $n = pq$, no evidence shows factorization of $n = p^2 q$ is easier. Also modulo $n = p^2 q$ was used in ESIGN many years ago, which still remains unbroken for $k > 3$.

In our scheme, we will use the following PKC.

Encryption Let x $(|x| < |p|)$ be a plaintext. The ciphertext of x is $C = g^x \bmod n$.

Decryption

$$x = \frac{(C^{p-1} \bmod p^2) - 1}{(g^{p-1} \bmod p^2) - 1} \bmod p$$

Notes

1. In the original Okamoto-Uchiyama PKC, two ways are adopted to strengthen the security. The first is that the encryption is made a randomized one for semantical security. The second is that the encryption is constructed to resist chosen ciphertext attack. (The above described scheme is apparently fragile to chosen ciphertext attack.)

2. In our scheme, we will not adopt randomized encryption since the security demanded here is the same as computing discrete logarithms. But we need to make the encryption immune to chosen ciphertext attack. However, we use a different way from that in [9] [3], because we need a way to fit our use: a proof that the encrypted message is smaller than p, while any party can verify the proof (without knowing p, q).

2.3 Description of Our VES

For the simplicity of description, we suppose three parties are involved in our scheme, namely

K: creates a pair of private/public keys of PKC, and publish the public key.
E: encrypts a message using K's public key and provide the proof.
V: verifies the ciphertext given by E is the encryption of a discrete logarithm.

Relevant Notations:
  G: a group in which computing discrete logarithm is hard.
  G: $G \in \mathbf{G}$. G and $\mathrm{ord}(G)$ are public.
  Y, x: $Y \in \mathbf{G}$, $Y = G^x$. Y is public. x is secretly held by E.
  p, q: primes selected by K, K's private key. $|p| > |\mathrm{ord}(G)|$ is published

n: $n = p^2q$, K's public key.

g: $g \in \mathbf{Z}_n$ and ord$(g \bmod p^2) = p(p-1)$, K's public key.

h: a one-way hash function, say, $\{0,1\}^* \longrightarrow \{0,1\}^{160}$.

An example of parameters' sizes: $|p| = 350$, $|n| = 1024$, $|\text{ord}(G)| = 160$. We will present our VES in these example sizes.

The Goal of the VES

E encrypts x to the ciphertext C and generates a certificate $Cert$ for proving that C is indeed the encryption of x such that $G^x = Y$. E gives $(C, Cert)$ to V. V verifies $(C, Cert)$. If the verification is passed, then the decryption result of C (by K's private key), say X, must satisfy $G^X = Y$.

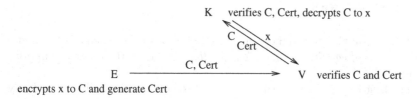

Fig. 1. The goal of the VES.

Security Requirements

1. K is always supposed to be honest(K plays the role of TTP in some applications). The security for K is that his private key won't be disclosed. More precisely, n should never be factorized even if E and V collude.

2. The security for V is that if he is honest(following the scheme properly), he won't be fooled by E. In other words, once he accept $(C, Cert)$, he can get the x such that $Y = G^x$ by the help from K.

3. The security for E is that x should not be disclosed to V unless V goes to K for help, i.e., without knowing the factorization of n, x is forever secret in the presence of $(C, Cert)$.

We present our VES in the following while leaving the proof of the security to the next section.

Verifiable Encryption Scheme

1. E encrypts x by setting $C = g^x \bmod n$.
2. E randomly choose w for $|w| = 380$, sets $a = g^w \bmod n$ and $A = G^w$, computes $r = h(C, Y, a, A)$. Then E computes $c = w - xr$ in $\mathbf{Z}$. The certificate is $Cert = (c, r)$, for proof of $\log_g C = \log_G Y \bmod \text{ord}(G)$. E gives $(C, Cert) = (C, c, r)$ to V.
3. V verifies $r = h(C, Y, g^c C^r, G^c Y^r)$ and $|c| \leq 380$. If OK, accept; otherwise, reject. ($g^c C^r$ should be $g^c C^r \bmod n$. We omit $\bmod\ n$ hereafter.)

4. Later when V submits (C, c, r) to K, K first verifies $r = h(C, Y, g^c C^r, G^c Y^r)$ and $|c| \leq 380$. If OK, K accepts the ciphertext and the certificate. K computes

$$X = \frac{(C^{p-1} \bmod p^2) - 1}{(g^{p-1} \bmod p^2) - 1} \bmod p$$

and checks which of (a) and (b) is correct:

$$\text{(a) } G^X = Y$$
$$\text{(b) } G^{X-p} = Y$$

One of them must hold. If (a) holds, K returns $X \bmod \mathrm{ord}(G)$. If (b) holds, K returns $X - p \bmod \mathrm{ord}(G)$.

3   Security Proof

Key Points for the Security: The step 2 (and 3) of the scheme is the non interactive *proof of equality of discrete logarithms* (PEDL). It plays two important roles in our VES.

1. The first is to guarantee that $|x| < |p|$ (except for a negligible probability). This property is required for resisting active attack(chosen ciphertext attack). This method has a good character for our use: any party can verify it without knowing factorization of n.

2. The second is to guarantee $\log_G Y = \log_g C \bmod \mathrm{ord}(G)$.

The following Lemmas are all related to the PEDL of our VES.

Lemma 1. *On the assumption that E cannot factorize n, E cannot find w, c and r such that $g^w = g^c C^r$ without $w = c + xr$ in $\mathbf{Z}$ except for a negligible probability.*

Proof. Suppose $g^w = g^c C^r$. We have $w = c + xr \bmod \mathrm{ord}(g)$. Since $\mathrm{ord}(g)$ is a large unknown number to E, we must have $w = c + xr$ in $\mathbf{Z}$. Otherwise, we have $w = c + xr + k\,\mathrm{ord}(g)$ for non-zero k. Remember p is a factor of $\mathrm{ord}(g)$. Then p can be found from n and $w - c - xr$.

In the next two lemmas, we consider the interactive version of the PEDL in our VES:

E: $w \in_R \{0,1\}^{380}$, $a = g^w \bmod n$, $A = G^w$, E $\xrightarrow{a, A}$ V.
V: $r \in_R \{0,1\}^{160}$, V $\xrightarrow{r}$ E.
E: $c = w - xr$ in $\mathbf{Z}$, E $\xrightarrow{c}$ V.
V: check $a = g^c C^r$ and $A = G^c Y^r$ and $|c| \leq 380$.

On the random oracle assumption of h, the non-interactive PEDL is equivalent to the interactive PEDL with V properly choosing random r.

Lemma 2. *Suppose E can pass the above interactive PEDL, we must have $|x| < |p|$ except for a negligible probability.*

Proof. Let $a = g^c C^r$ hold. From Lemma 1, this implies $c = w - xr$ in $\mathbf{Z}$ since E does not know the order of g. Remember that r is randomly chosen by V after V gets $a = g^w$ from E. r cannot be guessed before E fixing w. However, if $|x| \geq 350$, that E can find w such that $|c = w - xr| \leq 380$ before knowing r means that E can guess the r with an error not exceeding 2^{30}. The probability is 2^{-130} since $|r| = 160$.

Lemma 3. *E can pass the above interactive PEDL implies that* $\log_g C = \log_G Y$ *mod* $\mathrm{ord}(G)$ *except for a negligible probability.*

Proof. Let $C = g^X$ and $Y = G^x$. Let E first set $a = g^{w'}$ and $A = G^w$ ($w' = w$ if E is honest). Suppose E can pass the above interactive PEDL. Then we have $g^{w'} = g^c C^r$ and $G^w = G^c Y^r$. From Lemma 1, we have $c = w' - rX$ in $\mathbf{Z}$ and $c = w - xr$ mod $\mathrm{ord}(G)$. Now we must have $X = x$ mod $\mathrm{ord}(G)$. Otherwise, $r = (w' - w)/(X - x)$ mod $\mathrm{ord}(G)$, which means E can catch r before r is chosen by V.

Lemma 4. *It is hard to get any information about* x *from* C *and* $Cert$.

Proof. Getting x from C is like breaking the Okamoto-Uchiyama trapdoor one-way function. It has been shown that this is as hard as factorizing n. $Cert = (c, r)$ where $r = h(C, Y, g^w, G^w)$ and $c = w - rx$ for a randomly chosen $w \in \{0, 1\}^{380}$. If we take w as a random variable from $[0, \cdots, 2^{380} - 1]$, then c is a random variable from $[-rx, \cdots, 2^{380} - 1 - rx]$. Since we have $|r| \leq 160$ and $|x| \leq 160$, we have that $[0, \cdots, 2^{380} - 2^{320}]$ is the common domain of c for any x and any r. That means if c falls in $[0, \cdots, 2^{380} - 2^{320}]$, there is no way to tell that the c is from which x. In other words, if the c satisfies $0 \leq c \leq 2^{380} - 2^{320}$, zero-knowledge about x is disclosed. It is easy to see that for randomly chosen w, c will fall in $[0, \cdots, 2^{380} - 2^{320}]$ except for a probability of 2^{-60}.

Hence, the VES should be actually implemented like this:

in the step 2, if c falls beyond $[0, \cdots, 2^{380} - 2^{320}]$, E should give up the w and re-choose a w until the corresponding c falls in $[0, \cdots, 2^{380} - 2^{320}]$.

The zero-knowledge(on x) of our non-interactive scheme can be analogized in this formal way: Let $O_1, O_2, \cdots, O_N$ be N random oracles with output ranges $R_1, R_2, \cdots, R_N$, respectively. Let $R = \bigcap_{i=1}^{N} R_i$. Let S_i be a set of outputs of O_i for $i = 1, 2, ..., N$. Denote $T_i = S_i \bigcap R$ for $i = 1, 2, ..., N$. If we are given one of T_i's without being told i, there is no way to tell which O_i it is from. In other words, if we are given one of T_i's, it is equally probable to us that $i = 1, 2, ..., N$.

Proposition 1. *The security requirements of the VES are fulfilled under the assumption that* $n = p^2 q$ *is hard to be factorized and the random oracle assumption of* h. *We have 1) K's private key will not be disclosed; 2) V can get* x *such that* $Y = G^x$ *by the help of K if V properly follows the scheme; 3)* x *cannot be disclosed to V unless K decrypts* C *for V.*

Proof. 1) This is guaranteed by Lemma 2. If $r = h(C, Y, g^c C^r, G^c Y^r)$ and $|c| \leq 380$, we have $|x| < |p|$ except for a negligible probability. In this case, decrypting $C = g^x$ causes no problem.

2) From Lemma 3 and Lemma 2, if V properly conduct the verification and pass it, K will also pass it. In this case, K will decrypt C and the result will be the right value. One thing worth to mention is that although Lemma 2 guarantees $|log_g C| < p$, $log_g C$ is from $\mathbf{Z}$, i.e., it can be either positive or negative. Therefore, two values may be possible, $X = \frac{(C^{p-1} \bmod p^2)-1}{(g^{p-1} \bmod p^2)-1} \bmod p$ or $X - p$. From Lemma 3 $\log_g C = \log_G Y \bmod \operatorname{ord}(G)$. So by checking G^X and G^{X-p}, K can distinguish which one is the answer.

3) Lemma 4 guarantees this security.

4   Smart Card Implementation of the Scheme

As we know that some crypto-chips are available already for integrating into smart cards. A crypto-chip can conduct an exponential computation, conservatively, within 0.1 second. The certificate generation(including encryption) of our VES needs 3 exponential computations while the verification needs 4. Hence, a smart card with a crypto-chip can generate/verify a certificate of our VES within 0.5 second.

The most advantage of our scheme over the previous VESs for discrete logarithms is at its smaller requirement on RAM(i.e., the smaller size of intermediate data in certificate generation/verification). We know that a typical smart card has a RAM of several hundred Bytes. That is enough for our VES but not enough for the previous VESs for discrete logarithms, which have intermediate data size several dozens of ours. This makes our VES a big advantage in implementation in smart cards.

Acknowledgments. The author would like to thank Liqun Chen, Wenbo Mao and Markus Stadler for helpful comments and discussions.

References

1. N. Asokan, V. Shoup and M. Waidner, "Optimistic fair exchange of digital signatures", Proceedings of Eurocrypt'98.
2. F. Bao, R. H. Deng and W. Mao, "Efficient and practical fair exchange protocols with off-line TTP", Proceedings of the 1998 IEEE Symposium on Security and Privacy, IEEE Computer Press, Oakland, CA, 1998.
3. M. Bellare and P.. Rogaway, "Optimal asymmetric encryption—How to encrypt with RSA", Proceedings Eurocrypt'94, LNCS 950, Springer-Verlag, pp. 92-111, 1995.
4. J. Camenisch and M. Stadler, "Efficient group signature schemes for large groups", Proceedings of Crypto'97, LNCS, Springer-Verlag, 1997.
5. R. Canetti, O. Goldreich, and S. Halevi, "The random oracle methodology, revisit", Proceedings of STOC'98, 1998.

6. M. Girault, "Self-certified public keys", Proceedings of Eurocrypt'91, LNCS 547, Springer-Verlag, pp. 490-497, 1991.
7. L. C. Guillou and J. J. Quisquater, "A paradoxical identity-based signature scheme resulting from zero-knowledge", Advances in Cryptology - Crypto'88, LNCS 403, Springer-Verlag, pp. 216-231, 1988.
8. W. Mao, "Verifiable escrowed signature", Proceedings of ACISP'97, LNCS 1270, Springer-Verlag, pp.240-248, 1997.
9. T. Okamoto and S. Uchiyama, "A new public-key cryptosystem as secure as factoring" Proceedings of Eurocrypt'98, LNCS, Springer-Verlag, 1998.
10. M. Stadler, "Publicly verifiable secret sharing", Proceedings of Eurocrypt'96, LNCS 1070, Springer-Verlag, pp. 190-199, 1996
11. E. R. Verheul and H. C. Tilborg, "Binding ElGamal: a fraud-detectable alternative to key escrow proposals", Proceedings of Eurocrypt'97, LNCS, Springer-Verlag.

Efficient Smart-Card Based Anonymous Fingerprinting*

Josep Domingo-Ferrer and Jordi Herrera-Joancomartí

Universitat Rovira i Virgili, Department of Computer Science,
Autovia de Salou s/n, E-43006 Tarragona, Catalonia,
{jdomingo,jherrera}@etse.urv.es

Abstract. Thwarting unlawful redistribution of information sold electronically is a major problem of information-based electronic commerce. Anonymous fingerprinting has appeared as a technique for copyright protection which is compatible with buyer anonymity in electronic transactions. However, the complexity of known algorithms for anonymous fingerprinting is too high for practical implementation on standard computers, let alone smart cards. A scheme for anonymous fingerprinting is presented in this paper where all buyer computations can be performed by the buyer's smart card.

Keywords: Cryptographic protocols for IC cards, Electronic commerce, Anonymous fingerprinting, Intellectual property protection.

1 Introduction

In information-based electronic commerce, copyright protection of the information being sold is a key problem to be solved, together with secure payment. Fingerprinting is a technique which allows to track redistributors of electronic information. Given an original item of information, a tuple of *marks* is probabilistically selected. A mark is a piece of the information item of which two slightly different versions exist. At the moment of selling a copy of the item, the merchant selects one of the two versions for each mark; in other words, she hides an n-bit word in the information, where the i-th bit indicates which version of the data is being used for the i-th mark. Usually, it is assumed that two or more dishonest buyers can only locate and delete marks by comparing their copies (Marking Assumption, [Bone95]).

Classical fingerprinting schemes [Blak86][Bone95] are symmetrical in the sense that both the merchant and the buyer know the fingerprinted copy. Even if the merchant succeeds in identifying a dishonest buyer, her previous knowledge of the fingerprinted copies prevents her from using them as a proof of redistribution in front of third parties. In [Pfit96], asymmetric fingerprinting was proposed, whereby only the buyer knows the fingerprinted copy; the drawback

---

* This work is partly supported by the Spanish CICYT under grant no. TEL98-0699-C02-02.

J.-J. Quisquater and B. Schneier (Eds.): CARDIS 2000, LNCS 1820, pp. 221–228, 2000.

of this solution is that the merchant knows the buyer's identity even if the buyer is honest. Recently ([Pfit97]) the concept of anonymous fingerprinting was introduced; the idea is that the merchant does not know the fingerprinted copy nor the buyer's identity. Upon finding a fingerprinted copy, the merchant needs the help of a registration authority to identify a redistributor. In [Domi98], a scheme for anonymous fingerprinting is presented where redistributors can be identified by the merchant without help from the authority. The problem with the constructions [Pfit97][Domi98] is that, being based on secure multiparty computation ([Chau88a]), their complexity is much too high to be implementable on standard computers, let alone smart cards.

1.1   Our Result

Whereas algorithms for secure anonymous payment exist than can be implemented on a smart card on the buyer's side, no efficient anonymous fingerprinting algorithms exist in the literature where the buyer's computation can be carried out by the buyer's smart card. We describe in this paper a new construction for anonymous fingerprinting which keeps the buyer computation simple enough to be implemented by a smart card. In this way, all security functions needed to buy copyrighted information can be performed by a card.

Section 2 describes the new construction. Section 3 analyzes its security. Section 4 is a conclusion and a sketch of future work.

2   Anonymous Fingerprinting without Secure Multiparty Computation

In this section, a fingerprinting scheme is presented which provides anonymity and has the advantage of avoiding the secure two-party computation needed in previous asymmetric and anonymous fingerprinting schemes.

2.1   Merchandise Initialization

Let $H()$ be a cryptographically strong block hash function. Let n, l and u be nonnegative integer security parameters agreed upon by all parties, where $l < u < n$.

The merchant M splits the information $item$ to be fingerprinted into n disjoint subitems $item_1, item_2, \cdots, item_n$ of similar length all of which must be concatenated to reconstruct the original $item$. In addition, subitems $item_1, \cdots, item_u$ contain one mark (in the sense of Section 1), $i.e.$ there exist two slightly different versions $item_i', item_i''$ of each subitem $item_i$, for $i = 1$ to u.

Note 1 (Marking redundancy). The existence of two versions of $item_i$ allows to embed one bit in the subitem. To make subitem marking resilient to intentional modification, a redundancy scheme may be used. A simple redundancy scheme can be to replicate the bit value embedded in a subitem an odd number $m > 1$

of times so that the m-bit vector $(0,0,\cdots,0)$ is embedded in $item'_i$ instead of the bit 0, and the m-bit vector $(1,1,\cdots,1)$ is embedded in $item''_i$ instead of the bit 1. To extract the value embedded in a redistributed subitem $item^{red}_i$, all m marks are examined by M and a majority decision is made to determine whether the value is 0 or 1. Note that, by the Marking Assumption, dishonest buyers can only locate and delete marks by comparing their copies, so a single buyer is unlikely to modify a majority of marks while preserving the usefulness of the information in the subitem. Two colluding buyers can delete or alter all marks in the subitem if and only if one of them was given $item'_i$ and the other $item''_i$.

2.2 Buyer Registration

Let p be a large prime such that $q = (p-1)/2$ is also prime. Let G be a group of order p, and let g be a generator of G such that computing discrete logarithms to the base g is difficult. Assume that both the buyer B (in fact B is the buyer's smart card) and the registration authority R have ElGamal-like public-key pairs ([ElGa85]). The buyer's secret key is x_B and his public key is $y_B = g^{x_B}$. The registration authority R uses its secret key to issue certificates which can be verified using R's public key. The public keys of R and all buyers are assumed to be known and certified.

Protocol 1

1. *R chooses a random nonce $x_r \in \mathbf{Z}_p$ and sends $y_r = g^{x_r}$ to B.*
2. *B chooses secret random s_1 and s_2 in $\mathbf{Z}_p$ such that $s_1 + s_2 = x_B \pmod{p}$ and sends $S_1 = y_r^{s_1}$ and $S_2 = y_r^{s_2}$ to R. B convinces R in zero-knowledge of possession of s_1 and s_2. The proof given in [Chau88b] for showing possession of discrete logarithms may be used here. The buyer B computes an ElGamal public key $y_1 = g^{s_1} \pmod{p}$ and sends it to R.*
3. *R checks that $S_1 S_2 = y_B^{x_r}$ and $y_1^{x_r} = S_1$. R returns to B a certificate $Cert(y_1)$. The certificate states the correctness of y_1.*

By going through the registration procedure above several times, a buyer can obtain several different certified keys y_1.

2.3 Fingerprinting

Fingerprinting is in some respects similar to secure contract signing. The following protocol exploits such a similarity.

Protocol 2

1. *B sends $y_1, Cert(y_1)$ and text to M, where text is a string identifying the purchase. B computes an ElGamal signature sig on text with the secret key s_1; sig is sent to M.*

2. M verifies the certificate on y_1 and the signature sig on $text$.
3. For $i = 1$ to l, M sends one message out of the two messages $item'_i$ and $item''_i$ using the 1-2 provably secure oblivious transfer sketched in [Berg85]. If $item^*_i$ is the output of the oblivious transfer, it should be similar to the original meaningful $item_i$, so it should be easy for B to tell it from junk.
4. B computes an ElGamal signature $sig^*_{(l)}$ on $H(item^*_{(l)})$ using the key s_1, where

$$item^*_{(l)} = item^*_1 || item^*_2 || \cdots || item^*_l \qquad (1)$$

B returns $H(item^*_{(l)})$ and $sig^*_{(l)}$ to M. B proves to M in zero-knowledge that $H(item^*_{(l)})$ was correctly computed, i.e. that it was computed based on the outputs $item^*_i$ of the oblivious transfers, for $i = 1$ to l. If B fails to return $H(item^*_{(l)})$ and the zero-knowledge proof, then M quits the fingerprinting protocol.
5. For $i = l + 1$ to u, M sends one message out of the two messages $item'_i$ and $item''_i$ using the 1-2 provably secure oblivious transfer sketched in [Berg85].
6. B computes an ElGamal signature $sig^*_{(u)}$ on $H(item^*_{(u)})$ using the key s_1, where

$$item^*_{(u)} = item^*_{l+1} || item^*_{l+2} || \cdots || item^*_u \qquad (2)$$

B returns $H(item^*_{(u)})$ and $sig^*_{(u)}$ to M. B proves to M in zero-knowledge that $H(item^*_{(u)})$ was correctly computed, i.e. that it was computed based on the outputs $item^*_i$ of the oblivious transfers, for $i = l + 1$ to u. If B fails to return $H(item^*_{(u)})$ and the zero-knowledge proof, then M quits the fingerprinting protocol.
7. M sends $item_{u+1} || item_{u+2} || \cdots || item_n$ to B.

The following remarks on the security parameters n, l and u are in order:

– As will be justified in Section 3, it should be infeasible for M to figure out the values of $item^*_{(l)}$ and $item^*_{(u)}$ corresponding to a buyer B. Thus the sizes 2^l and 2^{u-l} of the spaces where $item^*_{(l)}$, respectively $item^*_{(u)}$, take values should be large enough (a good choice could be $l \geq 64$, $u - l \geq 64$ which implies $n \geq 128$).
– The buyer B can obtain up to l subitems from M and then quit Protocol 2 before Step 4. This means that up to l subitems can be obtained without copyright protection. *Thus l should be small as compared to n.*
– Once Step 6 is run, the first u subitems are copyright protected, but no protection is provided for the last $n - u$ subitems. *Thus u should not be much smaller than n.* However, the last $n-u$ subitems should contain enough information to deter B from quitting the Protocol 2 before Step 6, which in the worst case would leave subitems $l + 1$ up to u unprotected.

From the above remarks, a good choice would be to take $l = 64$, u such that $u - l \geq 64$, and n such that the last $n - u$ subitems contain the minimum amount of information needed to deter a standard buyer B from quitting Protocol 2 before Step 6.

If the computational resources of B are a bottleneck (as it may happen when B is a smart card), then a possibility is to suppress Steps 5 and 6 from Protocol 2 and send $item_{l+1}, \cdots, item_n$ in Step 7. In this case, the wisest choice is probably to take $l \approx n/2$.

Note 2 (Collusion-resistance). The information embedded in the fingerprinted copy is determined as the successive 1-2 oblivious transfers progress. If B takes part in the fingerprinting protocol through a tamper-proof device such as a smart card, then the 1-2 oblivious transfer from [Berg85] could be replaced by oblivious transfers where B's smart card can *choose* between $item_i', item_i''$ (the choice remains unknown to M, see [Crép88]). Otherwise put, the card chooses the bit b_i to be embedded during the i-th oblivious transfer. B. Then B's card could be programmed to choose the embedded bits as a random codeword of a c-secure code ([Bone95]), which would provide protection against buyer collusions. B should not learn the codeword chosen by his card.

2.4   Identification

Following [Pfit96], it only makes sense to try to identify a redistributor if the redistributed copy $item^{red}$ is not too different from the original $item$:

Definition 1. *Let sim be an arbitrary relation where $sim(item^{red}, item)$ means that a redistributed illegal copy $item^{red}$ is still so close to item that the merchant M wants to identify the original buyer.*

If $sim(item^{red}, item)$ holds, then it is reasonable to assume that $item^{red}$ contains a substantial number of subitems which are (perhaps modified) copies of $item_1^*, \cdots, item_u^*$, for some fingerprinted version $item^*$ of $item$.

It must be noted that no redistributor identification can be requested by M if Protocol 2 is quit before Step 4 is run (M gets no receipt). In the following two-party identification protocol between the merchant M and the registration authority R, we will assume that Step 4 of Protocol 2 was run and that $item^{red}$ contains enough (perhaps modified) copies of subitems among $item_1^*, \cdots, item_l^*$ to allow reconstruction of $item_{(l)}^*$ by M:

Protocol 3

1. *Upon detecting a redistributed $item^{red}$, M determines whether*

$$sim(item^{red}, item)$$

holds for some information item on sale. If yes, M uses the redundancy scheme to recover the bit value that was embedded in each subitem of $item^{red}$ (notice that $item^{red}$ may not exactly correspond to any fingerprinted $item^*$). If the redundancy scheme is sufficient and $item^{red}$ contains enough (perhaps modified) subitems among $item_1^*, \cdots, item_l^*$, M can reconstruct in this way the correct fingerprinted $item^*_{(l)}$ from which $item^{red}$ was derived (if a few subitems in $item^*_{(l)}$ had been suppressed or a majority of their marks had been modified in $item^{red}$, such subitems can be reconstructed by M using exhaustive search).

2. Once $item^*_{(l)}$ has been reconstructed, M retrieves the corresponding $sig^*_{(l)}$, text, sig, y_1 and $Cert(y_1)$ from her purchase record. Then M sends

$$proof = [item^*_{(l)}, sig^*_{(l)}, text, sig, y_1, Cert(y_1)] \qquad (3)$$

to R asking for identification of B.

3. R computes $H(item^*_{(l)})$ and uses the public key y_1 to verify that $sig^*_{(l)}$ is a signature on $H(item^*_{(l)})$. If the verification fails, this means that either M is trying to unjustly accuse a buyer or that the redundancy scheme was not sufficient to allow the correct reconstruction of $item^*_{(l)}$; in either case, identification fails. If the verification succeeds, the same key y_1 is used to verify that sig is a signature on the text identifying the purchase. Finally R searches its records to find the buyer B who registered the key y_1 and returns the name of B to M.

If $item^{red}$ does not allow reconstruction of $item^*_{(l)}$ and Step 6 of Protocol 2 was run, then reconstruction of $item^*_{(u)}$ (equation (2)) can be attempted. To do this, take Protocol 3 and replace l by u and $item^*_1, \cdots, item^*_l$ by $item^*_{l+1}, \cdots, item^*_u$. Since usually $u - l > l$, $item^{red}$ is likely to contain more subitems of $item^*_{(u)}$ than of $item^*_{(l)}$.

Note 3. If R refuses to collaborate in Protocol 3, its role can be performed by an arbiter except buyer identification. Replace "identify buyer" by "declare R guilty".

3   Security Analysis

We analyze in this section the security of the construction of Section 2.

Proposition 1 (Registration security). *Protocol 1 provides buyer authentication without compromising the private key x_B of the buyer.*

Proof. In registration, R sees S_1, S_2, y_1 and two zero-knowledge proofs. The latter leak no information. Without considering the zero-knowledge proofs, R needs no knowledge of x_B to find values S'_1, S'_2 and y'_1 which are related in the same way as S_1, S_2 and y_1. Take a random s'_1, then compute $y'_1 = g^{s'_1}$ and $S'_1 = y_r^{s'_1}$. Finally, $S'_2 = y_B^{x_r}/S'_1$.

Now consider the zero-knowledge proofs; imagine that an impersonator not knowing x_B can compute S_1, S_2 such that he/she can demonstrate possession of $\log_{y_r} S_1$ and $\log_{y_r} S_2$ and $S_1 S_2 = y_r^{x_B}$ holds. Then the impersonator can compute the discrete logarithm x_B. In general, if impersonation is feasible, so is computing discrete logarithms. ◇

Proposition 2 (Buyer anonymity). *Let l and u be the security parameters defined in Protocol 2. Then M must perform an exhaustive search in a space of size $\min(2^l, 2^{u-l})$ to unduly identify an honest buyer who correctly followed Protocol 2.*

Proof. In the fingerprinting protocol, M sees a pseudonym y_1, which is related to y_B by the equation $y_1^{x_r} S_2 = y_B^{x_r}$. Even knowledge of $\log_g y_r = x_r$ would not suffice to uniquely determine y_B from y_1, since S_2 is unknown to M.

Therefore, M must rely on Protocol 3 to unduly identify an honest buyer. In this protocol, M must figure out either the value $item^*_{(l)}$ or the value $item^*_{(u)}$. Since the oblivious transfer [Berg85] is provably secure and B's proofs on the correctness of $H(item^*_{(l)})$ and $H(item^*_{(u)})$ are zero-knowledge, the only conceivable attack is for M to start trying all possible values for $item^*_{(l)}$ or $item^*_{(u)}$ until one is found such that either $H(item^*_{(l)})$ is the value contained in $sig^*_{(l)}$ or $H(item^*_{(u)})$ is the value contained in $sig^*_{(u)}$. With subitems having two versions each, $item^*_{(l)}$ is uniformly and randomly distributed over a set of 2^l different values, and $item^*_{(u)}$ is uniformly and randomly distributed over a set of 2^{u-l} different values. $\diamond$

Merchant security depends on the marks being preserved. According to the Marking Assumption, marks can only be deleted by buyer collusion.

Definition 2 (Successful collusion). *A collusion of buyers is said to be successful if the colluding buyers manage to delete or modify a majority of marks of enough subitems to render reconstruction of $item^*_{(l)}$ and $item^*_{(u)}$ infeasible in Protocol 3.*

If no c-secure codes are used (see Note 2), then we can only say the following about collusions.

Proposition 3. *The expected percent of subitems whose marks can be deleted by a collusion of c buyers is $100(1 - 1/2^{c-1})$.*

Proof. As pointed out in Subsection 2.1, c colluding buyers can locate (and delete) all marks in the i-th subitem if and only if they can pool both versions $item'_i$ and $item''_i$ of the subitem. The probability that all c buyers were given the same version is $1/2^{c-1}$. Therefore, the probability that they can pool both versions is $1 - 1/2^{c-1}$. $\diamond$

Merchant security also depends on:

- The choice of the security parameters n, l and u (see Subsection 2.3).
- The resilience of the redundancy scheme used in fingerprinting. Even if one or several buyers cannot locate the marks in a subitem (because they all have the same subitem version), they could attempt a blind modification of the subitem with the hope of destroying its marks. Redundancy schemes are helpful against such blind modifications.
- The kind of similarity relation sim used (see Subsection 2.4). If sim is very loose, this means that M wishes to identify the original buyer of any redistributed item that vaguely resembles an item on sale; of course, identification may often fail in such cases.

4 Conclusion and Future Research

We have presented a protocol suite for anonymous fingerprinting which is computationally much simpler than previous proposals. The new scheme does not require secure multiparty computation and the buyer's computation can be performed by a smart card.

Future research should be directed to replacing the general zero-knowledge proof used in Protocol 2 with an efficient zero-knowledge proof specially designed for proving the correctness of a hash value.

References

Berg85.   R. Berger, R. Peralta and T. Tedrick, "A provably secure oblivious transfer protocol", in *Advances in Cryptology-EUROCRYPT'84*, LNCS 209. Berlin: Springer-Verlag, 1985, pp. 408-416.

Blak86.   G. R. Blakley, C. Meadows and G. B. Purdy, "Fingerprinting long forgiving messages", in *Advances in Cryptology-CRYPTO'85*, LNCS 218. Berlin: Springer-Verlag, 1986, pp. 180-189.

Bone95.   D. Boneh and J. Shaw, "Collusion-secure fingerprinting for digital data", in *Advances in Cryptology-CRYPTO'95*, LNCS 963. Berlin: Springer-Verlag, 1995, pp. 452-465.

Chau88a.   D. Chaum, I. B. Damgaard and J. van de Graaf, "Multiparty computations ensuring privacy of each party's input and correctness of the result", in *Advances in Cryptology - CRYPTO'87*, LNCS 293. Berlin: Springer-Verlag, 1988, pp. 87-119.

Chau88b.   D. Chaum, J.-H. Evertse and J. van de Graaf, "An improved protocol for demonstrating possession of discrete logarithms and some generalizations", in *Advances in Cryptology- EUROCRYPT'87*, LNCS 304. Berlin: Springer-Verlag, 1988, pp. 127-141.

Crép88.   C. Crépeau, "Equivalence between two flavours of oblivious transfer", in *Advances in Cryptology - CRYPTO'87*, LNCS 293. Berlin: Springer-Verlag, 1988, pp. 110-123.

Domi98.   J. Domingo-Ferrer, "Anonymous fingerprinting of electronic information with automatic identification of redistributors", *IEE Electronics Letters*, vol. 34, no. 13, June 1998.

ElGa85.   T. ElGamal, "A public-key cryptosystem and a signature scheme based on discrete logarithms", *IEEE Transactions on Information Theory*, vol. IT-31, July 1985, pp. 469-472.

Pfit96.   B. Pfitzmann and M. Schunter, "Asymmetric fingerprinting", in *Advances in Cryptology-EUROCRYPT'96*, LNCS 1070. Berlin: Springer-Verlag, 1996, pp. 84-95.

Pfit97.   B. Pfitzmann and M. Waidner, "Anonymous fingerprinting", in *Advances in Cryptology-EUROCRYPT'97*, LNCS 1233. Berlin: Springer-Verlag, 1997, pp. 88-102.

Implementation of a Provably Secure, Smartcard-Based Key Distribution Protocol

Rob Jerdonek [1,4], Peter Honeyman [2], Kevin Coffman [2], Jim Rees [2], and Kip Wheeler [3]

[1] Arcot Systems, Palo Alto, CA
jerdonek@ix.netcom.com
[2] Center for Information Technology Integration, University of Michigan, Ann Arbor
{honey, kwc, rees}@citi.umich.edu
http://www.citi.umich.edu/
[3] Personal Cipher Card Corporation, Lakeland, FL
smartcard1@compuserve.com

Abstract. We describe the implementation of the Shoup-Rubin key distribution protocol. This protocol stores long-term keys on a smartcard and uses the cryptographic capability of the card to generate and distribute session keys securely. The designers of the protocol provide a mathematical proof of its security, using techniques pioneered by Bellare and Rogaway. Combining this theoretical strength with our implementation on tamper resistant hardware results in practical and powerful middleware functionality, useful in applications that demand strong authentication and confidentiality.

1 Introduction

The Center for Information Technology Integration is a research laboratory that addresses near- and intermediate-term challenges to the University of Michigan's information technology environment. It does this by establishing collaborative relationships with industrial partners to explore and develop enterprise-scale information technology solutions. From the start, CITI's focus has been on middleware. In recent years, increasing amounts of attention have been focused on computer and network security.

Early in 1996, CITI began exploring ways to implement special functionality in smartcards to improve secure access to distributed services. The most prominent flaw in the University of Michigan computing environment (UMCE) is its reliance on the strength of user-selected passwords. UMCE makes heavy use of Kerberos IV for many secure services, such as login authentication, filing, email, and web access; regrettably, Kerberos IV admits an offline dictionary attack that is difficult to detect and defeat. Such an attack is likely to succeed any time users are responsible for selecting their own passwords or pass phrases [1]; indeed, it has long troubled CITI to confirm that many weak passwords are in daily use in the UMCE.[5]

---

4 This work was performed in partial fulfillment of Mr. Jerdonek's Master's degree requirements at the University of Michigan.

5 Although it is somewhat soothing to discover that the most common password is *love*.

J.-J. Quisquater and B. Schneier (Eds.): CARDIS 2000, LNCS 1820, pp. 229–235, 2000.
Springer-Verlag Berlin Heidelberg 2000

Our goal is to replace password-based authentication with stronger means. Smartcards bear particular attraction, as they are able to store securely moderate amounts of information, such as cryptographic keys; offer good tamper-resistance; and can even perform cryptographic calculations with modest performance.

Establishment of a session key is central to the goal of mutual authentication of cooperating principals in a security domain. Principals establish a security context by agreeing on a shared secret, which is used to authenticate or secure subsequent communications. An impractical approach is to arrange that all principals in a security domain share mutual secret keys; this arrangement breaks down from quadratic growth in the number of keys that must be set up in advance and the concomitant requirement that principals manage private databases of keys. Needham and Schroeder observe that a trusted third party can reduce these complexities by sharing a long-term key with each of the principals in the security domain [2]. This has two distinct advantages. First, $O(n)$ long-term keys are needed, instead of $O(n^2)$. Second, each principal must maintain only the key that it shares with the third-party, rather than one key for each of the other principals in the security domain.

While this reduces the obligations and bookkeeping for principals, it does not eliminate their responsibilities altogether, nor shield them from disaster in the event that control over the long-term key is lost. To assist principals in the secure management of their keys, Bellcore researchers Victor Shoup and Avi Rubin devised an innovative key distribution protocol that exploits the tamper-resistant properties of smartcards to provide a convenient and secure repository for cryptographic keys [3]. With the help of Personal Cipher Card Corporation (PC^3), CITI implemented the Shoup-Rubin protocol on smartcards and host workstations.

Shoup-Rubin uses two types of cryptographic keys. Long-term keys are securely stored on the card, never leaving its physical boundaries. These keys are shared with a trusted third-party and used to establish (short-term) session keys. Session keys are not (necessarily) stored on secure, tamper-resistant hardware, so they are vulnerable to compromise. In contrast, long-term keys must never be vulnerable.

The details of Shoup-Rubin, outlined in the next section, are fairly intricate, in part to satisfy the requirements of an underlying complexity-theoretic framework [4]. This inconvenience is balanced by the ability to prove powerful properties of the protocol. In particular, Shoup and Rubin are able to prove that the protocol does not disclose the session key to an adversary. The combined strength of mathematical proof of security and a tamper-resistant implementation lends good confidence in the overall security of our approach.

2 The Shoup-Rubin Key Distribution Protocol

The Shoup-Rubin key distribution protocol runs among three parties: the communicating peers, and a third-party that is trusted to hold long-term keys securely. Following Schneier [5], we call them ALICE, BOB, and TRENT, respectively. ALICE and BOB can each be viewed as a pair of agents, one responsible for holding long-term keys, and one with less stringent security requirements. The former agent is implemented on a secure token such as a smartcard, while the latter runs on an ordinary computer. We rely on the tamper-resistance inherent in smartcards to protect the long-term keys used by Shoup-Rubin. The host computers have less stringent security requirements; they rely on physical and other security properties inherent to the secure tokens holding the long-term keys.

We now describe the Shoup-Rubin session key distribution protocol, first in general terms, then in detail. We identify ALICE and BOB's computers with ALICE and BOB themselves. We assume that ALICE's and BOB's computers have smartcard readers attached, and that no computer other than the one to which it is attached can communicate with a smartcard reader.

Shoup-Rubin builds on the Leighton-Micali key distribution protocol [6], an inexpensive symmetric key distribution protocol. Leighton-Micali uses a construct known as a *pair key* to establish a shared secret between communicating parties.

Let $\mathbf{A}$ and $\mathbf{B}$ denote unambiguous identifiers for ALICE and BOB, and let K_A and K_B be their long term keys. These keys are shared with TRENT. DES encryption of message M with key K is denoted $\{M\}_K$. ALICE and BOB's *pair key* is defined

$$\text{AB} = \{\mathbf{A}\}_{K_B} \quad \{\mathbf{B}\}_{K_A}$$

TRENT calculates pair keys on demand; that is TRENT's entire role. Because a pair key reveals nothing about the long-term keys used in its calculation, it can be communicated in the clear.

With pair key $_{AB}$ in hand, ALICE computes $\{\mathbf{B}\}_{K_A}$. Combining this with the pair key yields $= \{\mathbf{A}\}_{K_B}$. BOB can compute   directly, so once ALICE has a pair key in hand, she and BOB can communicate privately using key   .

Shoup-Rubin extends Leighton-Micali in two ways:
-    is computed on ALICE's and BOB's smartcards, freeing ALICE and BOB from the responsibility of knowing their own long-term keys.
- ALICE and BOB then use   to secure the messages that provide for session key agreement.

Shoup and Rubin use Bellare and Rogaway's innovative complexity theoretic techniques [4] to prove that their key distribution algorithm does not disclose the session key, even to an extremely powerful adversary. We now describe the Shoup-Rubin protocol in detail.

2.1 Details

The following table defines the terms used in the Shoup-Rubin smartcard-based session key distribution protocol. Integer operands are concatenated to other protocol terms with the "dot" operator to satisfy requirements of the Bellare-Rogaway proof framework.

Term	Meaning
A, B	Unique identifiers
K_A, K_B	Long-term keys
K_{AC}, K_{BC}	Secret card keys
r, s	Nonces
$_{AB} = \{A\cdot0\}_{K_B} \quad \{B\cdot1\}_{K_A}$	Pair key
$= \{_{AB}\cdot B\cdot2\}_{K_A}$	Verifies $_{AB}$
$= \{r\cdot s\cdot1\}$	Verifies r and s
$= \{r\cdot1\cdot1\}_{K_{AC}}$	Verifies r
$= \{s\cdot0\cdot1\}$	Verifies s
$= \{A\cdot0\}_{K_B}$	See discussion
$= \{s\cdot0\cdot0\}$	Session key

Shoup-Rubin glossary

We now detail the steps of Shoup-Rubin.

From	To	Message	Meaning
ALICE	TRENT	**A, B**	ALICE wishes to initiate a session with BOB.
TRENT	ALICE	$_{AB}$,	$_{AB}$ is ALICE and BOB's pair key. is a verifier for $_{AB}$.

ALICE asks TRENT for the ALICE/BOB pair key. TRENT also returns a verifier, which ALICE's card uses to prevent masquerading.

From	To	Message	Meaning
ALICE	CardA	—	ALICE requests a nonce to verify subsequent communication with BOB.
CardA	ALICE	r,	r is a nonce, is a verifier for r.

ALICE's first card operation

ALICE initiates the protocol with BOB by requesting a nonce from her smartcard. ALICE retains the verifier for later use.

From	To	Message	Meaning
ALICE	BOB	**A, r**	BOB will use r to assure ALICE of his correct behavior.

By sending a nonce to BOB, ALICE requests establishment of a fresh session key.

From	To	Message	Meaning
BOB	CardB	A, r	BOB instructs his smartcard to construct a session key, and provides ALICE's nonce for her subsequent verification.
CardB	BOB	s, ,	s is a nonce used to construct the session key. is the session key. is ALICE's verifier for r and s. is BOB's verifier for s.

BOB's card operation

BOB sends ALICE's identity and her nonce to his smartcard. BOB's card calculates , then generates a nonce and a session key. BOB's card also generates two verifiers; one is used by ALICE's card to verify both nonces, the other is used by BOB to verify ALICE's subsequent acknowledgement. BOB retains the session key and his verifier.

From	To	Message	Meaning
BOB	ALICE	s,	ALICE needs s to construct the session key, and to verify r and s. BOB retains , the session key, and , a verifier for s.

BOB forwards his nonce, from which ALICE's card constructs the session key.

From	To	Message	Meaning
ALICE	CardA	B, r, s, $_{AB}$, , ,	Verify: $_{AB}$ with , r with , and BOB's use of r and s with . Use $_{AB}$ and s to construct the session key.
CardA	ALICE	,	is the session key. is sent to BOB to confirm ALICE's verification of s.

ALICE's second card operation

ALICE sends everything she has to her smartcard: BOB's identity, the pair key and its verifier, her nonce and its verifier, and BOB's nonce and its verifier. ALICE's card validates all the verifiers. If everything checks out, ALICE's smartcard derives , then constructs the session key from BOB's nonce and uploads it to ALICE along with a verifier to assure BOB that ALICE is behaving properly.

From	To	Message	Meaning
ALICE	BOB		Confirm

ALICE sends the verifier to BOB. BOB compares it to his retained verifier.

2.2 Implementation

To implement Shoup-Rubin, CITI turned to PC^3. PC^3 extended SCOS, a proprietary cryptographic smartcard operating system, to support four new operations, KeyDist$_1$, KeyDist$_2$, KeyDist$_{3a}$, and KeyDist$_{3b}$, and supplied CITI with SCOS cards that implement these operations. CITI tested the cards extensively, both for correctness and for performance. Performance is of interest because it affects usability of the implementation. If card operations take too many seconds, the user experience is adversely affected.

To gauge performance, CITI built SCOS drivers for UNIX, Windows 95, and NT that record communication time and elapsed time. The difference between elapsed time and I/O time is accounted to card processing time. For Shoup-Rubin operations that require more than one SCOS command, we also measure host processing time, but this is negligible in all cases.[6] Although this paper reports only UNIX performance, NT performance is comparable. We encountered timer granularity problems on Windows 95 that affected performance adversely.

ALICE's first card operation is implemented directly by $KeyDist_1$. This requires two I/O operations: one to send an SCOS command string, and one to read results from the card.

SCOS does not send both values and results in a single command, so BOB's card operation is broken into two SCOS commands: one to send the command and values, and one to read the results from an output buffer.

ALICE's second card operation also has values and results, requiring multiple SCOS commands. SCOS can send up to 64 bytes in one command, but this operation sends 72 bytes to the card, so we use three SCOS operations to effect $KeyDist_3$: $KeyDist_{3a}$ sends the first 64 bytes of values and $KeyDist_{3b}$ sends the remaining 8 bytes. Then an SCOS read command recovers the results from an output buffer.

2.3 Performance

PC^3's implementation of Shoup-Rubin runs on the SGS-Thomson ST16F48 card, which is based on an MC68HC05 microprocessor clocked at 3.57 Mhz, with 8 KB EEPROM, 16 KB ROM, and 384 bytes RAM. Version PC64T4 of SCOS uses 128 bytes of EEPROM, 6K of ROM, and 128 bytes of RAM. The Shoup-Rubin extensions to SCOS are written in 250 lines of Motorola 6805 assembler. This assembles to 430 bytes of code, which is stored in an executable EEPROM file.

ALICE runs on a 200 MHz Pentium running OpenBSD 2.2 and BOB runs on a 122 Mhz PowerPC running AIX 4.2. Serial communication with the card is 9600 bps.

The following table summarizes the number of bytes transmitted, and host, card, and communication times for the three card operations. Each figure represents the average of 10 time trials. Variance among the trials is negligible. All times are in msec.

operation	num cmds	num bytes	comm time	card time	clock time
$KeyDist_1$	1	32	32	63	95
$KeyDist_2$	2	80	306	147	454
$KeyDist_3$	3	112	133	241	374

Total time from the start of $KeyDist_1$ to the completion of $KeyDist_3$ is 3.1 sec. Most of the time is spent in network communications and protocol processing.

Our UNIX drivers write a byte at a time. Evidently OpenBSD handles this well, averaging slightly more than the expected msec per byte, while AIX is apparently tuned for larger transfers.

---

[6] < 1 msec

3 Discussion

To demonstrate the capabilities of our smartcard-based Shoup-Rubin implementation, we wrapped it in a GSS API interface library [7] on which we built a secure video-conferencing application [8]. While implementing in SCOS was a successful strategy, an approach that gives CITI more direct control over card programming would be more satisfactory.[7] But even at this writing, it is not easy for University developers to obtain cards and documentation for programmable smartcards capable of general-purpose cryptographic applications. For example, first generation JavaCards lack cryptography.

Yet more frustrating, on several occasions, CITI has been offered programmable cryptographic smartcards with embedded DES capability, only to find the DES engine "crippled" by key length or other limitations intended to satisfy US export regulations. (More than once, CITI has pled with manufacturers to consult an atlas.) These difficulties aside, this is an exciting time to be working with secure tokens: new companies and products are making custom programming of secure tokens fast and easy with user-friendly development kits that support high-level languages and rapid prototyping.

Acknowledgements

We thank Brahm Windeler for help in collecting the timings. This work was partially supported by a grant from Bellcore.

References

1. Robert Morris and Ken Thompson, "Password Security: A Case History," *Communications of the ACM* **22**(11) (November, 1979).
2. R.M. Needham and M.D. Schroeder, "Using Encryption for Authentication in Large Networks of Computers," *Communications of the ACM* **21**(12) (December, 1978).
3. V. Shoup and A.D. Rubin, "Session Key Distribution Using Smart Cards," in *Proc. of Eurocrypt '96* (May, 1996).
4. M. Bellare and P. Rogaway, "Provably Secure Session Key Distribution: The Three Party Case," in *Proc. ACM 27th Ann. Symp. on the Theory of Computing* (1995).
5. B. Schneier, *Applied Cryptography, Second Edition,* John Wiley & Sons, Inc. (1996).
6. T. Leighton and S. Micali, "Secret-Key Agreement Without Public-Key Cryptography," pp. 456 479 in *Proc of Crypto '93*, Santa Barbara (1993).
7. J. Linn, "Generic Security Service Application Program Interface, Version 2," RFC 2078 , USC/Information Sciences Institute (January, 10, 1997).
8. Peter Honeyman, Andy Adamson, Kevin Coffman, Janani Janakiraman, Rob Jerdonek, and Jim Rees, "Secure Videoconferencing," pp. 123 130 in *Proc. 7th USENIX Security Symp.*, San Antonio (January, 1998).

---

[7] To CITI.

The Block Cipher BKSQ*

Joan Daemen[1] and Vincent Rijmen[2]

[1] PWI
Zweefvliegtuigstraat 10
B-1130 Brussel, Belgium
Daemen.J@protonworld.com
[2] Katholieke Universiteit Leuven, ESAT-COSIC
K. Mercierlaan 94,
B-3001 Heverlee, Belgium
vincent.rijmen@esat.kuleuven.ac.be

Abstract. In this paper we present a new 96-bit block cipher called BKSQ. The cipher can be implemented efficiently on a wide range of processors (including smartcards) and in hardware.

1 Introduction

We present a new 96-bit block cipher called BKSQ. The cipher has been designed according to the principles of the 'Wide trail design strategy' [2] in order to guarantee its resistance against linear and differential cryptanalysis. The structure of the cipher is a generalisation of the SQUARE cipher structure [3]. It has already been shown that SQUARE can be implemented very efficiently on a wide range of platforms. However its structure only allows block lengths of $8n^2$ bits; e.g., $n = 4$ gives a block length of 128 bits. In this paper we generalize the structure of the round transformation in order to allow block lengths of $8nm$ bits without sacrificing cryptographic strength or implementation efficiency. This is accomplished by changing the linear layer in the round transformation.

BKSQ is especially suited to be implemented on a smart card. Its block length of 96 bits allows it to be used as a (2nd) pre-image resistant one-way function. Most available block ciphers have a block length of 64 bits, but this block length is currently perceived as being too small for a secure one-way function. The next option in currently available block ciphers is a block length 128 bit, but this leads to one-way functions that are significantly slower. The block cipher BKSQ is tailored towards these applications. Still, it can also be used for efficient MACing and encryption on a Smart Card.

The remainder of this paper is organized as follows. In Section 2 we explain the structure of BKSQ and introduce the various components. In Section 3 we discuss the resistance of the cipher against various cryptanalysis methods. We conclude with a discussion of some implementation aspects in Section 4.

---

* This research has been sponsored by PWI.

J.-J. Quisquater and B. Schneier (Eds.): CARDIS 2000, LNCS 1820, pp. 236–245, 2000.

2   Structure of BKSQ

BKSQ is an iterated block cipher with a block length of 96 bits and a key length of 96, 144 or 192 bits. The round transformation of BKSQ is *not* a Feistel network. In a typical Feistel network a part of the input bits of the round is transposed unchanged to another position at the output. This is not the case with BKSQ, where every bit of the input is treated in the same way. We call this type of round transformation a *uniform round transformation*. On the conceptual level, the round transformation is composed of four uniform invertible transformations. In an efficient implementation the transformations can be combined in a single set of table-lookups and exor operations.

Let the input of the cipher be denoted by a string of 12 bytes: $p_0 p_1 \ldots p_{11}$. These bytes can be rearranged in a 3×4 array, or 'state' a.

$$a = \begin{bmatrix} a_{0,0} & a_{0,1} & a_{0,2} & a_{0,3} \\ a_{1,0} & a_{1,1} & a_{1,2} & a_{1,3} \\ a_{2,0} & a_{2,1} & a_{2,2} & a_{2,3} \end{bmatrix} = \begin{bmatrix} p_0 & p_3 & p_6 & p_9 \\ p_1 & p_4 & p_7 & p_{10} \\ p_2 & p_5 & p_8 & p_{11} \end{bmatrix}$$

The basic building blocks of the cipher operate on this array. Figure 1 gives a graphical illustration of the building blocks.

2.1   The Linear Transformation θ

θ is a linear operation that operates separately on each of the four columns of a state. We have

$$\theta(a) = \begin{bmatrix} 3 & 2 & 2 \\ 2 & 3 & 2 \\ 2 & 2 & 3 \end{bmatrix} \cdot \begin{bmatrix} a_{0,0} & a_{0,1} & a_{0,2} & a_{0,3} \\ a_{1,0} & a_{1,1} & a_{1,2} & a_{1,3} \\ a_{2,0} & a_{2,1} & a_{2,2} & a_{2,3} \end{bmatrix} .$$

Both addition and multiplication are performed in the finite field $GF(2^8)$. This means that the addition operation corresponds to the bitwise exor and multiplication of two bytes is defined as a modular multiplication of polynomials with binary coefficients [10].

By defining the operations over a finite field and a careful choice of the coefficients of θ we can guarantee a high resistance against linear and differential cryptanalysis, following the design principles of the 'wide trail design strategy' [2, 13]. Furthermore, this choice for the coefficients makes it possible to implement θ very efficiently on an 8-bit processor with limited RAM.

2.2   The Nonlinear Transformation γ

γ is a nonlinear byte substitution, identical for all bytes. We have

$$\gamma : b = \gamma(a) \Leftrightarrow b_{i,j} = S_\gamma(a_{i,j}),$$

with S_γ an invertible 8-bit substitution table or S-box. The inverse of γ consists of the application of the inverse substitution S_γ^{-1} to all bytes of a state.

The design criteria for S_γ are minimal correlation between linear combinations of input bits and linear combinations of output bits, and a minimal upper bound for the entries in the exor-table (not counting the trivial (0,0) entry). For the construction of the S-box we started from the inverse mapping over GF(2), as explained in [12]. This mapping has very good resistance against linear and differential cryptanalysis. Subsequently we applied an affine transformation (over GF(2)) to the output bits, with the property that it has a complicated description in $GF(2^8)$ in order to thwart interpolation attacks [5]. We ensured that the S-box has no fixed points ($S_\gamma[x] = x$) and no 'opposite fixed points' ($S_\gamma[x] = \bar{x}$). The input-output correlations of this S-box are upper bounded by 2^{-3} and the entries of the exor-table are upper bounded by 4.

2.3   The Byte Permutation π

The effect of π is a shift of the rows of a state. Every row is shifted a different amount. We have

$$\pi : b = \pi(a) \Leftrightarrow b_{i,j} = a_{i,j-i}.$$

The effect of π is that for every column of a the three elements are moved to three different columns in $\pi(a)$. Such a byte permutation is called 'diffusion-optimal' with respect to θ and it enhances the effect of the linear transformation θ.

2.4   Bitwise Round Key Addition σ

$\sigma[k^t]$ consists of the bitwise addition of a round key k^t. We have

$$\sigma[k^t] : b = \sigma[k^t](a) \Leftrightarrow b = a \oplus k^t.$$

The inverse of $\sigma[k^t]$ is $\sigma[k^t]$ itself.

2.5   The Cipher BKSQ

The building blocks are composed into the round transformation denoted by $\rho[k^t]$:

$$\rho[k^t] = \sigma[k^t] \circ \pi \circ \gamma \circ \theta \tag{1}$$

BKSQ is defined as R times the round operation, preceded by a key addition $\sigma[k^0]$ and by θ^{-1}:

$$\text{BKSQ}[k] = \rho[k^R] \circ \rho[k^{R-1}] \circ \ldots \circ \rho[k^2] \circ \rho[k^1] \circ \sigma[k^0] \circ \theta^{-1} \tag{2}$$

The number of rounds depends on the key length that is used. For 96-bit keys, there are 10 rounds; for 144-bit keys, there are 14 rounds and for 192-bit keys, the number of rounds is 18.

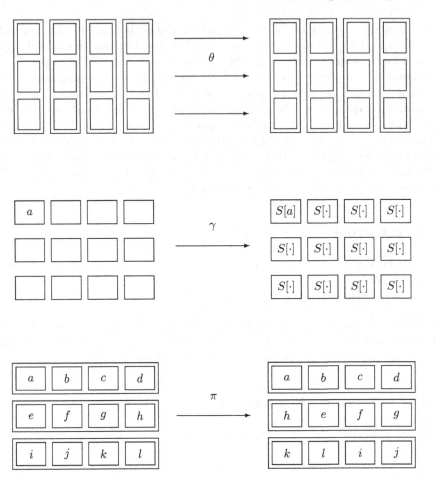

Fig. 1. Graphical illustration of the basic operations of BKSQ. θ consists of 4 parallel linear diffusion mappings. γ consists of 12 separate substitutions. π is a shift of the rows.

2.6   The Key Scheduling

The derivation of the round keys k^t from the cipher key K depends on the length of the cipher key. The key scheduling can be described as follows. The round keys have always a length of 96 bits. The cipher key K has a length of 96, 144 or 192 bits. All these lengths are multiples of 24, and all keys will be considered as an array of 24-bit columns. A round key has 4 columns, a cipher key has L columns, where $L = 4, 6$ or 8. We define an array w, consisting of $4(R+1)$ 24-bit columns, where R is the number of rounds in BKSQ. The array is constructed by repeated application of an invertible nonlinear transformation ψ: the first L

columns are the columns of K, the next L are given by $\psi(K)$, the following columns are given by $\psi(\psi(K))$, etc.

The round keys k^t are extracted in a simple way from w:

$$k^t = \begin{bmatrix} w_{4t} & w_{4t+1} & w_{4t+2} & w_{4t+3} \end{bmatrix} .$$

Note that this key scheduling can be implemented without explicit use of the array w. If the application requires that the implementation uses a minimal amount of RAM, it is possible to calculate the round keys during the round operation, thereby only requiring storage of L 24-bit columns.

2.7   The Round Key Evolution ψ

The transformation ψ is defined in terms of the exor operation, a byte-rotation rot that rotates the bytes of a column,

$$\text{rot}\left(\begin{bmatrix} a \\ b \\ c \end{bmatrix}\right) = \begin{bmatrix} b \\ c \\ a \end{bmatrix},$$

and a nonlinear substitution γ' that operates in exactly the same way as γ, but takes as argument column vectors instead of arrays:

$$\gamma'\left(\begin{bmatrix} a \\ b \\ c \end{bmatrix}\right) = \begin{bmatrix} S_\gamma(a) \\ S_\gamma(b) \\ S_\gamma(c) \end{bmatrix}.$$

The transformation ψ operates on blocks of L columns. For key lengths of 96 or 144 bits ($L = 4$ or 6), ψ is given by:

$$\psi([a_0 \dots a_{L-1}]) = [b_0 \dots b_{L-1}] \Leftrightarrow \begin{cases} b_0 = a_0 \oplus \gamma'(\text{rot}(a_{L-1})) \oplus C_t \\ b_i = a_i \oplus b_{i-1} & i = 1, 2, \dots, L-1. \end{cases}$$

For a key length of 192 bits ($L = 8$), an extra nonlinearity is introduced and ψ is given by:

$$\psi([a_0 \dots a_{L-1}]) = [b_0 \dots b_{L-1}]$$

$$\Leftrightarrow \begin{cases} b_0 = a_0 \oplus \gamma'(\text{rot}(a_{L-1})) \oplus c_t \\ b_i = a_i \oplus b_{i-1} & i = 1, 2, \dots, L/2 \\ b_{L/2} = a_{L/2} \oplus \gamma'(b_{L/2-1}) \\ b_i = a_i \oplus b_{i-1} & i = L/2+1, \dots, L-1. \end{cases}$$

The vectors c_t have as functionality to remove the symmetry in the transformation. They are given by:

$$c_t = \begin{bmatrix} d_t \\ 0 \\ 0 \end{bmatrix},$$

where $d_0 = 1$ and $d_{t+1} = 2 \cdot d_t$. Multiplication is done in the Galois field (modulo the same polynomial as for γ and θ).

2.8 The Inverse Cipher

The structure of BKSQ lends itself to efficient implementations. For a number of modes of operation it is important that this is also the case for the inverse cipher. Therefore, BKSQ has been designed in such a way that the structure of its inverse is equal to that of the cipher itself, with the exception of the key schedule. Note that this identity in *structure* differs from the identity of *components and structure* in IDEA [9].

By means of a mathematical derivation, very similar to the one given in [3], it can be shown that the inverse cipher is equal to the cipher itself with γ, θ and π replaced by γ^{-1}, θ^{-1} and π^{-1} respectively and with different round key values.

3 Cryptanalysis

We discuss the resistance of BKSQ against cryptanalytic attacks.

3.1 Linear and Differential Cryptanalysis

BKSQ has been designed according to the 'wide trail design strategy,' introduced by J. Daemen [2]. This strategy is used to guarantee a low maximum probability of differential trails and a low maximum correlation of linear trails.

The S-box is selected such that the maximal entry in the exor-table equals four, and the maximal correlation equals 2^{-3}.

The choice of the coefficients of θ gives it a branch number of four, which means that every two-round characteristic or linear approximation has at least four active S-boxes. The choice of π ensures that every four-round characteristic or linear approximation has at least 16 active S-boxes.

We wrote a program to count the minimum number of active boxes in an n-round characteristic or linear approximation, for n going up to 20. It turns out that for $n \geq 4$, there are at least $4n$ active S-boxes in every n-round differential characteristic and every n-round linear approximation

3.2 Truncated Differentials

The concept of truncated differentials was first published by L.R. Knudsen [7]. The idea can be summarized by stating that we don't look at the specific difference that the individual bytes have, but only take into account whether the bytes in position (i, j) are equal or not. Using truncated differentials, it is possible to cryptanalyse versions of BKSQ that are reduced to seven rounds or less. The attack is based on the fact that a (truncated) difference of the following form:

$$\begin{bmatrix} x & 0 & y & 0 \\ 0 & 0 & 0 & 0 \\ z & 0 & u & 0 \end{bmatrix},$$

at the input of a round transformation, goes with probability 2^{-16} to an output difference of the same form. This one-round characteristic can be concatenated with itself to produce a multi-round characteristic. A more detailed description of this attack is given in Appendix A. It seems not possible to cryptanalyse more than seven rounds with this attack.

3.3 The SQUARE Attack

In [3] a new attack is described, that works for up to six rounds of SQUARE. Because of the similarity between the round transformations of BKSQ and SQUARE, the same attack also applies here. Instead of repeating the description of the attack, we list the complexities for this attack on BKSQ in Table 1. While the requirements of the attack are smaller, it seems not possible to extend the attack with an additional round.

Table 1. Complexity of the SQUARE attack when applied to BKSQ.

Attack	# Plaintexts	Time	Memory
4-round	2^9	2^9	small
5-round	2^{11}	2^{32}	small
6-round	2^{24}	2^{56}	2^{24}

3.4 Timing Attacks

A class of timing attacks is described by Kocher in [8]. The underlying principle of the attacks is that if the execution time of an implementation depends on secret key bits, then a cryptanalyst can deduce information about these key bits. An implementation can be protected against timing attacks by removing all branches that are conditional on key bits. This can easily be done for BKSQ (cf. Section 4).

4 Implementation Aspects

The only operations required to implement BKSQ are exor, one-bit shifts and table-lookups. Therefore the cipher can be implemented efficiently on a wide range of processors and in hardware (no carry delays).

On 32-bit processors, the linear operations and the nonlinear substitution can be combined into a single set of table-lookups and exor operations. The key addition exists of a simple exor operation. This implementation requires about 1 kbyte of RAM for the tables.

On 8-bit processors, other optimisations are possible. The byte permutation can be combined easily with the nonlinear substitution and the key addition.

Typically RAM is scarce on 8-bit processors. In that case the additions (exors) and multiplications of the transformation θ will be implemented explicitly. This observation has influenced the choice for the coefficients of θ.

Multiplication with 2 can be implemented with one shift and a (conditional) reduction (i.e., an exor). However, in order to keep the implementation resistant against timing attacks, we implement this multiplication with a table lookup. This requires an additional 256 bytes of ROM. Multiplication with 3 can be implemented as a multiplication with 2 and an addition ($3x = 2x \oplus x$).

The design of the key scheduling facilitates 'just-in-time' calculation of the round keys, a necessity when the processor has not enough RAM to store all the round keys in advance.

A timing attack resistant implementation of BKSQ on the Motorola 68HC08 microprocessor fits easily in less than 1kbyte of ROM, requires 28 bytes of RAM and takes less than 7000 cycles (for the 10-round version).

References

1. E. Biham and A. Shamir, "Differential cryptanalysis of DES-like cryptosystems," *Journal of Cryptology*, Vol. 4, No. 1, 1991, pp. 3–72.
2. J. Daemen, "Cipher and hash function design strategies based on linear and differential cryptanalysis," *Doctoral Dissertation*, March 1995, K.U.Leuven.
3. J. Daemen, L.R. Knudsen and V. Rijmen, "The block cipher Square," Fast Software Encryption, LNCS 1267, E. Biham, Ed., Springer-Verlag, 1997, pp. 149–165. Also available as http://www.esat.kuleuven.ac.be/~rijmen/square/fse.ps.gz.
4. J. Daemen and V. Rijmen, "Linear frameworks for block ciphers," *COSIC internal report 96-3*, 1996.
5. T. Jakobsen and L.R. Knudsen, "The interpolation attack on block ciphers," *Fast Software Encryption, LNCS 1267,* E. Biham, Ed., Springer-Verlag, 1997, pp. 28–40.
6. J. Kelsey, B. Schneier and D. Wagner, "Key-schedule cryptanalysis of IDEA, G-DES, GOST, SAFER, and Triple-DES," *Advances in Cryptology, Proceedings Crypto'96, LNCS 1109*, N. Koblitz, Ed., Springer-Verlag, 1996, pp. 237–252.
7. L.R. Knudsen, "Truncated and higher order differentials," *Fast Software Encryption, LNCS 1008*, B. Preneel, Ed., Springer-Verlag, 1995, pp. 196–211.
8. P.C. Kocher, "Timing attacks on implementations of Diffie-Hellman, RSA, DSS and other systems," *Advances in Cryptology, Proceedings Crypto'96, LNCS 1109*, N. Koblitz, Ed., Springer-Verlag, 1996, pp. 146–158.
9. X. Lai, J.L. Massey and S. Murphy, "Markov ciphers and differential cryptanalysis," *Advances in Cryptology, Proceedings Eurocrypt'91, LNCS 547*, D.W. Davies, Ed., Springer-Verlag, 1991, pp. 17–38.
10. R. Lidl and H. Niederreiter, *Introduction to finite fields and their applications*, Cambridge University Press, 1986.
11. M. Matsui, "Linear cryptanalysis method for DES cipher," *Advances in Cryptology, Proceedings Eurocrypt'93, LNCS 765*, T. Helleseth, Ed., Springer-Verlag, 1994, pp. 386–397.
12. K. Nyberg, "Differentially uniform mappings for cryptography," *Advances in Cryptology, Proceedings Eurocrypt'93, LNCS 765*, T. Helleseth, Ed., Springer-Verlag, 1994, pp. 55–64.
13. V. Rijmen, "Cryptanalysis and design of iterated block ciphers," *Doctoral Dissertation*, October 1997, K.U.Leuven.

A   The Truncated Differential Attack

Using truncated differentials, reduced versions of BKSQ can be cryptanalysed. Up to seven rounds can be broken using the following approach. First we explain a one-round truncated differential, afterwards we describe how this can be used in an attack.

A.1   A One-Round Truncated Differential

Let a and b be two states, where $a_{i,j} = b_{i,j}$ for all (i,j), except for (i,j) equal to $(0,0)$, $(0,2)$, $(2,0)$, or $(2,2)$. We say then that $a \oplus b$ is an α-difference. Let $c = \theta(a)$ and $d = \theta(b)$. Since θ operates independently on every column, we have that

$$c_{i,j} = d_{i,j} \qquad i = 0,1,2; j = 1,3.$$

Our choice for the c_j coefficients ensures that in the first and the third column $(j = 0, 2)$ at least two of the three bytes differ between c and d. More precise, we have for $j = 0, 2$:

$$c_{i,j} \neq d_{i,j} \qquad i = 0, 2;$$

and

$$c_{1,j} = d_{1,j} \Leftrightarrow a_{0,j} \oplus b_{0,j} = a_{2,j} \oplus b_{2,j}. \tag{3}$$

Equation (3) shows that with probability $(2^{-8})^2$, an α-difference at the input of θ will go to an α-difference at the output.

Since γ and $\sigma[k^t]$ operate on the independent bytes, every truncated difference remains unchanged with probability one. Since π leaves the first row of a state unchanged, and shifts the third row by two positions, an α-difference at the input goes to an α-difference at the output with probability one.

We conclude that an α-difference at the input of a round transformation $\rho[k]$ goes to an α-difference at the output with probability 2^{-16}.

A.2   Constructing a Multiple-Round Truncated Differential

The one-round differential from the previous section can be concatenated. It can also be preceded and followed by a few special rounds with enhanced probability.

For the end rounds, we consider what happens when (3) is not followed: with a probability close to $1 - 2^{-7}$, an alpha difference at the input of a round will go to an output difference of the following form:

$$\begin{bmatrix} x_1 & 0 & x_2 & 0 \\ 0 & x_3 & 0 & x_4 \\ x_5 & 0 & x_6 & 0 \end{bmatrix}. \tag{4}$$

This difference is still highly structured: in the second an fourth column there is only one byte different from zero. This will be visible in the output of the next round, where the differences will show a specific relation. We conjecture that a differential attack will be possible if (4) is used in the last but one round. In the first rounds we can enhance the probability of our differential by guessing some key bits.

Summarising, we can attack seven rounds in the following way. We guess two bytes of information about the key. If we guess right we can construct pairs with an α-difference that pass the first two rounds of the truncated differential with probability one. The next three rounds are passed with probability 2^{-16} each. In the sixth round, we let the difference spread out (probability close to one) and in the seventh round we detect and/or verify the remaining structure. The probability of the characteristic is about 2^{-48}.

Note that it is not possible to extend this characteristic by adding a fourth $(\alpha \rightarrow \alpha)$-round. The probability that a random pair will produce an α-difference at the input of the last round is also given by 2^{-48} (6 bytes should be zero). Therefore it makes no sense to consider differential characteristics that will result in this difference with a lower probability. It might even be that the signal-to-noise ratio of the seven-round attack is already too low.

Serpent and Smartcards

Ross Anderson[1], Eli Biham[2], and Lars Knudsen[3]

[1] Cambridge University, England,
rja14@cl.cam.ac.uk
[2] Technion, Haifa, Israel,
biham@cs.technion.ac.il
[3] University of Bergen, Norway,
lars.knudsen@ii.uib.no

Abstract. We proposed a new block cipher, Serpent, as a candidate for the Advanced Encryption Standard. This algorithm uses a new structure that simultaneously allows a more rapid avalanche, a more efficient bitslice implementation, and an easy analysis that enables us to demonstrate its security against all known types of attack. Although designed primarily for efficient implementation on Intel Pentium/MMX platforms, it is also suited for implementation on smartcards and other 8-bit processors. In this note we describe why. We also describe why many other candidates are not suitable.

1   Introduction

For many applications, the Data Encryption Standard algorithm is nearing the end of its useful life. Its 56-bit key is too small, as the Electronic Frontier Foundation's keysearch machine has vividly demonstrated [15]. Although triple-DES can solve the key length problem, the DES algorithm was also designed primarily for hardware encryption, yet the great majority of applications that use it today implement it in software, where it is relatively inefficient.

For these reasons, the US National Institute of Standards and Technology has issued a call for a successor algorithm, to be called the *Advanced Encryption Standard* or *AES*. The AES call is aimed at Intel Pentium processors, but one of the evaluation criteria is that the algorithm should have the flexibility to be implemented on other platforms. As the majority of fielded block cipher systems use smartcards and other 8-bit processors and are found in applications such as electronic banking [2,3], prepayment utility meters [4] and pay-TV subscription enforcement systems [6], the performance of the Advanced Encryption Standard on such platforms will be critical to its acceptance worldwide.

2   Serpent

In [5], we presented Serpent, a candidate for AES. Our design philosophy was highly conservative; we did not feel it appropriate to use novel and untested ideas in a cipher which, if accepted after a short review period, will be used to protect

J.-J. Quisquater and B. Schneier (Eds.): CARDIS 2000, LNCS 1820, pp. 246–253, 2000.
© Springer-Verlag Berlin Heidelberg 2000

enormous volumes of financial transactions, health records and government information over a period of decades. We therefore devised a new structure which enabled us to use the S-boxes from DES, which have been studied intensely for many years and whose properties are thus well understood, in a manner suitable for efficient implementation on modern processors while simultaneously allowing us to apply the extensive analysis already done on DES.

The resulting design gave an algorithm (which we call Serpent-0) that was as fast as DES and yet resists all currently known attacks at least as well as triple-DES. It was published at the 5th International Workshop on Fast Software Encryption [9] in order to give the maximum possible time for public review. After that we worked hard to strengthen the algorithm and improve its performance, especially on 8-bit processors. The final submission has new, stronger, S-boxes and a slightly different key schedule. We can now show that our design (which we call Serpent-1, or more briefly, Serpent) resists all known attacks, including those based on both differential [10] and linear [20] techniques, with very generous safety margins. The improved key schedule ensures that it is also highly suitable for smartcards; in this context, we acknowledge useful discussions with Craig Clapp and Markus Kuhn on the hardware and low-memory implementation costs respectively.

The Serpent ciphers were inspired by recent ideas for bitslice implementation of ciphers [8]. However, unlike (say) the bitslice implementation of DES, which encrypts 64 different blocks in parallel in order to gain extra speed, Serpent is designed to allow a single block to be encrypted efficiently by bitslicing. This allows the usual modes of operation to be used, so there is no need to change the environment to gain the extra speed.

The basic idea is that a single round of Serpent has a key mixing step followed by 32 identical 4-bit S-boxes in parallel and finally a linear transformation (see [5] for full details). This conventional design enables the existing block cipher analysis machinery to be applied with ease. The radical performance improvement comes from the fact that, on a 32 bit processor such as the Pentium, one can implement each set of 32 S-boxes by bitslicing. Just as one can use a 1-bit processor to implement an algorithm such as DES by executing a hardware description of it (using one logical instruction to emulate each gate), so one can also use a 32-bit processor to compute 32 different DES blocks in parallel — in effect, using the CPU as a 32-way SIMD machine.

Serpent is optimised for bitsliced processing, and compared with DES, the performance gain is significant. 16-round Serpent resists all currently known attacks at least as well as triple-DES, and yet runs three times as quickly as single DES (about 50 Mbit/sec versus 15 Mbit/sec on a 200MHz Pentium). But as AES may persist for 25 years as a standard and a further 25 years in legacy systems, and will have to protect data for the lifetime of individuals thereafter, it will need a cover time of at least a century. In order to ensure that Serpent could withstand advances in both engineering and cryptanalysis for that length of time, we proposed 32 rounds to put its security beyond question. This gives a cipher that is faster than DES (i.e., about 26 Mbit/sec on a 200MHz Pentium Pro) but very much more secure than 3DES.

This is all very well for Pentium software, but what about smartcards?

3   Performance in Smartcard Applications

In a typical smartcard application, one performs a small number of encryptions or decryptions (typically 1–10 of them) in a transaction which should complete in well under a second in order not to inconvenience the user. In some applications, there is a smartcard at each end — one held by the customer, and another embedded in the merchant terminal, or parking meter, or whatever. So an encryption algorithm for use in smartcards should take at most a few tens of milliseconds to encrypt or decrypt a block. But that is not the only constraint.

3.1   EEPROM Usage Versus Speed

The most critical performance requirement is often memory usage rather than raw speed. In prepayment electricity meters, for example, code size was a determining factor in block cipher choice [4]. Fortunately, there is an implementation strategy for Serpent which yields a small code size. This is a bitslice implementation which uses table lookups for each S-box, thus avoiding the code size of the Boolean expression of the S-box.

An Ada implementation that uses this strategy indicates a code size of just under 1K and a computational cost of 34,000 clock cycles. Thus on the 3.5 MHz 6805 processor typical of low-cost smartcards, we expect a throughput of about 100 encryptions per second or 12.8 Kbit/s. A full bitslice implementation — with an unrolled Boolean implementation of the S-boxes rather than table lookup — should occupy 2K of memory but take 11,000 clock cycles and thus deliver 40.7 Kbit/s. These will be the relevant figures for some microcontroller applications; but as most smartcards do not have enough RAM to store Serpent's round keys, these will have to computed afresh with each block. Fortunately, round key computation takes only as many cycles as a single encryption, so the throughput figures for smartcards are about 6.4 and 20 Kbit/sec for 1K and 2K code size respectively.

This is still much faster than needed in most applications. In passing, we note that in applications where we only encrypt and never decrypt (such as some pay-TV and road toll tag systems), we can save 256 bytes from the 1K code size of the compact implementation by not including the inverse S-boxes.

3.2   RAM Usage

RAM requirements are also a critical factor in mass market applications as they make the difference between a 50 cent processor and a 90 cent processor. The sales projections of Gemplus, which has 40% of the smartcard market, indicate that in 2003 the world market will be about 1,885 million cards with small

RAM and shared-key cryptography, 400 million with large RAM and shared key cryptography, and 405 million with large RAM and public key cryptography [21]. Serpent can be implemented using under 80 bytes of RAM (current text, new text, prekey, working space); this is close to the minimum for a cipher with 128 bit blocks and a 256 byte key. It means that of the 128 bytes typically available in low cost smartcards, at least 48 bytes are left for the calling application.

Other candidates are not as frugal. For example, RC6 [23] takes 176 bytes for the round keys, 32 for the current and next text, plus storage for a number of transient variables, so it could be implemented in large RAM cards but not in low cost ones. MARS [13] is similar, needing 160 bytes for the round keys[1].

3.3 Key Agility

Key set-up time is critical in many smartcard applications. The UEPS system described at Cardis 94 is fairly typical, and has since been adapted by VISA as its COPAC product [2,3]. UEPS uses a three pass protocol in which a customer card transfers value to a merchant card. This involves two block encryptions by the customer card, then two decryptions and two encryptions by the merchant card, then two decryptions, two MAC computations and two encryptions in the customer card, and finally two decryptions by the merchant card. This makes a total of fourteen block cipher operations. But there are ten key set-up operations, and unless there is enough RAM to cache round keys, there are fourteen of them. If the protocol were re-implemented with AES, the longer key and block sizes might allow this number to be reduced to nine.

With Serpent, each key setup costs the same as one encryption, so fourteen of each will cost less than 300ms, and nine of each will cost less then 200ms, on a 3.5 MHz card. However, E2 [22] requires the equivalent of three encryptions per key setup, while LOKI-97 requires over 400,000 instructions to set up a key on an 8-bit processor [12] — which at an average of 8 clock cycles per instruction would take almost a second at 3.5 Mhz. This would be unacceptable.

On-the-fly round key computation introduces asymmetries as well as delays. For example, CAST-256 computes its round keys using a separate block cipher, so in order to decrypt, implementers would have to execute the whole key schedule and then reverse it a step at a time. Unless a separate decryption key is available, decryption should take about 246,000 operations versus 136,000 for encryption (based on the figures of [1]).

3.4 Embedded Crypto ASIC

In some smartcards, such as the Sky-TV series 10 subscriber card, a hardware encryption circuit has been bundled along with the CPU. For such applications, Serpent has a hardware implementation that iteratively applies one round at a time, while computing the S-boxes on the fly from table lookup. We estimate

---

[1] The MARS team has tweaked the key schedule since this paper was delivered at Cardis but performance on low-memory processors still appears to be poor

that the number of gates required for this is about 4,500 — roughly the same as the Sky-10 crypto ASIC.

It may be argued that given leading-edge fabrication technologies, custom cryptoprocessors containing tens of thousands of gates can be embedded in smartcard CPUs. This again ignores the realities of the smartcard industry: what can be done in theory, and what is economic in the mass market, are different animals. In particular, we know of no smartcard containing hardware crypto for symmetric key cryptography with more than 10,000 gates.

4   Smartcard Specific Security Issues

There has been much publicity recently about specialist attacks on smartcards, and ways in which these can interact with the design of algorithms and protocols [7]. In this section (which has been significantly expanded in the period between the conference and the final paper deadline) we will try to deal with these issues.

The main attacks on smartcards were described in [6] and are based on microprobing, timing analysis, power analysis and fault induction.

Most fielded attacks that did not exploit a protocol failure or other gross design flaw started off with an invasive attack on the card using microprobing techniques [6,18]. Once the card software had been extracted, it was usually possible to design non-invasive attacks that could be carried out quickly and with low cost equipment.

One example is the timing attack [16]. Here, one uses the fact that the time some encryption algorithms take to execute depends on the key, on the plaintext, or on some intermediate value which can help an attacker derive either the plaintext or the key. In the AES context, one possible timing attack would be on the data dependent rotations used, for example, in RC6; most smartcard processors support only a single bit shift, so a variable shift will typically be implemented as multiple single bit shifts in a loop. It is possible to design a constant time implementation, but this imposes a performance penalty.

In the case of Serpent, the number of instructions used to encrypt or decrypt does not depend on either the data or the key, and even cache accesses cannot help the attacker as we do not access different locations in memory for different plaintexts or keys. It follows that timing attacks are not applicable.

The second class of noninvasive attacks, known to the smartcard community as power analysis and to the military under the codenames 'Tempest', 'Hijack' and 'Nonstop', utilises the fact that many encryption devices leak key material electromagnetically, whether by variations in their power consumption [17,24] or by compromising electromagnetic radiation [19].

Two relevant papers were published at the second AES candidate conference. In the first, Chari et al. report a successful power analysis attack on the 6805 reference code for Twofish, implemented on an ST16 smartcard [14]; this exploits the key whitening process. In the second, Biham and Shamir observe that if the

Hamming weight of the current data word on the bus can be observed, then the key schedule of many AES candidate algorithms can be attacked.

This is only the tip of the iceberg. Firstly, different instructions have different power signatures, and so algorithms where the sequence of executed opcodes is a function of the data or the key (such as RC6 and MARS) might be particularly vulnerable. Secondly, the easiest parameter to measure on the typical card using power analysis appears to be the number of bits on the bus which change polarity at a given clock edge. This is not quite the same as parity, but given knowledge of the opcode sequence, it still amounts to about one bit of information about each data byte. Thirdly, values measured using these techniques are noisy, and so a real attack is less like simple linear algebra and more like the reconstruction of a noisy shift register sequence (this may give an advantage to algorithms such as Serpent where the linear relations in the key schedule are of relatively high Hamming weight). Fourthly, a number of defensive programming techniques are being increasingly used as a first line of defence against power analysis: the computation can be obscured in various ways such as by intercalating it with a pseudorandom computation. However, these techniques carry a performance cost – the typical slowdown can vary from two to five times.

Fault induction is the last main attack technique, and typically involves inserting transients ('glitches') into the clock or power lines to the card in order to cause targeted instructions to fail. In a typical attack, the power supply might be reduced to 2V for 40nS either side of the clock edge that triggers a jump instruction, which in some processors causes the instruction to become a no-op [6]. In this way, an access control check can be bypassed, or an output loop extended. This will usually be the preferred attack, but if for some reason the attacker wants to extract a key directly, then he can reduce the number of rounds in the cipher progressively and extract the round keys directly [7]. None of the AES candidates appears to offer much more resistance to this kind of attack than any other.

The main defences against attacks on smartcards are the concern of electrical and chemical engineers (e.g., refractory chip coatings, top layer metal grids, glitch and clock frequency sensors that reset the chip [18]), while secondary defences include defensive programming techniques that minimise the number of single instructions which are possible points of failure [6]. We suggest that a useful assessment of the AES finalists will consist of implementing them using defensive programming techniques, measuring their performance and doing actual attacks on them. We believe that as most operations in Serpent use all bits in their operands actively, as the avalanche is fast and as the code is independent of the data and the key, Serpent will do well in this exercise.

5   Conclusion

Serpent was engineered to satisfy the AES requirements. It is faster than DES, and we believe that it would still be as secure as three-key triple-DES against all currently known attacks if its number of rounds were reduced by half to sixteen.

Using twice the needed number of rounds gives a margin of safety which we believe to be prudent practice in a cipher with a cover time of a century.

Serpent's good performance comes from allowing an efficient bitslice implementation on a range of processors, including the market leading Intel/MMX and compatible chips. However, the 32-bit performance was not bought at the expense of imposing penalties on designers of low cost smartcard applications. The same cannot be said for many other AES candidates: some of them cannot be implemented on low cost smartcards at all, while many more would impose such constraints on system developers that they would undermine the goals of the AES programme.

Further information on Serpent, including the AES submission, the FSE and AES conference papers, this paper, and implementations in various languages, can be found on the Serpent home page at:

http://www.cl.cam.ac.uk/~rja14/serpent.html

References

1. CM Adams, "The CAST-256 Encryption Algorithm", available online from: http://www.entrust.com/resources/pdf/cast-256.pdf
2. RJ Anderson, "UEPS — a Second Generation Electronic Wallet" in *Computer Security — ESORICS 92*, Springer LNCS vol 648 pp 411–418
3. RJ Anderson, "Making Smartcard Systems Robust", in *Proceedings of Cardis 94* (Lille, October 1994) pp 1–14
4. RJ Anderson, SJ Bezuidenhoudt, "On the Reliability of Electronic Payment Systems", in *IEEE Transactions on Software Engineering* v 22 no 5 (May 1996) pp 294–301
5. RJ Anderson, E Biham, LR Knudsen, "Serpent: A Proposal for the Advanced Encryption Standard", available from http://www.cl.cam.ac.uk/~rja14/serpent.html
6. RJ Anderson, MG Kuhn, "Tamper Resistance — a Cautionary Note", in *The Second USENIX Workshop on Electronic Commerce Proceedings* (Nov 1996) pp 1–11
7. RJ Anderson, MG Kuhn, "Low Cost Attacks on Tamper Resistant Devices" in *Security Protocols – Proceedings of the 5th International Workshop* (1997) Springer LNCS vol 1361 pp 125–136
8. E Biham, "A Fast New DES Implementation in Software", in *Fast Software Encryption — 4th International Workshop, FSE '97*, Springer LNCS v 1267 pp 260–271
9. E Biham, RJ Anderson, LR Knudsen, "Serpent: A New Block Cipher Proposal", in *Fast Software Encryption — FSE 98*, Springer LNCS vol 1372 pp 222–238
10. E Biham, A Shamir, *'Differential Cryptanalysis of the Data Encryption Standard'* (Springer 1993)
11. E Biham, A Shamir, "Power Analysis of the Key Scheduling of the AES Candidates", *AES Second Candidate Conference*, http://csrc.nist.gov/encryption/aes/round1/conf2/papers/papers/biham3.pdf

12. L Brown, J Pieprzyk, "Introducing the new LOKI97 Block Cipher", http://www.adfa.oz.au/~lpb/research/loki97/

13. C Burwick, D Coppersmith, E D'Avignon, R Gennaro, S Halevi, C Jutla, SM Matyas Jr., L O'Connor, M Peyravian, D Safford, N Zunic, "MARS — a candidate cipher for AES", July 17th 1998; http://www.research.ibm.com/security/mars.html

14. S Chari, C Jutla, JR Rao, P Rohatgi, "A Cautionary Note Regarding Evaluation of AES Candidates on Smart-Cards", *AES Second Candidate Conference*, http://csrc.nist.gov/encryption/aes/round1/conf2/papers/chari.pdf

15. Electronic Frontier Foundation, *'Cracking DES — Secrets of Encryption Research, Wiretap Politics & Chip Design'*, O'Reilly (July 98) ISBN 1-56592-520-3

16. PC Kocher, "Timing Attacks on Implementations of Diffie-Hellman, RSA, DSS, and Other Systems", in *Advances in Cryptology — Crypto 96*, Springer LNCS v 1109 pp 104–113

17. PC Kocher, "Differential Power Analysis", available from: http://www.cryptography.com/dpa/

18. O Kömmerling, MG Kuhn, "Design Principles for Tamper-Resistant Smartcard Processors", USENIX Workshop on Smartcard Technology, Chicago, Illinois, USA (to appear); http://www.cl.cam.ac.uk/~mgk25/sc99-tamper.pdf

19. MG Kuhn, RJ Anderson, "Soft Tempest: Hidden Data Transmission Using Electromagnetic Emanations", in *Proceedings of the Second International Workshop on Information Hiding* (Portland, Apr 98), Springer LNCS vol 1525 pp 126–143

20. M Matsui, "Linear Cryptanalysis Method for DES Cipher", in *Advances in Cryptology — Eurocrypt 93*, Springer LNCS v 765 pp 386–397

21. D Naccache, *private communication*, 17 Aug 98

22. Nippon Telegraph and Telephone Corporation, "The 128-bit Block Cipher E2", July 1998, http://info.isl.ntt.co.jp/e2/

23. RL Rivest, MJB Robshaw, R Sidney, YL Lin, "The RC6 Block Cipher", July 1998, http://theory.lcs.mit.edu/~rivest/publications.html

24. P Wright, *'Spycatcher — The Candid Autobiography of a Senior Intelligence Officer'*, William Heinemann Australia, 1987, ISBN 0-85561-098-0

Decorrelated Fast Cipher: An AES Candidate Well Suited for Low Cost Smart Cards Applications

Guillaume Poupard and Serge Vaudenay

Ecole Normale Supérieure, Laboratoire d'informatique
45 rue d'Ulm, F-75230 Paris Cedex 05, France
{Guillaume.Poupard,Serge.Vaudenay}@ens.fr

Abstract. In response to the call for candidates issued by the National Institute for Standards and Technologies (the Advanced Encryption Standard project) the Ecole Normale Supérieure proposed a candidate called DFC as for "Decorrelated Fast Cipher", based on the decorrelation technique that provides provable security against several classes of attacks (in particular the basic version of Biham and Shamir's Differential Cryptanalysis as well as Matsui's Linear Cryptanalysis). From a practical point of view, this algorithm is naturally very efficient when it is implemented on 64-bit processors. In this paper, we describe the implementation we made of DFC on a very low cost smart card based on the Motorola 6805 processor. The performances we obtain prove that DFC is also well suited for low cost devices applications.

Since the beginning of commercial use of symmetric encryption (with block ciphers) in the seventies, construction design used to be heuristic-based and security was empiric: a given block cipher was considered to be secure until some researcher published an attack on.

The Data Encryption Standard [1] initiated an important open research area, and some important cryptanalysis methods emerged, namely Biham and Shamir's differential cryptanalysis [4] and Matsui's linear cryptanalysis [11], as well as further generalizations. Nyberg and Knudsen [14] showed how to build toy block ciphers which provably resist differential cryptanalysis (and linear cryptanalysis as well as has been shown afterward [3]). This paradigm has successfully been used by Matsui in the MISTY cipher [12,13]. However Nyberg and Knudsen's method does not provide much freedom for the design, and actually, this paradigm leads to algebraic constructions. This may open the way to other kind of weaknesses as shown by Jakobsen and Knudsen [8].

In response to the call for candidates for the Advanced Encryption Standard (AES) which has been issued by the National Institute of Standards and Technology (NIST) the ENS proposed in [6] the *Decorrelated Fast Cipher* (DFC)[1]. It is a block cipher which is faster than DES and hopefully more secure than triple-DES. It accepts 128-bit message blocks and any key size from 0 to 256.

---

[1] See http://www.dmi.ens.fr/~vaudenay/dfc.html

J.-J. Quisquater and B. Schneier (Eds.): CARDIS 2000, LNCS 1820, pp. 254–264, 2000.
© Springer-Verlag Berlin Heidelberg 2000

We believe that it can be adapted to any other cryptographic primitive such as stream cipher, hash function, MAC algorithm. The new design of DFC combines heuristic construction with provable security against a wide class of attacks. Unlike the Nyberg-Knudsen paradigm, our approach is combinatorial. It relies on Vaudenay's paradigm [15,16,17,18,19]. This construction provides much more freedom since it can be combined with heuristic designs.

In [6] we provided proofs of security against some classes of general simple attacks which includes differential and linear cryptanalysis. This result is based on the decorrelation theory. We believe that this cipher is also "naturally" secure against more complicated attacks since our design introduced no special algebraic property. Our design is guaranteed to be vulnerable against neither differential nor linear cryptanalysis with complexity less than 2^{81} encryptions. We believe that the best attack is still exhaustive search. Another theoretical result claims that if we admit that no key will be used more than 2^{43} times, then the cipher is guaranteed to resist to any iterated known plaintext attack of order 1.

From a practical point of view, the main computations are an affine mapping $x \mapsto P = ax + b$ where a, b and x are 64-bit operands and P a 128-bit quantity, followed by two reductions modulo $2^{64} + 13$, and modulo 2^{64} respectively. Modern computers, like those of the AXP family, have properties that make the implementation of DFC especially efficient because of there native 64-bit processor. As an example, we are able to encrypt 500 Mbps using the new Alpha processor 21264 600MHz provided that the microprocessor can input the plaintext stream and output the ciphertext stream at this rate (see [7]).

The aim of this paper is to describe the implementation we made of DFC on a very low cost smart card based on a 8-bit processor Motorola 6805, using less than 100 bytes of RAM and without the help of any kind of crypto-processor. This proves that DFC is well suited for a large range of applications.

Section 1 gives a high level overview of DFC (a full description can be found in [6]). Section 2 explains how to efficiently deal with the multiprecision arithmetic needed to implement the algorithm. Finally, section 3 exposes our implementation and the performances we obtained.

1 Definition of DFC

Notations

All objects are bit strings or integers. To any bit string $s = b_1 \ldots b_\ell$ we associate an integer $\bar{s} = 2^{\ell-1}b_1 + \ldots + 2b_{\ell-1} + b_\ell$ The converse operation of representing an integer x as an ℓ-bit string is denoted $|x|_\ell$. The concatenation of two strings s and s' is denoted $s|s'$. We can truncate a bit string $s = b_1 \ldots b_\ell$ (of length at least n) to its n leftmost bits $\text{trunc}_n(s) = b_1 \ldots b_n$.

High Level Overview

The encryption function DFC operates on 128-bit message blocks by means of a secret key K of arbitrary length, up to 256 bits. Encryption of arbitrary-length messages is performed through standard modes of operation which are independent of the DFC design (see [2]).

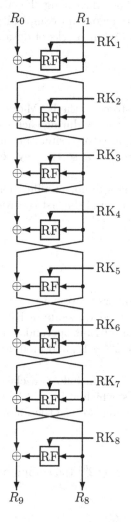

The secret key K is first turned into a 1024-bit "Expanded Key" EK through an "Expanding Function" EF, *i.e.* EK = EF(K). The EF function performs a 4-round Feistel scheme (see Feistel [5]).

The encryption itself performs a similar 8-round Feistel scheme. Each round uses the "Round Function" RF. This function maps a 64-bit string onto a 64-bit string by using one 128-bit string parameter.

Given a 128-bit plaintext block PT, we split it into two 64-bit halves R_0 and R_1 so that

$$PT = R_0|R_1$$

Given the 1024-bit expanded key EK, we split it into eight 128-bit strings

$$EK = RK_1|RK_2|\ldots|RK_8$$

where RK_i is the ith "Round Key".

We build a sequence $R_0,\ldots,R_9$ by the Equation

$$R_{i+1} = RF_{RK_i}(R_i) \oplus R_{i-1} \quad (i = 1,\ldots,8)$$

We then set CT = $DFC_K(PT) = R_9|R_8$.

The RF function (as for "Round Function") is fed with two 64-bit parameters, a and b. It processes a 64-bit input x and outputs a 64-bit string. We define $RF_{a|b}(x) =$

$$CP\left(\left|\left((\bar{a} \times \bar{x} + \bar{b}) \bmod (2^{64} + 13)\right) \bmod 2^{64}\right|_{64}\right)$$

where CP (as for "Confusion Permutation") is a permutation over the set of all 64-bit strings. It uses a look-up table RT (as for "Round Table") which takes a 6-bit integer as input and provides a 32-bit string output.

Let $y = y_l|y_r$ be the input of CP where y_l and y_r are two 32-bit strings. We define

$$CP(y) = \left|\overline{(y_r \oplus RT(\overline{trunc_6(y_l)}))|(y_l \oplus KC)} + \overline{KD} \bmod 2^{64}\right|_{64}$$

where KC is a 32-bit constant string, and KD is a 64-bit constant string.

In order to generate a sequence $RK_1,\ldots,RK_8$ from a given key K represented as a bit string of length at most 256, we first pad K with a constant pattern KS in order to make a 256-bit "Padded Key" string by PK = $trunc_{256}(K|KS)$. This allows any key size from 0 to 256 bits.

Then, the key scheduling algorithm consists in using the previously defined encryption algorithm reduced to 4 rounds instead of 8. This enables an efficient and secure (see [6]) generation of expanded keys without increasing the size of the program. We can observe that the key scheduling algorithm complexity is the same as the complexity of the encryption of four 128-bit blocks of data.

On the Fly Encryption and Decryption

The expanded key may be too large (128 bytes) to be stored in the RAM of some low cost smart cards. Anyway, it can be computed on the fly during each block encryption in such a way that only two round keys RK_i are stored simultaneously in memory. This makes the algorithm 5 times slower because the key setup requires 8 encryption using a 4-round version of DFC.

This strategy can also be used for decryption using a minor modification of the key scheduling algorithm based on the precomputation of the last two round keys RK_7 and RK_8.

2   Multiprecision Arithmetic

The internal operations deal with 64- and 128-bit numbers so we have to implement multiprecision arithmetic. The key operations, used to compute RF, are an affine mapping $x \mapsto P = ax + b$ where a, b and x are 64-bit operands and P a 128-bit quantity, followed by two reductions modulo $2^{64} + 13$, and modulo 2^{64} respectively.

The implementation of the multiprecision multiplication follows a classical scheme, without any optimization, such as Karatsuba's, which would not be worthwhile for so small operands. For the modular reduction, we use the following method. First we write

$$P = Q \times 2^{64} + R \tag{1}$$

where R is the remainder of the Euclidean division of P by 2^{64} (no computation is required for this). Then we rewrite (1) as:

$$P = Q \times (2^{64} + 13) + R - 13 \times Q \tag{2}$$

As we want to reduce modulo $2^{64} + 13$, the quantity $Q(2^{64} + 13)$ disappears. However, this is not yet perfect as we have to deal with two cases: $R - 13Q > 0$ and $R - 13Q < 0$. To avoid this, we rewrite (2) as:

$$P = (2^{64} + 13) \times (Q - 13) + (13 \times (2^{64} - 1 - Q) + 182 + R) \tag{3}$$

In (3), the quantity $2^{64} - 1 - Q$ is just the bitwise complement of Q. The modular reduction thus consists of the easy evaluation of:

$$P' = 13 \times (2^{64} - 1 - Q) + 182 + R \tag{4}$$

modulo $2^{64} + 13$. The result is always positive and, most of the time, greater than $2^{64} + 13$. We thus perform a second reduction, using the same formula. We rewrite (4)

$$P' = Q' \times 2^{64} + R' \tag{5}$$

and we define P'' as

$$P'' = 13 \times (2^{64} - 1 - Q') + 182 + R' \tag{6}$$

The result P'' verifies $0 \leq P'' < 2 \times 2^{64} + 13$ so the final value of the modular reduction is P'' if $P'' < 2^{64} + 13$ and $P'' - (2^{64} + 13)$ otherwise. These comparison and subtraction can be performed very efficiently because of the very special form of the binary representation of $2^{64} + 13$.

Timing Attacks

Implementations must be such that computations of the modular multiplication does not leak any information by time measurement (*i.e.* we must avoid tests and conditional branches that depend on the computation). Otherwise this may leak some information by Kocher's timing attacks [9].

The previous description of the modular reduction shows that the only step that does not require a fixed number of clock cycles is the last one. Consequently we always compute $P'' - (2^{64} + 13)$ even if the result is note always used.

The main problem with timing attacks appears during the computation of $P = ax + b$. Using the classical scheme for multiplication, differences of timing may appear because of carry propagation. A simple but not really efficient solution consists in removing all the conditional branches by propagating the carries as far as possible even if they are zeros.

3   Implementation on Smart Cards

We have implemented DFC on a cheap smart card based on a 8-bit processor Motorola 6805 running at 3.57 MHz. This microprocessor can perform very simple operations with two 8-bit registers. For example it can only perform rotations of one bit. Furthermore, a byte multiplication is implemented.

The smart card possesses three kinds of memory, a ROM of 4 KB, an EEPROM of 2 KB where the program and the data are stored and a 160-bytes RAM where only 120-bytes can be used. Furthermore, the stack is automatically set in its middle and consequently the available memory is not contiguous. The communication rate is 19200 bits per second and the server is a simple PC.

Two implementations of DFC are proposed:

- the first one performs the key scheduling just once and stores the expanded key EK (1024 bits) in RAM. It needs 171 bytes of memory.
- the second one needs 89 bytes of RAM but is 5 times slower because it computes the expanded key during encryption of each block. Anyway, it may be interesting for some applications to reduce the size of the RAM and accordingly the cost of the used smart cards.

The amount of ROM needed to store the program and constant data is less than two kilo-bytes. More precisely, the program needs 1600 bytes, half of which are used by the multiplication $P = ax + b$ for efficiency reasons. Consequently, the size of the program could be easily reduced at the cost of a slower execution.

The DFC algorithm depends on several constants whose total size is 348 bytes. In order to convince that this design hides no trap-door, we choose the constants from the hexadecimal expansion of the mathematical e constant. Furthermore, the size of the data can be reduced to 268 bytes since a part of the RT table can be reused for other constants.

The time needed to encrypt a 128-bit block is about 40.000 cycles (resp. 200.000 cycles for the second version). With a clock frequency of 3.57 MHz, our implementation is able to encrypt 1428 bytes per second (resp. 285 bytes per second). This is twice slower than the best known implementation of triple-DES on the same platform and such a rate is similar to the amount of data the card can exchange with the server per second.

	Version **1**	Version **2**
RAM used	171 bytes	**89** bytes
Size of the program (see the appendix)	1600 bytes	
Size of data	268 bytes	
Size of the needed EEPROM (or ROM)	< **2** KB	
Cycles to encrypt a 128 bit block	**40 000** cycles	200 000 cycles
Key setup (precomputation of EK)	160 000 cycles	~ 0
Blocks encrypted per second at 3.57 MHz	89 blocks	18 blocks
Data encrypted per second at 3.57 MHz	1428 bytes	285 bytes
Time to encrypt a 128 bit block at 3.57 MHz	11 ms	56 ms

Performances of two implementations of DFC on a 6805 based smart card

4   Conclusion

Even if DFC seems to be designed for powerful computers, the implementation we made of this algorithm on a very low cost smart card proves that it is well suited for a large range of applications. Hardware-based implementations require to implement the multiplication which may be painful for the designer, but efficiently possible. Although we did not investigate all possible applications, we believe that there is no restriction on the implementability of DFC.

References

1. Data Encryption Standard. *Federal Information Processing Standard Publication 46*, U. S. National Bureau of Standards, 1977.
2. DES Modes of Operation. *Federal Information Processing Standard Publication 81*, U. S. National Bureau of Standards, 1980.
3. K. Aoki, K. Ohta. Strict evaluation of the maximum average of differential probability and the maximum average of linear probability. *IEICE Transactions on Fundamentals*, vol. E80-A, pp. 1–8, 1997.
4. E. Biham, A. Shamir. *Differential Cryptanalysis of the Data Encryption Standard*, Springer-Verlag, 1993.
5. H. Feistel. Cryptography and computer privacy. *Scientific American*, vol. 228, pp. 15–23, 1973.
6. H. Gilbert, M. Girault, P. Hoogvorst, F. Noilhan, T. Pornin, G. Poupard, J. Stern, S. Vaudenay. Decorrelated Fast Cipher: an AES Candidate. Submitted to the call for candidate for the Advanced Encryption Standard issued by the National Institute of Standards and Technology.
7. O. Baudron, H. Gilbert, L. Granboulan, H. Handschuh, R. Harley, A. Joux, P. Nguyen, F. Noilhan, D. Pointcheval, T. Pornin, G. Poupard, J. Stern, S. Vaudenay. DFC Update. In *the Proceedings from the Second Advanced Encryption Standard Candidate Conference*, National Institute of Standards and Technology, 1999.
8. T. Jakobsen, L. R. Knudsen. The interpolation attack on block ciphers. In *Fast Software Encryption*, Haifa, Israel, Lectures Notes in Computer Science 1267, pp. 28–40, Springer-Verlag, 1997.
9. P. Kocher. Timing attacks in implementations of Diffie-Hellman, RSA, DSS and other systems. In *Advances in Cryptology CRYPTO'96*, Lectures Notes in Computer Science 1109, pp. 104–113, Springer-Verlag, 1996.
10. L. R. Knudsen, B. Preneel. Fast and secure hashing based on codes. In *Advances in Cryptology CRYPTO'97*, Santa Barbara, Californie, U.S.A., Lectures Notes in Computer Science 1294, pp. 485–498, Springer-Verlag, 1997.
11. M. Matsui. The first experimental cryptanalysis of the Data Encryption Standard. In *Advances in Cryptology CRYPTO'94*, Santa Barbara, Californie, U.S.A., Lectures Notes in Computer Science 839, pp. 1–11, Springer-Verlag, 1994.
12. M. Matsui. New structure of block ciphers with provable security against differential and linear cryptanalysis. In *Fast Software Encryption*, Cambridge, Royaume Uni, Lectures Notes in Computer Science 1039, pp. 205–218, Springer-Verlag, 1996.
13. M. Matsui. New block encryption algorithm MISTY. In *Fast Software Encryption*, Lectures Notes in Computer Science 1267, pp. 54–68, Springer-Verlag, 1997.
14. K. Nyberg, L. R. Knudsen. Provable security against a differential cryptanalysis. *Journal of Cryptology*, vol. 8, pp. 27–37, Springer-Verlag, 1995.
15. S. Vaudenay. Provable security for block ciphers by decorrelation. In *STACS 98*, Lectures Notes in Computer Science 1373, pp. 249–275, Springer-Verlag, 1998.
16. S. Vaudenay. The decorrelation technique home-page. URL:http://www.dmi.ens.fr/~vaudenay/decorrelation.html
17. S. Vaudenay. Adaptive-Attack Norm for Decorrelation and Super-Pseudorandomness. Tech. report LIENS-99-2, Ecole Normale Supérieure,1999.
18. S. Vaudenay. On the Lai-Massey Scheme. Tech. report LIENS-99-3, Ecole Normale Supérieure, 1999.
19. S. Vaudenay. Resistance against General Iterated Attacks. To appear in *Advances in Cryptology EUROCRYPT' 99*, Prague, Czech Republic, Lectures Notes in Computer Science 1592, Springer-Verlag, 1999.

ASM Implementation of DFC on Motorola 6805 (1/4)

```
lda    INS                         rts                             lda    EBP,x
       cmp    #$40        SwapMK clrx                                    sta    L,x
       beq    InKjmp      Lcle2  lda    X0,x                            clr    H,x
       cmp    #$41               sta    A,x                             incx
       beq    InData             lda    X1,x                            cpx    #$08
       cmp    #$42               sta    L,x                             bne    LEF21
       beq    Encrypt            clr    H,x                             jsr    RF
       jmp    COMMAND            sta    B,x                             clrx
InKjmp jmp    InKey              lda    MO,x            LEF22  lda    EAP,x
;***************************      sta    X0,x                            eor    RTO,x
;    BLOCK SETUP                  lda    M1,x                            sta    A,x
;***************************      sta    X1,x                            lda    EBP,x
InData jsr    OUT_BYTE           incx                                   eor    KB2,x
       clrx                      cpx    #$08                            sta    L,x
Lindata jsr   IN_BYTE           bne    Lcle2                           clr    H,x
       sta    MO,x               rts                                   incx
       incx              EncEF1 clrx                                   cpx    #$08
       cpx    #16        LEF11  lda    OAP,x                           bne    LEF22
       bne    Lindata            sta    A,x                             jsr    RF
       jmp    WAIT_COMMAND       lda    OBP,x                           clrx
;***************************      sta    L,x            LEF23  lda    EAP,x
;    ENCRYPTION                   clr    H,x                             eor    KA3,x
;***************************      incx                                   sta    A,x
Encrypt jsr   OUT_BYTE           cpx    #$08                            lda    EBP,x
       clrx                      bne    LEF11                           eor    KB3,x
Lcle0  clr    X0,x               jsr    RF                              sta    L,x
       clr    X1,x               clrx                                   clr    H,x
       incx              LEF12  lda    OAP,x                           incx
       cpx    #$08               eor    RTO,x                           cpx    #$08
       bne    Lcle0              sta    A,x                             bne    LEF23
       jsr    EncEF1             lda    OBP,x                           jsr    RF
       jsr    SwapMK             eor    KB2,x                           clrx
       jsr    RF                 sta    L,x            LEF24  lda    EAP,x
       jsr    SwapKM             clr    H,x                             eor    KA4,x
       jsr    EncEF2             incx                                   sta    A,x
       jsr    SwapMK             cpx    #$08                            lda    EBP,x
       jsr    RF                 bne    LEF12                           eor    KB4,x
       clr    cpt                jsr    RF                              sta    L,x
Lencryp jsr   SwapKM             clrx                                   clr    H,x
       jsr    EncEF1      LEF13  lda    OAP,x                           incx
       jsr    SwapMK             eor    KA3,x                           cpx    #$08
       jsr    RF                 sta    A,x                             bne    LEF24
       jsr    SwapKM             lda    OBP,x                           jsr    RF
       jsr    EncEF2             eor    KB3,x                           rts
       jsr    SwapMK             sta    L,x            ;***************************
       jsr    RF                 clr    H,x            ;    KEY SETUP
       inc    cpt                incx                  ;***************************
       lda    cpt                cpx    #$08           InKey  jsr    OUT_BYTE
       cmp    #3                 bne    LEF13                 ldx    #OAP
       bne    Lencryp            jsr    RF                    jsr    In4Byt
       lda    #16                clrx                         ldx    #EAP
       ldx    #X0         LEF14  lda    OAP,x                 jsr    In4Byt
       jsr    OUT_BUFFER         eor    KA4,x                 ldx    #EBP+4
       jmp    WAIT_COMMAND       sta    A,x                   jsr    In4Byt
SwapKM clrx                      lda    OBP,x                 ldx    #OBP+4
Lcle1  lda    X0,x               eor    KB4,x                 jsr    In4Byt
       sta    MO,x               sta    L,x                   ldx    #OBP
       lda    X1,x               clr    H,x                   jsr    In4Byt
       sta    M1,x               incx                         ldx    #EBP
       lda    A,X                cpx    #$08                  jsr    In4Byt
       sta    X0,x               bne    LEF14                 ldx    #EAP+4
       lda    B,X                jsr    RF                    jsr    In4Byt
       sta    X1,x               rts                          ldx    #OAP+4
       incx              EncEF2 clrx                          jsr    In4Byt
       cpx    #$08        LEF21  lda    EAP,x                 jmp    WAIT_COMMAND
       bne    Lcle1              sta    A,x            In4Byt jsr    IN_BYTE
```

ASM Implementation of DFC on Motorola 6805 (2/4)

```
        sta     0,x              sta     L+7             txa                      lda     A+2
        jsr     IN_BYTE          txa                     jsr     RL3              ldx     X1+3
        sta     1,x              jsr     RH0             lda     A+1              fcb     $42
        jsr     IN_BYTE          ; A*X1+1                ldx     X1+2             add     L+5
        sta     2,x              lda     A+0             fcb     $42              sta     L+5
        jsr     IN_BYTE          ldx     X1+1            add     L+3              txa
        sta     3,x              fcb     $42             sta     L+3              jsr     RL6
        rts                      add     L+1             txa                      lda     A+3
;**************************      sta     L+1             jsr     RL4              ldx     X1+3
;    Computation of RF           txa                     lda     A+2              fcb     $42
;    Multiplication              jsr     RL2             ldx     X1+2             add     L+6
;**************************      lda     A+1             fcb     $42              sta     L+6
        ; A*X1+0                 ldx     X1+1            add     L+4              txa
RF      lda     A+0              fcb     $42             sta     L+4              jsr     RL7
        ldx     X1+0             add     L+2             txa                      lda     A+4
        fcb     $42              sta     L+2             jsr     RL5              ldx     X1+3
        add     L+0              txa                     lda     A+3              fcb     $42
        sta     L+0              jsr     RL3             ldx     X1+2             add     L+7
        txa                      lda     A+2             fcb     $42              sta     L+7
        jsr     RL1              ldx     X1+1            add     L+5              txa
        lda     A+1              fcb     $42             sta     L+5              jsr     RH0
        ldx     X1+0             add     L+3             txa                      lda     A+5
        fcb     $42              sta     L+3             jsr     RL6              ldx     X1+3
        add     L+1              txa                     lda     A+4              fcb     $42
        sta     L+1              jsr     RL4             ldx     X1+2             add     H+0
        txa                      lda     A+3             fcb     $42              sta     H+0
        jsr     RL2              ldx     X1+1            add     L+6              txa
        lda     A+2              fcb     $42             sta     L+6              jsr     RH1
        ldx     X1+0             add     L+4             txa                      lda     A+6
        fcb     $42              sta     L+4             jsr     RL7              ldx     X1+3
        add     L+2              txa                     lda     A+5              fcb     $42
        sta     L+2              jsr     RL5             ldx     X1+2             add     H+1
        txa                      lda     A+4             fcb     $42              sta     H+1
        jsr     RL3              ldx     X1+1            add     L+7              txa
        lda     A+3              fcb     $42             sta     L+7              jsr     RH2
        ldx     X1+0             add     L+5             txa                      lda     A+7
        fcb     $42              sta     L+5             jsr     RH0              ldx     X1+3
        add     L+3              txa                     lda     A+6              fcb     $42
        sta     L+3              jsr     RL6             ldx     X1+2             add     H+2
        txa                      lda     A+5             fcb     $42              sta     H+2
        jsr     RL4              ldx     X1+1            add     H+0              txa
        lda     A+4              fcb     $42             sta     H+0              jsr     RH3
        ldx     X1+0             add     L+6             txa                      ; A*X1+4
        fcb     $42              sta     L+6             jsr     RH1              lda     A+0
        add     L+4              txa                     lda     A+7              ldx     X1+4
        sta     L+4              jsr     RL7             ldx     X1+2             fcb     $42
        txa                      lda     A+6             fcb     $42              add     L+4
        jsr     RL5              ldx     X1+1            add     H+1              sta     L+4
        lda     A+5              fcb     $42             sta     H+1              txa
        ldx     X1+0             add     L+7             txa                      jsr     RL5
        fcb     $42              sta     L+7             jsr     RH2              lda     A+1
        add     L+5              txa                     ; A*X1+3                 ldx     X1+4
        sta     L+5              jsr     RH0             lda     A+0              fcb     $42
        txa                      lda     A+7             ldx     X1+3             add     L+5
        jsr     RL6              ldx     X1+1            fcb     $42              sta     L+5
        lda     A+6              fcb     $42             add     L+3              txa
        ldx     X1+0             add     H+0             sta     L+3              jsr     RL6
        fcb     $42              sta     H+0             txa                      lda     A+2
        add     L+6              txa                     jsr     RL4              ldx     X1+4
        sta     L+6              jsr     RH1             lda     A+1              fcb     $42
        txa                      ; A*X1+2                ldx     X1+3             add     L+6
        jsr     RL7              lda     A+0             fcb     $42              sta     L+6
        lda     A+7              ldx     X1+2            add     L+4              txa
        ldx     X1+0             fcb     $42             sta     L+4              jsr     RL7
        fcb     $42              add     L+2             txa                      lda     A+3
        add     L+7              sta     L+2             jsr     RL5              ldx     X1+4
```

ASM Implementation of DFC on Motorola 6805 (3/4)

```
fcb    $42          sta    H+1          jsr    RH4                 ldx    X1+7
add    L+7          txa                 lda    A+6                 fcb    $42
sta    L+7          jsr    RH2          ldx    X1+6                add    H+6
txa                 lda    A+5          fcb    $42                 sta    H+6
jsr    RH0          ldx    X1+5         add    H+4                 txa
lda    A+4          fcb    $42          sta    H+4                 jsr    RH7
ldx    X1+4         add    H+2          txa                 ;********************
fcb    $42          sta    H+2          jsr    RH5          ; L+182+13*(2^64-1-H)
add    H+0          txa                 lda    A+7          ;********************
sta    H+0          jsr    RH3          ldx    X1+6                clr    L+8
txa                 lda    A+6          fcb    $42                 lda    L+0
jsr    RH1          ldx    X1+5         add    H+5                 add    #182
lda    A+5          fcb    $42          sta    H+5                 sta    L+0
ldx    X1+4         add    H+3          txa                        clra
fcb    $42          sta    H+3          jsr    RH6                 ldx    #1
add    H+1          txa          ; A*X1+7                          jsr    RLb
sta    H+1          jsr    RH4          lda    A+0                 clrx
txa                 lda    A+7          ldx    X1+7                stx    save1
jsr    RH2          ldx    X1+5         fcb    $42          Lmod1  lda    H,x
lda    A+6          fcb    $42          add    L+7                 coma
ldx    X1+4         add    H+4          sta    L+7                 ldx    #13
fcb    $42          sta    H+4          txa                        fcb    $42
add    H+2          txa                 jsr    RH0                 stx    save2
sta    H+2          jsr    RH5          lda    A+1                 ldx    save1
txa          ; A*X1+6                   ldx    X1+7                add    L,x
jsr    RH3          lda    A+0          fcb    $42                 sta    L,x
lda    A+7          ldx    X1+6         add    H+0                 lda    save2
ldx    X1+4         fcb    $42          sta    H+0                 inc    save1
fcb    $42          add    L+6          txa                        ldx    save1
add    H+3          sta    L+6          jsr    RH1                 jsr    RLb
sta    H+3          txa                 lda    A+2                 cpx    #8
txa                 jsr    RL7          ldx    X1+7                bne    Lmod1
jsr    RH4          lda    A+1          fcb    $42          ;********************
; A*X1+5             ldx    X1+6         add    H+1          ; L+14+(2^64-1-13*L8)
lda    A+0          fcb    $42          sta    H+1          ;********************
ldx    X1+5         add    L+7          txa                        lda    L+8
fcb    $42          sta    L+7          jsr    RH2                 ldx    #13
add    L+5          txa                 lda    A+3                 fcb    $42
sta    L+5          jsr    RH0          ldx    X1+7                coma
txa                 lda    A+2          fcb    $42                 add    L+0
jsr    RL6          ldx    X1+6         add    H+2                 sta    L+0
lda    A+1          fcb    $42          sta    H+2                 clra
ldx    X1+5         add    H+0          txa                        ldx    #1
fcb    $42          sta    H+0          jsr    RH3                 jsr    RLb
add    L+6          txa                 lda    A+4                 clr    L+8
sta    L+6          jsr    RH1          ldx    X1+7                ldx    #1
txa                 lda    A+3          fcb    $42          Lmod2  lda    #$FF
jsr    RL7          ldx    X1+6         add    H+3                 add    L,x
lda    A+2          fcb    $42          sta    H+3                 sta    L,x
ldx    X1+5         add    H+1          txa                        clra
fcb    $42          sta    H+1          jsr    RH4                 incx
add    L+7          txa                 lda    A+5                 jsr    RLb
sta    L+7          jsr    RH2          ldx    X1+7                cpx    #8
txa                 lda    A+4          fcb    $42                 bne    Lmod2
jsr    RH0          ldx    X1+6         add    H+4                 lda    L+0
lda    A+3          fcb    $42          sta    H+4                 add    #14
ldx    X1+5         add    H+2          txa                        sta    L+0
fcb    $42          sta    H+2          jsr    RH5                 clra
add    H+0          txa                 lda    A+6                 ldx    #1
sta    H+0          jsr    RH3          ldx    X1+7                jsr    RLb
txa                 lda    A+5          fcb    $42          ;********************
jsr    RH1          ldx    X1+6         add    H+5          ; test L>2^64+13 ?
lda    A+4          fcb    $42          sta    H+5          ;********************
ldx    X1+5         add    H+3          txa                        lda    L+8
fcb    $42          sta    H+3          jsr    RH6                 cmp    #0
add    H+1          txa                 lda    A+7                 beq    NO
```

ASM Implementation of DFC on Motorola 6805 (4/4)

```
         lda    L+0              add    KD,x         RH6      adc    H+6
         cmp    #13              eor    X0,x                  sta    H+6
         bhi    YES              sta    save1                 bcc    ExitR
         ldx    #1               lda    X1,x                  clra
Lcmp     lda    L,x              sta    X0,x         RH7      adc    H+7
         cmp    #0               lda    save1                 sta    H+7
         bne    YES              sta    X1,x         ExitR    rts
         incx                    incx               RLb      stx    save1
         cpx    #7               cpx    #8           LRLb     adc    L,x
         bne    Lcmp             bne    LaddD                 sta    L,x
         lda    L+7              rts                          bcc    ExitRb
         cmp    #0       ;*******************                 clra
         bne    NO       ; carry propagation                 incx
YES      dec    L+8      ;*******************                 cmp    #9
         lda    L+0      RL1      adc    L+1                   bne    LRLb
         sub    #13               sta    L+1         ExitRb   ldx    save1
         sta    L+0               bcc    ExitR                rts
         bcc    NO                clra               ;***********************************
         ldx    #1       RL2      adc    L+2         ;      CONSTANTS
Lyes     lda    L,x               sta    L+2         ;***********************************
         sbc    #0                bcc    ExitR       RT0  fcb  $B7,$E1,$51,$62,$8A,$ED,$2A,$6A
         sta    L,x               clra              KA3  fcb  $BF,$71,$58,$80,$9C,$F4,$F3,$C7
         bcc    NO       RL3      adc    L+3         KA4  fcb  $62,$E7,$16,$0F,$38,$B4,$DA,$56
         incx                     sta    L+3         KB2  fcb  $A7,$84,$D9,$04,$51,$90,$CF,$EF
         jmp    Lyes              bcc    ExitR       KB3  fcb  $32,$4E,$77,$38,$92,$6C,$FB,$E5
;*******************               clra              KB4  fcb  $F4,$BF,$8D,$8D,$8C,$31,$D7,$63
;     yr xor T(yL)       RL4      adc    L+4         KS   fcb  $DA,$06,$C8,$0A,$BB,$11,$85,$EB
;*******************               sta    L+4              fcb  $4F,$7C,$7B,$57,$57,$F5,$95,$84
NO       lda    L+7               bcc    ExitR       RT1  fcb  $90,$CF,$D4,$7D,$7C,$19,$BB,$42
         lsra                     clra                   fcb  $15,$8D,$95,$54,$F7,$B4,$6B,$CE
         lsra             RL5      adc    L+5              fcb  $D5,$5C,$4D,$79,$FD,$5F,$24,$D6
         tax                      sta    L+5              fcb  $61,$3C,$31,$C3,$83,$9A,$2D,$DF
         lda    RT0,x             bcc    ExitR            fcb  $8A,$9A,$27,$6B,$CF,$BF,$A1,$C8
         eor    L+4               clra                    fcb  $77,$C5,$62,$84,$DA,$B7,$9C,$D4
         sta    L+4      RL6      adc    L+6              fcb  $C2,$B3,$29,$3D,$20,$E9,$E5,$EA
         sta    L+8               sta    L+6              fcb  $F0,$2A,$C6,$0A,$CC,$93,$ED,$87
         lda    RT1,x             bcc    ExitR       RT2  fcb  $44,$22,$A5,$2E,$CB,$23,$8F,$EE
         eor    L+5               clra                    fcb  $E5,$AB,$6A,$DD,$83,$5F,$D1,$A0
         sta    L+5      RL7      adc    L+7              fcb  $75,$3D,$0A,$8F,$78,$E5,$37,$D2
         lda    RT2,x             sta    L+7              fcb  $B9,$5B,$B7,$9D,$8D,$CA,$EC,$64
         eor    L+6               bcc    ExitR            fcb  $2C,$1E,$9F,$23,$B8,$29,$B5,$C2
         sta    L+6               clra                    fcb  $78,$0B,$F3,$87,$37,$DF,$8B,$B3
         lda    RT3,x    RH0      adc    H+0              fcb  $00,$D0,$13,$34,$A0,$D0,$BD,$86
         eor    L+7               sta    H+0              fcb  $45,$CB,$FA,$73,$A6,$16,$0F,$FE
         sta    L+7               bcc    ExitR       RT3  fcb  $39,$3C,$48,$CB,$BB,$CA,$06,$0F
;*******************               clra                    fcb  $0F,$F8,$EC,$6D,$31,$BE,$B5,$CC
;     yl xor c           RH1      adc    H+1              fcb  $EE,$D7,$F2,$F0,$BB,$08,$80,$17
;*******************               sta    H+1              fcb  $16,$3B,$C6,$0D,$F4,$5A,$0E,$CB
         clrx                     bcc    ExitR            fcb  $1B,$CD,$28,$9B,$06,$CB,$BF,$EA
LxorC    lda    L,x               clra                    fcb  $21,$AD,$08,$E1,$84,$7F,$3F,$73
         eor    KC,x     RH2      adc    H+2              fcb  $78,$D5,$6C,$ED,$94,$64,$0D,$6E
         sta    save1             sta    H+2              fcb  $F0,$D3,$D3,$7B,$E6,$70,$08,$E1
         lda    L+4,x             bcc    ExitR       KD   fcb  $86,$D1,$BF,$27,$5B,$9B,$24,$1D
         sta    L,x      RH3      adc    H+3         KC   fcb  $EB,$64,$74,$9A
         lda    save1             sta    H+3         ;***********************************
         sta    L+4,x             bcc    ExitR       ;      THE END
         incx                     clra               ;***********************************
         cpx    #4       RH4      adc    H+4
         bne    LxorC             sta    H+4
;*******************               bcc    ExitR
;+KD mod 2^64 and swap             clra
;*******************      RH5      adc    H+5
         clc                      sta    H+5
         clrx                     bcc    ExitR
LaddD    lda    L,x               clra
```

Twofish on Smart Cards

Bruce Schneier[1] and Doug Whiting[2]

[1] Counterpane Systems, 101 E Minnehaha Parkway, Minneapolis, MN 55419, USA,
schneier@counterpane.com
[2] Hi/fn, Inc., 5973 Avenida Encinas Suite 110, Carlsbad, CA 92008, USA,
dwhiting@hifn.com

Abstract. Twofish is a 128-bit block cipher with a 128-, 192-, or 256-bit
key. The algorithm was designed with smart cards in mind, and can be
implemented on 8-bit CPUs with only 60 bytes of RAM. A variety of
implementation options allows Twofish to encrypt and decrypt quicker
if more RAM is available.

1   Introduction

The National Institute of Standards and Technology (NIST), in an initiative
designed to replace the aging Data Encryption Standard (DES), initiated a process to select the Advanced Encryption Standard (AES) [NIST97a,NIST97b,
NIST98]. Organizations were invited to submit candidate algorithms for the
standard, and NIST received fifteen submissions. The selection process will result in about five algorithms chosen for the second round sometime in mid 1999,
and one single algorithm chosen as the standard sometime in early 2000.

In choosing an AES, NIST will be defining the block encryption standard
for the next several decades. AES will be used in a wide variety of applications
with a wide variety of performance requirements and constraints. Hence, good
performance on smart cards and other low-end CPUs is essential. The majority of
encryption applications are on weak CPUs, and there will always be requirements
to implement AES on these platforms.

Twofish [Seu60,SKW+98a,SKW+99a] is our submission into the Advanced
Encryption Standard (AES) process. Our design process stressed performance on
32-bit CPUs, 8-bit low-RAM CPUs, and hardware, and resulted in an algorithm
that is conservative in design, fast, and flexible.

2   Twofish

A full description of Twofish can be found in [SKW+98a,SKW+98b,Sch98,
SKW+99a]. Briefly, Twofish is a symmetric block cipher with a 128-bit block.
There are three basic key lengths, 128, 192 and 256 bits, but Twofish can accept
key lengths less than those values by padding the key. Twofish is a 16-round Feistel network. Before the first round and after the final round, whitening key bits
are XORed into the text. In each round, two 32-bit words are the input into the

bijective F-function. The second word is rotated 8 bits, and each words is broken up into bytes and sent through one of four key-dependent 8-by-8-bit S-boxes. The four output bytes of each word are then combined using a fixed maximum distance separable (MDS) matrix over $GF(2^8)$. This results in two 32-bit output words, which are combined with each other using addition (a pseudo-Hadamard transform). A word of expanded key material is added to each word, and the results are XORed with the other half of the text to complete the Feistel structure. Finally, one bit rotations are added; one before and one after this XOR.

The key schedule produces the four key-dependent S-boxes, the 32 round subkeys, and the 8 subkey words for input and output whitening. The key schedule uses two fixed 8-by-8-bit S-boxes and key bits to create these constructs. Details of the key schedule can be found in [SKW+98a,SKW+98b,SKW+99a]. Basically, the same structure is used to create the key-dependent S-boxes and the round keys.

We have spent considerable effort analyzing both reduced-round Twofish and simplified Twofish (i.e. Twofish with some of the complexity removed). Details of our initial cryptanalysis of Twofish are in [SKW+98a,SKW+98b,F98,WW98, SKW+99a]. Our best attack breaks 5 rounds with $2^{22.5}$ chosen plaintexts and 2^{51} effort [SKW+98a,SKW+99a].

2.1 Performance and Flexibility

Because of our performance-driven design methodology [SW97], Twofish is the fastest AES submission on the Pentium and weaker 32-bit CPUs, and the second fastest on the Pentium Pro and Pentium II. It is also one of the fastest on the Alpha and Merced. On all of these platforms, Twofish encrypts and decrypts in approximately 18 clock cycles per byte.

As impressive as these numbers are, the full range of performance is much more complicated than that. Twofish was designed to have considerable implementation flexibility. The design of both the round function and the key schedule permits a wide variety of tradeoffs between speed, software size, key setup time, gate count, and memory.

On 32-bit CPUs, there are five different implementation options that trade off key setup time for encryption time: compiled, full, partial, minimum, and zero.[1] These implementations all interoperate; it is possible to encrypt data with one implementation option and decrypt it with another. Some applications encrypt large amounts of data with a single key (e.g., secure video distribution), while others need to change keys after encrypting only a few blocks (e.g., electronic-cash protocols); Twofish can be made efficient in each case.

---

[1] The names refer to the amount of precomputation done to the key-dependant S-boxes. The "zero keying" option does no precomputation. One layer of the S-boxes are computed in the "minimal keying" option. The "partial keying" option precomputes the four 8-by-8-bit S-boxes, and the "full keying" option combines the four S-boxes and MDS matrix into four 8-by-32-bit S-boxes. In the "compiled" option, the subkey constants are directly embedded into a key-specific copy of the code.

Table 1. Twofish Pentium assembly-language performance with different implementation options and key lengths

Keying Option	Code Size	Clocks to Key 128-bit	192-bit	256-bit	Clocks to Encrypt 128-bit	192-bit	256-bit
Compiled	9100	12300	14600	17100	290	290	290
Full	8200	11000	13500	16200	315	315	315
Partial	10300	5500	7800	9800	430	430	430
Minimum	12600	3700	5900	7900	740	740	740
Zero	8700	1800	2100	2600	1000	1300	1600

Table 1 gives performance numbers for the Pentium; further discussions of Twofish's performance can be found in [SKW+98a,Sch98,WS98,SKW+99a]. For applications with large amounts of memory available (256 KBytes or more), the Twofish key schedule can be implemented using large (fixed) precomputed tables to reduce key setup time [WS98].

Similar performance trade-offs are possible in hardware implementations and implementations on 8-bit CPUs; these will be discussed in detail below.

3   Smart Cards and Cryptography

Although most AES candidates concentrated on performance on state-of-the-art 32-bit CPUs, the majority of symmetric cryptography occurs on much smaller chips, either in dedicated hardware or small 8-bit CPUs. As a first approximation, all DES implementations in the world are on 8-bit CPUs. Examples include satellite TV decoders, automatic teller machines, eftpos, cellular telephones, telephone cards, electronic cash cards, prepaid electricity meters, computer access tokens, building access tokens, burglar alarms, automobile remote locking devices, road toll and parking garage tokens, automatic garage-door openers, tachographs, lottery ticket terminals, and postal franking machines.[2] None of these applications can afford the luxury of a Pentium-class microprocessor; they have to make do with embedded CPUs, smart card chips, or custom silicon.

Higher-end smart card CPUs that implement public-key cryptography have between 512- and 2304-bytes of RAM, 14- and 32 KBytes of ROM, and 4- and 32-KBytes of EEPROM [NM96a,NM96b,HP98], but lower end smart cards still have nowhere near this capacity. Until two years ago, virtually all smart cards had 4K of ROM or less, and only 128 bytes of RAM. An example is the Motorola MC68HC05SC80, which entered production at the end of 1997; it has 4K ROM, 128 bytes RAM, and 1K EEPROM. RAM-poor smart card chips such as this are currently fielded in most smart card-based applications, and are likely to dominate the market for years to come. According to Gemplus, which has about 40% of the smart card market, the world market in 2003 will be about 1.885 billion cards with small RAM and shared key cryptography, 400 million with

---

[2] Many of these examples came from [And96].

Table 2. Twofish performance on a 6805 smart card

RAM, ROM, or EEPROM for key	Working RAM	Code and Table Size	Clocks per Block	Time per block @ 4MHz
24	36	2200	26500	6.6 msec
24	36	2150	32900	8.2 msec
24	36	2000	35000	8.7 msec
24	36	1750	37100	9.3 msec
184	36	1900	15300	3.8 msec
184	36	1700	18100	4.5 msec
184	36	1450	19200	4.8 msec
1208	36	1300	12700	3.2 msec
1208	36	1100	15500	3.9 msec
1208	36	850	16600	4.2 msec
3256	36	1000	11900	3.0 msec

large RAM and shared key cryptography, and 405 million with large RAM and public key cryptography [Gem98].

While smart cards will continue to get more powerful—the newer smart card chips have more RAM, more ROM, and 16- or even 32-bit CPUs—it is unreasonable to assume the death of the small 8-bit microprocessors. From past experience we know that every time a new generation of more powerful CPUs appears, a much larger new generation of applications for the low-end CPUs, now much cheaper, also appears. When electronic cash cards and cellular telephones are using 32-bit CPUs, 8-bit CPUs will become the platform of choice for the next wave of miniaturization. Today, the Motorola and Intel 8-bit architectures are more common than they were when they controlled desktop computers. Tomorrow, these architectures will be even cheaper and smaller, and there is every reason to believe that they will be even more plentiful.

4   Twofish and Smart Cards

Twofish is ideally suited for smart cards. It can fit on the smallest smart cards while exhibiting reasonable performance, and can take advantage of more RAM or more powerful processors with increased performance. It can operate efficiently in environments that require rapid key changes, and can be implemented in dedicated hardware in only a few gates.

We implemented Twofish on a 6805 CPU (a typical smart card processor) to obtain our smart card performance data. A summary of our results are shown in Table 2, and are explained in more detail in the subsequent sections. The lack of a second index register on the 6805 has a significant impact on the code size and performance, so a different CPU with multiple index registers (e.g., 6502, 6811) might be a better fit for Twofish. However, the 6805 is one of the most widely used smart card CPUs, so performance on this platform is important. We have not yet implemented Twofish for the 8051 architecture.

4.1   RAM Usage

For any encryption algorithm, memory usage can be divided into two parts: that required to hold the expanded key, and that required as working space to encrypt or decrypt text (including the text block). In applications where a smart card holds a single key for a long period of time, the key can be put into EEPROM or even ROM, greatly reducing RAM requirements. Most applications, however, require the smart card to encrypt using session keys, which change with each transaction. In these situations, the expanded key must be stored in RAM, along with working space to perform the encryption.

Twofish—the 128-bit key version—can be implemented in a smart card in 60 bytes of RAM. This includes the text block, key, and working space. If a slightly expanded key (24 bytes instead of 16) can be stored in ROM or EPROM, then Twofish can be implemented in only 36 bytes of RAM. In either case, there is zero key-setup time for the next encryption operation with the same key.

Larger key sizes require more RAM to store the larger keys: 36 bytes for 192-bit keys and 48 bytes for 256-bit keys. If these applications can store key material in ROM or EPROM, then these key lengths can be implemented on smart cards with only 36 bytes of RAM. All of this RAM can be reused for other purposes between block encryption operations.

For smart cards with larger memory to hold key-dependent data, encryption speed can increase considerably. This is because the session keys can be precomputed as part of the expanded key, requiring a total of 184 bytes of key memory. As shown in Table 2, this option nearly halves the encryption time. If the smart card has enough additional memory available to hold 1 kilobyte of precomputed S-box in either RAM, ROM, or EEPROM (for a total of 1208 bytes), performance improves further. Finally, as shown in the final row of Table 2, if the entire precomputed S-box plus MDS table can be held in memory (3256 bytes), the speed can again be increased slightly more. Although this type of implementation is unlikely to be suitable for a smart card, it can be used in terminals which often have an 8-bit CPU and 32 Kbyte of RAM or so. It should be noted that some of these "large RAM" implementations save 512 bytes of code space by assuming that certain tables are not required in ROM, with the entire precomputation being instead performed on the "host" that sets the key in the smart card. If the card has to perform its own key expansion, the code size increases although this increase again has a significant flexibility in space-time tradeoffs.

This flexibility is unique in all AES submissions: Twofish works in the most RAM-poor environments, while at the same time is able to take advantage of both moderate RAM cards and large-RAM cards.

4.2   Encryption Speed and Key Agility

On a 6805 with only 60 bytes of RAM, Twofish encrypts at speeds of 26,500 to 37,100 clocks per byte, depending on the amount of ROM available for the code. On a 4 MHz chip, this translates to 6.6 msec to 9.3 msec per encryption. In these implementations, the key-schedule precomputation time is minimal: just over 1750 clocks per key. This setup time could be cut considerably at the cost of two additional 512-byte ROM tables, which would be used during the key schedule.

If ROM is expensive, Twofish can be implemented in less space at slower speeds. The space-speed tradeoffs are of two types: unrolling loops and implementing various lookup tables. By far, the latter has the larger impact on size and speed. For example, Twofish's MDS matrix can be computed in three different ways:

- Full table lookups for the multiplications. This is the fastest, and required 512 bytes of ROM for tables.
- Single table lookup for the multiplications. This is slower, but only requires 256 bytes of ROM for the table.
- No tables, all multiplies in done with shift/XOR. This is the slowest, and the smallest.

Longer keys are slower, but only slightly so. Twofish's encryption time per block increases by less than 2600 clocks per block (for any of the code size/speed tradeoffs) for 192-bit keys, and by about 5200 clocks per block for 256-bit keys[3]. Similarly, the key schedule precomputation increases to 2550 clocks for 192-bit keys, and to 3400 clocks for 256-bit keys.

As shown in Table 2, in smart card CPUs with sufficient additional RAM storage to hold the entire set of subkeys, the throughput improves significantly, although the key setup time also increases. The time savings per block is over 11000 clocks, cutting the block encryption time down to about 15000 clocks; i.e., nearly doubling the encryption speed. The key setup time increases by roughly the same number of clocks, thus making the key setup time comparable to a single block encryption. This approach also cuts down the code size by a few hundred bytes. It should be noted further that, in fixed key environments, the subkeys can be stored along with the key bytes in EEPROM, cutting the total RAM usage down to 36 bytes while maintaining the higher speed.

As another tradeoff, if another 1K bytes of RAM or EPROM is available, all four 8-bit S-boxes can be precomputed. Clearly, this approach has relatively low key agility, but the time required to encrypt a block decreases by roughly 6000 clocks. When combined with precomputed subkeys as discussed in the previous paragraph, the block encryption time drops to about 9000 clocks, nearly three times the best speed for "low RAM" implementations. In most cases, this approach would be used only where the key is fixed, but it does allow for very high throughput. Similarly, if 3K bytes of RAM or EEPROM is available for tables, throughput can be further improved slightly.

The wide variety of possible speeds again illustrates Twofish's flexibility in these constrained environments. The algorithm does not have one speed; it has many speeds, depending on available resources.

---

[3] The only exceptions are the very-large RAM implementations that precompute complete tables for the S-boxes. The encryption speed is independent of the key length for these implementations.

Table 3. Hardware tradeoffs (128-bit key)

Gate count	Clocks/ block	Interleave Levels	Clock Speed	Throughput (Mbits/sec)	Startup clocks
8000	324	1	80 MHz	32	20
14000	72	1	40 MHz	71	4
19000	32	1	40 MHz	160	40
23000	16	1	40 MHz	320	20
26000	32	2	80 MHz	640	20
28000	48	3	120 MHz	960	20
30000	64	4	150 MHz	1200	20
80000	16	1	80 MHz	640	300

4.3 Code Size

Twofish code is very compact: 1760 to 2200 bytes for minimal RAM footprint, depending on the implementation. Unlike some of the other AES submissions, the same code base can be used for both encryption and decryption. If only encryption is required, minor improvements in code size can be obtained (on the order of 150 bytes). The extra code required for larger keys is fairly negligible: less than 100 extra bytes for a 192-bit key, and less than 200 bytes for a 256-bit key.

For ultra-low-ROM applications, the ROM tables can be computed using 64 bytes of tables and some code. This will save approximately 350 bytes of ROM, at a performance decrease of a factor or ten or more. Although only useful in applications where ROM is critical but performance is not, this implementation shows how flexible Twofish really is.

4.4 32-bit Smart Cards

Microprocessors on 32-bit smart cards have relatively simple instruction sets and only one pipeline. Although we haven't implemented Twofish on any of these processors, a reasonable performance assumption is twice the Pentium clock cycles: see Table 1. The doubling is due to the fact that the Pentium has two parallel instruction paths, while the smart card chip has one.

4.5 Twofish in Hardware

The flexibility of Twofish reflects in the wide variety of possible hardware implementations; Table 3 is only a handful of the possibilities. The numbers in this table are based on our estimates of the complexity of various implementation options.

The low-end hardware design requires only 8000 gates. This is a "byte-serial" implementation: four clocks per dword for the S-boxes plus MDS, four dwords (two subkey, two text) per round, plus two clocks of PHT "overhead." The design can be very easily pipelined internally, with 80 MHz operation implying a throughput of 32 Mbits/sec. This approach has very high key agility (20 clocks, or about 6% of a block time).

The next line is a slightly higher performance hardware implementation that uses only 14,000 gates but still computes the round keys on the fly. The other versions all precompute the round subkeys. The last line is a version that pre-computes the S-boxes in to dedicated RAM instead of computing the S-boxes on the fly. Depending on the architecture, the logic will grow somewhat in size for larger keys, and the clock speed may decrease.

These estimates are all based on existing 0.35 micron CMOS technology. All the examples in the table are actually quite small in today's technology, except the final (highest performance non-interleaved) instance, but even that is very doable today and will become fairly inexpensive as the next generation silicon technology (0.25 micron) becomes the industry norm. No full custom layout is assumed, although it is clearly possible to achieve even higher speeds and lower areas using a custom layout if desired.

4.6 Smart-Card-Specific Cryptanalytic Attacks

Recently, cryptographers have developed a new class of attacks against encryption algorithms in smart card hardware: attacks that rely on the leakage of additional information about the encryption operation. Timing attacks [Koc96], differential power analysis [Koc98] are both specific examples of this "side-channel cryptanalysis" [KSWH98], as are attacks based on NMR scanning and electronic emanations.

With Twofish, the number of instructions for both encryption and decryption does not depend on either the key or the text. Additionally, there are no operations that take variable lengths of time depending on the inputs, like data-dependent rotations or multiplications[4]. Timing attacks based on cache hits are not applicable to smart cards as they typically do not have a cache. Timing differences induced by cache behavior are a concern in other platforms; most AES candidates use some form of S-box table which can lead to data-dependent timing of an encryption.

The same properties make Twofish more resistant to power and radiation attacks. All rounds of Twofish operate in the same way, regardless of the key and text inputs. Twofish only uses simple operations that execute independent of either key or text values. There are no obvious operations that can leak information about their operands[5].

---

[4] On some CPUs the multiply instruction uses an "early out" algorithm. This makes the multiply instruction a bit faster on average, but the execution time now depends on the data being multiplied. This is an obvious source of timing differences which could be used in an attack.

[5] It seems that differential power analysis is powerful enough to "read" individual bits within the computations of the cipher. It is clear that no cipher can be secure against such an attack, and countermeasures will have to be taken in other areas.

Table 4. RAM Requirements and 32-bit Smart-Card Performance for Selected AES Candidates

Algorithm Name	Smart Card RAM (bytes)	32-bit Speed (clock cycles)
CAST-256	?	1630*
Crypton	52*	780*
DEAL	50*	4400*
DFC	200*	?
E2	300*	820*
Mars	195*	1100*
RC6	210*	1400*
Rijndael	52	640*
SAFER+	50*	2200*
Serpent	50*	2200*
Twofish	60	580*

While total resistance to side-channel cryptanalysis is probably impossible, and in the end resistance is dependent on the implementation far more than the algorithm, we believe that achieving practical resistance is far easier with Twofish than it is with many of the other AES submissions.

5   Comparing AES Candidates on Smart Cards

The speed of almost all the candidate algorithms on common 8-bit CPUs seems to be acceptably fast, given certain assumptions. It is fairly difficult to compare the speeds given in the AES submission papers, since most involve different CPUs, different clock rates, and different assumptions about subkey precomputation vs. on-the-fly computation. For our purposes here, we will concentrate more on how well each algorithm fits on a smart card CPU rather than exactly how fast it runs.

One major concern is how much RAM is used. Most commodity smart card CPUs today include from 128 to 256 bytes of on-board RAM. Each CPU family typically contains members with more RAM and a correspondingly higher cost. Table 4 summarizes the RAM usage for 8-bit implementations of the various AES submissions. Some of these numbers are estimates that do not derive from an actual implementation; these are marked with an asterisk. Several of the algorithms—DFC, E2, Mars, and RC6—have no way to compute subkeys on-the-fly, thus requiring that all the subkeys be precomputed whenever a key is changed. These subkeys can consume from 150 to 256 bytes of "extra" RAM, which means they cannot possibly fit on a smart card with only 128 bytes of RAM.

By Gemplus's sales projections [Gem98], in 2003 70% of the word's smart cards will still not be able to run these AES candidates. Although 30% of the smart card CPUs will have enough RAM to hold the subkeys, it is naive to assume that such a large fraction of the RAM (or any other system resource for that matter) can be dedicated solely to the encryption function. Clearly, if a given algorithm cannot fit on a smart card's CPU, it cannot be used whether or not it is a standard.

On 32-bit smart-card CPUs speed is likely to be more of a concern, since these more-expensive CPUs will be used in high-end smart card applications. Although we have not implemented the AES candidates on 32-bit smart card CPUs, a reasonable performance estimate is to double the number of clock cycles on the Pentium (see Table 4). For most algorithms, smart-card performance will be within 10% of this number; for Mars and RC6, which make heavy use of data-dependent rotations and multiplications, actual performance will probably be worse. Given these estimates, the fastest algorithm is Twofish, followed by Rijndael, Crypton, and E2. A more extensive comparison would also include key setup times (which is important in protocols that change keys frequently and encrypt very little text with each key); the interested reader is referred to [SKW+99b].

Some of the AES candidates have obvious timing problems on small CPUs (e.g., RC6 and Mars with their data-dependent rotations and 32-bit multiplications). These operations, not easily available on 8-bit CPUs, are also very slow. Even on 32-bit smart cards, multiplications and data-dependent rotations can take multiple clock cycles, making these algorithms significantly slower than others (just as RC6 and Mars are significantly slower on a Pentium than a Pentium Pro or II).

One final note: When comparing the performance of different AES candidates on smart cards, it is important to make the comparison on a single platform. It is *very* difficult to compare performance numbers on different microprocessors: for example, a 6805 vs. a 8051. To give a concrete example of this problem, Ron Rivest mentioned in his RC6 presentation that their performance numbers were on a 1 MHz 8051 while many people used 4 MHz 6805s, implying that RC6 should be faster [Riv98]. The problem is that the clocking scheme for an 8051 is dramatically different, with the 1 MHz number actually being a cycle time, not a clock frequency, since an 8051 "cycle" consists of 12 clocks. Thus his "MHz" 8051 is actually very comparable to a 4 MHz 6805 in terms of the time to process a "typical" opcode.

6   Conclusions

If the past 30 years of microcomputer applications has taught us anything, it is that the high end always improves while the low end becomes more ubiquitous. The AES, by virtue of it becomming a government and then an industry standard, will be required in a wide variety of cryptographic applications. In order to be "buzzword compliant," products will have to implement AES, just as today they must implement DES. Given this reality, it makes sense to choose an AES that can work everywhere: one that is both suitable for the cheapest smart-card processors and that can take advantage of the additional capabilities of the more powerful processors.

Twofish's design philosophy can be summed up in three words: conservative, fast, flexible. The wide variety of implementation trade-offs make it possible to implement Twofish on the most low-powered smart card, while at the same time to take advantage of the increased memory capabilities of the more powerful smart cards. It can fit in hardware in a very small number of gates, or can run faster with more gates. Any set of design constraints—encryption speed, key setup speed, gate count, code and table size, RAM usage, EEPROM usage—can be optimized for. This capability is unique among all AES candidates.

Further information on Twofish, including the AES submission, a series of Twofish Technical Reports announcing new cryptographic and performance results, and Twofish implementations in C, Pentium assembly, Java, 6805 assembly, and other languages, can be found at the Twofish home page at:

http://www.counterpane.com/twofish.html

Additional information on the AES competition can be found on NIST's AES home page at:

http://www.nist.gov/aes/

We welcome additional data to better compare the AES submissions, and hope that some laboratory will implement the submissions on a common platform.

References

[And96]   R. Anderson, "Crypto in Europe — Markets, Law, and Policy," *Cryptography: Policy and Algorithms International Conference*, LNCS #1029, Springer-Verlag, 1996, pp. 75–90.

[F98]   N. Ferguson, "Upper bounds on differential characteristics in Twofish," Twofish Technical Report #1, Counterpane Systems, Aug 1998.

[Gem98]   Gemplus, corporate presentation slides, 1998.

[HP98]   H. Handschuh and P. Paillier, "Smart Card Coprocessors for Public-Key Cryptography" *Third Smart Card Research and Advanced Applications Conference (CARDIS) Proceedings*, Springer-Verlag, 1999, this volume.

[KSWH98]   J. Kelsey, B. Schneier, D. Wagner, and C. Hall, "Side Channel Cryptanalysis of Product Ciphers," *ESORICS '98 Proceedings*, Springer-Verlag, 1998, pp. 97–110.

[Koc96]   P. Kocher, "Timing Attacks on Implementations of Diffie-Hellman, RSA, DSS, and Other Systems," *Advances in Cryptology—CRYPTO '96 Proceedings*, Springer-Verlag, 1996, pp. 104–113.

[Koc98]   P. Kocher, "Differential Power Analysis," available online from http://www.cryptography.com/dpa/.

[NIST97a]   National Institute of Standards and Technology, "Announcing Development of a Federal Information Standard for Advanced Encryption Standard," *Federal Register*, v. 62, n. 1, 2 Jan 1997, pp. 93–94.

[NIST97b]   National Institute of Standards and Technology, "Announcing Request for Candidate Algorithm Nominations for the Advanced Encryption Standard (AES)," *Federal Register*, v. 62, n. 117, 12 Sep 1997, pp. 48051–48058.

[NIST98]   NIST, AES website, http://www.nist.gob/aes/.

[NM96a]   D. Naccache and D. M'Raihi, "Cryptographic Smart Cards," *IEEE Micro*, June 96, pp. 14–24.

[NM96b]   D. Naccache and D. M'Raihi, "Arithmetic Co-processors for Smart Cards: The State of the Art," *Proceeings 1996 CARDIS Smart Card Research and Advanced Applications*, CWI, 1996, pp. 39–58.

[Riv98]   R. Rivest, "RC6 Presentation," First AES Candidate Conference, place, date. ((get this data))

[Sch98]   B. Schneier, "The Twofish Encryption Algorithm," *Dr. Dobbs Journal*, v. 23, n. 12, Dec 1998, pp. 30–38.

[Seu60]   Seuss, Dr.,]it One Fish, Two Fish, Red Fish, Blue Fish, Beginner Books, 1960.

[SKW+98a]   B. Schneier, J. Kelsey, D. Whiting, D. Wagner, C. Hall, and N. Ferguson, "Twofish: A 128-Bit Block Cipher," NIST AES Proposal, 15 June 1998.

[SKW+98b]   B. Schneier, J. Kelsey, D. Whiting, D. Wagner, C. Hall, and N. Ferguson, "On the Twofish Key Schedule," *Proceedings of the 1998 SAC Conference*, Springer-Verlag, 1998, to appear.

[SKW+99a]   B. Schneier, J. Kelsey, D. Whiting, D. Wagner, C. Hall, and N. Ferguson, *The Twofish Encryption Algorithm*, Springer-Verlag, 1999.

[SKW+99b]   B. Schneier, J. Kelsey, D. Whiting, D. Wagner, C. Hall, and N. Ferguson, "Performance Comparison of the AES Submissions," to appear.

[SW97]   B. Schneier and D. Whiting, "Fast Software Encryption: Designing Encryption Algorithms for Optimal Speed on the Intel Pentium Processor," *Fast Software Encryption, 4th International Workshop Proceedings*, Springer-Verlag, 1997, pp. 242–259.

[WS98]   D. Whiting and B. Schneier "Improved Twofish Implementations," Twofish Technical Report #3, Counterpane Systems, to appear.

[WW98]   D. Whiting and D. Wagner, "Empirical Verification of Twofish Key Uniqueness Properties," Twofish Technical Report #2, Counterpane Systems, 22 Sep 1998.

The Block Cipher Rijndael

Joan Daemen[1] and Vincent Rijmen[*2]

[1] Proton World Int'l
Zweefvliegtuigstraat 10
B-1130 Brussel, Belgium
`Daemen.J@protonworld.com`
[2] Katholieke Universiteit Leuven, Dept. Electrical Engineering–ESAT
Kardinaal Mercierlaan 94, B–3001 Heverlee, Belgium
`vincent.rijmen@esat.kuleuven.ac.be`

Abstract. In this paper we present the block cipher Rijndael, which is one of the fifteen candidate algorithms for the Advanced Encryption Standard (AES). We show that the cipher can be implemented very efficiently on Smart Cards.

1   Introduction

The US National Institute of Standards and Technology (NIST) issued a call for an Advanced Encryption Standard (AES) to replace the current Data Encryption Standard (DES). The AES call asks for a 128-bit block cipher whith a variable key length. (At least key lengths of 128, 192 and 256 bits are to be supported.) The cipher should be efficient on a Pentium platform, 8-bit processors and in hardware. Rijndael is one of the fifteen submissions that have been accepted as a candidate algorithm.

We describe the block cipher in Section 2 and discuss its Smart Card implementation in Section 3. We give some performance figures in Section 4 and we conclude in Section 5.

2   Description of Rijndael

Rijndael is an iterated block cipher with a variable block length and a variable key length. The block length and the key length can be independently specified to 128, 192 or 256 bits. Like SQUARE [2] and BKSQ [4], Rijndael has been designed following the wide trail strategy [1,7]. This design strategy provides resistance against linear and differential cryptanalysis. In the strategy, the round transformation is divided into different components, each with its own functionality. In this section we explain the cipher structure and the component transformations. For implementation aspects, we refer to Section 3.

---

[*] F.W.O. postdoctoral researcher, sponsored by the Fund for Scientific Research – Flanders (Belgium).

J.-J. Quisquater and B. Schneier (Eds.): CARDIS 2000, LNCS 1820, pp. 277–284, 2000.

2.1   The State, the Cipher Key, and the Number of Rounds

We define the *state* of the block cipher as the intermediate result of the encryption process. The state is initialised with the plaintext, in the order $a_{0,0}$, $a_{1,0}$, $a_{2,0}$, $a_{3,0}$, $a_{0,1}$, $a_{1,1}$, ... The round transformations are built from component transformations that operate on the state. Finally, at the end of the cipher operation, the ciphertext is read from the state by taking the state bytes in the same order.

The state can be pictured as a rectangular array of bytes. This array has four rows, the number of columns is denoted by N_b and is equal to the block length divided by 32. The cipher key is similarly pictured as a rectangular array with four rows. The number of columns of the cipher key is denoted by N_k and is equal to the key length divided by 32. This is illustrated in Figure 1. Sometimes the Cipher Key is pictured as a linear array of four-byte words. The words consist of the four bytes that are in the corresponding column.

$a_{0,0}$	$a_{0,1}$	$a_{0,2}$	$a_{0,3}$	$a_{0,4}$	$a_{0,5}$
$a_{1,0}$	$a_{1,1}$	$a_{1,2}$	$a_{1,3}$	$a_{1,4}$	$a_{1,5}$
$a_{2,0}$	$a_{2,1}$	$a_{2,2}$	$a_{2,3}$	$a_{2,4}$	$a_{2,5}$
$a_{3,0}$	$a_{3,1}$	$a_{3,2}$	$a_{3,3}$	$a_{3,4}$	$a_{3,5}$

$k_{0,0}$	$k_{0,1}$	$k_{0,2}$	$k_{0,3}$
$k_{1,0}$	$k_{1,1}$	$k_{1,2}$	$k_{1,3}$
$k_{2,0}$	$k_{2,1}$	$k_{2,2}$	$k_{2,3}$
$k_{3,0}$	$k_{3,1}$	$k_{3,2}$	$k_{3,3}$

Fig. 1. Example of state layout (with $N_b = 6$) and cipher key layout (with $N_k = 4$).

The number of rounds is denoted by N_r and depends on the values N_b and N_k. It is given in Table 1.

Table 1. Number of Rounds (N_r) as a function of the block and key length.

		N_b		
		4	6	8
	4	10	12	14
N_k	6	12	12	14
	8	14	14	14

2.2   The Round Transformation

The round transformation is composed of four different component transformations. In pseudo C notation we have:

```
Round(State,RoundKey) {
ByteSub(State);
ShiftRow(State);
MixColumn(State);
AddRoundKey(State,RoundKey);
}
```

The final round of the cipher is slightly different. It is defined by:

```
FinalRound(State,RoundKey) {
ByteSub(State);
ShiftRow(State);
AddRoundKey(State,RoundKey);
}
```

It can be seen that in the final round the MixColumn step has been removed. The component transformations are specified in the following subsections.

The ByteSub Transformation. The ByteSub transformation is a non-linear byte substitution, operating on each of the state bytes independently. The substitution table (or S-box) is invertible and is constructed by the composition of two transformations:

1. First, taking the multiplicative inverse in $GF(2^8)$ [6], the zero element is mapped onto itself.
2. Then, applying an affine transformation (over $GF(2)$).

The application of the described S-box to all bytes of the state is denoted by ByteSub(State).

The ShiftRow Transformation. In ShiftRow, the last three rows of the state are shifted cyclically over different offsets. Row 1 is shifted over C_1 bytes, row 2 over C_2 bytes and row 3 over C_3 bytes. The shift offsets C_1, C_2 and C_3 depend on the block length N_b. The different values are specified in Table2.

Table 2. Shift offsets for different block lengths.

N_b	C_1	C_2	C_3
4	1	2	3
6	1	2	3
8	1	3	4

The operation of shifting the last three rows of the state over the specified offsets is denoted by ShiftRow(State).

The MixColumn Transformation. In MixColumn, the columns of the state are considered as polynomials over $GF(2^8)$, and multiplied modulo $x^4 + 1$ with a fixed polynomial $c(x)$, given by $c(x) = 3x^3 + x^2 + x + 2$. This can also be written as a matrix multiplication. Let $b(x) = c(x) \otimes a(x)$, then

$$\begin{bmatrix} b_0 \\ b_1 \\ b_2 \\ b_3 \end{bmatrix} = \begin{bmatrix} 2 & 3 & 1 & 1 \\ 1 & 2 & 3 & 1 \\ 1 & 1 & 2 & 3 \\ 3 & 1 & 1 & 2 \end{bmatrix} \times \begin{bmatrix} a_0 \\ a_1 \\ a_2 \\ a_3 \end{bmatrix}.$$

The application of this operation on all four columns of the state is denoted by MixColumn(State).

The Round Key Addition. In this operation, a round key is applied to the state by a simple bitwise EXOR. The round key is derived from the cipher key by means of the key schedule. The round key length is equal to the block length N_b. The transformation that consists of EXORing a round key to the state is denoted by AddRoundKey(State,RoundKey).

2.3   Key Schedule

The round keys are derived from the cipher key by means of the key schedule. This consists of two components: the key expansion and the round key selection. The basic principles are the following.

- The total number of round key bits is equal to the block length multiplied by the number of rounds plus 1. (e.g., for a block length of 128 bits and 10 rounds, 1408 round key bits are needed).
- The cipher key is expanded into an expanded key.
- Round keys are taken from this expanded key in the following way: the first round key consists of the first N_b words, the second one of the following N_b words, and so on.

Key Expansion. The expanded key is a linear array of four-byte words and is denoted by $W[N_b(N_r + 1)]$. The first N_k words contain the cipher key. All other words are defined recursively in terms of words with smaller indices. The key schedule depends on the value of N_k: there is a version for $N_k \leq 6$, and a version for $N_k > 6$. For $N_k \leq 6$, we have:

```
KeyExpansion(CipherKey,W) {
    for(i = 0; i < Nk; i++) W[i] = CipherKey[i];
    for(j = Nk; j < Nb(Nr + 1); j += Nk) {
        W[j] = W[j − Nk] ⊕ SubByte(Rotl(W[j − 1])) ⊕ Rcon[j/Nk];
        for(i = 1; i < Nk && i + j < Nb(Nr + 1); i++)
            W[i + j] = W[i + j − Nk] ⊕ W[i + j − 1];
    }
}
```

When the cipher key words are used, every following word $W[i]$ is equal to the EXOR of the previous word $W[i-1]$ and the word N_k positions earlier $W[i - N_k]$. For words in positions that are a multiple of N_k, a transformation is applied to $W[i-1]$ prior to the EXOR and a round constant is EXORed. This transformation consists of a cyclic shift of the bytes in a word, denoted with Rotl, followed by SubByte, the application of a table lookup to all four bytes of the word.

The key expansion for $N_k > 6$ is very similar, but uses an extra application of SubByte. It is described in detail in [3].

The round constants are independent of $N - k$ and defined by: $\mathsf{Rcon}[i] = (RC[i], 0, 0, 0)$, with $RC[0] = 1$, $RC[i] = 2 \cdot RC[i-1]$ (multiplication in the field $\mathrm{GF}(2^8)$).

Round Key Selection. Round key i is given by the round key buffer words $W[N_b i]$ to $W[N_b(i+1)]$. The key schedule can be implemented without explicit use of the array W. For implementations where RAM is scarce, the round keys can be computed just-in-time using a buffer of N_k words.

2.4   The Cipher

The cipher Rijndael consists of

− an initial round key addition,
− $N_r - 1$ rounds,
− a final round.

In pseudo C code, this gives:

```
Rijndael(State,CipherKey) {
KeyExpansion(CipherKey,ExpandedKey);
AddRoundKey(State,ExpandedKey);
for(i = 1; i < Nr; i++) Round(State,ExpandedKey + Nbi);
FinalRound(State,ExpandedKey + NbNr);
}
```

The Key Expansion can be done on beforehand and Rijndael can be specified in terms of this expanded key.

```
Rijndael(State,ExpandedKey) {
AddRoundKey(State,ExpandedKey);
For(i = 1; i < Nr; i++) Round(State,ExpandedKey + Nbi);
FinalRound(State,ExpandedKey + NbNr);
}
```

3   Implementation Aspects

The Rijndael cipher is suited to be implemented efficiently on a wide range of processors and in dedicated hardware. We will concentrate on 8-bit processors, typical for Smart Cards.

3.1 Implementation on Eight-Bit Processors

Rijndael can be programmed by simply implementing the different component transformations. This is straightforward for RowShift and for the round key addition. The implementation of ByteSub requires a table of 256 bytes. The round key addition, ByteSub and RowShift can be efficiently combined and executed serially per state byte. Indexing overhead is minimised by explicitly coding the operation for every state byte. The transformation MixColumn requires matrix multiplication in the field $GF(2^8)$. The choice for the coefficients of the polynomial $c(x)$ (cf. Section 2.2 has been influenced by implementation considerations. We define the 256-byte table $X2$ as follows: $X2[i] = i \cdot 2$, whith multiplication in the Galois Field. Thus, $X2$ implements the multiplication with two. We can now implement the matrix multiplication very efficiently. Indeed, the matrix has only entries 1, 2 and 3. Multiplication with 3 can be done by multiplying with 2 and then adding the argument. We illustrate it for one column:

$p = a[0] \oplus a[1] \oplus a[2] \oplus a[3];$ /* a is a byte array */
$q = X2[a[0] \oplus a[1]]; a[0] = a[0] \oplus q \oplus p;$
$q = X2[a[1] \oplus a[2]]; a[1] = a[1] \oplus q \oplus p;$
$q = X2[a[2] \oplus a[3]]; a[2] = a[2] \oplus q \oplus p;$
$q = X2[a[3] \oplus a[0]]; a[3] = a[3] \oplus q \oplus p;$

Instead of using the table $X2$, the multiplication with two can be implemented with a shift and a conditional exor. In a straightforward implementation, the execution time of this operation will depend on the input value. This may allow an attacker to mount a timing attack [5]. The timing attack can be countered by inserting additional NOP-operations to make the execution time of both branches equal to one another, but this will probably introduce weaknesses with respect to a power analysis attack. The use of a table effectively counters these types of attacks.

Obviously, implementing the key expansion in a single shot operation is likely to occupy too much RAM in a Smart Card. Moreover, in most applications, such as debit cards or electronic purses, the amount of data to be enciphered, deciphered or that is subject to a MAC is typically only one or two blocks per session. Hence, not much performance can be gained by expanding the key only once for multiple applications of the block cipher. The key expansion can be implemented in a cyclic buffer of $4N_b$ bytes. The round key is updated in between rounds. All operations in this key update can be efficiently implemented on byte level. If the cipher key length is equal to the block length or an integer multiple of it, the implementation is straightforward. If this is not the case, an additional buffer pointer is required.

3.2 The Inverse Cipher

The round transformation of Rijndael is not a Feistel network. An advantage of a Feistel cipher is that the inverse cipher is almost the same as the cipher. Since the round transformation of a Feistel cipher is an involution, only the order of the round keys has to be inverted. For Rijndael, this is not the case. In principle, the decryption has to be done by applying the inverses of the component transformations in inverse order.

However, the round transformation and the cipher structure have been designed to alleviate this problem partially. By using some algebraic properties we can derive an equivalent representation for the inverse cipher, that has the same *structure* as the cipher. This means that a round of the inverse cipher looks the same as a round of the cipher, except that ByteSub, MixColumn and ShiftRow have been replaced by their inverses. The round keys in this representation are different from the round keys used in the encryption mode.

The elements in the matrix corresponding to the inverse operation of Mixcolumn, have other values than 1, 2 and 3. Therefore, the multiplication cannot be done with the same efficiency. If we use only the table $X2$, the performance of the cipher drops with about 50%. The performance loss can be alleviated by using additional tables to define multiplications with other field elements.

4   Performance

Rijndael has been implemented in assembler on two different types of microprocessors that are representative for Smart Cards in use today. In these implementation the round keys are computed in between the rounds of the cipher (just-in-time calculation of the round keys) and therefore the key schedule is repeated for every cipher execution. This means that there is no extra time required for key set-up or a key change. There is also no time required for algorithm set-up. Only the forward operation of the cipher has been implemented, backwards operation is expected to be slower by a factor of 1.5 to 2, as explained in Section 3.2.

4.1   Intel 8051 Processor

Rijndael has been implemented on the Intel 8051 microprocessor, using 8051 Development tools of Keil Elektronik: μVision IDE for Windows and dScope Debugger/Simulator for Windows. Execution time for several code sizes is given in Table 3 (1 cycle = 12 oscillator periods).

Table 3. Execution time and code size for Rijndael in Intel 8051 assembler.

(Key, block length)	Number of cycles	Code size (bytes)
(128,128)	4065	768
	3744	826
	3168	1016
(192,128)	4512	1125
(256,128)	5221	1041

4.2   Motorola 68HC08 Processor

Rijndael has been implemented on the Motorola 68HC08 microprocessor using the 68HC08 development tools by P&E Microcomputer Systems, Woburn, MA USA, the IASM08 68HC08 Integrated Assembler and SIML8 68HC08 simulator. Execution time, code size and required RAM for a number of implementations are given in Table 4 (1 cycle = 1oscillator period). No optimization of code length has been attempted for this processor.

Table 4. Execution time and code size for Rijndael in Motorola 68HC08 Assembler.

(Key, block length)	Number of cycles	Required RAM (bytes)	Code size (bytes)
(128,128)	8390	36	919
(192,128)	10780	44	1170
(256,128)	12490	52	1135

5   Conclusions

Rijndael is a very fast block cipher. It can be implemented very efficiently on a Smart Card with a small amount of code, using a small amount of RAM and taking a small number of cycles. Some ROM/performance trade-off is possible. It is easy to make the implementation of the cipher resistant to timing attacks. The variable block length allows the construction of a collision-resistant hash function with Rijndael as compression function.

The most important disadvantage is the fact that the inverse cipher is different from the cipher. The inverse cipher is typically 1.5 to 2 times slower on Smart Card (or takes more ROM).

References

1. J. Daemen, "Cipher and hash function design strategies based on linear and differential cryptanalysis," *Doctoral Dissertation*, March 1995, K.U.Leuven.
2. J. Daemen, L.R. Knudsen and V. Rijmen, "The block cipher Square," Fast Software Encryption, LNCS 1267, E. Biham, Ed., Springer-Verlag, 1997, pp. 149–165. Also available as http://www.esat.kuleuven.ac.be/~rijmen/square/fse.ps.gz.
3. J. Daemen and V. Rijmen, "The Rijndael block cipher," presented at the First Advanced Encryption Standard Conference, Ventura (California), 1998, available from URL http://www.nist.gov/aes.
4. J. Daemen and V. Rijmen, "The block cipher BKSQ," *this volume*.
5. P.C. Kocher, "Timing attacks on implementations of Diffie-Hellman, RSA, DSS and other systems," *Advances in Cryptology, Proceedings Crypto'96, LNCS 1109*, N. Koblitz, Ed., Springer-Verlag, 1996, pp. 104–113.
6. R. Lidl and H. Niederreiter, *Introduction to finite fields and their applications*, Cambridge University Press, 1986.
7. V. Rijmen, "Cryptanalysis and design of iterated block ciphers," *Doctoral Dissertation*, October 1997, K.U.Leuven.

Secure Log File Download Mechanisms
for Smart Cards

Constantinos Markantonakis *

Information Security Group,
Royal Holloway, University of London,
Egham, Surrey, TW20 0EX,
United Kingdom
C.Markantonakis@rhbnc.ac.uk
http://www.dcs.rhbnc.ac.uk/~costasm

Abstract. The necessity of auditing mechanisms for smart cards is currently under thorough investigation. Both current and future real world applications impose requirements which suggest the storage of sensitive information in log files. In this paper we present various applications that demonstrate the use of audit logs, justifying their practical advantages and disadvantages. We propose computationally practical methods for creating and maintaining such log files in the light of the limited memory of smart cards. We conclude with a brief discussion of design principles for future implementations and guidelines for further research.

1 Introduction

Audit log mechanisms [14,20,23] upon their successful definition, installation and operation are very powerful tools for monitoring a system's activity. Through their application, malicious users are discouraged from attempting to violate the security of a system, since the operations of such attempts are tracked and measures can be applied to restrict the likelihood of future attempts.

Although much work [24] has been done in the area of audit log design and implementation for databases and general computer systems, the distinctive nature and technological characteristics of current smart card technology impose specific constraints that demand careful investigation.

Among the most important issues which seriously restrict the design and usage of such mechanisms, is the limited storage capacity of current smart cards, along with the restricted functionality of smart card operating systems. Recent improvements on existing smart card operating systems [12,17,32,33] along with related theoretical work [10,13,25,26] and further improvements in the hardware level [5,8,11,19], have made the whole idea more feasible. We certainly believe that audit logs for smart cards are helpful, since they increase the evidence

---

* The author's research is funded by Mondex International Ltd. This work is the opinion of the author and does not necessarily represent the view of the funding sponsor.

available in the event of fraud, whilst at the same time providing evidence of the completion of important events. This is particularly true nowadays, as smart cards are moving away from their traditional focus on single applications [4,7, 21] towards multi-application environments [6,27].

Specific application prerequisites, different operating environments or even slight variations of the trust relationships among participants, often impose different audit log usages. It is thus important to outline the exact dimensions of the problems arising from the use of audit log files in smart cards. This will help the reader to obtain a deeper understanding of any requirements and restrictions whilst avoiding confusions with other proposals [18,30].

As previously stated, it might be necessary to maintain a log file on a smart card. Obviously whatever space is allocated for the storage of such a log file will not be enough, as sooner or later it will fill up. Our goal here is to push the state-of-the-art a little further and deal with the complex and realistic issue of extracting the log files from the card and storing them in some other medium. Upon the successful transmission and storage of the log file, the card holders, card issuers and application providers are provided with accurate information, either for their own reference or for use as evidence in cases of dispute.

In this paper we discuss protocols and policies that need to be considered when the space available for audit log files in smart cards is filling up and the log file is about to be downloaded to some other device. Firstly we survey the current status of applications that might make use of an audit log file. We then describe our model for the card environment, followed by a proposed log file download protocol. Finally, we discuss several practical issues that impose design restrictions and introduce some new concepts to act as directions for further research.

2   Applications

When looking into audit log mechanisms, we need to clarify their necessity in real world smart card applications. Nowadays, the risks of having more than one application residing on the same smart card have increased. There are certainly more entities involved in the smart card life cycle and in every day transactions. As a result these entities might gain potential benefits from attacking, denying or forging transactions. Although some applications try to avoid the need for log files by providing sufficient security assurance within their transaction protocols, there are occasions when further evidence is required. It would then be beneficial to distinguish between the different entities supporting the provision of audit log mechanisms in particular smart card applications.

We split the participants into two groups. The first group comprises the card holders involved in a transaction who might not be the actual owners of all the secrets on their cards. The second group includes other entities (banks, service providers, card issuers, application developers) that might have the opportunity to download applications onto the card holders' smart cards. These entities might own the card or some of its secrets (certain files, cryptographic keys, etc.).

2.1   Smart Card Holders

Applications where card holders have an interest in the existence of audit log mechanisms abound.

One example is provided by a scenario presented in detail in [13] and referred to as application monitoring. Currently the favoured approach stipulates that application certificates should be verified prior to downloading and installing an application on a smart card. This will verify that applications have "trust-worthy" origins but will not provide any guarantees about the content of these applications. In the future, users and applications developers might favour a more "liberal" infrastructure that will allow card holders to visit web pages and download "untrusted" or "unsigned" applications. Through the existence of a mechanism (placed within the smart card operating system) that records certain operations (downloading, execution problems and other "sensitive operations") of these untrusted applications within the smart card, users can check that the applications do not perform unauthorised actions.

Another example of application monitoring could be the monitoring of digital signatures performed by the smart card. In certain financial applications, in order to authorise transactions the card is asked to produce a digital signature. It is however, very difficult to keep track of what the card is actually signing and when the signature occurred. In such a case, a signature manager [13] that will record the computation of digital signatures in a log file, coupled with the corresponding log files, should improve user confidence.

Particular electronic commerce applications may keep a small file for logging transaction details. This file overwrites itself in a cyclic manner, whenever a new transaction is performed. It would be very helpful to maintain an externally shared copy of the log file containing the details of a larger number of transactions.

2.2   Service Providers

The service providers might also have some interest in the existence of a smart card log file.

Consider the following scenario where an electronic purse application performs the following transactions, (1:Debit, 2:Debit, 3:Payphone Credit, 4:Payphone Credit, 5:Debit). The user goes back to the companies offering the aforementioned services and claims that something went wrong between transactions 2 and 5. The companies could then very easily run through the log file providing both their customers and themselves with enough evidence of what exactly happened.

Similarly the service providers might wish to obtain specific feedback concerning the testing of certain functions or applications or even evidence from any intrusion detection mechanisms within the cardholder's smart card. Moreover these entities might need to use information stored in the log files in order to identify licensing details or even roll back any uncommitted transactions. Thus the audit log file technology provides extra assurance not only in cases of disputes.

3   Model for Smart Card Environment

In this section we describe a model for the use and operation of a smart card. This model is designed to be as general as possible, and is intended to capture the principal entities and inter-entity relationships which are likely to arise in smart card applications. This model is used in all subsequent discussions of smart card auditing mechanisms.

We start by defining the principle entities within the model. We then describe the operation of the model as it relates to the generation and management of the auditing information.

3.1   Entities of the Smart Card Model

The principal participants and relationships between participants are depicted in Figure 1.

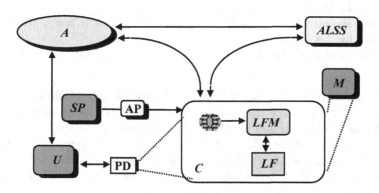

Fig. 1. Graphical representation of the relationships among the participants.

1. C represents the smart card. Typically a sufficiently tamper resistant device which is relatively difficult to compromise, it has access to a variety of cryptographic algorithms and a good pseudorandom number generator.
2. U is a smart card holder, the user.
3. AP is an application running in the smart card.
4. SP is a service provider which offers certain services and develops applications for the cards.
5. M is a malicious user with possibly enough knowledge of the internal structure of card along with the format of the messages exchanged during the download procedure.
6. ALSS stands for an Audit Log Storage Server. This entity will receive and store the transmitted log files in dedicated locations. Depending on the environment the ALSS could be a "smart wallet", a personal computer used in conjunction with the smart card or even a repository server connected in the Internet.

7. LF is the log file which will be downloaded.
8. LFM is the log file manager, a smart card operating system entity. This is the only authorised entity for updating and writing in the log files in the card.
9. A is the arbitrator who receives the downloaded log files in case of a dispute and subsequently informs the entities involved in order to resolve any disputes.
10. PD is the smart card reader/writer or personal wallet used by the smart card in order to communicate with the outside world.

3.2   Operation of the Model

Within our model, we divide the audit related operation of the smart card into three phases.

- In the first phase, the card C generates evidence which is stored and managed by the LFM.
- In the second phase, the LF stored within the card is transmitted to and stored by the ALSS.
- In the third phase the log files are used, e.g. for arbitration in the case of a dispute.

In this paper we are primarily concerned with the second phase in this process. For clarity we state the main requirements of the other two phases, but their detailed behaviour and implementation are outside the scope of this paper.

The generation of the evidence (LFs) is a very critical operation and we have to provide strong guarantees about the log file origins. In other words we need to make sure that legitimate log files are only generated by the LFM. There are two different methods that will help to achieve this aim.

Firstly we have to assume that the log file construction in the card is a LFM task, and no other entity will be able to interfere. The write and update permissions for the log file are totally under the control of the LFM. Furthermore we assume that the LFM has access to the cryptographic primitives-functions residing in the card, and is capable of assigning unique sequential numbers to the newly generated log files. Secondly we require that the log files will be linked with each other in a way that would make difficult to add, delete or modify any entries without such changes being evident. When the log files are linked together this also creates substantial auditing evidence. However in order to ensure the integrity of the log files and their appropriate log file chaining we require the use of cryptography.

The main use of cryptography here is that the LFM appends a cryptographic check value (MAC) on the downloaded LFs. In our proposals we require that the key used will only be known internally in the card [3] and will never appear in clear outside the card. This key will be generated by an arbitrator (based on some information submitted by each user). Subsequently it will most likely be stored in the card most likely during the personalisation phase, along with publishing the key identification number or a corresponding public key certificate.

In the second phase we would like to ensure that a log file stored in the card is securely transmitted and stored in an ALSS with the minimal amount of interactions. The steps involved in order to establish and accomplish communication with an ALSS is another responsibility of the LFM. For example the next time the card is used and the default storage space for the log file is full, the LFM has to decide (depending on the type of the application, the card, along with the applications predefined security policy) either to block the card, allow further transactions or proceed and download the log files. In the latter case, the LFM initiates the process key, displaying a message in the PD's screen, that the card holder needs to contact its issuer or some other specific terminals (ATMs). When the card is next inserted in such a terminal the LFM proceeds with one of the download mechanisms below. Upon the successful completion of the download process the LFM will permanently flush the space occupied by the log file, only after it receives an acknowledgement by the ALSS indicating that the log file is successfully received.

While the log files are stored in the ALSS we assume that they are adequately protected against deletion. In one of our proposed solutions we favour the idea of assigning a more active role for the ALSS than just simply accepting any LFs. We require the ALSS to accept only legitimate log files along with identifying modifications or alterations in the transmitted LFs. This feature will simplify the arbitration procedure and make it more faster and efficient.

In the third phase we present the notion of the arbitrator (A) and we explain how the arbitration procedure takes place. The arbitration procedure starts with the arbitrator receiving an arbitration request. Subsequently the arbitrator verifies certain details (if exactly similar requests have been raised in the past, etc.) of the request. The next step requires the arbitrator to inform all the parties involved (users, ALSSs). The users could be informed by using conventional communication methods like telephone, mail, or even email when applicable. Informing the ALSS's could be easier since they might be on line connected with other ALSSs or even with the arbitrators. The exact behaviour and requirements of both the arbitrators and the ALSS depend on the actual implementation.

Finally in all the protocols described below, we require the parties involved to have access in accurate directories that provide specific details on digital user IDs and key certificate IDs. Similarly, some of the protocols require the entities (C, A) to establish a secure connection [31] in order to exchange various messages. Finally we assume that all entities have access to a trusted time-stamping service.

4   An Approach to Secure Log File Transfer

In this section we present our proposed protocols for downloading log files into some external storage entity (ALSS). We assume throughout that the ALSS has unlimited storage capabilities (a not unreasonable assumption given the current low price of high-speed disk storage). We start by outlining our assumptions regarding the contents of the log file. We then describe three different sets of protocols for downloading log files to an ALSS, appropriate for three different scenarios.

- The first scenario applies to the case where the ALSS is implemented on a cardholder-controlled device, e.g. their own PC (§4.3).
- The second scenario covers the use of a remote ALSS, where confidentiality of the log file contents is not an issue (§4.4).
- The third scenario again applies to a remote ALSS, and this time provides confidentiality protection for the log file, i.e. the ALSS cannot read the log file contents (§4.5).

We summarise the notation we use in Table 1. This notation is an extended version of the notation defined in [16,22].

Table 1. Notation and terminology.

Notation	Description
$e_K(Z)$	is the result of encipherment of data Z with a symmetric encipherment algorithm (DES) using key K.
$h(Z)$	is the one way hash of data Z using an algorithm such as SHA-1.
$f_K(Z)$	is the result of applying the cryptographic check function f using as input a secret key K; and an arbitrary data string Z.
$z_{V_X}(Z)$	is the result of encipherment of data string Z using a public key algorithm (RSA) with key V_X.
$s_{S_X}(Z)$	is the signature resulting from applying the private signature transformation on data Z using the private signature key S_X.
K_{XY}	is a secret key shared between entities X and Y; used in symmetric cryptographic techniques only.
I_K	a unique key identification information for key K.
T_X	is a timestamp issued by entity X.
N_X	is a sequence number issued by entity X.
S_X	is a private signature key associated with entity X.
P_X	is a public verification key associated with entity X.
B_X	is a private encryption key associated with entity X.
V_X	is a public encryption key associated with entity X.
E_X	the unique identification information for entity X.
$X \longrightarrow Y : C$	implies that entity X sends entity Y a message with contents C.
$Y \parallel Z$	represents the concatenation of the data items Y, Z in that order.

Descriptions of cryptographic algorithms appropriate for use in the protocols defined below can be found, for example, in [28].

4.1 Security Requirements for Log File Storage and Management

1. Privacy and Integrity. The system must be secure in the sense that it should be very difficult for the participants (U, SP, A, ALSS) involved to deny the existence and origin of the log files. Similarly it would very difficult for an attacker to create log files that appear to be legitimate and falsify the

system. The privacy and integrity of the log files should be addressed by using encryption and Message Authentication Codes (MACs).

2. Cheap to Operate. The operation of the system will not require the purchase of additional expensive equipment either by users or by the merchants.

3. Fast. Communication between the entities should take place with a minimal exchange of messages. Moreover the messages exchanged between the participants should minimise the use of cryptography (given the limited computational capabilities of smart cards).

4. Auditable. The log file chain should be auditable. It will also be necessary to be able to identify changes and modifications in the log entries after the log files have been transmitted.

5. Efficient. The system's operation should not seriously restrict the normal participants behaviour.

4.2 Contents of a Log File

We start by specifying the form of the log file (note that this log file structure applies to all three protocols described below). The log file is a cyclic file (i.e. one which is over-written on a cyclic basis) of size dependent on the application and the card; a typical file might have size around 1 Kbytes. We assume that the log file consists of a serial list of entries, each assigned a unique serial number in numerically increased order. Each entry corresponds to a single auditable "event", and takes the form specified below. Note that, as already specified, we assume that the card's LFM is responsible for generating the entries in the log file. We denote the ith entry in log file by DE_i . We further assume that

$$DE_i = (D \parallel T_C \parallel N_C)$$

where D is data regarding the logged event, T_C is a timestamp, and N_C is a monotonically increasing sequence number. Given that the card will not possess a real time clock, the card will rely on external devices for the value of the time-stamp. Hence the time-stamp value may only be of limited value for auditing purposes.

We assume that the sequence number N_C is generated using a counter held internally to the card, and which cannot be reset or otherwise modified by any external events. In particular, downloading the log file contents to an ALSS will not involve resetting the sequence number counter. The sequence numbers of the data entries can thus be used to order down-loaded log files, and gaps in numbers can be used to indicate lost or deleted log file entries. When downloaded from a card, the log file F will consist of an ordered sequence of w log file entries. The size of F will be fixed (predefined) and will allow for a fixed number w of entries.

$$F = (DE_1 \parallel \ldots \parallel DE_w)$$

We also assume that when the log file is about to fill up the available space within the card, the cardholder is given a warning, e.g. via a PD on the next occasion the card is used. The protocols below then describe how a log file F might be downloaded to an ALSS.

4.3   Using an ALSS on a Cardholder-Controlled Device

Our first scenario involves the cardholder downloading the log file information to an ALSS controlled by the cardholder, e.g. a PC, PD belonging to the card holder. This might be appropriate in situations where the cardholder does not trust a third party ALSS.

In the following protocol we assume that the card shares a key (K_{AC}) with an arbitrator. This key can be stored in the card during the personalisation phase. The card should not be able to communicate with an ALSS if it does not possess such a key. Additionally we assume that the card is maintaining a sequence number N_C which cannot be modified by any external events. The initial value of the message sequence number variable will be $(N_C = 0)$. The initial value of $CBind_{N_C}$ variable could be a standard pre-defined string of fixed length. Prior to start downloading any log files we require that the cardholders will be authenticated by the cards. Thus, an existing unilateral authentication scheme can be used but its details are not within the scope of this paper. The generation of evidence (LF construction) is taking place by the LFM as described previously. The protocol starts with the LFM sending message (1) to the ALSS.

$$1) C \longrightarrow ALSS : M_{N_C} \parallel fK_{AC}(M_{N_C})$$

where

$$M_{N_C} = (F \parallel T_C \parallel N_C \parallel I_{AC} \parallel CBind_{N_C})$$

F is the log file data (containing w entries), T_C is a newly generated time-stamp, N_C is a sequence number (current message sequence number stored internally in the card and incremented by one), I_{AC} is the unique key identifier for key K_{AC} (which allows the arbitrator to identify which key to use in order to verify the cryptographic check value of the message), and

$$CBind_{N_C} = h(h(M_{N_C-1}) \parallel N_C)$$

The $CBind_{N_C}$ variable serves the role of the linking information. When adding some linking information in the form of a hash chain [1,9] of all the previously generated messages into the current messages, we create extra auditing evidence [2,29]. Thus, this variable links the previously send message (M_{N_C-1}) with the current message sequence number (N_C). At this stage the LFM stores in the card (in protected memory) a hash of the current file (F) and a hash of the current message sent (M_{N_C}). Note that the LFM has not yet flushed the space occupied by the log file.

Depending on the system design, the ALSS could perform various checks on the validity of the previous message (1) received. For reliability purposes in this protocol we simply require the ALSS to acknowledge every message received, despite the fact that it might not be an actual log file (as we will see later on).

On receiving message (1) the ALSS informs the cardholder, by displaying a notification message on the PD's screen, that the message has been successfully received. Subsequently it extracts the log file (F) from message (M_{N_C}). The ALSS reply to the card consists of the following message (2).

$$(2)ALSS \longrightarrow C : SBind$$

where

$$SBind = (h(F) \parallel \text{``Log File Received''} \parallel T_S)$$

$h(F)$ is a hash of the log file received, along with a data string indicating that the message is successfully received, and a time-stamp (T_S).

On receiving the response message, the card checks for the correct hash value of the log file (F). In case a correct hash value of the log file is present, the LFM proceeds with flushing the memory space utilised by the log file along with replacing the previous value of M_{N_C-1} with the current value of M_{N_C}.

Supposedly users having some interest in the information stored in the log files at the same time they have to ensure their adequate protection after they are downloaded and stored in the ALSS. However it is clear that this solution does not prevent the users from downloading their log files and subsequently deleting them, "Watergate Attack" [29]. Similarly we realise that this solution does not prevent Ms from modifying the communication path between a card and an ALSS.

When a dispute arises the arbitrator will have to inform, using conventional methods (telephone, email) the user involved in order to obtain a copy of the log files. The users will have to establish a secure connection with the arbitrator and send over their log files. The arbitrators by using their copy of the shared key (K_{AC}), they can easily verify the linking information on every message.

What Can Go Wrong? In case the card receives an invalid reply, it will request the ALSS to resent message (2) once more. If problems persist the LFM will assume that most probably there is a communication error and it will refrain from sending further messages. If that is the case, the LFM performs certain roll back operations [34] in order to return the system in its previous state. Another problem which might arise is the possibility of M attacking the ALSS and getting hold of the downloaded log files. Obviously M will gain access to the content of the log files but since they are protected with a MAC, any alterations will be detected.

4.4   Using an ALSS in a Remote Location

Our second scenario involves the cardholders securely transmitting the log files in a physically secure ALSS located remotely in the network. The major difference from the previous proposal is that the ALSS is not within the immediate control of the user. Evidently this approach prevents the "Watergate Attack" and also removes the user anxieties on where exactly the log files will be downloaded, keeping backup copies, etc.

This protocol requires that all the participants have access to a number of cryptographic algorithms along with means of establishing secure connections between each other. Additionally, we assume that the unique key ID's, certificate ID's are sufficient for each entity to retrieve the actual corresponding public keys, or certificates.

We also assume that the ALSSs have the ability (processing and communication power) to deal with a large number of card requests for service, at the same time. On the other hand the cards will be dealing with a single ALSS. Furthermore we assume that ALSSs are trusted entities in a sense that they will never loose or disclose any received log files.

A further major difference from the previous proposal is that the ALSS is assigned with a more active role. This implies that the ALSS has to verify the integrity of the transmitted log files prior to their acceptance. The verification aims to simplify the arbitration procedure since in case of a dispute the arbitrators will have to verify less details due to the already "filtered" information.

In this scenario we favour the idea of public key cryptography which has its advantages and disadvantages. The main advantage is that it simplifies the verification procedure, as it will be shown later. On the other hand public key cryptography is computationally expensive and it might involve validating chains of key certificates. For the sake of brevity, we omit the details of how the card obtains a pair of cryptographic keys from the arbitrators. The card's private key will be available only internally in the card and the corresponding public key will become widely known by being published in public directories. Communication with an ALSS involves two phases.

- The Card and Server Registration phase, where the entities are introduced to each other.
- The Secure Log File Transmission phase, where the log files are being transmitted to the ALSS.

Card and ALSS Registration. The card and ALSS registration phase takes place once, in order to establish a fixed relationship between the card and the ALSS. This phase could be omitted from our proposals, if all the necessary information (ALSS related public keys and certificates) is burned into the cards memory during the personalisation phase. The real benefit of this phase is that it offers the users the freedom to select their preferred ALSS or re-establish communication with an ALSS in case of key and certificate revocation problems [15].

The smart card holders will have the opportunity to select an ALSS from a regularly and accurately updated list of ALSSs, available either in their PD's or PC's. We assume that the card uses a copy the TTP's public verification key (obtained from the TTP's web server or stored internally), in order to verify the ALSS's certificate. This verification will also reveal both the ALSS's public encryption key (V_S) and its unique identification information (E_S). The protocol starts with the LFM sending the following message to the ALSS:

$$1)C \longrightarrow ALSS : z_{V_S}(M_{N_C}) \parallel s_{S_C}(M_{N_C})$$

where

$$M_{N_C} = (\text{"Directory Initialisation"} \parallel T_C \parallel N_C \parallel CBind_{N_C})$$

a text entry to denote the card's intention for future communication, T_C is a newly generated time-stamp, N_C the incremented internally stored sequence number and

$$CBind_{N_C} = (E_S \parallel E_C \parallel I_C \parallel \text{"Directory Initialisation"})$$

E_S is the ALSS's unique identification information, E_C the card's identification information, I_C is the unique identification information of the card's public verification key, and finally the text entry. The actual role of the M_{N_C} variables is to prevent any reply attacks. Additionally the LFM stores $h(CBind_{N_C})$ internally.

On receiving the first message the ALSS decrypts its first part. Subsequently it checks the following: if it has already received a similar message before (i.e. if the timestamp is within its current window along with a valid sequence number), and finally if the message was intended for it. The next step requires the ALSS to obtain (by using the I_C value as an index), a copy of card's public verification key. This key will be used in order to verify the signature in the second part of the message. Upon the successful signature verification the ALSS sends the following message to the card.

$$2)ALSS \longrightarrow C : z_{V_C}(L_{N_S}) \parallel s_{S_S}(h(L_{N_S}))$$

where

$$L_{N_S} = (\text{"Initialisation Message Received"} \parallel T_S \parallel N_S \parallel SBind_{N_S})$$

a text entry to denote the successful receipt of the previous sent message, T_S is a newly generated time-stamp, N_S the server incremented sequence number which is unique for each card, and

$$SBind_{N_S} = (E_C \parallel h(M_n) \parallel \text{"Initialisation Message Received"})$$

The linking variable ($SBind_{N_S}$) contains the identity of the card (E_C), along with a hash of the previous received message (M_{N_S}) and the text entry indicating the successful message receipt .

On receiving the response message, the LFM decrypts its first part by using its private encryption key (B_C). Subsequently it checks if the timestamp (T_S) is within its current window, if the unique identification string (E_C) is included and finally for a correct hash of the linking variable (M_{N_C}). Similarly by using the ALSS public signature key (PS which is previously obtained) it verifies the digital signature in the second part of the message. Successful signature verification will indicate that both entities have successfully completed the registration phase. Finally the LFM copies the linking variable $SBind_{N_S}$ to the $CBind_{N_C}$ variable ($CBind_{N_C} = SBind_{N_S}$).

What can go wrong? If the ALSS receives the first message invalid or not within its current time window, it will then sent back to the card a message with a data entry "Error Message" (out of time limits, invalid signature, etc.). When the LFM receives such a message, it resends the original message once more with updated the freshness mechanisms $(T_S \parallel N_S)$.

If the card does not receive a reply from the ALSS it assumes that either message (1) never reached the ALSS or message (2) never reached the card. In either case it will resend the messages once more. Finally if problem persist both the ALSS and the card will not keep exchanging messages forever and after a short period of time they terminate their communication. Upon the successful completion of the registration protocol both entities have successfully established the required relationship and we set up the stepping stone of the required linking information.

Log File Transmission. The second phase involves the actual transmission of the log files to the ALSS. From the previous phase we assume that the LFM obtained the exact details of the ALSS along with a copy of its public encryption key and signature verification key. Similarly we assume that the ALSS posse a copy of the cards public encryption key and the signature verification key. The protocol starts with the LFM sending the following message to the ALSS.

$$1)C \longrightarrow ALSS : z_{V_S}(M_{N_C}) \parallel s_{S_C}(M_{N_C})$$

where

$$M_{N_C} = (F \parallel T_C \parallel N_C \parallel E_S \parallel CBind_{N_C})$$

F is the log file data containing w entries), T_C is a newly generated timestamp, N_C is a sequence number (current message sequence number stored internally in the card), E_S is the ALSS's unique identification information, and

$$CBind_{N_C} = h(h(CBind_{N_C-1}) \parallel N_C \parallel h(F))$$

once more, the $CBind_{N_C}$ variable serves the role of the linking information. Thus it contains a hash of the following: a hash of the previous sent message $(h(Cbind_{N_C-1}))$ stored internally, a message sequence number (N_C) and a hash of the current log file. At this stage the LFM stores internally a copy of $h(M_{N_C})$.

On receiving message (1) the ALSS decrypts the first part of the message by using its private encryption key (B_S). Subsequently it verifies the details of the message (M_{N_C}) by checking for a valid timestamp (T_C), a sequence number (N_C) along with the ALSS identification information (E_S). If these details are present and valid, the ALSS assembles the message data (M_{N_C}) in order to verify (by using a widely available copy of the cards public key (PC)) the digital signature on the second half of the message. Upon the successful signature verification the ALSS assumes that the message originated from a card which knows the secret signing key (S_{SA}) and subsequently it sends the following message.

$$2)ALLS \longrightarrow C : z_{V_C}(L_{N_S}) \parallel s_{S_S}(L_{N_S})$$

where

$$L_{N_S} = (\text{"Log File Received"} \parallel T_S \parallel N_S \parallel E_C \parallel SBind_{N_S})$$

a text entry to denote the successful receipt of the log file, T_S is a newly generated time-stamp, N_S the ALSS incremented sequence number for this card, the
identification information of the card, and

$$SBind_{N_S} = h(h(CBind_{N_C}) \parallel N_S \parallel \text{"Log File Received"})$$

the $SBind_{N_S}$ variable serves the role of the linking information maintained by
the ALSS. Thus it links the previous information sent to the ALSS, with the
current sequence number and text entry.

On receiving message (2) the card decrypts (by using its private encryption key B_C) the first part of the message. Subsequently it checks the freshness
mechanisms (N_S, T_S), and also makes sure that its name is correctly present.
Subsequently it assembles the linking variable (L_{N_S}) in order to verify the signature in the second half of the message. If everything appears to be correct the
LFM is confident that message (2) is a reply for message (1). In that case it flushes the space occupied by the current log file, deletes the value of the previous
stored message (M_{N_S}) and finally overwrites the value of the old linking variable
($CBind_{N_C-1}$) with the most recent one ($CBind_{N_C}$). In case of any problems in
the messages exchanged both entities proceed as described in §4.4.1.1.

During a dispute, the ALSS will be asked to submit a copy of the log files
to the arbitrator or any other interested party. The interested party could very
easily verify the authenticity of the log files simply by using the widely known
public encryption key (B_C) of the card.

4.5   Using an ALSS in a Remote Location and Encrypted Log Files

In our previous example we successfully addressed the problem of securely transmitting the log files in a ALSS. However we realise that in this particular example
we were not concerned about the confidentiality of the log files while stored in
the ALSS. This means that while the log files are stored in the ALSS, their
content is accessible by the ALSS.

In this example we slightly modify our requirements and advocate a solution
which increases the users confidence that ALSSs do not have access to the content of the log files. The proposed solution is an extended combination of the
previous two. Please note that the initialisation phase remains exactly the same
as presented in §4.4.1. The protocol starts with the LFM sending the following
message.

$$1)C \longrightarrow ALSS : z_{V_S}(M_{N_C}) \parallel s_{S_C}(M_{N_C})$$

where

$$M_{N_C} = (T_C \parallel N_C \parallel E_C \parallel E_S \parallel eK_{AC}(F) \parallel CBind_{N_C})$$

T_C is a newly generated time-stamp, N_C is a sequence number (current message sequence number stored internally in the card), E_C, E_S the identities of the card and ALSS respectively, $eK_{AC}(F)$ is the log file encrypted under the key shared between the card and the arbitrator, and

$$CBind_{N_C} = h(h(Cbind_{N_C-1}) \parallel h(eK_{AC}(F)) \parallel N_C)$$

which contains a hash of the card's previous linking variable $h(Cbind_{N_C-1})$, a hashed copy of the encrypted log file $(h(eK_{AC}(F))$, along with the current message sequence number (N_C). Note that the log file (F) is encrypted before it is actually included in the linking variable. At this stage the card stores internally a hashed copy of the encrypted log file $(h(F))$.

On receiving the message, the ALSS decrypts the first half by using its private encryption key (B_S). Subsequently it looks for an appropriate sequence number (N_C) and a time-stamp (T_C), along with the correct entity identifiers (E_C, E_S), and a valid hash value on the $CBind_{N_C}$ components. Then by using a copy of the public signature key of the card (PC) it verifies the digital signature in the second part of the message. If everything is correct, both the message decrypted correctly and a valid digital signature the ALSS sends the following message.

$$2)ALSS \longrightarrow C : zV_C(L_{N_S}) \parallel sS_S(L_{N_S})$$

where

$$L_{N_S} = (\text{``Log File Received''} \parallel T_S \parallel N_S \parallel E_C \parallel SBind_{N_S})$$

a text entry to denote the successful receipt of the log file, T_S is a newly genera-ted time-stamp, N_S the ALSS incremented sequence number for this card, the identification information of the card (E_C), and

$$SBind_{N_S} = h(\text{``Log File Received''} \parallel N_S \parallel h(CBind_{N_C}))$$

once more the $SBind_{N_S}$ variable serves the role of the linking information main-tained by the ALSS. Thus, it links the previous information sent by the ALSS, with the current sequence number and text entry.

On receiving the message, the LFM uses its private decryption key (V_C) and decrypts the first half. It then checks for a valid hash of the linking variable and for a correct unique card identifier. This will ensure that the ALSS has correctly received the transmitted log file. Subsequently by using the public verification key (PS) of the ALSS if verifies the signature in the second part of the message. If everything appears to be correct the LFM flushes the space occupied by the log file, deletes the value of the previous stored message (M_n) and finally overwrites the value of the old linking variable $(CBind_{N_C-1})$ with the most recent one $(CBind_n)$.

Identify Invalid Submitted Log Files. The purpose of having the ALSS simply accepting and acknowledging any received messages without checking the integrity of the transmitted log file is the following: We assume that in a real world implementation of the scheme the ALSSs will communicate with a large number of cards. Due to the possible large number of transactions involved we would like to ensure that ALSSs will be able to respond back to the cards within a reasonable time. If the ALSSs had to verify the linking information of every transmitted log file of every card, their task would be extremely time consuming. In other words we would like to transfer the task of verifying the integrity of the transmitted log files in the arbitrators when a dispute arises.

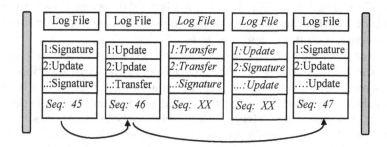

Fig. 2. Sequence of log files stored in the ALSS.

In case of a dispute the A will contact the ALSS in order to get the transmitted log files. In that case, let us suppose that the ALSS transmits the received log files received in the following order $(45, 46, XX, XX, 47)$ figure 2. Suppose that the valid sequence of log files from 45 to 47 is interrupted with two invalid log files with sequence numbers XX. These non legitimate log file entries might contain any user assembled data, properly acknowledged by the ALSS, but not encrypted with the key shared between the card and the arbitrator (since it is only known internally in C). When the arbitrator starts verifying the linking information, it will easily identify and discard the two fake entries firstly because they are not encrypted with the valid key and secondly because they do not reassemble correctly the linking information.

4.6   Terminate the ALSS and Card Relationship

During the period of communication between the ALSS and the card, either of the two entities might decide to terminate the existing relationship. The reasons which might cause such a decision to be made could be the following: the ALSS might discover that its keys have been compromised or expired and they need to be revoked. Similarly the cardholders might decide to terminate the existing relationship in case they prefer to establish a relationship with a different ALSS.

We believe that in a real world implementation of the aforementioned proposals, the cards will not be permitted to switch to a different ALLS. We also believe that offering the ability to terminate an existing ALSS and card relationship increases the confidence of both the cardholders and the ALSS. Although this is an implementation decision which depends on the systems security policy we very briefly describe the operations involved, when either of the entities decide to terminate their relationship.

In case the ALSS decides to terminate its relationship with a specific card, we encounter the following procedure. The next time the ALSS is contacted by the specific card, depending on the security policy, the ALSS decides whether to accept or reject the received log file. In either case, the ALSS forms a reply as described in either of the protocols but with a single difference. The text entry of the reply message will look like ("Terminate Relationship" || ("Log File Received" or "Log File Rejected")). On receiving the message, the card verifies both the digital signature and the linking information, subsequently it switches into the registration mode described in §4.4.1.

The card can also issue a similar message according to the following procedure: the LFM generates message Mn following the steps described in the previous sections. Subsequently it includes an additional text entry "Terminate Relationship" along with the current log file depending on whether is permitted to submit it or not. On receiving such a message the ALSS verifies its details and acknowledges with a reply similar to the one described above. In both cases the additional text entry is also included in the linking variable ($CBind_n$).

4.7   Verification of the Log Files While Stored in the Card

Let us suppose that a dispute arises while the log files are still stored in the card. A simple solution to this problem requires that the card should offer the functionality of enforcing the LFM to download the log files on the cardholders request. This functionality will also allow the log files to be downloaded even when the log file space is not yet full.

In such a case the LFM generates a text entry *"Enforced Log File Download"* which is appended in the current message (M_n) variable and in the linking variable ($CBind_n$). Subsequently it follows one of the protocols described in the previous sections in order to securely download the log files to an ALSS.

5   Conclusions and Directions for Further Research

We believe that audit log mechanisms for smart cards are a very powerful tool which builds extra confidence among users in the event of attempted fraud.

In this paper we have presented several variations of a scheme that allows the log files to be securely transmitted from a card to another device which does not suffer from immediate storage restrictions. Our proposals successfully address the aim of transmitting the auditing information, by using the minimal exchange of messages between the participants along with only the necessary computationally expensive cryptographic protection.

The implementation of these proposals is highly related with the following: the type of the card (merchant card, user card, high value transaction card, etc.), its technological characteristics and limitations (size of EEPROM memory, operating system functionality, etc.) along with the whole surrounding infrastructure (number of ALSSs, number of supporting ATMs, etc.). Another very significant factor is the need to define specific security policies that clearly address the relationships of the participants and the exact legal framework concerning the arbitration procedure.

In our proposals we require that only the log files are linked together. Under certain circumstances we might require that every single entry in the log file is linked with each other. Similarly it would also be useful to be able to perform complete anonymous log file submission to the ALSS. This would make it harder for the attackers to perform network spoofing attacks and subsequently construct consumer profiles simple by monitoring the ALSS communication line.

Currently, in order to investigate the complete practicality issues behind our proposals, we are implementing the protocols by using the Multos and the JavaCard platforms. Finally we believe that the acceptance of the aforementioned proposals is dependent on whether users are willing to sacrifice some extra time waiting for the log files to be downloaded.

6   Acknowledgement

The author would like to thank Dieter Gollmann, Chris Mitchell, Dimitrios Markakis, Pierre Paradinas for their helpful comments and endless reviews of the early drafts of this paper, Kostas Rantos for discussing issues related with the application level of the proposed solutions, various anonymous reviewers, and finally Prof. Fred Piper and Mondex International Ltd. for helping fund the author's research.

References

1. Ross Anderson. Robustness principles for public key protocols. *Advances in Cryptology CRYPTO'95*, pages 236–247., 1995.
2. Ross J. Anderson. UEPS - a second generation electronic wallet. *ESORICS 92, Springer Verlag Lecture Notes in Computer Science*, 648:411–418, 1992.
3. Europay-Mastercard-Visa. EMV-96 integrated circuit card specification for payment systems. Technical report, Europay-Mastercard-Visa, 1996.
4. Gemplus. *MCOS 16K EEPROM DES Reference Manual Ver 2.2*. Gemplus, 1990.
5. Gemplus. The first 32-bit risc processor ever embedded in a smart card. http://www.gemplus.fr/presse/cascade2uk.htm, 1996.
6. Gemplus. Gemxpresso reference manual. July 1998.
7. General Information Systems Ltd. (GIS). Oscar, specification of a smart card filling system incorporating data security and message authentication. http://www.gis.co.uk/oscman1.htm, 1997.
8. UCL Crypto Group. A smarter chip for smart cards. http://www.dice.ucl.ac.be.crypto/cascade, 1996.

9. Stuart Haber and W.Scott Stornetta. How to time-stamp a digital document. *Journal of Cryptology*, 3(2):99–111, 1996.

10. P. H. Hartel and E. K. de Jong Frz. Smart cards and card operating systems. In *Uniforum'96*, pages 725–730, 1996.

11. Hitachi. Hitachi 8bit microcontroler for smart card IC's. http://www.halsp.hitachi.com/smartcard/index.html, 1997.

12. MAOSCO. Multos reference manual Ver 1.2. www.multos.com, July 1998.

13. Constantinos Markantonakis. The case for a secure multi-application smart card operating system. In *Springer-Verlag Lecture Notes in Computer Science Vol. 1396*, pages 188–197, October 1997.

14. Constantinos Markantonakis. An architecture of audit logging in a multi-application smart card environment. *EICAR'99 E-Commerce and New Media Managing Safety and Malware Challenges Effectively*, October 1999.

15. Constantinos Markantonakis and Konstantinos Rantos. On the life cycle of the certification authority key pairs in emv'96. *EUROMEDIA 99*, to be published, May 1999.

16. Alfred Menezes, Paul van Oorschot, and Scott Vanstone. *Handbook of Applied Cryptography*. Boca Raton CRC Press, 1997.

17. Sun Microsystems. The Java Card API Ver 2.0 specification. http://www.javasoft.com/products/javacard/, 1998.

18. Mondex. Brief description of the mondex log file. http://www.mondex.com/mondex/cgi-bin/printpage.plenglish+global-technology-security, 1996.

19. Motorola. M68hc05sc family - at a glance. http://design-net.com/csic/SMARTCRD/sctable.htm, 1997.

20. Ajitkumar Natarajan and Cjin Pheow Lee. An ARIES log manager for Minirel CS 764. http://www.cs.ndsu.nodak.edu/-tat.minibase/logMgr/report/main.html, 1994.

21. International Standard Organisation. *ISO/IEC 7816-4, Information technology - Identification cards - Integrated circuits(s) cards with contacts*. International Standard Organization, 1995.

22. International Standard Organisation. *(ISO/IEC) 9798-1, Information technology - Security Techniques - Entity Authentication - Part 1: General*. International Standard Organization, 1997.

23. Vikram Persati, Thomas Keefe, and Shankar Pal. The design and implementation of a multilevel secure log manager. In *IEEE Symposium on Security and Privacy 1081-6011/97*, pages 55–64, 1997.

24. Vikram Persati, Thomas F. Keefe, and Shankar Pal. A guide to understanding audit in trusted systems. Technical report, NCSC-TG-001 Library No. S-228-470, July 1987.

25. Patrice Peyret. Application-enabling card systems with plug-and-play applets. In *Smart Card'96 Conference Proceedings*, 1996.

26. Jean-Marie Place, Thierry Peltier, and Patrick Trane. Secured co-operation of partners and applications in the blank card. In *GDM-Darmstadt 95 - Struif Editors*, July 1995.

27. Schlumberger. Cyberflex smart card series developers manual. http://www.cyberflex.austin.et.slb.com/cyberflex/cyberhome, 1997.

28. Bruce Schneier. *Applied Cryptography*. John Wiley and Sons, 1996.

29. Bruce Schneier and John Kelsey. Automatic event-stream notarization using digital signatures. In *Security Protocols, International Workshop April 1996 Proceedings*, pages 155–169. Springer-Verlag, 1996.

30. Bruce Schneier and John Kelsey. Cryptographic support for secure logs on untrusted machines. *The Seventh USENIX Security Symposium Proceedings Usenix Press*, pages 53–62, January 1998.

31. Adam   Shostack.   SSL   3.0   SPECIFICATION. http://www.homeport.org/ adam/ssl.html, May 1995.

32. SIEMENS. STARCOS. http://www.gdm.de/index.htm, 1996.

33. SIEMENS. CardOS. http://www.ad.siemens.de/cardos/index76.htm, September 1997.

34. Patrick Trane and Sylvain Lecomte. Failure recovery using action logs for smart cards transactions based systems. In *Third IEEE International On-Line Testing Workshop*, July 1997.

The Vault, an Architecture for Smartcards to Gain Infinite Memory

Patrick Biget

Gemplus Research Group,
Avenue du Pic de Bertagne, B.P. 100,
13881 Gémenos Cedex France
Patrick.Biget@gemplus.com

Abstract. Smartcard chips vendors have always done their best to embed more memory inside cards. These efforts are driven to allow their customers - smartcard manufacturers - to mask more software inside cards (in ROM) but, above all, to help them to provide cards with more memory dedicated to the application (EEPROM). Even if the geometry is getting smaller and smaller, some applications do not match with the current memory limitations due to smartcard constraints making impossible for the chips to be more than just a few millimeter square. The goal of the Extended Memory Card project is to suggest an architecture in which smartcards can securely "contain" more data than their own memory allows it. The card acts as a key to access information stored outside of it.

1 Introduction: The WebCard Prototype

1.1 Presentation

The basis of the *Extended Memory Card* project lies on an earlier work performed at the RD2P laboratory (Research and Development on Portable File), a research laboratory of USTL (University of Science and Technology of Lille - France). A prototype called WebCard has been developed and is described in [1].

WebCard has chosen a medical portable file as the reference application. A medical portable file smartcard is a secure container of personal medical information. Each patient is given a card in which his medical file may be stored (details, history of diseases...). The card is a part of a global medical information system in which information relative to each patient is secured.

The card used to store the personal medical information is the CQL card in which data can be directly modelled into an entity-relation scheme (CQL stands for Card Query Language and comes from SQL). The CQL card does not manage file, as all the other cards do, but tables. In each table, you can store character strings of any size (the memory is allocated dynamically at each cell writing or updating). Some access rights (or privileges) can be associated to each table to restrict its use to a category of users. In the application, depending on their profiles, doctors, nurses and medical hostesses will not be granted the same privileges. Thus they will not be able to read and/or write the same kind of information.

J.-J. Quisquater and B. Schneier (Eds.): CARDIS 2000, LNCS 1820, pp. 305–312, 2000.

In this architecture, the card provides the security of personal and private information. With a 10-kilobyte memory inside the card dedicated to the application, the file must be restricted to the critical information. How may we store X-ray photographs that are part of the medical file and which require several hundreds of bytes?

To counterbalance these card restrictions, the idea is to store a part of the medical file outside the card. The information, too large to reside on the card, may be stored on servers that are part of the medical information system. In that case, instead of containing the whole information, the card just keeps a reference to it (a non-ambiguous way to address it).

1.2 The Integration Platform: The World Wide Web

The WWW platform offers a suitable support to this application since it provides a uniform way of location all around the Web as well as easy interfacing facilities via Web browsers applications managing HTML documents.

The WebCard has chosen to store URLs in its table to reference external data. As URLs are character strings, they can be easily stored into table cells. To browse and update information inside the card, a set of HTML forms has been designed to consult card content after having presented the correct login and password to identify the user's profile.

1.3 A CGI-Based Architecture

An architecture based on CGI scripts has been designed for the application that is located on a Web server of the medical information system to gain access to the card inserted in a smartcard reader on the client station. CGI is the *Common Gateway Interface* which allows to create Web pages on the fly based on information from buttons, checkboxes, text input and so on.

A script, called CGI-W2C (CGI-Web To Card), is implemented on the server station. It is a gateway between the server and a program running on the client station, called *CQL Socket Driver*, which is the piece of code that makes the real requests to the card. Fig. 1 presents this architecture by underlying the multiple data exchanges between all the entities taking part in any transactions involving the card.

2 Security Architecture

2.1 Security Requirements

The architecture described in the previous chapter shows two terrible weaknesses in terms of security.

First, the information stored on the Web servers outside the card are totally unsecured (not encrypted) although they may be private and confidential. Even if a part of the information retained by the card is outside it, the idea here is to provide the same level of security for those deported data.

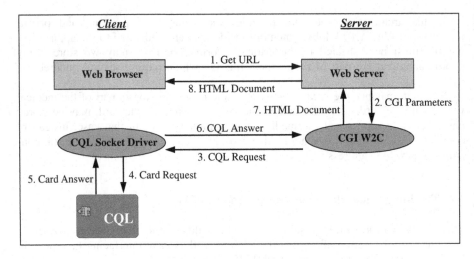

Fig. 1. The WebCard Architecture

The first solution that may be considered regarding this problem consists in securing servers physically and logically. But to reach your Web browser, an HTML page travels all around the net following an unpredictable path (possibly through all the WWW servers of the world!). At each node of the Web, this page may be easily copied for harmful usages. That is why data should never be transmitted plainly. This makes obvious that the information must at least travel over the net in an encrypted form. There are two solutions that meet these requirements.

The first one consists in building a security protocol performing a mutual authentication between the client and the server in order to establish a session key, when an external information must be accessed. This implies to set up a complete certification chain where certificates (like X.509 certificates) are distributed by an authority to all the entities involved in the transaction (servers and clients). According to the potential number of servers and mainly of clients, this solution is very difficult to implement.

Another method making the system much easier to manage is to encrypt the documents at their creation when they are stored in the remote severs. This is also a more economical way to solve the security issues of the architecture since the application may use a large number of external servers (in this case, securing all the servers may require lots of efforts). Here the key used to cipher documents is a private key owned by the card and documents are directly encrypted by the card. This method allows to avoid a mutual authentication. The server does not need to authenticate the client since the delivered document is encrypted and therefore usable only by the right person. The client does not need to authenticate the server since nobody could be able to build a valid document without the right key.

The issue for this solution is now to find a way to encrypt and decrypt the documents using some secrets stored inside the card pursuant to two constraints:

- the documents may be larger than card memory capacity so they cannot be totally encrypted/decrypted inside the card,
- and the secrets must never go out of the card.

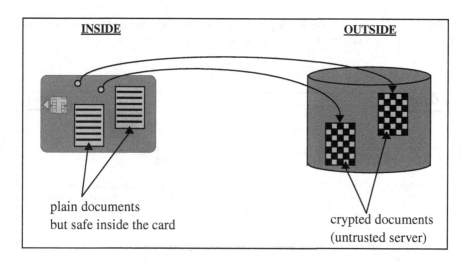

INSIDE   **OUTSIDE**

plain documents
but safe inside the card

crypted documents
(untrusted server)

Fig. 2. The Vault principle

The second security weakness of the WebCard architecture is that even data stored inside the card are made unsecure because of the architecture since all the answers from the card travel plainly on the network (see Fig. 1). The new architecture must be designed so that transactions with the card are locally performed to the client station.

2.2 The Remotely Keyed Encryption Protocol

[2] proposes a solution that authorizes a secure, but bandwidth-limited, cryptographic smartcard to function as a high-bandwidth secret-key encryption and decryption engine for an unsecure, but fast, host processor.

The host wants to encrypt and decrypt large blocks under a secret key stored in the card without knowing it. The card knows the key K but is computationally and bandwidth limited and cannot process entire blocks within the time required by the host. The Remotely Keyed Encryption Protocol (RKEP) allows the host to perform a single, fixed-size low-bandwidth interaction with the card to obtain enough information in order to encrypt or decrypt a given arbitrary length block.

RKEP requires from the smartcard and the host to share a block cipher algorithm that operates on b-bit cipherblocks keyed with a k-bit key. We have chosen to use the DES algorithm, then we can assume that we will use 64-bit cipherblocks and 56-bit key.

The host operates on large blocks of plaintext (P) and ciphertext (C), each consisting of a serie of n individual 64-bit cipherblocks, denoted $P_1...P_n$ and $C_1...C_n$, respectively. $I_1...I_n$ denote temporary "intermediate" cipherblocks internally used on the host by the protocol.

We denote encryption of plaintext block p under key K as $E_K(p)$ and decryption of ciphertext c under key K as $D_K(c)$. $\oplus$ denotes bitwise exclusive-OR. It is assumed that the host can efficiently calculate a public function $H(t)$ that returns a 64-bit cryptographic (one-way and collision-free) hash of arbitrary length bitstring t.

The encryption of n-cipherblock plaintext block P producing ciphertext C is shown in Fig. 3. Decryption of C is shown in Fig. 4.

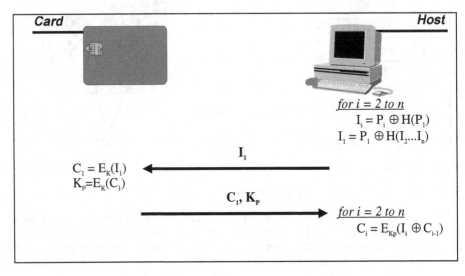

Fig. 3. RKEP encryption of P to obtain C

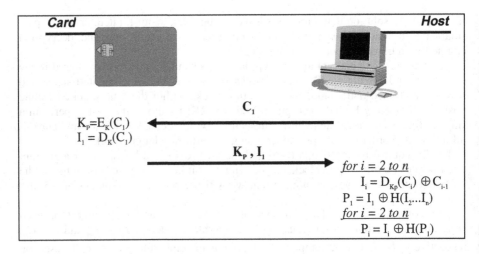

Fig. 4. RKEP decryption of C to obtain P

3 A New Application Architecture

3.1 Inadequacy of the WebCard Architecture

The choices we made by building the security architecture lead us to break the application architecture designed in the WebCard project. Once the external information are encrypted, it becomes impossible to build dynamically the HTML pages on the server. Before being displayed on the client browser, data need now to be decrypted by the smartcard which is attached the client station. Thus the manipulated data must be handled locally by the client.

We have actually to modify the architecture in the way the main process takes place on the client side. Then the role of the server moves to the simple data storage.

This solves another issue of the old architecture : the availability of the resources on the Web. Effectively, in the WebCard way of running, all the process is performed by the server. Even the accesses to smartcards that are performed on the client station by the *CQL Socket Driver* (see Fig. 1) are controlled directly by the server. This application « strategy » is to be reviewed for a more optimized version with respect to the Web transfer rates. So an architecture in which a major part of the work is performed on the client station is also be much preferable for efficiency reasons.

The last limitation of the WebCard prototype is the most pragmatic one. The prototype has been implemented on a Sun/Solaris platform in native code. It does not run on another platform. A more portable approach may be considered for the *Extended Memory Card* demonstration.

3.2 An Improved Architecture Using Java Technologies

Using a Java applet on the client station to access the card makes the architecture much more valuable. First, Java applets are dynamically loaded on the browser. Thus, there is no need to install a dedicated software on the possibly huge pool of client stations. Then, the browser may directly interact with the applet, consequently with the card, to retrieve the required information. In this way, the card accesses are stand-alone. Finally, before being executed, an applet is carefully checked by the sandbox of the Java Virtual Machine.

The sandbox is the module that verifies the adequacy of the applet with the security policy defined in the environment. For example, an applet would not satisfy the security rules of any environment if it tries to access the local disks or use any peripheral device. This last point solves the security issues raised in the previous chapter but introduces an important constraint: it forbids a "pure Java" applet to use a smartcard reader as it can only be a peripheral device. That is why the communication layers with the reader must be written in native code. This native code can be called from an applet using Java Native Interface, a standard interface to call external native programs. But this implies that the client has to trust this native library.

On the server side, the recently issued Java Servlet API proposes a very interesting alternative to CGI scripts. A servlet is the opposite end of an applet. It can almost be thought of as a server-side applet. Servlets run inside the Web server in the same way as applets run inside the Web browser to generate dynamic HTML pages. Basically, CGI scripts and servlets offer exactly the same services but servlets provide better features in term of security, efficiency and usability.

Here, our concerns are mostly focused on efficiency. In addition to the classical advantages brought by Java (platform independence, code reusability, programming language efficiency), the main improvement with servlets is performance. Servlets only need to be loaded once, while CGI programs need to be loaded for each request. The servlet init() method allows programmers to perform resource intensive actions (such as database connections) at startup and reuse them across servlet invocations. To know more about servlet, refer to [4] and [5].

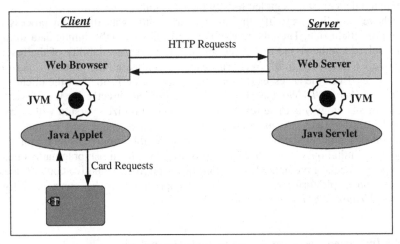

Fig. 5. A Full-Java Architecture

Figure 5 illustrates the new architecture we have build for the project. *CGI W2C* is replaced by a servlet and the *CQL Socket Driver* is replaced by an applet. The applet on the browser allows to perform the main part of the application using local resources without any network request (we especially think here of card accesses). The servlet just provides a data storage service. This service is invoked by the applet using HTTP-POST requests that deliver to the server the data to be stored as well as a filename on the server.

The URL stored into the smart card as a reference to the information is broken up into two parts : a machine name identifying the server where to find the running servlet and a filename to be used as a local name on the server.

4 Industrial Challenges and Perspectives

The final goal of this project is to tackle the never-ending problem of the lack of memory inherent to smartcards. As said in the introduction, it's unreasonnable to think that we will have one day a smart card embedding « enough » memory since the requirements grow as fast as the technology improvements are able to provide. Storing data outside the card but secured by the card has appeared to us a good solution to solve the problem.

Our short-term objective in order to evaluate the potential market for such kind of solution is to build rapidly a demonstrator illustrating functionally the principles described in this paper. Then, the next step will be to use this demonstrator to promote the concept of an extended memory card and find some industrial partners to initiate a real application.

The application demonstrator we have chosen is an health-care portable file application since we think it illustrates perfectly the issues and it is easily understandable. Such a portable file requires indeed a strong security (since it refers to stricly private information) as well as large storage capacity (for a real and complete medical file).

Another objective of the project is to demonstrate the power of the new JavaCards and their efficiency to develop rapidly software inside smartcards. Effectively, even if the role of the card is here mainly limited to a data repository, the card takes an active part in the encryption/decryption process. That is why the card software has to be customized to follow our requirements. Moreover, using a JavaCard, gives a general coherence to the architecture from Web servers to smartcards passing through Web clients.

This project, based on a full-java architecture, has also been used to evaluate the valuable interest of the OpenCard Framework [6]. The OpenCard Framework is an architecture developped by IBM in collaboration with the major smart card manufacturers and IT industry actors which aims at providing a framework for smart card solutions interoperability. As the OpenCard Framework architecture is Java-based, using it in our context has been very natural and efficient.

5 Conclusion

The project brings an opportunity to investigate new businesses in the development of smart card solutions and promotes the use of smart cards to secure private data storage. Its development has been an occasion to gather a pool of recent standardization initiatives to illustrate the high interoperability introduced by these emerging standards and the simplicity induced in the development of applications using smartcards.

This will undoubtedly reinforce potential markets for smart cards by breaking once for all the false image generally attached to smart cards : small memory capacity and difficult integration into applications. These constraints will no more be a barrier for developping new innovative highly secured applications.

References

[1] Vandewalle, J.-J.: Projet OSMOSE: modélisation et implémentation pour l'interopérabilité de services carte à microprocesseur par l'approche orientée objet. PhD Thesis, Université des Sciences et Technologies de Lille (1997) 50-56
[2] Blaze,   M.:   High-Bandwith   Encryption   with   Low-Bandwith   Smartcards.
    ftp://ftp.research.att.com/dist/mab/card_cipher.ps
[3] Hui, E.: CGI, Plug-ins, & etc... Course of the Department of Computer Science at the University of Calgary.
    http://www.cpsc.ucalgary.ca/~kremer/courses/547/CGIandPlugins.
[4] Dougherty, D.: Understanding Java Servlets.
    http://webreview.com/97/10/10/feature/colton.html
[5] Crawford, W.: Developing Java Servlets.
    http://webreview.com/97/10/10/feature/main.html
[6] Hermann, R., Husemann, D.: OpenCard Framework 1.0 White Paper.
    http://www.opencard.org/docs/whitepaper

A Data Driven Model for Designing Applications with Smart Cards

William Caelli[1], Vincent Cordonnier[2], and Anthony Watson[3]

[1] School of Data Communications, Queensland University of Technology
head.dc@qut.edu.au
[2] University of Sciences and Technology of Lille
vincent.cordonnier@univ-lille1.fr
[3] School of Computer and Information Science, Edith Cowan University, Perth
a.Watson@cowan.edu.au

Abstract. Developing smart card applications to work in massively distributed environments requires consistency to ensure reliable functionality. A likely point of error occurs at the boundaries of interlinked applications or transactions. Every individual access to a service maybe represented as a transaction between the partners of the information system. Using a focus on the data as the universal element for creating the transaction a concept of modules based on data entities is introduced. The module becomes the atomic object for describing the transactions which in term describe the application outcomes. A significant advantage of the data driven model is that correctness analysis is possible revealing the correctness of the transaction and the real flow of data across module boundaries. The model includes the description of the synchronisation of the module interaction and the possibility of code importation.

1 Introduction

Smart cards are usually considered as components of distributed information systems. It is commonly agreed that smart cards are presently the best solution to drive secure and reliable transactions between a large population of users and services providers. But there are many and unresolved discussions about what a card must be able to store, deliver and consequently process.

On one side, some people argue that the cards must contain as much data as possible when that is technically feasible. Hardware (flash memory) and software (CQL cards, JavaCard) offer a large spectrum of possibilities and promises. This option will be considered as the totally distributed model of data and processing sites.

To the other side, people who invest in networks and distributed systems suggest that centralized storage is more reliable and cheaper, easier to maintain and permanently accessible. This possibility is the totally centralized option. The only data to be stored in the card is that which is necessary to identify and authenticate the user.

Assuming that data must be used by the information system, one of the most important questions the application designer has to look at is the location of that data, which could be the card, a terminal or a server. It is noticeable, for example with

J.-J. Quisquater and B. Schneier (Eds.): CARDIS 2000, LNCS 1820, pp. 313–325, 2000.
© Springer-Verlag Berlin Heidelberg 2000

telephone cards, that the same service can be provided by using either model. Obviously many aspects of the service such as security, cost, user's comfort are different in each case.

This paper is an attempt to propose a methodology as a guideline to better discuss and manage the data distribution within the overall information system.

Every individual access to a service may be presented as a transaction between the partners of the information system. Some specific characteristics of these transactions including smart cards can be taken into account by creating a general model for any type of transaction. In particular, such a model must be capable of determining the movements of data and programs which better fit with the requirements of the application provider : Efficiency, security, flexibility, price of the components, cost of transmissions, etc. A data driven approach looks appropriate as it is able to clearly express these properties of data for both storage and communication

2   Definitions

A *digital transaction* is the set of operations, communications, processing and data management activities which offers a consumer a complete service and results in a coherent state of the overall information system.

A transaction may be seen as the implementation of a protocol between the entities which are implied in the service provision and consumption. When using a smart card, these entities usually are : the application issuer, the service provider and the client using the service. These entities are : *Partners of the transaction*. Very often an application needs to include a few other partners such as the communication suppliers, banks, vendors or complementary services providers.

A transaction with a card will necessarily imply a distributed system. *A site* of the information system is a physical component, fixed of mobile, which is capable of proceeding and/or storing data and to communicate with the other sites

3   Notion of Module

A data driven oriented model is based upon entities which receive and produce data. We assume that the scheme of a transaction, corresponding to a well identified service can be described by many existing tools such as entity analysis. The aim is to propose a model which will permit the designer to locate the different elements of the transaction according to the specific requirements of a card based application.

Smart cards are characterized by a high level of security but their storage and processing capabilities are limited. The other possible sites are smart cards readers, terminals and any remote server. Then the most important issue is to determine what part of the transaction must necessarily be performed by the card itself, what must be performed by other sites and what has to be discussed as alternate possibilities.

As applications and transactions may differ from each other, the entity which will be used to describe a transaction must be a fine grain description of every activity. We identify a *module* as an elementary atomic object which is the reunion of four elements :

The site were the module will be activated : S;
Data which have to be provided by other modules : D_{in}
Data which are produced by the module to other ones : D_{out}
The action of that module represented by a program or a process: P.

$$M := \{ \ S, D_{in}, P, D_{out} \ \}$$

A transaction can be described as a set of modules $T := \{M1, M2, ..Mi, ...Mn\}$ which communicate data to each other. Data location and movements can then be described by examining the interactions between these modules.

If $Mi := \{ \ Sa, Dx, Pa, Dy\}$ and $Mj := \{ \ Sa, Dy, Pb, Dz\}$
Mi and Mj are implemented on the same site Sa, Dy will reside on that site.
If $Mi := \{ \ Sa, Dx, Pa, Dy\}$ and $Mj := \{ \ Sb, Dy, Pb, Dz\}$
Mi and Mj are implemented on two different sites Dy will have to move from Sa to Sb.

In some cases the quadruplet may be simplified by observing that some elements do not exist or introduce redundancy:

1) So far, neither smart cards, nor the servers have to import the code they execute. It is likely that, in the very near future this feature will bring many new possibilities for developing innovative applications. But for the moment, with many applications, S and P have the same meaning, assuming that a site always contains the code it has to work with. Current transactions may then be described by a triplet such as :

$$Mi := \{ \ Site, Data\ Input, Data\ Output \ \}$$

2) The first module of a transaction has no input

$$Mj := \{ \ Site, 0, Data\ Output \ \}$$

3) Some modules may have not output to another module. In particular the one which concludes the transaction.

$$Mk := \{ \ Site, Data\ Input, 0 \ \}$$

The module description allows the application designer to identify data movements between the various sites of the information system. As one of the most important issues of the method is to decide where data have to be permanently located, sites are not yet identified. That can be represented by the following expression where Sx is not yet indentified :

$$Mi := \{ \ Sx, Data\ input, Data\ output, Program \ \}$$

We assume that the data which are local to a module and never move are located in the site where the module will be executed. These data will not be mentioned because they do not cross module boundaries. Finally, it is interesting to notice that data movements of the model are very similar to the communications by messages in an object oriented method.

The aim of the method is not to design a supervisor which would be able to synchronize the modules of a transaction. It can rather be seen as a data flow chart. Then we can assume that all necessary D_{in} are made available to the module before it starts working. Similarly, the module is supposed to produce D_{out} after having completed its process.

4   Example

Analysis of a transaction for automatic telephone payment. Telephone numbers, dialing operations and transmission are not represented because they do not present a risk from the security point of view and also because there is no choice for their location or the communication links they must use.

For any implementation, the transaction comprises five modules:

M1 : Money control
Input Data : Available money or number of tokens: MONEY.
Action : If MONEY > 0 then ACK else NAK
Output Data: ACK or NAK.

M2: Money Withdraw
Input data : MONEY, TAX PULSE
Action : MONEY = MONEY - 1
Output data: MONEY

M3 : Line control
Input Data: ACK or NAK
Action : If ACK then keep the line ELSE cut the line
Output data : LINE ON/OFF

M4 : Tax pulse generator
Input data : LINE ON/OFF
Action: according to the communication rate : send TAX PULSE
Output Data : TAX PULSE

M5 : Display money (optional)
Input Data : MONEY
Code : display
Output : no

Module M3 and M4 are necessarily located in the central server (CS); module M5 is optional but it represents an interesting facility for the consumer; it must be located in the local terminal (T), if it exists. The formal representation of the transaction is:

```
M1:= { X1, MONEY, MONEY = 0 ? , ACK or NAK, }
M2:= { X2, MONEY and PAYMENTPULSE, MONEY =MONEY - 1, MONEY }
M3:= { CS, ACK or NK , Line control, LINE ON/OFF }
M4:= { CS, LINE ON/OFFPAYMENT POLICY, PAYMENT PULSE }
M5:= { T, MONEY, 0, DISPLAY }
```

The only choices are for M1 and M2 which can be either on the card or on the server. It is interesting to notice that both solutions exist in use. Each implies very different communications between the sites.

Solution 1 - The prepaid token card with three partners : The card (C), the telephone box (B), the central server CS). M1 and M2 take place in the card. The model must take into account that there is no possibility for a direct communication between the card and the server. If necessary this communication will go through the local terminal by creating two new gateway modules (M6 and M7) in the telephone box.

```
M1:= { C, MONEY, MONEY=0 ?, ACK or NAK and MONEY }
M2:= { C, MONEY and PAYMENTPULSE-2, MONEY =MONEY -1, MONEY }
M3:= { CS, ACK or NK , Line control, LINE ON/OFF }
M4:= { CS, LINE ON/OFF,  PAYMENT POLICY, PAYMENT PULSE-1 }
M5:= { T, MONEY, 0, DISPLAY }
M6:= { T, PAYMENT PULSE-1, 0, PAYMENT PULSE-2 }
M7:= { T, ACK or NAK, 0, ACK or NAK }
```

As every module is now located in a physical site, two diagrams can easily be extracted from the model. The functional communication flow between the modules and the physical communication flow between the sites (diagram 2).

M1→M2: MONEY	M1→ M5: MONEY
M1→ M7: ACK or NAK	M2→M1: MONEY
M→M4: LINE ON/OFF	M4→M6: TAX PULSE-1
M6→M2: TAX PULSE-2	M7→M3: ACK or NAK
Diagram 1	Diagram 2

The physical site to site description does not need to take in account movements between two modules which are located in the same site; for example M1 and M2, inside the card or M4 and M6, inside the server.

C →T : MONEY, ACK or NAK	T → S : ACK or NAK,
CS → T : PULSE-1	T → C : PULSE-2

Solution 2 - The centralized data based prepaid card with only two sites : The user (U), the central server (CS). The telephone handset itself serves as the local terminal. The user provides data thanks to the keyboard and can only receive vocal messages. All modules M1, M2, M3 and M4 are located in the server. The module M5 cannot be implemented because it would interfere with the voice.

But another module is necessary to address M1 which needs to select one out of the possible many records located in the central server. This module is:

$$M0 := \{ U, 0, 0, SECRET\ CODE \}$$

And M1 becomes

$$M1 := \{ CS,\ SECRET\ CODE,\ MONEY=0?,\ ACK\ or\ NAK \}$$

These two examples, show how the same service can be provided by two different implementations. The most significant difference is the location of money and the way this money is made available. But there are many more differences which will be revealed later by the analysis of the description.

5   Exploitation of the Model

Basically, the model allows a transaction to be described in terms of elementary functional modules and observe the data flow between these modules. It can be seen as a tool for designing the overall architecture of an application by taking into account various criteria such as security, communication, cost, quality of services etc.

5.1   The Correctness Analysis

By analysing communications between modules the data driven model allows the designer to detect unused output data and not provided input data. Diagram 3 shows an example of this analysis.

	M1	M2	M3	M4	M5	M6
M1		D1	D2		D2	
M2			D3			D3
M3	D8			D4		D5
M4					D6	
M5					D7	
M6						

Diagram 3

It also reveals loops in the data flow diagram (in the previous example an error can be detected as a loop between modules M1 and M3 through D2 and D8).

It is quite simple to automatically verify the correctness of the application by using a program which is very similar to the first pass of a data driven compiler. This program could also provide information about the synchronization of the existing modules.

5.2 Real Movements of Data

Another aspect of the design is the evaluation of data movements. The decision to locate a module in a site enables the communications between that module and the ones which are functionally linked to it as data providers or consumers.

Let us assume that three sites A, B, and C are used according to the following distribution:

A for (M1, M2), B for (M3, M4), C for (M5, M6).

		M1	M2	M3	M4	M5	M6
A	M1		D1	D2		D2	
	M2			D3			D3
B	M3				D4		D5
	M4					D6	
C	M5					D7	
	M6						

Diagram 4

It is first possible to ignore data movements which remain inside a unique site. These movements will only be utilised by an internal memory access. The diagram 4 shows that D1, D4 and D7 may be ignored and only real communications are the ones which are out of the gray areas.

		A		B		C	
		M1	M2	M3	M4	M5	M6
A	M1			D2		D2	
	M2			D3			D3
B	M3						D5
	M4					D6	
C	M5						
	M6						

Diagram 5

The physical links which are needed are:

A → B for D2 and D3; A→C for D2 and D3; B→C for D5 and D6.

Each of these links must be realized and it is easy to discuss their ability to transport the data which are involved in the transaction. The model enlightens the overall need for communications and consequently the protocol to be used, the price and the complexity of the selected data distribution.

5.3   The Security Approach

There are two different possibilities for attacks. Those which target one of the sites involved in the transaction and those which target communications between these sites. The security level of a site is established as well as possible by physical and logical means. The model allows the application designer to discuss the overall distribution of data among sites according to their robustness.

Another interest of the model is for an evaluation of the communication risks. The previous stage gave a clear view of the physical communications which are imposed by the choices involved in implementing the transaction. The element which must be observed is :

Data out from module M_i(Site A) → Data in to module M_j (Site B)

Every movement of data from one site to another one is a threat which can be analyzed and discussed. For example, the smart card telephone application has to provide the following movements:

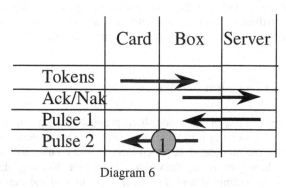

	Card	Box	Server
Tokens	⟶		
Ack/Nak		⟶	
Pulse 1		⟵	
Pulse 2	⟵①		

Diagram 6

Every arrow of the data flow model can be examined as a possible weakness of the system and used as an element of the overall security evaluation.
The following is a brief analysis of the communications represented by these arrows:

Number of tokens :
Storage security: the security level is rated by the tamper resistance of the card.
Communication security : No major risk as this number is just used for display.
Ack or Nak : There is no risk on Nak messages as it does not give any advantage; the
risk occurs if a Nak message is replaced by an Ack response.
Pulse 1 : moving from the server to the telephone box; the link offers good security.
Pulse 2 : This is the weakest component of the transaction because the physical
access to that link is easy and there is no possibility to cipher the communication. For
some time it was observed that some telephone boxes could be easily and indefinitely
used by preventing the payment pulse-2 from being transmitted to the card (arrow 1).
Then when the fraud was detected, a new module has been added to the transaction.
This module has been located in the telephone box and verifies that the amount of
tokens in the card has been diminished by one after a pulse.

$$M7 := \{ \text{ B, Number of tokens, Control, Ack or Nak } \}$$

The communication diagram of the centralised solution is simpler : the only site to
site message is:

$$M0 \rightarrow \text{Secret code} \rightarrow M1$$

The solution does not require any equipment at the terminal level and is compatible
with any telephone set. This code cannot be ciphered but the service provider only
assumes that there are a very few meaningful codes among all possible ones. The
secret code is composed of 12 digits leading to one chance out of a million or so to
find a correct code by chance. Some hackers have written programs to repetitively try
numerous codes.

The main difference between the two solutions is the consequence of an attack. If
the money is distributed an attack will only threaten the owner or the server at the
individual level. With a centralized money store, an attack may be a disaster.

6   A General Decision Model

An interesting application of the model is to propose a design method by analysing
the consequences of locating a module on a site. These consequences apply to data
which are local on the module, data which have to move either as input or as output.
Assuming that there are more than one choice for locating data, the various
possibilities may be examined and discussed according to the major criteria of the
application.

6.1   Stage 1 : The Functional Model

It is first possible to produce a functional description of the transaction by the list of
its modules without any previous decision for a possible choice of locations.

Then the modules which necessarily must be located in a given site will be allocated to that site. The other modules which can be seen as floating ones are the arguments for a variety of possible architectures. A module such as:

$$Mi := \{ X, \text{Data input, Data output, Code}\}$$

can be located in one site Sj (X = Sj) because of many possible arguments:

1) The code can only be executed on a site because of its size or because it requires much more processing power than any other site can provide.
2) The module uses data which cannot move off the site for security reasons.
3) The amount of communication required by the module leads to preferably select the site which has the best data rate and the most flexible protocol.
4) The module must closely and securely cooperate with another module which has previously been allocated to a site.

Finally, there are a few possible architectures that remain as possible options for the applications. Each of these architectures must now be examined from a security perspective.

6.2   Stage 2 : The Physical Model

Every possible architecture imposes communication of data between the sites of the distributed system. Assuming that communication is the weakest element of security, the best physical architecture can both limit the communication of important data and define the link which must be secured.

The following example allocates the six modules of a transaction described in Diagram 4. The three sites A (the card), B (the terminal) and C (the server) may be envisaged according to two different distributions. Diagram 7 illustrates 2 different distributions of the 6 modules.

Architecture 1
M1 and M2 are in the card
M3 and M4 are in the terminal
M5 and M6 are in the central server
Architecture 2
M1 and M3 are in the card
M2 and M4 are in the terminal
M5 and M6 are in the central sever.

The architecture 1 will be preferred if the communication between M1 and M2, M3 and M4 must be secured by priority. To the contrary, the architecture 2 will be selected to better protect the communication between M2 and M4, M1 and M3.

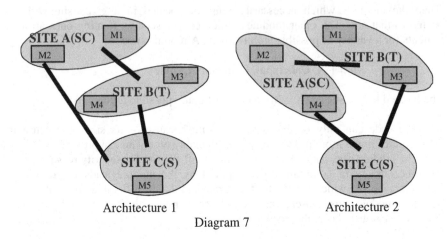

Architecture 1   Architecture 2

Diagram 7

The model reveals the need for physical communication between sites. It leads to preferential selection of one architecture because the physical link is either more secure, cheaper, more reliable or better adapted to transport the data to be exchanged.

Eventually, it is possible to have an idea of the cost of the components including specifically the smart card. With both architectures, the card will have to accommodate the module M1. According to the selected architecture, it will also have to support either M2 or M3 and associated local data. It then becomes possible to specify the characteristics of the appropriate card.

7   Synchronization of the Modules

A data driven description of a transaction automatically provides a synchronization scheme provided that a module can be executed as soon as its input data are made available. For many reasons the data flow control may not be sufficient and other sources of triggers are necessary:

1) A message, especially by considering that the module will start working as soon as its input data are available,
2) A clock,
3) An internal trigger which detects that a starting condition has become true.
4) The user via the interface of the terminal.
5) Any external event such as unexpected card withdrawl or any failure. This could be useful for example to control an extra module which will be responsible of recovering a coherent status for stored data.

There are many possibilities to express the synchronization element. As the triggering sources may be very different, the most general representation should be an explicit condition which can be considered as a guarded command:

$$Mi := Condition < S, D_{in}, C, D_{out}>$$

This condition enables the designer to verify that every module will properly play its role in due time and under the right conditions with an appropriate temporal and logical relationship with the other modules.

This synchronization toll looks to be especially useful with the new concept of active card where a module can be activated without receiving any explicit command or message. The guarded command which is associated with the module describes a set of conditions under which the module has to be executed. For example:

A data which have been updated (elementary level)
A file or a table which has been modified. (group level)
An external command (global level)

The module itself is able to produce messages to other modules by issuing extra output data according to the current data driven model of time control and synchronization. It must also be noted that this solution takes into account, in a unified presentation, the communication with the user via the interface of the terminal. Then the user may be considered as responsible for executing its own modules. For example , the user will deliver a PIN as an input data to a verification module located in the card.

8   Code Importation

For most current applications the code is located in the site where the module must be executed. With the first generation of cards, the code was stored in ROM memory and was the completely determined and fixed at the point of manufacture.

Recently there were announcements from the manufacturers for new technologies which could offer the application designer improved flexibility:

1)   Possibility to add extra code at the personalisation level.
2)   Updating the code by special and well protected transactions during the life of the card.
3)   Code importation during regular transactions.

The third possibility is the most innovative and ambitious one. It offers a lot of facilities to permanently adapt a card to many different environments.

If we consider that code to be imported can be seen as data which must be transferred from the code server to the card, the code appears as a new input data for the corresponding module or set of modules. Then the same considerations about security and other aspects apply to imported programs. The availability of the program becomes another synchronisation condition for the module to be executed.

9   Conclusion

Many smart card projects have been driven on a quite empirical basis by deciding that the card should store a given but arbitrary subset of the data that are required by the application. The method does not proposes to automatically lead to the best solution. This final solution remains under the responsibility of the project designer. He or she must take in account many criteria which are either too complex or not easy to compare and evaluate.

As the main role of a smart card is to act as a memory or a data manager, it seemed natural and efficient to select a data driven approach. In information technology this approach is usually implemented thanks to a Single Assignment Language where the atomic element is an instruction. Because of the specific requirements of distributed applications and a larger grain analysis, we proposed to replace instructions by modules as previously defined.

As the smart cards technology, especially when associated with networks, proposes more and more possibilities, it seems important to better analyse an application and to use a top down approach which can take in account the numerous parameters which can influence the design of the application, namely the distribution of data and the consequences for security, cost, reliability and flexibility.

References

1. Balme, L., Silvy, C., Project Smart Power card, Activity report, Laboratorie TIMA, Techniques de l'Informatique et de la Microelectronique pour l'Architecture d'ordinateurs, University de Grenoble, 1992.
2. Castellani, "Methode generale d'analyse et de conception des systemes d'objects", Masson, 1993.
3. CNET. Special - "Paiement Electronique". *L'echo des RECHERCHES*, No 158, Centre National d'Etudes des Telecommunications, Issy-les-Moulineaux, France, December 1994.
4. Cordonnier, V. "Assessing the Future of Smart Cards". *Proceedings, Card Tech '92*, Washington DC, USA, April 1992.
5. Cordonnier, V., - The future of smart cards : Technology and applications. Invited paper. *IFIP world conference*. Canberra September 1996.
6. Cordonnier, V., Watson, A.C., "Access Control Determination of Multi-Application Smartcards Using a Security Index", Third Australasian Security Research Symposium, Queensland University of Technology, July, 1997.
7. Guillou, L C and Ugon, M. "Smart Card, A Highly Reliable and Portable Security Device". *Advances in Cryptology - Crypto '86 Proceedings*, ed. Odlyzko, A M, *Lecture Notes in Computer Science*, No 263, Springer-Verlag, Berlin, Germany, 1987.
8. Ugon, M. "Future of Smartcard Operating Systems". *Proceedings, Card Tech '94*, pp 69 - 96, Washington DC, USA, April 1994.
9. Verjus, R., "Towards autonomous description of synchronisation modules", Proceedings IFIPWorld Conference 1977.

Secure Personalization Using Proxy Cryptography

Pierre Girard

GEMPLUS, Cryptography and Security R&D
Parc d'activité de Gémenos – B.P. 100
13881 Gémenos CEDEX – France
Pierre.Girard@gemplus.com

Abstract. In this paper we describe new secure personalization schemes using proxy cryptography. We first introduce the context of a large scale smart card application such as an electronic purse, the current personalization schemes and the security requirements. We recall the notion of proxy cryptography and we consider an actual proxy cryptosystem based on ElGamal public key encryption. With this proxy cryptosystem we setup new security schemes for smart cards personalization and we show that they are more secure, flexible and cheap than existing ones.

1 Introduction

Smart card applications have grown recently in such a way that they now often include numerous industrial and commercial partners. But, when the number of partners increase, the confidence level in each one proportionally decreases as it becomes impossible to individually assess each actor. Moreover the global security is never stronger then the weakest point of the application.

Smart cards security problems (either in hardware or in software) have been carefully studied in the past years from an end–user point of view, but organizational problem arising within the manufacturing process have not often been addressed. However, it turns out that cards and data at various stages of the manufacturing process are vulnerable to numerous attacks leading to severe security breaches in the overall application.

As usual, the security solutions should be of little impact on the process flexibility, scalability and cost. It is not often the case and some parts of the process such as cards personalization are actually constrained by a security vs cost/flexibility tradeoff.

In this paper, we describe new secure personalization schemes using proxy cryptography. We show that they improve the cost vs security tradeoff and that they implement in software the features of secure devices currently used in personalization schemes.

2 The Context

In this paper, we consider a large scale application, such as a country wide electronic purse. An organization (called the issuer) drives the overall application

J.-J. Quisquater and B. Schneier (Eds.): CARDIS 2000, LNCS 1820, pp. 326–335, 2000.

and generates data to be stored in the cards when required by a purse retailer. These data generally include secret keys used to authenticate the cards and sign transactions. The secret keys are usually diversified from a mother key using the user identifier (UID) which is supposed to be unique. The issuer relies on a manufacturing infrastructure to obtain a personalized card with the generated data and to deliver it to the end-user as shown on figure 1.

We suppose that crediting the electronic purse is an on–line transaction whereas debit is processed off–line.

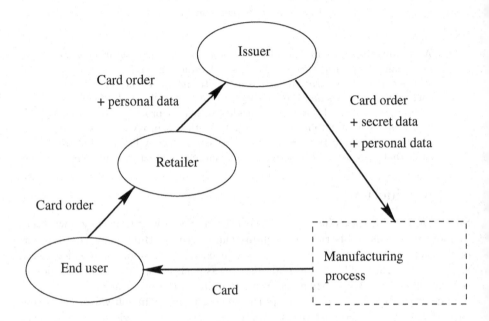

Fig. 1. Card issuing scheme

The next sections explain how the cards are manufactured and personalized and what security threats should be addressed.

2.1   Cards Life-Cycle

Large batches of blank smart cards are usually provided by a few manufacturers to the personalization centers. These centers receive data from the issuer and personalize the requested cards accordingly (see figure 2).

The number of centers could be rather large as the personalization should take place close to the end user. The cards could even be personalized in real-time at the point of sale (POS) by the retailer itself. On the opposite, manufacturing the blank card is a heavier industrial activity and although each personalization center should deal with several manufacturers for reliability reasons, the overall number of manufacturers remains small.

2.2 Security Requirements

The main security threat is the theft of keys which could be used to forge an electronic purse, and to create electronic money. This could be achieved by using a smart card of any origin with an embedded fake purse, but the simplest way to do it is to wire the smart card reader to a PC simulating the smart card application. Although the latter approach can't be used in a real store, it should be seriously considered in an Internet based commerce context.

Cloning a smart card without knowing its secret key is not considered as a threat because the clone must go on–line to be credited and the fraud will be detected at this stage. Credit transaction use the internal state of the card which depends on previous credit transactions and random numbers generated by the card. Since the internal state of the real card and its clones will differ, all the credit transactions of all but one card will be blocked.

During the manufacturing process a lot of attacks could take place especially at the personalization stage. The secret keys of a card should consequently be securely transmitted to the personalization center in such a way that the other personalization centers and the cards manufacturer cannot retrieve them.

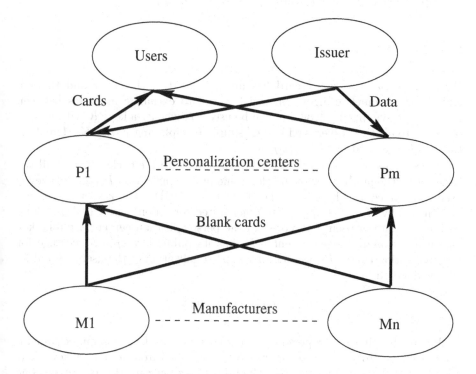

Fig. 2. Card life-cycle

The internal security of the personalization centers and the manufacturers could be physically assessed by frequent audits. However, these audits are costly and even impracticable if the number of personalization centers is too large or if the personalization takes place in a POS where minimum internal security requirements can't be reached. For all these reasons, it is safer to require that even if the security of one point fails, the overall personalization scheme is still secure. In this case, two parties (a smart card manufacturer and a personalization center) must collude to conduct a successful attack and a center alone cannot retrieve the keys although the card can be personalized. In the next section we show how these requirements can be fulfilled.

3   Personalization Schemes

In this paper the symmetric encryption key of holder h will be denoted by K_h and a ciphering public key by e_h, a deciphering private key by d_h. The ciphering of a message m by a key k will be denoted by $E(m, k)$ or $[m]_k$. The deciphering of a ciphertext c by a key k will be denoted by $D(c, k)$.

3.1   Used Keys

We assume that the smart card has an embedded block–cipher and that an additional asymmetric algorithm can be used to exchange messages between parties. The symmetric algorithm can be used to diversify a key[1] K with a piece of data x to obtain a diversified key K' simply by ciphering x with K. Hereafter, this will be denoted by: $K' = [x]_K$.

Three kinds of keys must be used during the card life-cycle. First of all the issuer owns the mother key of the electronic purse application K_{AM}. This key is used to produce user keys from theirs identifiers (UID). The key of user u will be denoted by $K_{Au} = [u]_{K_{AM}}$. Once generated for an end–user, the key along with other data are sent encrypted to the personalization center. A public key algorithm is used, and each center P_x has its public key e_{Px}. A message for personalization center P_4, asking for the personalization of the users 23 and 34 will be denoted by:

$$[(K_{A23}, data), (K_{A34}, data)]_{e_{P4}}$$

Before shipping to the personalization centers, smart card manufacturer initializes each card i with a secret key K_{Ci} diversified from a mother key K_{CM} and the chip serial number (CSN) which is unique per card. In some cases, one may have to secretly communicate with the manufacturer M_n using his public key e_{Mn}.

---

[1] The same purpose can be acheived as well by using a MAC function (e.g.:HMAC [5]).

3.2   Personalization with a Trusted Center

The simpliest personalization scheme is as follows: the issuer sends to the personalization center the data for user u encrypted with the center's public key. The center decrypts the message and re–encrypts it with the card's secret key.

The main point here is that the user's application key is exposed when deciphered even if it is possible to shorten the exposure time. It should be noticed as well that the issuer can't encrypt data directly with the card secret key as he doesn't know in advance which card will be used by the personalization center.

Finally the smart card manufacturer has to give its mother key K_{CM} to the personalization center (the center must derive from it each card secret key K_{Ci}). As a result, either each personalization center can personalize all cards or the manufacturer has to manage a different mother key for each center which is likely undesirable.

Consequently, this scheme is only to be used with trusted personalization centers.

3.3   Personalization with an Untrusted Center

When personalization centers are untrusted, the decryption/re–encryption process of the user application key must take place in a tamperproof device[2] which contains the center's private key and the secret mother key of the card manufacturer. The keys are entered respectively by the issuer and the manufacturer and can't be extracted.

In this case, the application's user keys are no longer exposed, but two drawbacks should be considered: the tamper proof devices are costly and the procedural complexity to safely initialize and maintain them is far from being insignificant.

In the next section, we recall the basics of proxy cryptography that we will use to build–up a new secure personalization scheme that does not require tamperproof devices.

4   Proxy Cryptography

4.1   Overview of Proxy Cryptography

An *atomic proxy function* is a function used to convert a ciphertext for one key to a ciphertext for another key without revealing the secret decryption keys nor cleartext messages. Although the concept applies both to symetric and asymetric cryptography, it has not been yet proven usefull in the symetric case. Consequently we will only deal with the asymetric case.

The atomic proxy function could be given to an untrusted third party without introducing threats against plaintext messages or secret keys. We will denote by Π the atomic proxy function and by $\pi_{A \to B}$ the proxy key used to convert text

---

[2] Racal devices are one concrete example of such high–speed devices (see www.racal.com). Smart card can be used as well as a cheaper, yet slower, encryption "black–box".

encrypted with the public key e_A held by user A to a ciphertext for user B such that:

$$D(\Pi(E(m, e_A), \pi_{A \to B}), d_B) = m$$

Function Π is atomic in the sense that it computes $E(D(c, d_A), e_B)$ on a ciphertext c without revealing the intermediate result $D(c, d_A)$.

Proxy schemes have been categorized by the trust relationship between A and B. The scheme is qualified as *symmetric* if and only if A and B must trust each other in the sense that A (resp. B) can retrieve the private key d_B (resp. d_A) of B (resp. A) based on the knowledge of its private key d_A (resp. d_B) and the proxy key $\pi_{A \to B}$. Otherwise proxy schemes are defined as *asymmetric*.

Clearly the proxy relationship is transitive. This means that if there exist two proxy keys $\pi_{A \to B}$ and $\pi_{B \to C}$ everyone can compute a third proxy key $\pi_{A \to C}$.

Proxy cryptosystems have been introduced for signatures in [7] and extended in [6] to specific ciphertexts. Blaze and Strauss generalized proxy encryption and classified proxy schemes in [2,1]. They give an atomic proxy function for an ElGamal–based cryptosysytem, called cryptosystem χ, and note that the original ElGamal cryptosystem could have been used as well. In the next section we recall the cryptosystem χ and the associated proxy function.

4.2   Cryptosystem χ

To generate a key pair, one has to choose a prime p of the form $2q+1$ for a prime q and g a generator in $\mathbb{Z}_p^*$. A random number x relatively prime to $p-1$ is used as the private key. In a second step, a value of y is computed such as: $y = g^x \bmod p$. The public key is (p, g, y), and the private key is x. The parameters p and g can be shared by a group of users.

Encryption consists in computing:

1. Choose k, a random number relatively prime to $p - 1$.
2. Compute (a, b) the ciphertext of a message M ($M < p$) such as $a = g^k \times M \bmod p$ and $b = y^k \bmod p$.

The decrypting process simply computes:

$$\frac{a}{b^{x^{-1}}} \bmod p = \frac{g^k \times M}{g^{x \times k \times x^{-1}}} \bmod p = M$$

Note that the ciphertext is twice the size of the plaintext, which is unoptimal. However, a proxy function can easily be obtained for this scheme as exposed in the next subsection.

4.3   Proxy Function for χ Encryption

Let p and g be the parameters shared by users 1 and 2. The public keys are y_1 and y_2 and the private keys are x_1 and x_2. In this case, the proxy key $\pi_{1 \to 2}$ will be: $\pi_{1 \to 2} = x_1^{-1} \times x_2$ and the proxy function $\Pi((a, b), \pi_{1 \to 2}) = (a, b^{\pi_{1 \to 2}} \bmod p)$.

It can be observed that only the b part of the ciphertext should be modified. A ciphertext (a_1, b_1) of message m for user 1, will be transformed as follow:

$$\Pi((a_1, b_1), \pi_{1 \to 2}) = (a_1, b_1^{\pi_{1 \to 2}} \bmod p)$$
$$= (a_1, (g^{x_1 \times k})^{x_1^{-1} \times x_2} \bmod p)$$
$$= (a_1, g^{x_2 \times k} \bmod p) = (a_1, b_2) = (a_2, b_2)$$

This proxy scheme is symmetric as it is possible for one user (given his private key) to pull–out the other user's private key out of $\pi_{1 \to 2}$. It has been proved in [2] that the scheme is at least as hard as the Diffie-Hellman key-exchange scheme.

5   New Secure Personalization Schemes

We now assume that the χ algorithm is embedded in the cards as well as its associated proxy function. Each card i has its own key pair $(e_{Ci}, d_{Ci}) = (y_{Ci}, x_{Ci})$. The public parameters p and g are shared by all cards, the centers and the issuer.

We further assume that each personalization center P_x owns a key pair as well: $(e_{Px}, d_{Px}) = (y_{Px}, x_{Px})$.

5.1   Personalization with a Trusted Center

The smart card manufacturer releases a proxy key $\pi_{P_x \to C_i}$ for each card sent to the personalization center. The center uses it to convert each ciphertext with its public key to a ciphertext for the card to be personalized. In this scheme, the personalization center can still retrieve data sent by the issuer, but now, as the proxy function is atomic, sensitive data are no longer exposed by the decryption/re–encryption process. If the personalization center is trusted and keeps his private key secure, the overall process is safe. The table 1 summarizes the scheme at the initialization phase which takes places once or when needed (if a key expire or has been compromised, etc.). A message sent to all means that it is publicly available. The table 2 summarizes the computations and exchanges that take place for each card being personalized.

Table 1. Personalization with a trusted center: initialization

Entity	Generates	Sends	To
Issuer			
Manufacturer M_n	(e_{Mn}, d_{Mn})	e_{Mn}	all
Center P_x	(e_{Px}, d_{Px})	e_{Px}	all
		$[d_{Px}]_{e_{Mn}}$	M_n

Table 2. Personalization with a trusted center: processing one card

Entity	Generates	Sends	To
Issuer	$DataC_i$	$[DataC_i]_{e_{Px}}$	P_x
Manufacturer M_n	(e_{Ci}, d_{Ci})	d_{Ci}	C_i
	$\pi_{P_x \to C_i}$	$\pi_{P_x \to C_i}$	all
Center P_x	$Msg = [[DataC_i]_{e_{Px}}]_{\pi_{P_x \to C_i}}$	Msg	C_i

5.2 Personalization with an Untrusted Center

The problem of an untrusted personalization center can be solved if the key pair of a personalization center P_x is generated by the issuer and the secret key d_{Px} is only given to the smart card manufacturer in order to compute the proxy keys when needed. This only modify the initialization phase as shown in table 3.

Table 3. Personalization with an untrusted center: initialization

Entity	Generates	Sends	To
Issuer	(e_{Px}, d_{Px})	$[d_{Px}]_{e_{Mn}}$	M_n
Manufacturer M_n	(e_{Mn}, d_{Mn})	e_{Mn}	all
Center P_x			

In this context a center can no longer retrieve the application's user secret key contained in the issuer's ciphertexts. The first goal of implementing a safe "black–box" in software is achieved. This is a real benefit when dealing with numerous and uncontrolled personalization centers. However, the smart card manufacturer has still to be trusted. It owns both the secret keys of personalization centers and of all smart cards. It would consequently be able to retrieve the plaintext of messages sent by the issuer to the personalization center.

5.3 Personalization with an Untrusted Center and an Untrusted Manufacturer

We refine the previous scheme by adding two other key pairs. The first one, (e_{MnPx}, d_{MnPx}) is generated by the issuer, for each link between a manufacturer M_n and a personalization center P_x. The second one, (e_{PxI}, d_{PxI}) is generated by the personalization center and used to set up a secure channel between it and the issuer. The issuer computes $\pi_{P_x \to MnPx}$ and ships it to the personalization center (using e_{PxI}), keeps d_{Px} unrevealed and sends d_{MnPx} to the manufacturer who will be able to compute $\pi_{MnPx \to C_i}$ for each card. The proxy key $\pi_{P_x \to MnPx}$ must be kept secret by the center P_x.

The initiation phase and the personalization phase are now as shown in the tables 4 and 5.

Table 4. Personalization with an untrusted center and an untrusted manufacturer: initialization

Entity	Generates	Sends	To
Issuer	(e_{Px}, d_{Px})		
	(e_{MnPx}, d_{MnPx})	$[d_{MnPx}]_{e_{Mn}}$	M_n
	$\pi_{Px \to MnPx}$	$[\pi_{Px \to MnPx}]_{e_{PxI}}$	P_x
Manufacturer M_n	(e_{Mn}, d_{Mn})	e_{Mn}	all
Center P_x	(e_{PxI}, d_{PxI})	e_{PxI}	all

Table 5. Personalization with an untrusted center and an untrusted manufacturer: processing one card

Entity	Generates	Sends	To
Issuer	$DataC_i$	$[DataC_i]_{e_{Px}}$	P_x
Manufacturer M_n	(e_{Ci}, d_{Ci})	d_{Ci}	C_i
	$\pi_{MnPx \to C_i}$	$\pi_{MnPx \to C_i}$	all
Center P_x	$Msg = [[[DataC_i]_{e_{Px}}]_{\pi_{Px \to MnPx}}]_{\pi_{MnPx \to C_i}}$	Msg	C_i

To steal the secret data $DataC_i$, an attacker must have access either to the secret key d_{Px} or to both $\pi_{Px \to MnPx}$ and d_{MnPx}. One should note that there is no reason to store d_{Px} when $\pi_{Px \to MnPx}$ has been computed and that the first threat is easy to avoid by destroying d_{Px}. The second threat assumes that an external attacker has to target two sites or that an untrusted party has to collide with another one to succeed.

6   Limitations and Future Work

As all public key algorithms, the computation of χ encryption is costly compared to block–ciphers such as DES. For this reason, this cryptosystem won't be used after the personalization stage. As the ROM capacity of all the available chips is limited, the code of proxy cryptography functions should be located in EEPROM and erased after the personalization.

It should be noticed that a lot of complexity in our scheme is induced by the symmetry of the proxy function and the fact that given a proxy key and a private key it is possible to compute the other private key. The existence of asymmetrical proxy functions could be investigated to avoid this drawback.

Finally, we have not considered an application with multiple issuers. Such a situation would probably lead to a more complex scheme although structurally similar.

7   Conclusion

The new secure personalization schemes introduced in this paper resolve the problem of sharing secret keys between entities (perhaps competing each–other)

within the manufacturing process. The issuer takes a central position and keeps under its control the secret data introduced in the cards. We avoid the usage of costly and unpractical security devices. In addition the schemes can be used by untrusted and uncontrolled parties such as POS.

Acknowledgments. The author is grateful to Pierre Bieber, Jean-Luc Giraud, David Naccache, and Ludovic Rousseau for their corrections, suggestions and improvements.

References

1. Matt Blaze, Gerrit Bleumer, and Martin Strauss. Divertible protocols and atomic proxy cryptography. In Kaisa Nyberg, editor, *Advances in Cryptology EUROCRYPT'98*, volume 1403 of *LNCS*, pages 127–144, Espoo, Finland, May 31 – June 4, 1998. Springer.
2. Matt Blaze and Martin Strauss. Atomic proxy cryptography. TR 98.5.1, AT&T Labs–Research, February 23, 1998. URL: http://www.research.att.com/library/trs.
3. Taher ElGamal. A public-key cryptosystem and a signature scheme based on discrete logarithms. In *Advances in Cryptology: Proceedings of CRYPTO'84*, pages 10–18. Springer–Verlag, 1985.
4. Taher ElGamal. A public-key cryptosystem and a signature scheme based on discrete logarithms. *IEEE Transactions on Information Theory*, IT–31(4):469–472, 1985.
5. H. Krawczyk, M. Bellare, and R. Canetti. HMAC: Keyed-hashing for message authentication. Internet Engineering Task Force, Request for Comments 2104, February 1997.
6. Masahiro Mambo and Eiji Okamoto. Proxy cryptosystem: Delegation of the power to decrypt ciphertexts. *IEICE Transactions on Fundamentals*, E80–A(1):54–63, 1997.
7. Masahiro Mambo, Keisuke Usuda, and Eiji Okamoto. Proxy signatures: Delegation of the power to sign messages. *IEICE Transactions on Fundamentals*, E79–A(9):1338–1354, 1996.

Recent Results on Modular Multiplications for Smart Cards

(Extended Abstract)

J.-F. Dhem[*1] and J.-J. Quisquater[2]

[1] R&D - Gemplus Software - Security,
GEMPLUS Card International,
13881 Gemenos,
France
`jean-francois.dhem@gemplus.com`
[2] Université catholique de Louvain, UCL Crypto Group,
Laboratoire de microélectronique (DICE),
Place du Levant 3, B-1348 Louvain-la-Neuve, Belgium.
`jjq@dice.ucl.ac.be`
`http://www.dice.ucl.ac.be/crypto`

Abstract. In most currently used public-key cryptographic systems, including those based on the difficulty to either factorize large numbers like the RSA [RSA78] or to extract a discrete logarithm of a large number [Elg85,DH76,US 94], the most time consuming part is modular exponentiation. The base of this computation is modular multiplication. We demonstrate the ability to implement very efficiently public-key cryptographic algorithms on nearly standard processors. Furthermore, as our study is also oriented to smart cards, we focus on algorithms minimizing the RAM needed for the computations as well as the ROM code.

1   Introduction

At first glance, a modular reduction is simply the computation of the remainder of an integer division. But as we know, the division is very slow, compared to the other operations, even to the multiplication.

$$A \bmod N = A - \left\lfloor \frac{A}{N} \right\rfloor N$$

To fix the problem, let us examine the number of computations requested for a trivial reduction using the "hand" division method. Suppose we want to calculate the remainder of the division of a $2k$ bit number by a k bit modulus. For that, k subtractions and shifts must be performed on long numbers with in mean $k/2$ restoring (if the result is negative, the previous value must be restored) of k bit

---

* Work done when he was research assistant at the Université catholique de Louvain, Laboratoire de microélectronique (DICE), UCL Crypto Group. See also the thesis [Dhe98]

J.-J. Quisquater and B. Schneier (Eds.): CARDIS 2000, LNCS 1820, pp. 336–352, 2000.
© Springer-Verlag Berlin Heidelberg 2000

numbers to obtain the quotient. After that, it must be multiplied by the modulus before doing the final subtraction to obtain the remainder. By comparison, this is much slower than multiplying two k bits numbers to obtain a $2k$ bit one.

The first progress of the"hand" division was probably the one described in the 1969 edition of Knuth [Knu97] where the quotient is estimated and only a part of the whole division is performed.

Mainly two ways are followed by people implementing modular reduction (multiplications). The first one is done by building an architecture with large data path, larger than 100 bits and the other one by doing computations with more conventional architectures (typically 32 bits). These orientations will greatly influence the algorithms used. With more than 100 bits data paths, every operation will be basic and mainly limited to shifts and additions. On more conventional architectures, hardware multipliers will be intensively used and the clock speed will be generally faster. Algorithms for fast evaluations of quotient may normally be adapted to both methods.

The first well known implementations are the Brickell [Bri83], Sedlak [Sed88], multiplication by the inverse (for example, see Knuth [Knu97] p.312) and computations in residue/redundant number systems (RNS).

Today, the most effective used methods for modular reduction are all variations of the Knuth (improved by Sedlak), Barrett, Quisquater (yet an improvement of Barrett) or Montgomery methods.

After the notations given in section 2, we describe, in section 3, an improved version of Barrett modular reduction algorithm interleaving the modular multiplication. It allows to minimize the error on the quotient reducing its correction during a whole modular exponentiation to only one at the end of the exponentiation. It may be very efficient for RSA exponentiations even when working with intermediate numbers of the size used in conventional CPU (e.g. 32-bits).

In section 4, we extend our results for Barrett to the Quisquater modular reduction algorithm.

In section 5, we compare the previous methods with the well known Montgomery one, we give an optimized software implementation of the algorithms on a standard RISC CPU (the ARM 7M) and we further optimize the implementations giving some small hardware modifications to obtain a nearly optimal software implementation. We compare our various implementations in terms of speed and code size and we conclude that the three algorithms described give very similar results when optimized.

For this extended abstract we omit most proofs: the symbol $(\lozenge)$ will be used to indicate these omissions.

2   Notations

A multi-precision number A may be represented in *radix-b* with $|A| = n \cdot b$: $A = A_{n-1}b^{n-1} + A_{n-2}b^{n-2} + \ldots + A_1 b + A_0$. When working with a processor, we have $b = 2^t$ where t is 32 for a 32-bits processor.

Large integers will be represented by arrays of words. The Most Significant Word (the last word) represents the b most significant bits of the integer. Within a word, the Most Significant Bit represents the most significant bit of this part of the binary representation of the integer.

When modular multiplications are performed on large numbers as for the computation of an RSA, an efficient implementation interleaving the multiplication and the reduction phases dramatically reduce the size of the needed RAM memory.

The interleaving of multiplication and reduction may be seen as follows:

$$AB \bmod N = ((...((A_{n-1}B \bmod N)2^t + A_{n-2}B \bmod N)2^t + ...$$
$$+ A_1 B \bmod N)2^t + A_0 B) \bmod N \qquad (1)$$

This last equation only requires a temporary variable of size $t(n+1)$ instead of $2tn$ for the often used "multiply all and after reduce" method.

3   Improved Barrett Algorithm

The initial algorithm was first proposed by Barrett in 1984 [Bar84,Bar87]. To improve his model we extend here the results introducing more variable parameters [Dhe94]. Some papers expose similar works as Barrett's idea [PP90].

With $n = |N|$, we may write the quotient q as:

$$q = \left\lfloor \frac{U}{N} \right\rfloor = \left\lfloor \frac{\frac{U}{2^{n+\beta}} \frac{2^{n+\alpha}}{N}}{2^{\alpha-\beta}} \right\rfloor$$

β and α are two parameters.

The estimation of the suggested quotient is now (Barrett only considers the case $\alpha = n$ and $\beta = -1$):

$$\hat{q} = \left\lfloor \frac{\left\lfloor \frac{U}{2^{n+\beta}} \right\rfloor \left\lfloor \frac{2^{n+\alpha}}{N} \right\rfloor}{2^{\alpha-\beta}} \right\rfloor \qquad (2)$$

The value

$$R = \left\lfloor \frac{2^{n+\alpha}}{N} \right\rfloor \qquad (3)$$

is constant for a fixed modulus N and may be precomputed. As $|N| = n$ we have $2^\alpha < R < 2^{\alpha+1}$.

The introduction of the new parameter α is of great importance and will allow us to refine the estimation on the quotient.

3.1   Bounds on the Error on the Quotient

The error on the quotient can be limited to 1 when choosing adequate values for the parameters α and β.

The following inequalities occur ($\Diamond$):

$$\left\lfloor \frac{U}{N} \right\rfloor \geq \hat{q} > \left\lfloor \frac{U}{N} \right\rfloor - 2^{\gamma-\alpha} - 2^{\beta+1} - 1 + 2^{\beta-\alpha} \tag{4}$$

The estimated quotient $\hat{q}$ is therefore always smaller than q and it is possible to choose α, β and γ to have a maximal error of 1 on this estimated quotient.

If we want to minimize the error and the computations to evaluate the quotient we must choose $\beta \leq -2$ and $\alpha > \gamma$. R will always be $\alpha + 1$ bits.

3.2   Interleaved Reduction and Multiplication

Suppose that the numbers to multiply, A and B, are smaller than N. It does not decrease the generality of the computations as A and B are generally reduced by N before the modular reduction itself.

Considering Barrett algorithm applied to the computation of each intermediate U_i, we prove that it is possible to improve the speed of the whole computation by correcting the estimated quotient $\hat{q}$ at the end of the whole process. To this purpose, we ensure that the intermediate results are not growing uncontrollably.

If we note e as the error on the quotient, we have ($\Diamond$):

$$(2 + e)2^t - 1 - 2^{t-N} < 2^\gamma \tag{5}$$

Three *important results* can be directly deduced:

- The equation (5) gives the minimum value of γ for an error of e. Since the minimal error on the quotient is 1 ($e = 1$), the first acceptable value of γ is $t + 2$.
- It also proves that $\hat{q}$ will be less than 2^{t+2} since (5) also gives a superior bound of $\hat{q}$ $((2 + e)2^t - 1 - \frac{2^t}{N} < 2^\gamma)$.
- With $e = 1$, if the bit $n + t + 2$ of U_i is a 1, the bit $n + t + 1$ must always be a 0. It also implies that $\hat{q}$ (2), that has maximum $t + 2$ bits has also its bit $t + 1$ always equal to zero when the $t + 2$ equals one. It allows to simply replace the multiplication by $\hat{q}$ by a t-bit multiplication and a conditional addition sometimes shifted left of one bit.

3.3   Choice of the Parameters to Avoid Corrections During a Modular Exponentiation

When doing a modular exponentiation, it may be interesting to see if it will also be possible to bound the computations in such a way that no intermediate correction on the quotient is necessary. To this purpose, we need to fix the parameters so that there is no growth of intermediate results. We suppose here that we already have an error of the quotient of maximum 1 ($e = 1$).

The following theorem can be proved ($\Diamond$):

Theorem 1. *If $A, B < 2^{n+1}$ then $(A \cdot B) \mod N < 2^{n+1}$ if $\gamma \geq t + 2$*

Thus for $\gamma = t + 2$, $\alpha = t + 3$ and $\beta = -2$ we may realize an exponentiation with only one correction at the end of the whole process. Additionally, we can see that it is without additional cost compared to the choices that we have an interleaved modular reduction without additional error corrections.

3.4   Conclusion

The values we obtained when using our modified Barrett method in a (by words) interleaved modular multiplication with a maximal error of 1 ($e = 1$):
$$\alpha = t+3, \; \beta = -2, \; \gamma = t+2, \; R < 2^{t+4}, \; \left\lfloor \frac{U}{2^{n+\beta}} \right\rfloor \text{ and, most important: } \hat{q} < 2^{t+2}$$
with the second bit after the MSB always equal to zero when $|\hat{q}| = t + 2$.

4   Quisquater's Algorithm

This algorithm was first presented by Quisquater at the rump session of Eurocrypt '90 [Qui90,Qui92]. This method has a lot of similarities with the one of Barrett except that the number R is taken here as a normalization factor for the modulus N. The advantage is that the estimation of the quotient is immediate. The method is used in Philips smart card chip P83C852 and P83C855 using CORSAIR crypto coprocessor [QdB91,dWQ91] and P83C858 that uses FAME crypto co-processor [FMM+96]. The same method was proposed later by other people [BW95,Wal91].

When computing $T = U - qN$, the quotient q may be written:

$$q = \left\lfloor \frac{U}{N} \right\rfloor = \left\lfloor \frac{U}{2^{n+c}} \cdot \frac{2^{n+c}}{N} \right\rfloor$$

In Quisquater's method, the reduction is the following one:

$$T = U - \left\lfloor \frac{U}{2^{n+c}} \right\rfloor \cdot \left\lfloor \frac{2^{n+c}}{N} \right\rfloor \cdot N$$

The difference with Barrett's method is that the computations will now be done with a larger modulus $N' = \delta N = \left\lfloor \frac{2^{n+c}}{N} \right\rfloor \cdot N$. This new modulus has its c highest bits equal to 1.

With this new modulus, the evaluation of the new quotient $\hat{q} = \left\lfloor \frac{U}{2^{n+c}} \right\rfloor$ is immediate since it is simply the most significant part of the number to reduce.

We can notice that if the 2'complement $\overline{N'} = 2^{n'} - N'$ is used, the reduction can be computed by $U - \hat{q} \cdot N' = U - \hat{q} \cdot 2^{n'} + \hat{q} \cdot \overline{N'} = U \mod 2^{n'} + \hat{q} \cdot \overline{N'}$

The method needs a denormalization to retrieve the result modulo N. If U' is the remainder modulo N', we have that $T = U \mod N = (U \mod N') \mod N = U' \mod N$. Computing only modulo N', it immediately follows that: $T = \frac{\delta U' \mod N'}{\delta}$.

From this last point, it is obvious that the method is especially efficient when the normalization operations are not the most time consuming. Such a situation appears when doing RSA signatures. We have then to evaluate an expression of the form $C = M^e \bmod N$. If the modulus N is normalized to $N' = \delta N$, the computation of C can be obtained by:

$$C = \frac{\left(\delta(M^e \bmod N')\right) \bmod N'}{\delta}. \tag{6}$$

We have shown [DJQ97] that δ can be very efficiently computed by $\hat{\delta} = \left\lfloor \frac{2^{2c+2}}{N} \right\rfloor$ with $\delta \leq \hat{\delta} \leq \delta + 1$

The value of δ may also often be minimized, reducing the size of N' and thus also the number of computations during the reduction phase [Dhe98].

4.1 Bounds on the Error on the Quotient

A similar result ($\Diamond$) than the one obtained for Barrett can be achieved if the normalization is two bits greater than the size of the first operand of the multiplication. In this case an overflow is avoided and the error on the estimation of the quotient is limited to 1.

4.2 Choice of the Parameters to Avoid Corrections During a Modular Exponentiation

When a RSA is made by using the algorithm, we notice that there may be an overflow caused by the growth of the error on $\hat{q}$. With a t-bit normalization (i.e. $c = t$), it can be shown that the error on the quotient estimation $\hat{q}$ grows by three at each step in the worst case.

It is quite simple to take this overflow into account as done in some versions of Philips CORSAIR chip [dWQ91]. The idea is to provide room for this overflow in an adequate register. In the above realization, the algorithm works with a 24-bit long normalization and a 32-bit long quotient $\hat{q}$. Therefore, there may be at the most 256 overflows, or equivalently, $\lfloor 256/3 \rfloor = 85$ iterations in the interleaved multiplication/reduction (loop) step. The problem of this approach lies on the reduction of the result (up to 256 times) and on the fact that $\hat{q}$ becomes greater, in the worst case, at each iteration involving extra computations.

This problem can be solved by performing a larger normalization. The following Lemma can be proved ($\Diamond$):

Lemma 1. *If a $t + 2$ bit normalization is used, the intermediate result U is bounded by $2^{n'+1}$.*

At each step of the exponentiation process, at each intermediate multiplication, we have a number U that may be greater than the modulus N'. This number may be re-injected in the same algorithm again without intermediate reduction. A final reduction will only be performed at the end of all the successive multiplications.

5   Number of Operations and Implementation

There are basically two approaches for implementing computations on very large
integers. The first one is by using "complex" operations on reduced size integers
and the second one is the use of very simple operations directly on the "very"
large integers. These two methods have their advantages and their drawbacks.
The first one is well suited for "software" implementations on "standards" ALU
(CPU) working on reduced size integers. Nevertheless, it implies some modifications (often minor on carries, memory access,...) in the hardware to obtain the
fastest implementations. On the other hand dedicated hardware [Sed88,Bri83]
using very simple operations like 256-bit additions may be very efficient and
have similar results in terms of speed. Nevertheless, the use of very large busses
requires a large space and the speed of very large adders is often dramatically
reduced due to the time for internal carry propagation. It is also less flexible
than the other method in terms of size of the operands. Using 257 bits numbers
with a 256-bit architecture often takes as long as working on 512-bits numbers!

Our study is focused on the first method since it may be applied to a wide
range of existing hardware and is often more flexible. This choice was also led
by the implementation we did at the same time in CASCADE project funded by
the European Community (see http://www.dice.ucl.ac.be/crypto/cascade) on a
"standard" ARM7M RISC processor.

The following important result in computer arithmetic regarding simultaneous multiplications and additions has important implication on our implementation:

Theorem 2. *If $A, C < b^{\alpha}$ and $B, D < b^{\beta}$ then $A \cdot B + C + D < b^{\alpha+\beta}$*

Such a multiplication with two simultaneous accumulates does not generate
an additional carry.

5.1   Implementation

The programs in pseudo code described here after are very near to a generic
assembly language but with higher level of abstraction for some functions like
loops. It must be clear that languages like C(++), Pascal and other high level
languages are very inefficient for implementations of multi-precision arithmetic.
The main inefficiency is due to the lack of access to carries in the standard
arithmetic operations.

Our implementation is also more suited for processors having several (Rx)
registers of size t, like most RISC processors.

Specific used operations not directly available in C like language are:

- *Addition* with (without) carry. Example: $(C, Rc) = Ra + Rb(+C)$ where C
  is a carry. (C, Rc) means that the result is put in register Rc of size t and
  the bit $t + 1$ (the carry) in C if necessary.

– *Multiplication.* Example: $(Rc, Rd) = Ra*Rb+Rc+Rd$ where (Rc, Rd) means that Rc is the superior part of the result (t MSB) and Rd the inferior one (t LSB).

Globally, the modular multiplication $A \cdot B \bmod N$ will be made in two nested loops. The external one on the number of words in A and the inner one on the ones in B and N.

The graphical representation of the computations for an A_i is shown in figure 1. A rectangle with a light gray line in the middle represents the two registers which are the result of a multiplication. The rectangles aligned vertically must be added. This disposition is similar for every algorithm described.

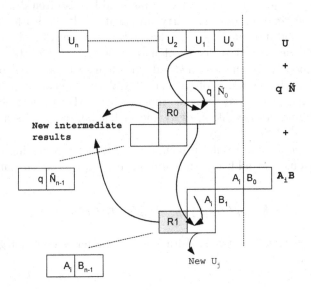

Fig. 1. Interleaved multiplication/reduction with advance on A_i.

As explained before, additional carries are avoided by first doing $(R_0, R_k) = qN_j + R_0 + U_j$ and then $(R_1, U_j) = A_iB_j + R_1 + R_k$ where R_0 and R_1 are temporary registers between iterations on B_j's.

This addition process does not generate any carry between two consecutive iterations which speeds up the implementation. It can be seen that whatever the chosen configurations are, the use of a "conventional" DSP $32 \times 32 + 64$ multiplier generates less simple operations with additional carries that must coexist. Furthermore, these carries are generally not directly available without some manipulations or are purely not available. Indeed, as the carry is not directly reusable in the next multiplication operation but some cycles later, the larger accumulators on most DSP like DSP56000 or TMS320 are not very useful.

An important directive about the implementation is the necessity to minimize memory access. Indeed, the numbers used are too large to be retained in register and the RAM memory accesses are often far slower than working directly with registers. If the external loop is carried out on A, the current value A_i is often maintained in a register but for this value it is also important to avoid multiple accesses to the temporary value U, B and N. The only means to do so is to perform the addition by qN at the same time as the one by A_iB.

Since we cannot know the evaluation of the quotient q in advance, the only way to access U only once per iteration on A_i is to delay by one cycle, the subtraction by q_iN. In other words, at step i, we subtract $q_{i-1}N$ to A_iB. The first loop with the computation of A_0B is done without any subtraction of N and an additional iteration will be added at the end (after treating $A_{n-1}B$ and $q_{n-2}B$) for subtracting $q_{n-1}B$. It takes a lot of space in code size but it is much faster on most architectures.

The detailed pseudo code is given in figure 2 and is organized as follows:

- In the first loop, A_nB is computed to be able to evaluate the first quotient q,
- Two nested loop, the outer one incrementing A_i and the inner one on B_j and N_j,
- The quotient is first evaluated in the outer loop,
- Since the computation on A_i is in advance on the one on q_i, the addition of A_iB is delayed by one cycle with a consequence that the computation of A_iB_0 is put in the outer loop (figure 1),
- qN is subtracted in the inner loop with a test and an addition if q is on 33 bits and an additional shift if it is on 34 bits (see the remark at the end of section 3.2),
- A_iB is added,
- As A_i is in advance, the termination, after the two nested loops is equivalent to one inner loop without the line with $Q * B_i$,
- Finally, U[N] and U[N+1] (two bits in U[N+1]) are the quotient by which U must be reduced in the next outer loop for Quisquater algorithm and the number (minus 2) for computing the quotient in the case of Barrett algorithm.

Since on standard architectures "square" multipliers are used, the multiplication by the 34 bits of q is very inconvenient. Since the two MSB are '1' or '10' it is replaced by a 32 × 32 bit multiplication and a test on the MSB's with conditional additions (with a shift if the MSB is 1).

This fact is very inconvenient for a pure software implementation of Barrett or Quisquater algorithms as compared to a Montgomery implementation.

The quotient evaluation for Quisquater's method is simply the superior part of the computed intermediate value U: $U[n]$ and $U[n+1]$ in figure 2. The computation of $\hat{q}$ (Qh and Ql in lines 9 and 10 in figure 2) for Barrett method is a little more complicated. The additional computations are shown in figure 3 where Rl and Rh respectively contain the inferior ($t = 32$ bits) and the superior (4 bits) part of R defined in equation 3.

```
1:    Rh=0
2:    for  j=0 to  n-1
3:        (Rh,Rl)=A[n-1]B[j]+Rh
4:        U[j]=Rl
5:    endfor
6:    U[n]=Rh
7:    for  i=n-1 to  0
8:        Ra = A[i]
9:        Qh = MSB of U/N
10:       Ql = LSB of U/N
11:       R0 = R1 = tmp = 0
12:       C = C1 =0
13:       Ru=U[0]
14:       Rb=B[0]
15:       (R1,Rl)=Ra·Bb
16:       U[0]=Rl
17:       for  j=1 to  n-1
18:           Rn=N[j-1]
19:           (R0,Rl)=Ql·Rn+Ru+R0
20:           if (Qh==2) then
21:               (C1,Rn)=Rn≪1+C1
22:           if (Qh!=0) then
23:               (C,R0)=R0+Rn+C
24:           Rb=B[j]
25:           (R1,Rl)=Ra·Rb + Rl + R1
26:           Ru=U[j]
27:           U[j]=Rl
28:       endfor
29:       Rn=N[n-1]
30:       (R0,Rl)=Ql·Rn+Ru+R0
31:       if (Qh==2) then
32:           (C1,Rn)=Rn≪1+C1
33:       if (Qh!=0) then
34:           (C,R0)=R0+Rn+C
35:       U[n-1]=Rl
36:       U[n]=R0            // Ru=U[n+1] and U[n+1]=Ru+C+C1
37:       U[n+1]=C+C1        // for Quisquater's method.
38:   endfor
```

Fig. 2. Primary software implementation.

```
(R1,R0) = Ul·Rl
(R1,R0) = R1 + Uh·Rl + Rh·Ul
R1 = R1 + Rh·Uh
Ql = (R0 ≫4) + (R1 ≪ 28)
Qh = R1 ≫ 4
```

Fig. 3. Evaluation of the quotient for Barrett algorithm.

The resulting quotient in Qh and Ql is on $t + 2$ (34) bits (see section 3.2).

This will slow the algorithm as compared to Quisquater one but it is compensated by the fact that Quisquater algorithm needs one additional iteration more for the inner and outer loop of the algorithm since the normalized numbers are larger.

To the algorithm presented here, we should also add the normalization/denormalization phase for Quisquater's method and the additional final test for correcting the error on the quotient. Since these computations are only performed once (or less) for a whole exponentiation (multiplication) and are very fast, they may be considered as second order computations for which the influence on the whole timing is very low.

5.2   Comparison between Barrett and Quisquater Methods

The only difference between Quisquater and Barrett algorithms lies in the computation of the estimated quotient $\hat{q}$ which is immediately available in Quisquater method but must be computed for Barrett's. Indeed, the precomputed value R in Barrett algorithm is the equivalent of δ in Quisquater method.

Both methods use an estimated quotient $\hat{q}$ of $t + 2$ bits.

Barrett's method presents a real advantage if the multiplication $(t+4) \times (t+4)$ can be speeded up or more precisely, if it can be done in the same time as a normal $t \times t$ multiplication. In this case, the additional multiplication appearing n times is superseded by the additional computations needed by Quisquater algorithm which requires one more iteration for the outer and/or the inner loop of the algorithm. Indeed, the modulus is at most 34 bit larger and if an RSA is done, the intermediate values to multiply are also larger since they are the result of a previous calculation.

Furthermore, if the system using one of the algorithms must be able to generate its own modulus, or if the modulus must change very often, Barrett's method is also somewhat more advantageous:

- No denormalization is needed,
- Computations of δ and R are similar but no normalization is necessary.

As a conclusion, it brings advantage to use the modified Barrett's method if a computation $(t + 4) \times (t + 4)$ can be done very efficiently and if the modulus must be changed very often. In terms of code space, if the normalization / denormalization is included, it is also more advantageous. Quisquater's algorithm is preferred if δ may be reduced with, as a consequence, a normalized modulus smaller than 2^{n+t+2}.

5.3   Evaluation of the Number of Operations

We consider multi-precision integers of size n for Barrett's method and size $n+1$ for the Quisquater's one. The size of the intermediate variable U is inferior to $2^{n+\gamma} = 2^{n+t+2}$ for Barrett's algorithm and $2^{n+c'+t+2} = 2^{n+2t+4}$ for the

Quisquater's one. The size of U is then $n + 2$ for Barrett's method and $n + 3$ for the Quisquater's one.

Integers of size $n + 1$ could be multiplied by others of size n for Quisquater's method when doing, for example, a modular exponentiation using the square and multiply method. Indeed, in this case an intermediate value of size $n + 1$ is multiplied by one of size n when doing a multiplication or one of size $n + 1$ is squared in the other case. The inner loop of the algorithm must always be the one with the $n + 1$ iterations as the temporary variable U in this loop must have $n + 1$ elements. This only implies variations in the constant terms in the evaluation of the number of operations and will not influence the results.

We consider four different types of operations for the evaluation of the number of operations since they generally have different timings. Nevertheless, in some processor architectures, some of them may have similar timings and may then be put together.

Moves from registers to registers, additions, tests and shifts are considered as elementary operations with the same timing.

In table 1, the second column represents the number of operations outside the two nested loops, the third one is the operations only in the outer nested loop and the last one the operations located in the inner nested loop. n must be replaced by $n + 1$ in Quisquater's method.

Tests for the conditional instructions (lines 20, 22, 31 and 33 in figure 2) are always executed. But in general, the instruction for the test (Qh!=0) is executed in 50% of the cases and the other test in 25%. Furthermore, since these instructions imply carries which must probably always be saved in registers between two executions, the first case will be considered as a simple instruction and the other one as half of a simple one.

Table 1. Number of operations for a "pure" software implementation.

	external	outer	inner
Elementary	1	$\frac{17}{2}n$	$\frac{7}{2}(n-1)^2$
Multiplications	n	$2n$	$2(n-1)^2$
Read	1	$4n(+n)$	$3(n-1)^2$
Store	n	$4n$	$(n-1)^2$
Loop	n	n	$(n-1)^2$

To table 1, we have to add some additional operations for Barrett quotient estimation. The estimation is very difficult to realize since it implies "small" multiplications that may be speeded up on most hardwares. Considering that a 32×32 multiplication is often executed in four clock cycles (with a 8×32 hardware multiplier) and that the multiplication only takes one cycle if the first 24 bits of the multiplicand are '0', the three multiplications implying that Uh or Rh (figure 3) may be done using a quarter of the operations of the last one. The additional operations are then:

- Multiplications: $\frac{7}{4}n$
- Elementary operations: $3n$

The total number of operations for both methods is then (table 2):

Table 2. Number of operations for Barrett and Quisquater's algorithms.

	Barrett	Quisquater $((n+1) \times (n+1))$
Elementary	$\frac{7}{2}n^2 + \frac{9}{2}n + \frac{9}{2}$	$\frac{7}{2}n^2 + \frac{17}{2}n + \frac{19}{2}$
Multiplications	$2n^2 + \frac{3}{4}n + 2$	$2n^2 + 3n + 3$
Read	$3n^2 - 2n + 4$	$3n^2 + 5n + 6$
Store	$n^2 + 3n + 1$	$n^2 + 5n + 4$
Loop	$n^2 + 1$	$n^2 + 2n + 2$

These results reflect one possible architecture but may vary depending on the architecture used. Implementation of such algorithm is very hardware dependent. As said before, Barrett's algorithm is more advantageous here as in this case, the quotient may be efficiently evaluated and it does not take into account the possible δ reduction for Quisquater method. The small expense for Quisquater's method in terms of memory access is due to the larger normalized numbers that must be fetched to and from memory.

We can also conclude here that both methods give very similar results.

In hardware implementations, the choices made here, due for example to the use of tests, are irrelevant. Hardware tests allow transparent choices. For example, hardware tests on the $t+1$ and $t+2$ bit of $\hat{q}$ permit to directly present a word of N to the adder (or this word shifted right of one bit).

5.4   "Hardware" Implementation

The "software" implementation given before had a major disadvantage due to the impossibility to work with $t + 2$ bit numbers because of the conventional t-bit architectures.

Suppose we have access to a specialized DSP having this capacity to multiply a $t + 2$ bit number with a t bit one. As seen in Theorem 2 we could multiply a $t + 2$ bit number by a t bit one without having an additional carry. This would help us here and directly permit to eliminate the lines with tests in the previous implementation.

Let us call $R0_{ext}$ as the $t + 2$ bits register used in the multiplication. It may simply be an accumulator linked to the multiplier for which the two MSB are only accessible by a shift right of its value as it is in the case for some DSP's.

The pseudo-code is shown in figure 4.

The critical (more time consuming) part of our algorithm is the inner loop. It is written here such that each multiplication is followed by two instructions independent from the multiplication itself.

```
1:   Rh=0
2:   for  j=0 to  n-1
3:        (Rh,Rl)=A[n-1]B[j]+Rh
4:        U[j]=Rl
5:   endfor
6:   U[n]=Rh
7:   for  i=n-1 to  0
8:        Ra = A[i]
9:        Qh = MSB of U/N
10:       Ql = LSB of U/N
11:       R0 = R1 = tmp = 0
12:       C = C1 =0
13:       Ru=U[0]
14:       Rb=B[0]
15:       (R1,Rl)=Ra·Rb
16:       U[0]=Rl
17:       Rk=0
18:       Rn=N[0]
19:       for  j=1 to  n-1
20:            (R0_{ext},Rl)=Ql·Rn + Ru + R0_{ext}
21:            U[j]=Rk
22:            Rb=B[j]
23:            (R1,Rk)=Ra·Rb + Rl + R1
24:            Ru=U[j]
25:            Rn=N[j-1]
26:       endfor
27:       Rn=N[n-1]
28:       (R0_{ext},Rl)=Ql·Rn+Ru+R0_{ext}
29:       U[n-1]=Rl
30:       U[n]=R0
31:       U[n+1]=R0_{ext} ≫ t
32:  endfor
```

Fig. 4. Final version of Barrett/Quisquater pseudo-code.

Therefore it is not a drawback for us to have a multiplication in several cycles, if it is possible to perform other instructions at the same time. Indeed, several processors like Sparc's (namely used in the Sun workstations) have an instruction pipeline allowing to execute several instructions at the same time. The fact that an instruction takes more than one cycle to execute, do not prevent other ones to be carried out. Of course, this is only possible when these instructions do not depend on results of the slower preceding one or if they do not use buses or other parts of the data-path at the same time.

Furthermore, a hardware multiplier is a non negligible part of a CPU. By comparison, a 32×32 multiplier in a standard 0.6 μm technology with two metal layers has a surface near to 1.5 mm^2 and a 32-bit RISC ARM7M processor (with a 8×32 multiplier) has a size inferior to 5 mm^2 in the same technology. A 32×32

multiplier is clearly too large and especially for a smart card. Furthermore, the delay may be important and consequently reduce the speed of the whole processor. Therefore, most microprocessor manufacturers propose multiplication instructions in several cycles with internally smaller multipliers like a 8×32 as in the ARM7M.

Assuming now that the processor has a 8×32 hardware multiplier emulating a 32×32 multiplication in four cycles and the external memory access takes only one cycle for execution, it is then possible to execute the inner loop in only $8n^2$ cycles with this multiplier. *A real one cycle* 32×32 *multiplier would not be able to do it quicker.* Furthermore, if the architecture allows it, it will be possible to carry out the inner loop in $6n^2$ cycles with a 11×32 multiplier.

We have supposed that the **memory accesses** only take **one** cycle. This is not the case on lots of processors but is nevertheless possible with longer pipelines. It also implies a separated bus for data and code or a memory bus working at twice the speed of the CPU. Most of the time spent by our algorithms is used for memory access or multiplication. It is thus very important to have very short cycles also for this memory access. We may think about a sort of memory stack for storing data such that no address has to be computed as they will be automatically incremented or decremented. This kind of implementation may be very efficient for dedicated hardware. It implies very specific hardware like several address counters. We will not discuss this more deeply.

5.5   Timing of our Algorithms with All the Improvements

After all these optimizations, supposing that we may realize with one instruction a multiplication 36×36 in Barrett method and 34×34 in Quisquater one, and that a final reduction is always done for the Montgomery one, the number of operations is given in table 3. The details for the Montgomery implementation can be found in [Dhe98].

Table 3. Optimized number of operations.

	Barrett	Quisquater	Montgomery
Elementary	$5n + 1$	$5n + 6$	$5n + 3$
Multiplications	$2n^2 - n + 2$	$2n^2 + 3n + 2$	$n^2 + \frac{5}{2}n$
Read	$3n^2 - 2n + 4$	$3n^2 + 5n + 6$	$3n^2 + 11n + 1$
Store	$n^2 + 3n + 1$	$n^2 + 5n + 4$	$n^2 + 4n$
Loop	$n^2 + 1$	$n^2 + 2n + 2$	$n^2 + 3n + 1$

This table shows once more that timings are very similar and lead to nearly the same results if hardware optimizations are possible.

To compare, on ARM7M, a memory read takes three cycles, a store, two cycles and the equivalent multiplication, nine cycles. Only for memory access it takes $11n^2$ cycles. The total number of cycles for the inner loop is $29n^2$ without the treat of the loop itself that takes $4n^2$ cycles for decrementing a counter and going back until the value is zero.

Another improvement can be made by implementing a very efficient loop instruction suited for our particular purpose [Dhe98]. The number of needed cycles may be reduced to n^2 and may be combined with a multi-cycle multiplier as well as the read and store operations for minimizing the size of this multiplier without reducing the speed of the overall algorithm.

6 Conclusion

We have presented an alternative to Montgomery modular multiplication algorithm when performing such very efficient computations on new powerful RISC processors usable in smart cards. It allows, with only small modifications to standard processors, to obtain better results (see table 3) than with Montgomery algorithm or other methods using dedicated hardware. Another main advantage when using the modified Barrett or Quisquater methods is that they use a non negligible less overall code space due to the uselessness to implement a heavy normalization/denormalization as in Montgomery method.

References

[Bar84]   P. Barrett. *Communications authentication and security using public key encryption - A design for implementation -*. Master's thesis, Oxford University, Sep 1984.

[Bar87]   P. Barrett. Implementing the Rivest Shamir and Adleman public key encryption algorithm on a standard digital signal processor. In *Advances in Cryptology - CRYPTO '86, Santa Barbara, California* (edited by A.M. Odlyzko), vol. 263 of *LNCS*, pp. 311–323. Springer, 1987.

[Bri83]   E.F. Brickell. A fast modular multiplication algorithm with application to two key cryptography. In *Advances in cryptology Proc. of CRYPTO '82* (edited by D. Chaum, R.L. Rivest and A.T. Sherman), pp. 51–60. Plenum Press, 1983.

[BW95]   J. Benaloh and Wei Dai. Fast modular reduction. Rump Session of CRYPTO '95, Santa Barbara, California, Aug 1995.

[DH76]   W. Diffie and M.E. Hellman. New directions in cryptography. In *IEEE transactions on information theory*, vol. 22, pp. 644–654. IEEE, Nov 1976.

[Dhe94]   J.-F. Dhem. Modified version of the Barrett algorithm. Technical report, Jul 1994.

[Dhe98]   J.F. Dhem. *Design of an efficient public-key cryptographic library for RISC-based smart cards*. Ph.D. thesis, Université catholique de Louvain - UCL Crypto Group - Laboratoire de microélectronique (DICE), May 1998.

[DJQ97]   J.-F. Dhem, M. Joye and J.-J. Quisquater. Normalisation in diminished-radix modulus transformation. In *Electronics letters*, vol. 33, p. 1931, 6th Nov 1997.

[DVQ96]   J.-F. Dhem, D. Veithen and J.-J. Quisquater. SCALPS: Smart Card for Limited Payment Systems. *IEEE Micro*, pp. 42–51, Jun 1996.

[dWQ91]   D. de Waleffe and J.-J. Quisquater. CORSAIR: a smart card for public key cryptosystems. In *Advances in Cryptology - CRYPTO '90, Santa Barbara, California* (edited by A.J. Menezes and S.A. Vanstone), vol. 537 of *LNCS*, pp. 502–513. Springer, 1991.

[Elg85]   T. Elgamal. A public key cryptosystem and a signature scheme based on discrete logarithms. In *IEEE transactions on information theory*, vol. 31, pp. 469–472. IEEE, jul 1985.

[FMM+96]   R. Ferreira, R. Malzahn, P. Marissen, J.-J. Quisquater and T. Wille. FAME: A 3rd generation coprocessor for optimising public key cryptosystems in smart card applications. In *Proc. CARDIS 1996, Smart Card Research and Advanced Applications* (edited by P.H. Hartel, P. Paradinas and J.-J. Quisquater), pp. 59–72. Stichting Mathematisch centrum, CWI, Amsterdam, The Netherlands, Sep 16–18 1996.

[Knu97]   D.E. Knuth. *The art of computer programming*, vol. 2 Seminumerical Algorithms of *Computer science and information processing*. Addison-Wesley, third edn., 1997.

[PP90]   K.C. Posch and R. Posch. Approaching encryption at ISDN speed using partial parallel modulus multiplication. In *Microprocessing and microprogramming, North-Holland*, vol. 29, pp. 177–184, 1990.

[QdB91]   J.-J. Quisquater, D. de Waleffe and J.-P. Bournas. CORSAIR: A chip with fast RSA capability. In *Proc. Smart Card 2000* (edited by D. Chaum), pp. 199–205. Elsevier Science Publishers, Amsterdam, 1991.

[Qui90]   J.-J. Quisquater. Procédé de codage selon la méthode dite RSA, par un microcontrôleur et dispositifs utilisant ce procédé. Demande de brevet français. No de dépôt 90 02274, 23 Fev 1990.

[Qui92]   J.-J. Quisquater. Encoding system according to the so-called RSA method, by means of a microcontroller and arrangement implementing this system. U.S. Patent # 5,166,978, Nov 24, 1992.

[RSA78]   R.L. Rivest, A. Shamir and L. Adleman. A method for obtaining digital signatures and public-key cryptosystems. In *Proc. Communications of the ACM*, vol. 21, pp. 120–126. ACM, Feb 1978.

[Sed88]   H. Sedlak. The RSA cryptography processor. In *Advances in Cryptology - EUROCRYPT '87, Amsterdam, The Netherlands* (edited by D. Chaum and W.L. Price), vol. 304 of *LNCS*, pp. 95–105. Springer, 1988.

[US 94]   US DEPARTMENT OF COMMERCE - National Institute of Standards and Technology. FIPS PUB 186: Digital Signature Standard (DSS), May 19, 1994.

[Wal91]   C.D. Walter. Faster modular multiplication by operand scaling. In *Advances in Cryptology - CRYPTO '91, Santa Barbara, California* (edited by J. Feigenbaum), vol. 576 of *LNCS*, pp. 313–323. Springer, 1991.

RSA Signature Algorithm for Microcontroller Implementation

Guopei Qiao and Kwok-Yan Lam

Dept of Computer Science
National University of Singapore
S119260, Singapore

Abstract. In this paper, we present a fast method for generating RSA signature. The method is based on the Chinese Remainder Theorem and Wiener's conjecture. Using this method, one can efficiently generate a RSA signature on a low-cost microcontroller. Hence it is suitable for the MCU IC in a typical smart card.

Keywords. Fast RSA Signature Algorithm, Microcontroller, Smart card, Chinese Remainder Theorem.

1 Introduction

Digital signature is an essential mechanism for enabling electronic commerce. Most of the widely used public key signature algorithms are based on computing intensive operations such as modular exponentiation. In fact, the Secure Electronic Transaction (SET) payment mechanism developed by major credit card companies adopted the 1024-bit RSA algorithm for generating electronic signatures.

With today's microprocessor technology, an ordinary personal computer can generate a 1024-bit RSA signature in the order of milliseconds. This makes it realistic for electronic commerce applications on home computers. However, it is dangerous to store the private key, and generate RSA signatures, on a personal computer because of virus threats, potential design flaws in Internet browsers, as well as the possibility of hostile JAVA applets from malicious web sites. It is therefore highly desirable to store the private key and perform signature operations outside of the PC memory. Portable intelligent devices such as smart cards, or intelligent smart card readers, are obvious choices for meeting the security requirements of electronic commerce applications.

Nevertheless, low-cost microcontrollers typical in smart cards are not powerful enough to generate 1024-bit RSA digital signatures within the acceptable timeframe of several seconds. In order to surmount this difficulty, many methods based on the concept of server-aided computation were developed [6,7]. However, almost all of the server-aided schemes are considered insufficiently secure under stringent security assumptions. Burns and Mitchell [2] presented another method to overcome this problem, which uses small private keys to accelerate

J.-J. Quisquater and B. Schneier (Eds.): CARDIS 2000, LNCS 1820, pp. 353–356, 2000.

the computation of signature. With this method, the private key can be chosen to be at least 128 bits long in order to withstand Shank's baby-step-giant-step search attack [5]; however, the corresponding public key must be at least 1.5 times longer than the modulus due to Wiener's attack [1]. In this paper, we present a new method for speeding up the signature operations by means of short private keys.

2   The New Method

The design of this new method is based on the Chinese Remainder Theorem while its security is based on an open problem of Weiner's [1]. Weiner pointed out that one could reduce the signature generation time by choosing a private key s such that both $s_p = s \bmod (p-1)$ and $s_q = s \bmod (q-1)$ are small, and $s_p \neq s_q$. However, the probability of having a randomly chosen private key satisfying this condition is very low. In the following, we give a method for creating such a private key.

According to the generalized Chinese Remainder Theorem, s_p and s_q must satisfy $\gcd(p-1, q-1) | s_p - s_q$, where $a|b$ means that a divides b; and we can also construct s that satisfies the congruences

$$s = s_p \bmod (p-1), s = s_q \bmod (q-1)$$

if we choose two numbers s_p, s_q such that $\gcd(p-1, q-1) | s_p - s_q$. Since s is the private key, we have that $s \cdot e = 1 \bmod lcm(p-1, q-1)$, and $\gcd(s_p, p-1) = \gcd(s_q, q-1) = 1$. If we choose p, q such that $\gcd(p-1, q-1) = 2$, then $2|s_p - s_q$. For generating RSA keys, we usually require that p and q are strong primes, in this case the probability that $\gcd(p-1, q-1) = 2$ are very high, so most RSA keys satisfy this condition.

Therefore, we choose secret s such that $s_p - s_q = 2$, so for the private key of the RSA with CRT, we only need to store p, q and s_q. Our key generation algorithm is as follows:

1. Randomly choose a pair of large strong primes p and q such that $\gcd(p-1, q-1) = 2$.
2. Randomly choose a k-bit natural number s_q such that

$$\gcd(s_q, q-1) = \gcd(s_q + 2, p-1) = 1.$$

3. Compute

$$s = (s_q + (q-1)((\frac{q-1}{2})^{-1} \bmod \frac{p-1}{2})) \bmod lcm(p-1, q-1).$$

If $l(s) < min\{l(p), l(q)\}$ or $\gcd(s, lcm(p-1, q-1)) \neq 1$, go to step 2.
4. Output the private s_q, p, q and public key $e = s^{-1} \bmod lcm(p-1, q-1)$.

The signature S of message M can be computed using the Chinese remainder theorem as follows [3]:

$$S = ((S_p - S_q)w \bmod p)q + S_q$$

where $S_p = M^{s_p} \bmod p$, $S_q = M^{s_q} \bmod q$, and $w = q^{-1} \bmod p$.

To compute a RSA signature using this scheme, we need at most $2 * l(s_p) + 2 * l(s_q) + 1$ half-sized modular multiplications where $l(x)$ represents the length (in bits) of integer x. Note that the system parameter k controls the size of s_p and s_q and hence determines the efficiency of the modular exponentiation. In order to allow signatures to be generated efficiently, one needs to choose a small value for k. Whereas this parameter also controls the security level of the system. Hence there is a trade-off between the security level and efficiency when choosing the value of k.

3   Choosing the Parameters

First of all, one can attack this algorithm by a brute-force search for s_p or s_q. The cryptanalyst may pick any value s_p' and compute $G = gcd(N, (S - M^{s_p}) \bmod N)$. If $s_p' = s_p$, then there is a high probability that G equals to p. Since s_p and s_q must be odd, one can break this scheme by searching all k-bit odd numbers, i.e. $O(2^{k-1})$. In order to achieve a (2^{60})-level security, we may choose k to be 64.

Nevertheless, it was pointed out that this search can be improved by means of the Baby-Step Giant-Step method [9] as follows:

1. Divide the s_p into two parts s_h and s_l, where $s_p = s_h 2^r + s_l$, $l(s_h), l(s_l) \leq r$ and $r = \lceil k/2 \rceil$.
2. Compute two lists, say, L_1 and L_2: L_1 consists of numbers of the form $M^{r_1 2^r} \bmod N$ and L_2 consists of numbers of the form $SM^{-r_2} \bmod N$, where r_1 and r_2 represent all r bits numbers.
3. When $r_1 * 2^r + r_2 = s_p$, the lists L_1 and L_2 will have a common element modulo p, since $M^s = M^{s_p} \bmod p$.

The technique of Strassen [8] can be used to find a repetition modulo p in a list of numbers known only in modulo N. The time complexity of the technique is $L^{1+\epsilon}$ where $L = |L_1| + |L_2| = 2^{r+1}$. Hence the complexity of attack is reduced to $O(2^{\frac{k}{2}+\epsilon})$. For the (2^{60})-level security, we must choose $k = 128$. Note that this improved search needs 2^{r+1} intermediate results to be stored, thus each search step is much slower than that in the original search.

For experimental analysis, we choose $k = 96$ since it will be secure enough to withstand the above attacks in practice. Experimental results showed that when $k = 96$, this scheme can generate a RSA signature using approximately 200 half-sized modular multiplications. With a fast modular multiplication algorithm [4], a 1024-bit signature can be generated in 0.04 seconds by a 120MHZ Pentium PC. Suppose that the microcontroller in a typical smart card is 100 times slower than the Pentium 120 microprocessor, a 1024-bit signature can be generated in about four seconds by a smart card. It is therefore suitable for implementation in a low-cost smart card.

4 Conclusion

In this paper, we presented a new method for generating RSA signatures in a low-cost microcontroller environment. The security of this scheme is based on an open problem of Weiner's. Experimental results showed that this RSA signature operations can be performed efficiently by a low-cost microcontroller. Hence it can be used to implement signature operations in a smart card or a low-cost intelligent smart card reader. Unlike server-aided schemes, our method does not require the participation of the host computer. This method is therefore suitable for applications, such as payment protocols in electronic commerce, that require a secure environment for generating digital signatures and yet is affordable to ordinary PC users.

Acknowledgement. The authors would like to thank Dr R.G.E Pinch for helpful comments about the security of algorithm.

References

1. M. J. Wiener, Cryptanalysis of short RSA secret exponents, IEEE Trans. Information Theory, vol. IT-36, pp.553-558,1990.
2. J. Burns and C.J. Mitchell, Parameter Selection for Server-aided RSA Computation Schemes, IEEE Trans. on Computers, vol.43, pp.163-174, 1994.
3. J.J. Quisquater and C. Couvreur, Fast Decipherment Algorithm for RSA Public-key Cryptosystem, Electron. Lett., vol.18, no.21, pp.905-907, Oct.1982.
4. C.K. Koc, T. Acar and B.S. Kaliski, Analyzing and Comparing Montgomery Multiplication Algorithms, IEEE Micro, pp.26-33, June 1996.
5. A.J. Menezes, Elliptic Curve Public Key Cryptosystems, Kluwer Academic Publishers, pp.50, 1993.
6. P. Beguin and J. J. Quisquater, Fast Server-Aided RSA Signatures Secure Against Active Attacks, Crypto'95, pp.57-69.
7. C.H. Lim and P.J. Lee, Security and Performance of Server-aided RSA Computation Protocols, Crypto'95, pp.70-83.
8. V. Strassen, Einige Resultate über Berechnungskomplexität, Jahresber. Deutsch. Math.-Verein. 78 (1976/77), pp.1-8
9. R.P.E. Pinch, Private Communication, May 1997.

Efficient Ways to Implement Elliptic Curve Exponentiation on a Smart Card

Alain Durand

Oberthur Smart Cards
12 bis rue des Pavillons
92804 Puteaux Cedex, France

Abstract. Most of publications on Elliptic Curve Cryptosystem implementations concentrates on characteristic 2 case. We show here that advantage can be taken of the good performances of processors or coprocessors to compute RSA ([4]) calculus to get fast implementations of elliptic curve exponentiation in a field of characteristic p. We compare also known and less known algorithms performances to make this calculus.

1 Introduction

The main asymmetric cryptographic algorithm nowadays used by smart card is RSA ([4]). Thus, many card manufacturers such as SGS-Thomson, Motorola or Philips have developed specific coprocessors or modified existing processors to speed up the RSA calculus and then the modular multiplication. RSA cryptosystem presents the main inconvenient to repose on the factorization problem. Works of many mathematicians have been for years concentrating on this problem. 1024 bits modulus size is now generally considered as minimal. This makes harder its implementation on a smart card which has only a little RAM size.

Elliptic Curve Cryptosystem reposes on the discrete logarithm problem. This problem better resists (until today) to the cryptographic community attacks. It presents the advantage to use smaller key size which speed up the computations and saves some RAM. Thus, it can appear as a good replacement solution to RSA cryptosystem. Implementations in characteristic 2 have been widely studied because of their good fitness to microprocessors environment. It presents two major drawbacks :

- it requires to design specific processors or coprocessors to speed up the calculus.
- optimizations are often linked to a specific field : it's not flexible.

Furthermore, until the next few years, chips will still have to keep the ability to make RSA calculus for marketing reasons. A processor speeded up for both calculus would be much more expensive.

We try to show here that advantage can be taken of the optimizations made for RSA calculus to obtain fast implementation of elliptic curve exponentiation

J.-J. Quisquater and B. Schneier (Eds.): CARDIS 2000, LNCS 1820, pp. 357–365, 2000.
© Springer-Verlag Berlin Heidelberg 2000

in characteristic p where p is a prime number. The framework of this article is not to find optimizations valid for only specific fields but to explore which algorithm is the best for any field.

The most adapted algorithm to compute elliptic curve exponentiation is the left to right binary method because of its poor memory requirements. This algorithm can be speeded up with some precomputations but the available size on a smart card is generally not sufficient to their storage.

Algorithm 1. Left to right binary method.

INPUT : P, a point on an elliptic curve $(E) : y^2 = a.x^3 + b.x + c$;
a positive integer e whose sparse signed-digit representation with radix 2 is $(e_{t-1}, e_{t-2}, \cdots, e_0)$ (e_i can be 0,1 or -1).
OUTPUT : $e.P$.

1. $A \leftarrow e_{t-1}.P$
2. For i from $t - 2$ to 0 do the following
   a) $A \leftarrow 2.A$
   b) If $e_i \neq 0$, $A = A + e_i.P$
3. Return(A)

The signed-digit representation is to be preferred to the binary one since computing the opposite of a point does not require any extra calculus. It allows to save one third of the multiplications (see [1]). Thus, the expected numbers of doubling of the above algorithm will be $t - 1$ and the expected number or adding (or subtracting) will be $\frac{t-1}{3}$.

We remind the addition formula in non-projective coordinates :
If $P = (x_1, y_1)$ and $Q = (x_2, y_2)$, we note $P + Q = (x_3, y_3)$ and we have :

$$x_3 = \lambda^2 - x_1 - x_2$$

$$y_3 = \lambda(x_1 - x_3) - y_1$$

where

$$\lambda = \begin{cases} \dfrac{y_2 - y_1}{x_2 - x_1}, \text{ if } P \neq Q \\ \dfrac{3x_1^2 + a}{2y_1}, \text{ if } P = Q \end{cases}$$

As we see, each addition or doubling involves one modular division, two modular multiplications and four modular additions. As the cost of the multiplications and the additions is negligible compared with the division one, we will from now consider only the latter, which cost is crucial.

Most of the cryptoprocessors can compute a modular inverse. But, this operation is often not optimized since it will be only used once to compute the CRT constants of an RSA calculus. For instance, the algorithm used by ST-coprocessors is the modular exponentiation with an exponent $\varphi(n) - 1$. As we will see, it is not envisageable to use this algorithm to compute a modular exponentiation on an elliptic curve because it would not be efficient.

Overview We are presenting five methods to compute the modular division. Three of them are the extension of three well-known GCD's algorithms : Euclidean algorithm, Stein's algorithm and Lehmer's algorithm. Another is less known. It's obtained from Stein's algorithm by the same way as Lehmer's algorithm is from the Euclidean one. Finally, we will try to avoid most of the modular inversions by using projective coordinates.

2   Extended Euclidean Algorithm and Extended Stein's Algorithm

We present here the two most famous extended GCD's algorithm. As in the present case we can assume that GCD will always be 1, we have a little modified them in order to improve the inverse calculus. Usual description of these algorithms can be found in [3] while their analysis is made in [2].

Algorithm 2. Extended Euclidean Algorithm

INPUT : n and y, two coprimes integers so that $y < n$.
OUTPUT : $y^{-1} \bmod n$.

1. $b \leftarrow 0$; $d \leftarrow 1$
2. while $y > 1$ do
   a) $q \leftarrow \lfloor \frac{n}{y} \rfloor$; $r \leftarrow n - q.y$; $t \leftarrow b - q.d$
   b) $n \leftarrow y$; $y \leftarrow r$; $b \leftarrow d$; $d \leftarrow t$
3. if $d < 0$ then $d \leftarrow d + n$.
4. Return(d)

Proof (Sketch). It's easy to see by induction that the two following identities always holds :
$$b.y_0 = n \bmod n_0$$
$$d.y_0 = y \bmod n_0$$
where n_0 and y_0 are the initial values of variables n and y. As the sequence of the (y) decreases strictly and as we assumed that n_0 and y_0 where coprime, the value $y = 1$ will be reached. The fact that $|d|$ is bounded by n_0 is well known and can be easily deduced from the usual description of the algorithm.

Analysis. We can find in [2] the average number of divisions in algorithm 2 :

$$\tau_n = \frac{12 \ln 2}{\pi^2} \ln n + 0.467 \approx 0.584.log_2(t) + 0.467$$

We can also note that the inequality $b.d \leq 0$ always hold : t is obtained in fact by addition.

The main operation involved here is the euclidean division. This operation is very expensive : most of the processors don't have any division instruction and the overhead in this operation (normalization and unnormalization particuraly) is huge. However, processors in which RSA has been implemented (and optimized) with the standard multiplication-division algorithm can dispose of a good division algorithm.

Stein's algorithm replaces all the expensive integer division by division by 2 which can be made only by right shifts with carry propagation.

Algorithm 3. Extended Stein's Algorithm

INPUT : n, x and y three integers with n odd, $x < n$, $y < n$ and $\gcd(y, n) = 1$
OUTPUT : $x.y^{-1} \bmod n$

1. $v \leftarrow n$; $c \leftarrow 0$;
2. while $x > 1$ or $v > 1$ do the following
   a) while y even do
      i. $y \leftarrow y/2$
      ii. if x even, $x \leftarrow x/2$ else $x \leftarrow \frac{x+n}{2}$
   b) while v even do
      i. $v \leftarrow v/2$
      ii. if c even, $c \leftarrow c/2$ else $c \leftarrow \frac{c+n}{2}$
   c) If $y > v$,
      then $y \leftarrow y - v$ and $x \leftarrow x - c$. If $x < 0$, $x \leftarrow x + n$
      else $v \leftarrow v - y$ and $c \leftarrow c - x$. If $c < 0$, $c \leftarrow c + n$
3. if $v = 1$, return(c) else return(x).

Proof (Sketch). It's easy to see by induction that the two following identities always hold :

$$c.y_0 = x_0.v \bmod n$$

$$x.y_0 = x_0.y \bmod n$$

where x_0 and y_0 are the initial values of variables x and y. As the sequences of the (y) and the (v) decrease strictly and as we assumed that n and y_0 where coprime, the value $v = 1$ will be reached. It is easy to see that all along the algorithm, tha values taken by c and x are positive and less than n.

Analysis. The first remark is that the algorithm allows to make directly a modular division. In the Euclidean algorithm we could have initialized d by x instead of by 1 but each multiplication should have been replaced by a modular one.

Knuth ([2]) showed that the average number of steps involving divisions by 2 (which are in fact simple right shifts) is $1.41.t - 2.7$ and that of steps involving subtractions is $0.7.t - 0.5$. The number of steps is higher than in the Euclidean algorithm but each step involves only additions, subtractions or right shifts. These operations are much more simple than those of Euclidean algorithm and we will see that Stein's algorithm is more efficient than the Euclidean one.

3   Extended Lehmer's Algorithm

In the extended Euclidean algorithm, we said that the most expensive step was the multiple-precision division. The main idea of the Lehmer's algorithm is to simulate most of the multiple-precision division steps by simple-precision division steps. This idea has come from the constat that more than 99.8 % of the quotients computed in the Euclidean algorithm are less than 1000 (see [2]).

The algorithm is the following :

Algorithm 4. Extended Lehmer's Algorithm

INPUT : n and y, two coprimes integers such that $y < n$; w the processor word size.
OUTPUT : $y^{-1} \bmod n$.

1. $v \leftarrow n$; $A \leftarrow 0$; $C \leftarrow 1$.
2. while $y \geq 2^w$, do the following
   a) If h is the bit length of string v, set $\tilde{v} \leftarrow \lfloor \frac{v}{2^{h-w}} \rfloor$ and $\tilde{y} \leftarrow \lfloor \frac{y}{2^{h-w}} \rfloor$
   b) $a \leftarrow 1$; $b \leftarrow 0$; $c \leftarrow 0$; $d \leftarrow 1$.
   c) while $\tilde{y} + c \neq 0$ do
      i. $q \leftarrow \lfloor \frac{\tilde{v}+a}{\tilde{y}+c} \rfloor$.
      ii. if $\tilde{v} + b - q * (\tilde{y} + d) < 0$ goto step 2d
      iii. $t \leftarrow a - q.c$; $a \leftarrow c$; $c \leftarrow t$.
      iv. $t \leftarrow b - q.d$; $b \leftarrow d$; $d \leftarrow t$.
      v. $t \leftarrow \tilde{v} - q.\tilde{y}$; $\tilde{v} \leftarrow \tilde{y}$; $\tilde{y} \leftarrow t$.
   d) if $b = 0$ do the following :
      i. $t \leftarrow v \bmod y$; $q \leftarrow \lfloor \frac{v}{y} \rfloor$; $v \leftarrow y$; $y \leftarrow t$.
      ii. $t \leftarrow A - q.C$; $A \leftarrow C$; $C \leftarrow T$.
      else do
      i. $t \leftarrow a.v + b.y$; $y \leftarrow c.v + d.y$; $v \leftarrow t$.
      ii. $t \leftarrow a.A + b.C$; $C \leftarrow c.A + d.C$; $A \leftarrow t$.
3. Thanks to the usual extended Euclidean algorithm, compute a and b such that $a.y + b.v = 1$.
4. $A \leftarrow a.A + b.C$.
5. if $A < 0$ then $A \leftarrow A + n$.
6. Return(A).

Proof (Sketch). Instead of computing the same quotient as in the Euclidean algorithm, the computed quotient is a value by excess of this quotient. Then we compare it to a value by default (in fact, we compare it to $q' \leftarrow \lfloor \frac{\tilde{v}+b}{\tilde{y}+d} \rfloor$ but the solution proposed above avoids an extra division). If the two values are the same, there is no need to make the whole division. The algorithm just computes the coefficient of the extended Euclidean algorithm to keep track of the made operations. If they are not equal, we compute the result of all the precedents simulations or, if there were no simulation step (condition $B = 0$), we would compute a normal step of the Euclidean algorithm.

Analysis. The first thing to emphasize is that, in the main loop, only the step 2d is a multiple-precision step. The second thing is the initialization of values $\tilde{y}$ and $\tilde{v}$: We must *not* take the most significant digit of the basis 2^w representation (as suggested in [2] and [3]) but the w leading bits : That way, the very expensive step of multiple-precision division will scarcely happen (it occurs 0.4 % of the time against almost 25 % of the time in the other way). Jon Sorenson gave in [5] an analysis of a slightly modified version of the algorithm : The number of iterations of the main loop is $O(\frac{t}{w} + w)$. As we will see, this algorithm is much faster than the Stein's one.

4 Applying Lehmer's Idea to Stein's Algorithm

As we did for the Euclidean algorithm, we could try to simulate most of the multiple-precision steps of the Stein's algorithm by single-precision one. Knuth (see [2]) suggested the main ideas to build this algorithm (in a non-extended version) and asserted that its implementation was much faster than Lehmer's one. The full description of the algorithm is not given. We provide it here in its extended version.

Algorithm 5. Stein's algorithm for big numbers

INPUT : n, x and y three integers with $x < n$, $y < n$ and $\gcd(y, n) = 1$; w the word size of the processor.
OUTPUT : $x.y^{-1} \bmod n$

1. Compute $R \leftarrow 2^{-w} \bmod n$ thanks to an optimized Stein's algorithm.
2. $v \leftarrow n$; $A \leftarrow 1$; $C \leftarrow 0$.
3. While $y > 1$ or $v > 1$ do the following :
   a) $a \leftarrow 1$; $b \leftarrow 0$; $c \leftarrow 0$; $d \leftarrow 1$.
      $ly \leftarrow y \bmod 2^w$; $lv \leftarrow v \bmod 2^w$.
   b) If h is the bit length of string v, set $mv \leftarrow \lfloor \frac{v}{2^{h-w}} \rfloor$ and $my \leftarrow \lfloor \frac{y}{2^{h-w}} \rfloor$;
      $sh \leftarrow 0$.
   c) while $sh < w$ and $ly \neq lv$ do the following
      i. While ly even and $sh < w$
         $ly \leftarrow \frac{ly}{2}$, $mv \leftarrow 2.mv$, $c \leftarrow 2.c$, $d \leftarrow 2.d$, $sh \leftarrow sh + 1$.
      ii. While lv even and $sh < w$
         $lv \leftarrow \frac{ly}{2}$, $my \leftarrow 2.my$, $a \leftarrow 2.a$, $b \leftarrow 2.b$, $sh \leftarrow sh + 1$.
      iii. if $sh = w$ or $ly = lv$ goto 3d.
      iv. if $my \geq mv$, $my \leftarrow my - mv$, $a \leftarrow a - c$, $b \leftarrow b - d$, $ly \leftarrow ly - lv$
         else $mv \leftarrow mv - my$, $c \leftarrow c - a$, $d \leftarrow d - b$, $lv \leftarrow lv - ly$.
   d) if $sh < w$ $a \leftarrow a.2^{w-sh}$, $b \leftarrow b.2^{w-sh}$, $c \leftarrow c.2^{w-sh}$, $d \leftarrow d.2^{w-sh}$
   e) if $a = 0$, $v \leftarrow \frac{c.y+d.v}{2^w}$; if $v < 0$, $v \leftarrow -v$, $c \leftarrow -c$ and $d \leftarrow -d$.
      $C \leftarrow (c.A + d.C).R \bmod n$; go to step 3.
   f) if $d = 0$, $y \leftarrow \frac{a.y+b.v}{2^w}$; if $y < 0$, $y \leftarrow -y$, $a \leftarrow -a$ and $b \leftarrow -b.A \leftarrow$
      $(a.A + b.C).R \bmod n$; go to step 3.

g) $t \leftarrow \frac{a.y+b.v}{2^w}$; if $t < 0$, $t \leftarrow -t$, $a \leftarrow -a$ and $b \leftarrow -b$. $v \leftarrow \frac{c.y+d.v}{2^w}$; if $v < 0$, $v \leftarrow -v$, $c \leftarrow -c$ and $d \leftarrow -d$. $y \leftarrow t$.

h) $t \leftarrow (a.A + b.C).R \bmod n$; $C \leftarrow (c.A + d.C).R \bmod n$; $A \leftarrow t$.

4. if $y = 1$, return(A) else return(C).

Proof (Explanations). Stein's algorithm's steps are leaded by two things : Which of y or v is the greater and what is their parity. Thus, we have to keep track of both w least significant and most significant bits of these words. Steps 3(c)i and 3(c)ii enable the simulation : if we want to restore values of A and C at the end of the single-precision step, we can't allow steps of division by 2 (because we may need to add n to get the good parity). So, we replaced it by multiplication by 2 of the other value (if ly is odd, we multiply mv, c and d by 2 and inversely). We should also multiply lv by 2 (thus, ly and lv would be both multiple of 2^{sh}) but we prefer keep track of the parity. This way, new values calculated for y and v are both divisible by 2^w which implies no multiple-precision right shifts but just a pointer incrementation. To obtain right values for A and C, we have to multiply by the inverse of 2^w.

Analysis. While designing the algorithm we met essentially two problems. The first was to keep a good track of the greatest element. As we can't care with word carry propagation, my and mv can only be estimations of the greatest one (that's why we have to check the new sign of y and v). So, we could either design the algorithm such that calculus involving mu and mv were only single-precision (and having a greatest imprecision) or allow double-precision calculus and avoid most of the sign regularisation step. Simulations have showed that the latter gave the best performances. The other problem was to get the right values for A and C. We could either count the number of main loop iterations and reduce the value of A at the end or reduce both values at each step. The former was implying to handle with very large values for A and C whereas the latter was forcing to make modular multiplications at each step. Simulations have again showed which was the best solution.

Each iteration of the main loop corresponds to the usual Stein's algorithm on two w-bits words. Then, if we made $1.41.w$ steps of shifting, we would reduce the greatest value of y and v by one word at each iteration. As we only make w shifts, we only reduce the size by on average $\frac{w}{1.41}$ bits. Thus, we will need in average $1.41\lceil\frac{t}{w}\rceil$ iterations of the main loop to terminate the algorithm. It means that we reduced the number of steps by w comparing with Stein's algorithm. But, as we need the extended version of the algorithm, we have to handle with modular multiplication at each step. This involves a big overhead. Even if this algorithm was faster than the Lehmer's one in a non-extended version, we would see that this overhead is too important to keep this advantage.

5   Using Projective Coordinates

All the modular divisions except one could be avoided by the use of projective coordinates. It means that we introduce a third coordonnate z and that we consider that two points $P(x, y, z)$ and $Q(x', y', z')$ are equivalent if there is λ such that $(x', y', z') = \lambda(x, y, z)$. Thus, we can find another addition law on the elliptic curve that induces no inversion. At the end of the elliptic curve exponentiation, a modular inversion (using one of the above algorithms) has to be performed to obtain the unique element of the equivalent class such that $z = 1$.

In the left-to-right binary exponentiation algorithm, we have two figures : either we have to double a point $P(x_1, y_1, z_1)$ or we have to add P with $Q(x_2, y_2, 1)$. We note (x_3, y_3, z_3) the coordonates of the result and we have in the former case :

$$\begin{cases} x_3 = B(z_1 A^2 - 2x_1 B^2) \\ y_3 = 3x_1 AB^2 - z_1 A^3 - y_1 B^3 \\ z_3 = z_1 B^3 \end{cases} \quad \text{with} \quad \begin{aligned} A &= 3x_1{}^2 + a z_1{}^2 \\ B &= 2y_1 z_1 \end{aligned}$$

In the second case, we will have :

$$\begin{cases} x_3 = B[z_1 A^2 - (x_1 + x_2 z_1)B^2] \\ y_3 = (2x_1 + x_2 z_1)AB^2 - z_1 A^3 - y_1 B^3 \\ z_3 = z_1 B^3 \end{cases} \quad \text{with} \quad \begin{aligned} A &= y_1 z_2 - y_2 z_1 \\ B &= x_1 z_2 - x_2 z_1 \end{aligned}$$

Analysis. We can see that almost 18 multiple-precision multiplications are needed for each case.

6   Conclusion

All the above algorithms have been tested on a RISC 32-bit processor from SGS-Thomson, the ST20-C1. This processor was initially not designed for cryptographic purposes. We give now evaluations for 1024 bits RSA exponentiation and 160 bits elliptic curve exponentiations. **These evaluations are given according to OSC Implementation.**

Table 1. ST20-C1 Running Time Evaluations

ST20-C1 @40 MHz	Operation	Size (bits)	Inner Loop Iterations	Running Time (ms)
RSA	$x \to x^d[n]$	1024	1537	1 212
Inverse calculus by $x^{-1} = x^{\varphi(n)-1}$	$n \to n.P$	160	239	1 485
Extended Euclidean	$n \to n.P$	160	94	594
Extended Stein's	$n \to n.P$	160	223	306
Extended Lehmer's	$n \to n.P$	160	10	144
Stein's for big numbers	$n \to n.P$	160	7.5	372
Projective coordinates	$n \to n.P$	160	239	249

These data allow us to see that Lehmer's algorithm seems to be the best for this size of modulus. We also see that the version adapted for big numbers of Stein's algorithm is more expensive than the usual one. It is mainly due to the modular multiplications (more than 66 % of the time is spent in these operations).

The second thing we can underline is the good efficiency of the elliptic curve exponentiation : While RSA exponentiation performance cannot be seen as sufficient, we have very good performances for that exponentiation without any further optimization.

Within MASSC (Multi-Application Secure Smart Card) project, ST20-C1 has been optimized for RSA calculation to give the processor ST22-SC1. We made the same evaluations on that processor :

Table 2. ST22-SC1 Running Time Evaluations

ST22-SC1 @40 MHz	Size (bits)	Running Time (ms)	Savings %
RSA	1024	474	-61.9
Inverse calculus by $x^{-1} = x^{\varphi(n)-1}$	160	865	-41.8
Extended Euclidean	160	487	-18.0
Extended Stein's	160	247	-19.3
Extended Lehmer's	160	119	-17.4
Stein's for big numbers	160	247	-33.6
Projective coordinates	160	154	-38.2

References

1. Dieter Gollman, Yongfei Han and Chris J. Mitchell *Redundant Integers Representations and Fast Exponentiation* Designs, Codes and Cryptography, 7. p 135-151 (1996)
2. Donald E. Knuth *The Art of Computer Programming Vol 2 : Seminumerical Algorithms* Second Edition, Addison Wesley. p 316-336. 1981
3. Alfred J. Menezes, Paul C. van Oorshot and Scott A. Vanstone *Handbook of Applied Cryptography* CRC Press. p 606-610. 1997
4. Ron L. Rivest, Adi Shamir and Leonard M. Adleman *A method for obtaining digital signatures and public-key cryptosystems* Communications of the ACM, 21 p 120-126. 1978
5. Jonathan Sorenson *An Analysis of Lehmer's Euclidean GCD Algorithm* ISSAC'95. p 254-258. 1995

Reducing the Collision Probability of Alleged Comp128

Helena Handschuh[1,2] and Pascal Paillier[1,2]*

[1] GEMPLUS
Cryptography Department
34 Rue Guynemer
F-92447 Issy-Les Moulineaux
handschuh@gemplus.com
paillier@gemplus.com
[2] ENST
Computer Science Department
46, rue Barrault
F-75634 Paris Cedex 13
handschu@enst.fr
paillier@enst.fr

Abstract. Wagner, Goldberg and Briceno have recently published an attack [2] on what they believe to be Comp128, the GSM A3A8 authentication function [1]. Provided that the attacker has physical access to the card and to its secret PIN code (the card has to be activated), this chosen plaintext attack recovers the secret key of the personalized SIM (Secure Identification Module) card by inducing collisions on the second (out of 40) round of the compression function. In this paper we suggest two different approaches to strengthen the alleged Comp128 algorithm with respect to this attack. An evaluation of the number of chosen plaintexts and the new complexity of the attack are given.

Keywords. Alleged Comp128, chosen plaintext attack, authentication, compression function, cryptanalysis, smart cards, GSM.

1 Introduction

GSM networks use an authentication and session key generation algorithm called A3A8. An example of A3A8 is the Comp128 algorithm. An alleged version of Comp128 (we shall call it AComp128 hereafter) was recently published on the Web [1]. AComp128 is a compression function that takes the card's secret key Ki and a challenge sent over the air by the base station as an input to compute a MAC and a session key. The SIM card sends the MAC back to the base station for authentication and uses the session key for voice encryption with A5.

Briceno, Goldberg and Wagner's attack [2] is a chosen plaintext attack which induces collisions on the second round of the compression function and performs

---

* Both authors jointly work with Gemplus and ENST.

J.-J. Quisquater and B. Schneier (Eds.): CARDIS 2000, LNCS 1820, pp. 366–371, 2000.

a 2R-attack to recover the secret key Ki. Details of AComp128 and of the attack are given in the next two sections.

In this paper we suggest two ways to prevent this attack; the first is by slightly modifying the protocol in order to disable any collisions after the second or third round, and the second is by changing the structure of the inner permutations of indices referred to as a butterfly structure. Both methods offer protection against this attack but may also be of independent interest.

2   The AComp128 Algorithm

The compression function takes 256 bits as an input and computes a hash value of 128 bits. The 32 leftmost bits are used as a MAC and sent back to the basestation, and the 64 rightmost bits are used as a session key for voice encryption with the A5 algorithm.

Let Ki be the secret key of the target SIM card, and R the challenge sent to the card by the base station. Ki and R are each 16 bytes long. Let $X[0..15]$ = Ki and $X[16..31]$ = R be the 32 byte input to the compression function. Let $T0[0..511]$, $T1[0..255]$, $T2[0..127]$, $T3[0..63]$ and $T4[0..31]$ be the four secret tables. Then there are 8 loops of the following compression function: apply 5 rounds of table lookups and substitutions using tables T0 to T4, and except in the last loop, perform a permutation on the 128 output bits before entering the next loop.

In order to achieve a better comprehension of the attack, we will describe the 5 rounds inside one loop in pseudocode:

For i = 0 to 4 do:
For j = 0 to $2^i - 1$ do:
For k = 0 to $2^{4-i} - 1$ do:
{
$s = k + j*2^{5-i}$
$t = s + 2^{4-i}$
$x = (X[s] + 2X[t]) \bmod 2^{9-i}$
$y = (2X[s] + X[t]) \bmod 2^{9-i}$
$X[s] = Ti[x]$
$X[t] = Ti[y]$
}

The way the substitutions are performed in each round is referred to by Wagner et al. as a butterfly structure.

The size of the elements in the tables decreases from one table to the next. Starting from 8 bit outputs for table T0, and 7 bit outputs for table T1, we get down to 4 bit outputs in table T4. Actually, the 32 output bytes only have 4 significant bits each. Therefore these 32 bytes are reorganised into 16 bytes. After the permutation, the 16 byte output updates $X[16..31]$, and $X[0..15]$ is updated with the key Ki.

3   BGW's Attack

After the second round of the first loop, the bytes X[i],X[i+8],X[i+16],X[i+24] depend only on the input bytes having the same indexes. Two of these bytes are key bytes, namely X[i] = Ki[i] and X[i+8] = Ki[i+8] (for every i from 0 to 7). Thus, performing a chosen challenge attack, we can hope to find a collision on the four bytes after the second round. The birthday paradox guarantees that with 2^{14} random challenges, a collision most probably occurs on the corresponding 28 bit output (table T1 has 7 bit outputs).

Once a collision occurs on the second round, it propagates right through the compression function until the end of the last round. Comparing the MACs that are sent back by the card, this collision can be recognized.

Next, perform a 2R-attack to recover the two secret key bytes involved in the collision. This attack can be iterated for each pair of key bytes (i.e. for i from 0 to 7), and the whole secret key Ki can be recovered. The attack requires approximately $8*2^{14} = 2^{17}$ chosen plaintexts and can be performed on a card within 8 hours.

4   Modifying the Authentication Protocol

The first suggestion we make in order to fix the flaw in AComp128, is to reduce the size of the input challenge in a specific way.

The first thing to mention here is that collisions cannot occur after the first round. Actually, T0 has the following property:

Consider the function t(x,y) = T0[(x + 2y) mod 512]. When either x or y are fixed, the partial functions t(x,.) and t(.,y) of one variable are both permutations. Thus no collision can occur after the first round.

Let us now consider the second and the following rounds. The birthday paradox guarantees that with enough random challenges a collision can be found on each combination of four output bytes as mentioned in the last section.

The idea is to fix some parts of the challenge to a constant value in order to reduce the probability that there exists a collision. Say we fix for example the 8 first bytes of the challenge to a given value. Then 2^8 random challenges will almost certainly not produce a collision on 28 output bits.

Let N be the maximum number of challenges that can be issued to the card. Actually the probability to have no collision on these 28 bits can be approximated to:

$$P_i = e^{-\frac{N^2}{2 \times 2^{28}}} = e^{-2^{-13}}$$

This probability is very close to 1. The probability to have no collision on either of the 8 combinations of four input bytes (two key bytes, one constant challenge byte, and one variable challenge byte) is approximately:

$$P = (e^{-\frac{(2^8)^2}{2 \times 2^{28}}})^8 = e^{-2^{-10}}$$

There are many different ways to fix parts of the challenge, each one with a corresponding probability to get no collision at all. We suggest fixing half of the challenge, but considering each pair of bytes R[i],R[i+8] involved in a birthday attack, one might want to fix only l_i bits out of the 16. The location of those bits is not relevant. The l_i parameter may even vary for each index i. Different combinations can be found giving a satisfactory probability to be protected from the BGW attack. We can even allow some of the key bytes to be found, leaving the rest to be found by exhaustive search, but this game seems rather dangerous to us.

Note that collisions on the third or even fourth round seem easier to achieve as the size of the outputs of tables T2 and T3 decreases, but if we fix some parts of the challenge this will not be the case any more. At round 3 for example, 8 bytes (4 key bytes and 4 challenge bytes) are involved in a collision search. In the BGW case, 2^{32} random challenges eventually lead to a collision on 48 bits (8 times 6 output bits). Nevertheless, with only half of the bits available for collision search, the probabilities are even worse than in the 2 round case.

5   Using Mix-Optimal Permutations

The birthday attack works out fine because there is a "narrow pipe" in this compression function that causes bad diffusion of small changes in the input. We suggest to change the indexes to the table lookups in a way such that no narrow pipe subsists. In other words, if you choose one byte of the challenge and follow the bytes that are modified at the second round, going upwards in that network, far more than four bytes should be involved in the structure.

Here is the second modification we suggest in order to repair AComp128. Following the analysis of the previous section, we suggest a new structure for the diffusion network instead of the butterfly structure used in the actual version of AComp128. We still use one key byte and one random byte for the index of every table lookup at the first and the following rounds, but we change the byte permutations in the first and second rounds, such that the collision-free property is still valid on the first round, and such that the probability of having a collision on the second or the next rounds is optimally low.

We analyse the new probability of success for a "narrow pipe" attack, and deduce the number of cards needed in order for one of them to reveal it's secret key.

5.1   Round1

Let f be the permutation on byte indexes at the first round; the butterfly struc-ture mixes X[i] and X[i+16], which means that indexes i and i+16 are used to update indexes i and i+16. We adopt the following notation:

$$f = (0, 16)(1, 17)(2, 18)(3, 19)...(14, 30)(15, 31)$$

This means that index 0 updates itself and index 16, index 16 updates itself and index 0, index 1 updates itself and index 17, etc. f is to be read as a permutation on indexes: the current butterfly structure is therefore represented with 16 transpositions. It is easy to see that f is an involution.

For a new first round function we suggest a cyclic f' function which destroys part of the symmetry. Nevertheless, keep in mind that one key byte and one challenge byte are requested to update each byte of X at the first round.

$$f' = (0, 16, 1, 17, 2, 18, ..., 14, 30, 15, 31)$$

Index 0 updates itself and index f'(0) = 16, index 16 updates itself and index f'(16) = 1, etc. f' is no more involutive and its cyclic structure guarantees a minimal cycle length of 32, whereas the minimal cycle length of f is only 2.

5.2   Round2

The cyclic structure is not enough in the first round. The new permutation on the second round, noted g' hereafter, is mix-optimal in the sense that for a realistic collision search (no more than 8 challenge bytes involved), the bytes involved after round 2 are sufficiently numerous to achieve optimally low collision probabilities. An exhaustive search of the best g' led us to the following results: we can achieve at least a factor 3 between the number of involved challenge bytes, and the number of bytes involved in a collision after round 2. In the butterfly structure, this factor is only 2, which makes BGW's birthday attack feasible.

In order to define g', let us introduce the following notation. If f' is read from left to right, we call f'(k)(0), the k-th element in the list, i.e. if f' is applied k times the index of the involved byte is f'(k)(0). There are 2 mix-optimal g' functions defined as follows:

$$g'(k)(0) = f'(9k + 3 mod 32)(0) \tag{1}$$

and

$$g'(k)(0) = f'(9k + 2 mod 32)(0) \tag{2}$$

For example (1) has a maximal cycle length of 16 and two cylces of length 8.

5.3   New Probabilities

With a factor of at least 3 between the number of bytes involved at the second round and the number i of challenge bytes on which an attacker chooses to perform a collision search, the probabilities of such a collision drop to a reasonable value. For small i values (such as $i = 1$), the factor is at least 4 or 5. More details will be given in the full paper.

For large i (at least 3), we achieve the following lower bound on the probability of having no collision:

$$P = e^{-\frac{(2^{8*i})^2}{2 \times 2^{7*3i}}} = e^{-2^{-5*i-1}}$$

These mix-optimal permutations at rounds 1 and 2 suggest that the attacker has to have a fair amount of different activated cards in order to recover at least one secret key, which achieves some improvement over the actual performance of AComp128 with respect to BGW's attack. Attacks on subsequent rounds are even harder.

6   Conclusion

We have shown two ways to fix the flaw in AComp128, an example of the GSM A3A8 authentication algorithm. We analysed the probability of success of a narrow pipe attack in a general case with different permutation structures. These results may lead to the implementation of algorithms with higher collision-resistance derived from AComp128-like algorithms with butterfly structures, by introducing only minor changes.

References

1. http://www.scard.org/a3a8.txt
2. http://www.isaac.cs.berkeley.edu/isaac/gsm-faq.html

Smart Card Crypto-Coprocessors for Public-Key Cryptography

Helena Handschuh and Pascal Paillier*

[1] GEMPLUS
Cryptography Department
34 Rue Guynemer
F-92447 Issy-Les Moulineaux
handschuh@gemplus.com
paillier@gemplus.com
[2] ENST
Computer Science Department
46, rue Barrault
F-75634 Paris Cedex 13
handschu@enst.fr
paillier@enst.fr

Abstract. This paper intends to provide information about up-to-date performances of smart-card arithmetic coprocessors regarding major public-key cryptosystems and analyze the main tendences of this developing high-tech industry and related markets. We also comment hardware limitations of current technologies and provide a technique for extending them by virtually doubling their capacities.

1 Introduction

In recent years, public key cryptography [4] has gained increasing attention from both companies and end users who wish to use this technology to securize a wide variety of applications. One consequence of this trend has been the growing importance of public-key smart cards to store the user's private keys and provide a secure computing environment for private key operations. As such, smart cards can be seen as secure tokens.

Many chip manufacturers are therefore proposing ever better and faster implementations of public key algorithms using dedicated crypto-coprocessors on their chips. Two years ago the main focus of attention was on established public-key techniques such as RSA and Discrete Logarithm based signature schemes [14]. Main industrial efforts concentrated on the performance of these algorithms with key sizes that were lying around the 512-bit range. A survey of the state of the art at that time was published in [11]. This paper is intended to give an overview of recent evolutions in the crypto-coprocessor market and the latest achievements in terms of speed and available modulus size ranges. We also include consideration of implementations of other public-key techniques such as elliptic curve signature schemes [9].

---

* Both authors jointly work with Gemplus and ENST towards their PhD thesis.

J.-J. Quisquater and B. Schneier (Eds.): CARDIS 2000, LNCS 1820, pp. 372–379, 2000.
© Springer-Verlag Berlin Heidelberg 2000

2   The Public-Key Battlefield

The most widely used smart card chips with crypto-coprocessors are listed here. The usual manufacturers such as SGS-Thomson, Siemens, Philips and Motorola (now part of Atmel) still lead the market, but new manufacturers have more actively joined the public-key battlefield since 1996, such as NEC, Hitachi and Toshiba. Table 2 and 4 given in appendix list the standard field size of such chips in terms of on-board memory sizes (RAM, ROM, EEPROM), operating voltage and frequency, abnormal behaviour sensors (high or low voltage (HV/LV/V), frequency (HF/LF/F) or temperature (HT/LT/T)), maximum key size supported for RSA or DSA public moduli, and elliptic curve characteristic as appropriate.

It can be observed that new trends include increasing RAM and EEPROM sizes for user customized applications, faster internal clocks, improved security features such as new sensors or address scrambling and security matrices, and growing public modulus sizes. In other words, cryptographic chips are becoming bigger, more versatile, faster and increasingly secure.

The new range of key sizes for RSA and DSA is now generally up to 1024 bits, and some chips even handle 2048-bit computations. But as the need for ever bigger moduli becomes less acute, one future direction for improvement is clearly in a battle for increased performance. Public key algorithms are currently used only for authentication or access control as they are much too slow for stream encryption.

Every architecture presents its own optimizations for computing modular multiplications and exponentiations which are the basic operations in most public key cryptosystems. See [11] for some examples. But basically most chips end up achieving comparable speed. Tables 3 and 5 list the computing times on different platforms regarding various public key algorithms, with the most widely implemented system being RSA. However, DSA [7] and its elliptic curve version ECDSA, as well as other schemes such as ESIGN or zero-knowledge identification techniques [6] appear in some applications.

With regard to RSA signature generation, only 1024-bit implementations run with perfomance times of less than a second for now, but we suspect it will not be too long before 2048-bit RSA becomes practical as well. As a matter of fact, in one of Gemplus' custom implementations, 2048-bit signatures can already be computed in a reasonable time (around 1.5 seconds) using the Chinese Remainder Theorem and a signature verification using a small exponent (typically $e = F_4 = 2^{16} + 1$) can be computed in about 270 ms by applying what we call *size-doubling techniques* (see below).

3   Modular Arithmetics on CCPs

Modular multiplication, the computation[1] of $Z = XY\,[N]$ for given k-bit numbers X, Y and N, is certainly the most useful operation in public key cryptogra-

---

[1] we denote by $X\,[N]$ the residue of X modulo N seen as an element of $\mathbb{N}$, so that the equality $X\,[N] = Y$ be properly defined.

phy, and its efficiency in terms of hardware throughput remains highly critical for modular exponentiation-based schemes [13,5]. There exist many different ways of performing a modular multiplication, among which Montgomery [10], De Waleffe and Quisquater [2], Barrett [1] or Sedlak [15] provide techniques that are still the most commonly used in hardware implementations. Naturally, the internal architecture of an arithmetic coprocessor relies strongly on the choice of the multiplication technique (see [8,12] for details).

4   Size-Doubling Techniques: Algorithmic Tools for Emulating a $2k$-bit CCP from a k-bit One

There exist some tricky algorithmic infrastructures that allow one to virtually increase (typically double) the size of the crypto-coprocessor being used. Basically, these techniques allow the execution of a 1024-bit (resp. 2048-bit) exponentiation on a 512-bit (resp. 1024-bit) processor. They consist in an additional API layer which implements an up-to-$2k$-bit arithmetic engine out of an k-bit one, thereby providing up-to-$2k$-bit modular addition, multiplication, and exponentiation. Applied to a 1024-bit processor, this would allow 2048-bit DSA, 2048-bit Diffie-Hellman Key Exchange, 2048-bit ESIGN, 2048-bit RSA verification, 4096-bit RSA signature generation, and so on.

A particularly interesting case is the instanciation of a fast 2048-bit RSA on a 1024-bit chip ($k = 1024$). As only a few manufacturers have planned 2048-bit plateforms so far, this seems to be the most useful context in which to apply such size-doubling techniques. These arithmetic algorithms rely on several simultaneous computation strategies including:

1. modular representation of long operands,
2. low-storage Chinese remaindering combinations,
3. new parallelizable Montgomery-like operations, and
4. fast modular computation techniques.

These methods make previously unavailable operations on large numbers (2048-bit regular multiplication, 2048-bit addition, 2048-bit modular addition, multiplication and squaring) available and at the disposal of public key cryptographic algorithms so that they can be used with a larger key size.

4.1   Modular Representations

Long operands (ranging from 1025 to 4096 bits) are usually given under a radix form in base 2^{1024}. To be computationally exploitable, they are at first splitted into (at most) four workable 1024-bit words

$$X \to \langle X \rangle = (X[a_1], X[a_2], X[a_3], X[a_4]) \,,$$

where a_1, a_2, a_3 and a_4 are relatively prime easy-to-generate 1024-bit constants. Clearly the representation conversion $X \to \langle X \rangle$ consists solely of four modular reductions with a 1024-bit modulus, which is usually already implemented and directly available from the underlying arithmetic engine. Larger data appears to be much easier to handle under such a form, as computing

$$\langle X \rangle, \langle Y \rangle \rightarrow \langle X + Y \rangle \,, \tag{1}$$

or

$$\langle X \rangle, \langle Y \rangle \rightarrow \langle XY \rangle \,, \tag{2}$$

is carry-free and can be performed by independent parallel computations. It is worthwhile noticing that multiplication (2) presents a lower time complexity than would a 2k-bit classical multiplication since:

$$\sum (\log a_i)^2 < (\log \prod a_i)^2 \,. \tag{3}$$

Hence, this representation leads to time savings when compared to classical radix-form oriented manipulations. Obviously one has to be carefull that the cost of recombining the operand afterwards does not reduce the newly gained benefit too much. A set of moduli $\{a_1, a_2, a_3, a_4\}$ that offers this property is said to be *radix-compliant*.

4.2   Fast CRT Combinations

The original form of operands is re-obtained, after various calculations, by combining coordinates according to Garner's Chinese remaindering implementation

$$X\left[a_1 a_2\right] = \left(\frac{X\left[a_2\right] - X\left[a_1\right]}{a_1} \left[a_2\right] \right) a_1 + X\left[a_1\right] \,, \tag{4}$$

which can be cascaded to obtain a modular-to-radix representation conversion

$$\langle X \rangle = (X\left[a_1\right], X\left[a_2\right], X\left[a_3\right], X\left[a_4\right]) \rightarrow X\left[a_1 a_2 a_3 a_4\right] = X \,.$$

The use of a radix-compliant set of moduli allows the recombination of the correct operands at almost no extra cost (only linear operations), thus leading to high-speed representation conversions.

4.3   Modular Montgomery Reduction

Once two operands $\langle X \rangle$ and $\langle Y \rangle$ are given under their modular representation, one will typically wish to compute $\langle XY\left[N\right]\rangle$ where N may be up-to-2048-bit long. For that purpose, a newly discovered efficient algorithm for computing

$$\langle X \rangle, \langle Y \rangle, \langle N \rangle \rightarrow \langle XYK\left[N\right]\rangle \,, \tag{5}$$

where K is some modulus-dependent constant, can be implemented (contact the authors for further information). Routines for 2048-bit (both modular and non modular) multiplication and 4096-bit modular reduction can be directly obtained from this procedure.

4.4 Constructing a 2048-bit Exponentiation

Classically, a Square-and-Multiply implementation will call the 2048-bit modular multiplication routine that we previously discussed while bit-scanning the exponent. As a consequence, the whole algorithm remains fully compatible with exponent-relative precomputations (signed-digit, redundant representations, $d + k\phi(N)$, and so forth).

As far as we know, only this size-doubling technique makes it possible to execute on board a 1024-bit smart card any personalized version of RSA with keysize ranging continuously from 1025 to 2048 bits, and while using any public exponent. The required key material (N, e, constants) is proportional in length to the chosen RSA-size and Table 3 gives an illustration of the memory requirements for implementing a k-bit version of RSA ($1025 \leq k \leq 2048$).

Table 1. Key Size In Size-Doubling Techniques

EEPROM (key size)	$0.875 \times k$ bytes
Required RAM	$0.875 \times k$ bytes

5 Conclusion

In this brief article we have presented the data obtained during a study of the current state of the art public-key implementations on smart cards. We have also added some information on the performance of popular secret key algorithms and hash functions such as DES, SHA-1 and MD5. Although most of the performance improvements are still made for public key implementations, some chips already feature dedicated secret key coprocessors. One question for the future is whether it will be possible to embed both on the same chip, and/or whether 16-bit and 32-bit processors (like the CASCADE chip [3]) will spark a revolution in the developing smart card market.

6 Acknowledgements and Contacts

We would like to give special thanks to all interested parties who kindly helped us to gather the technical details for the survey, particularly those that could not be found in the usual documentation. Hereafter are listed some contact names and phone numbers that the reader might find useful.

References

1. P. Barrett, *Implementing the Rivest, Shamir and Adleman Public-Key Encryption Algorithm on a Standard Digital Signal Processor*, Advances in Cryptology : Crypto'86 (A. M. Odlyzko ed.), LCNS 263, Springer-Verlag, pp. 311-323, 1987.

Company	Contact Name	Phone/Fax No	Email Adress
Hitachi	Nicolas Prawitz	+33 1 3463 0500 +33 1 3463 3431	`Nicolas.Prawitz` `@hitachi-eu.com`
NEC	Nicolas Bérard	+33 1 3067 5800 +33 1 3067 5899	`BerardN` `@ef.nec.de`
Philips GmbH	Stefan Philipp	+49 405613 2747 +49 405613 3045	`Stefan.Philipp` `@hamburg.sc.philips.com`
SGS-Thomson	Frédéric Barbato	+33 1 47407575 +33 1 47407910	`Frederic.Barbato` `@st.com`
Siemens	Laurent Deloo	+33 1 4922 3100 +33 1 4922 3413	`Laurent.Deloo` `@pl.siemens.fr`
Atmel	Benoit Makowka	+33 4 4253 6129 +33 4 4253 6001	`bmakowka` `@atmel.com`

2. D. de Waleffe and J.J. Quisquater, *CORSAIR, A Smart Card for Public-Key Cryptosystems*, Advances in Cryptology : Crypto'90 (A. Menezes and S. Vanstone ed.), LNCS 537, Springer-Verlag, pp. 503-513, 1990.

3. J. F. Dhem, *Design of an Efficient Public-Key Cryptographic Library for RISC-based Smart Cards*, PhD Thesis, UCL, 1998.

4. W. Diffie and M. Hellman, *New Directions in Cryptography*, IEEE Transactions on Information Theory, vol IT-22, n 6, pp. 644-654, november 1976.

5. T. El-Gamal, *A Public-Key Cryptosystem and a Signature Scheme based on Discrete Logarithms*, IEEE TIT, vol. IT-31:4, pp 469-472, 1985.

6. A. Fiat and A. Shamir, *How to prove yourself: Practical solutions to Identification and Signature Problems*, Advances in Cryptology : Crypto'86 (A. M. Odlyzko ed.), LCNS 263, Springer-Verlag, pp. 181-187, 1987.

7. FIPS PUB 186, February 1, 1993, *Digital Signature Standard*.

8. D. Knuth, *The Art of Computer Programming*, vol. 2, Seminumerical Algorithms, pp. 248-250, 1969.

9. V. S. Miller, *Use of Elliptic Curves in Cryptography*, Advances in Cryptology: Crypto'85, Springer Verlag, pp. 417–426, 1986.

10. P. Montgomery, *Modular Multiplication without Trial Division*, Mathematics of Computations, vol. 44(170), pp. 519-521, 1985.

11. D. Naccache and D. M'Raïhi *Arithmetic Coprocessors for Public-Key Cryptography : The State of the Art*, IEEE Micro, pp. 14-24, June 1996.

12. J. Omura, *A Public Key Cell Design for Smart Card Chips*, IT Workshop, Hawaii, USA, November 27-30, pp. 983-985.

13. R. Rivest, A. Shamir and L. Adleman, *A Method for Obtaining Digital Signatures and Public- Key Cryptosystems*. Communications of the ACM, vol. 21, n 2, p.120-126, February 1978.

14. C. Schnorr, *Efficient Identification and Signatures for Smart-Cards*, Advances in Cryptology: Eurocrypt'89 (G. Brassard ed.), LNCS 435, Springer-Verlag, pp. 239-252, 1990.

15. H. Sedlak, *The RSA Cryptographic Processor : The First High Speed One-Chip Solution*, Advances in Cryptology : Eurocrypt'87 (C. Pomerance ed.), LNCS 293, Springer-Verlag, pp. 95-105, 1988.

A   Technical Carateristics of CCPs

Note that we call maximum modulus size (Max $|N|$) the size of the underlying architecture; algorithms using bigger moduli are achieved on some chips, but need additional software implementations. In Table 2, stars (*) indicate that the product is expected in the forthcoming months. In Table 5, they indicate actual measurements by Gemplus. Given figures for Atmel's MSC1114 are target ones whilst those of MSC0501 are actual. All RSA verifications are measured with $e = F_4$. In all the DSA entries, the subgroup size is standard, that is, set to 160 bits.

Table 2. Technical Caracteristics of CCPs

Chip Name	Manufacturer	μ-P core	CCP name	Max $|N|$	RAM	ROM
H8/3111	Hitachi	H8/300	CoProcessor	576 bits	800 B	14 KB
H8/3112	Hitachi	H8/300	CoProcessor	576 bits	1312 B	24 KB
H8/3113*	Hitachi	H8/300	CoProcessor	1024 bits	1.5 KB	32 KB
T6N29	Toshiba	Z80	1024B	1024 bits	512 B	20 KB
T6N37*	Toshiba	Z80	1024B	1024 bits	512 B	20 KB
T6N39*	Toshiba	Z80	1024B	1024 bits	512 B	20 KB
T6N42*	Toshiba	Z80	2048B	2048 bits	512 B	20 KB
SLE44CR80S	Siemens	80C51	CCP	540 bits	256 B	17 KB
SLE66CX160S	Siemens	80C51	ACE	1100 bits	1280 B	32 KB
μPD789828*	NEC	78K0S	SuperMAP	2048 bits	1 KB	24 KB
ST16CF54B	SGS-Thomson	8-bit MCU	MAP	512 bits	512 B	16 KB
ST19CF68	SGS-Thomson	8-bit CPU	MAP	512 bits	960 B	23 KB
ST19KF16	SGS-Thomson	8-bit CPU	MAP	1088 bits	2 KB	32 KB
P83W854	Philips	80C51	FameX	2048 bits	800 B	20 KB
P83W858	Philips	80C51	FameX	2048 bits	800 B	20 KB
P83W8516	Philips	80C51	FameX	2048 bits	2304 B	32 KB
P83W8532	Philips	80C51	FameX	2048 bits	2304 B	32 KB
SmartXA	Philips	16 bits CPU	FameX	2048 bits	1.5/2 KB	32 KB
MSC0501	Atmel	68HC05	MEU	2048 bits	896 B	20 KB
MSC1114	Atmel	68HC05	MEU	2048 bits	1664 B	32 KB
AT90SCC	Atmel	AVR Risc	SC16	1024 bits	1/2.5 KB	-

Table 3. Public-Key Timings

Chip Name	H8/3111-3112	H8/3113	ST16CF54B	ST19CF68	ST19KF16	MSC0501
Internal Clock	3.57 MHz	14 MHz	5 MHz	10 MHz	10 MHz	5 MHz
DES 64 bits	-	-	10 ms	-	-	4.5 ms
SHA 512 bits	-	-	15.2 ms	8.2 ms	8.2 ms	17 ms
MD5 512 bits	-	-	12 ms*	-	-	-
RSA 512 Sign CRT	202 ms	-	142 ms	70 ms	20 ms	86 ms
RSA 512 Sign	514 ms	68 ms	389 ms	195 ms	55 ms	-
RSA 512 Verify	-	-	9 ms	4.5 ms	2 ms	14 ms
RSA 768 Sign CRT	-	-	377 ms	189 ms	50 ms	222 ms
RSA 768 Sign	-	210 ms	-	-	165 ms	621 ms
RSA 768 Verify	-	-	190 ms	100 ms	3 ms	28 ms
RSA 1024 Sign CRT	-	-	800 ms	400 ms	110 ms	460 ms
RSA 1024 Sign	-	480 ms	-	-	380 ms	1416 ms
RSA 1024 Verify	-	-	265 ms	150 ms	5 ms	47 ms
RSA 2048 Sign CRT	-	-	-	-	780 ms	-
RSA 2048 Verify	-	-	-	-	100 ms	-
DSA 512 Sign	-	-	163 ms	84 ms	25 ms	-
DSA 512 Verify	-	-	283 ms	146 ms	40 ms	-
DSA 768 Sign	-	-	-	-	50 ms	-
DSA 768 Verify	-	-	-	-	80 ms	-
DSA 1024 Sign	-	-	-	-	100 ms	-
DSA 1024 Verify	-	-	-	-	160 ms	-
ECDSA 255 Sign	-	-	-	-	555 ms	-

Table 4. Technical Caracteristics of CCPs (continued)

Name	EEPROM	Voltage	Ext Clock	Int Clock	Techno.	Sensors
H8/3111	8 KB	3V/5V	10 MHz	10 MHz	0.8 μm	LV, LF
H8/3112	8 KB	3V/5V	10 MHz	10 MHz	0.8 μm	LV,LF,HF
H8/3113*	16 KB	3V/5V	10 MHz	14.32 MHz	0.5 μm	LV,HV,LF,HF
T6N29	8 KB	3V/5V	-	-	0.6 μm	V
T6N37*	8 KB	3V/5V	-	-	-	V/T/F
T6N39*	8 KB	3V/5V	-	-	-	V/T/F
T6N42*	8 KB	3V/5V	-	-	-	V/T/F
SLE44CR80S	8 KB	3V to 5V	7.5 MHz	7.5 MHz	0.7 μm	-
SLE66CX160S	16 KB	2.7V to 5.5V	7.5 MHz	7.5 MHz	0.6 μm	-
μPD789828*	8 KB	1.8V to 5.5V	5 MHz	40 MHz	0.35 μm	-
ST16CF54B	4 KB	5V $\pm$ 10%	5 MHz	5 MHz	-	-
ST19CF68	8 KB	3V/5V $\pm$ 10%	10 MHz	10 MHz	0.6 μm	-
ST19KF16	16 KB	3V/5V $\pm$ 10%	10 MHz	10 MHz	0.6 μm	-
P83W854	4 KB	2.7V to 5.5V	8 MHz	-	-	V/T/F
P83W858	8 KB	2.7V to 5.5V	8 MHz	-	-	V/T/F
P83W8516	16 KB	2.7V to 5.5V	8 MHz	-	-	V/T/F
P83W8532	32 KB	2.7V to 5.5V	8 MHz	-	-	V/T/F
MSC0501	4 KB	2.7V to 5.5V	5 MHz	5 MHz	0.8 μm	-
MSC1114	32 KB	2.7V to 5.5V	20 MHz	10 MHz	0.4 μm	-
AT90SCC	8/48 KB	3V to 5V	-	16 MHz	0.5 μm	V/F

Table 5. Public-Key Timings (continued)

Chip Name	P83W854/8	P83W8516/32	SLE44CR80S	SLE66CX160S	μPD789828	MSC1114
Internal Clock	-	-	5 MHz	5 MHz	40 MHz	10 MHz
DES 64 bits	10 ms	10 ms	3.7 ms*	3.7 ms*	4 ms	2.2 ms
SHA 512 bits	10 ms	5 ms	5.6 ms*	5.6 ms*	$\leq$ 2 ms	8 ms
MD5 512 bits	-	-	9 ms*	9 ms*	-	-
RSA 512 Sign CRT	45 ms	37 ms	60 ms	37 ms	16 ms	34 ms
RSA 512 Sign	140 ms	93 ms	220 ms	110 ms	52 ms	-
RSA 512 Verify	22 ms	10 ms	20 ms*	10.3 ms*	2 ms	5 ms
RSA 768 Sign CRT	182.5 ms	88 ms	250 ms*	124 ms*	52 ms	80 ms
RSA 768 Sign	385 ms	220 ms	-	437 ms*	164 ms	210 ms
RSA 768 Verify	36 ms	18 ms	-	18.4 ms*	4 ms	9 ms
RSA 1024 Sign CRT	250 ms	160 ms	450 ms	230 ms	100 ms	165 ms
RSA 1024 Sign	800 ms	400 ms	-	880 ms	360 ms	480 ms
RSA 1024 Verify	50 ms	25 ms	-	24 ms*	7 ms	16 ms
RSA 2048 Sign CRT	2180 ms	1100 ms	-	1475 ms*	750 ms	-
RSA 2048 Sign	21 s	6.4 s	-	44 s*	-	-
RSA 2048 Verify	156 ms	54 ms	-	268 ms*	45 ms	-
DSA 512 Sign	75 ms	58 ms	95 ms	50 ms	31 ms	-
DSA 512 Verify	115 ms	82 ms	175 ms	90 ms	70 ms	-
DSA 768 Sign	145 ms	100 ms	-	-	57 ms	-
DSA 768 Verify	230 ms	145 ms	-	-	150 ms	-
DSA 1024 Sign	215 ms	150 ms	-	143 ms*	-	-
DSA 1024 Verify	355 ms	225 ms	-	271 ms*	-	-
ECDSA 135 Sign	-	-	185 ms	185 ms	-	-
ECDSA 135 Verify	-	-	360 ms	360 ms	-	-
ECDSA 255 Sign	-	-	-	-	81 ms	-
ECDSA 255 Verify	-	-	-	-	380 ms	-

Author Index

Lecture Notes in Computer Science

For information about Vols. 1–1825
please contact your bookseller or Springer-Verlag